T0312001

Japanese
Project Management

KPM — Innovation, Development and Improvement

Japanese Management and International Studies
(ISSN: 2010-4448)

Editor-in-Chief: Yasuhiro Monden *(University of Tsukuba, Japan)*

For the complete list of titles in this series, please go to
http://www.worldscientific.com/series/jmis

Monden Institute of Management
Japanese Management and International Studies – Vol. 3

Japanese Project Management

KPM — Innovation, Development and Improvement

editors

Shigenobu Ohara
Nippon Institute of Technology, Japan

Takayuki Asada
Osaka University, Japan

 **World Scientific**

NEW JERSEY · LONDON · SINGAPORE · BEIJING · SHANGHAI · HONG KONG · TAIPEI · CHENNAI

Published by

World Scientific Publishing Co. Pte. Ltd.

5 Toh Tuck Link, Singapore 596224

USA office: 27 Warren Street, Suite 401-402, Hackensack, NJ 07601

UK office: 57 Shelton Street, Covent Garden, London WC2H 9HE

British Library Cataloguing-in-Publication Data
A catalogue record for this book is available from the British Library.

First published 2009 (Hardcover)
Reprinted 2016 (in paperback edition)
ISBN 978-981-3203-46-4

Japanese Management and International Studies — Vol. 3
JAPANESE PROJECT MANAGEMENT
KPM — Innovation, Development and Improvement

Copyright © 2009 by World Scientific Publishing Co. Pte. Ltd.

ISBN-13 978-981-277-873-4
ISBN-10 981-277-873-X

Typeset by Stallion Press
Email: enquiries@stallionpress.com

Printed in Singapore

Monden Institute of Management

The Mission of the Institute and Editorial Information

For the purpose of making a contribution to the business and academic communities, Monden Institute of Management is committed to publishing the book series coherently entitled *Japanese Management and International Studies*, a kind of book-length journal with a referee system.

Focusing on Japan and Japan-related issues, the series is designed to inform the world about research outcomes of the new "Japanese-style management system" developed in Japan. It includes the Japanese version of management systems developed abroad. In addition, it publishes research by overseas scholars and concerning overseas systems that constitute significant points of comparison with the Japanese system.

Research topics included in this series are management of organization in a broad sense (including the business group) and the accounting that supports the organization. More specifically, topics include business strategy, organizational restructuring, corporate finance, M&A, environmental management, business models, operations management, managerial accounting, financial accounting for organizational restructuring, manager performance evaluation, remuneration systems, and management of revenues and costs. The research approach is interdisciplinary, which includes case studies, theoretical studies, normative studies, and empirical studies.

Each volume contains the series title and a book title which reflects the volume's special theme.

Our institute's board of directors has established an editorial board of international standing. In each volume, guest editors who are experts on the volume's special theme will serve as the volume editors.

Editorial Board of
Japanese Management and International Studies

Yoshiteru Minagawa, Nagoya Gakuin University, Japan
Kanji Miyamoto, Osaka Gakuin University, Japan
Tengku Akbar Tengku Abdullah, Universiti Kebangsaan Malaysia,
    Malaysia
Jimmy Y.T. Tsay, National Taiwan University, Taiwan
Susumu Ueno, Konan University, Japan
Eri Yokota, Keio University, Japan
Walid Zaramdini, UAE University, United Arab Emirates

Preface

In the 1990s, Japanese companies experienced a deflationary depression called the "lost ten years". To survive the depression, they looked for solutions in the *kaikaku* (reforms) of business management, organizations and technology, while struggling to regain their global competitiveness. We have observed that the companies that utilized the intellectual property of the entire organization were more successful in their reforms than those who focused only on their technological abilities. Specifically, such successful companies made efforts in the planning and execution of strategic businesses that would change the framework of value creation for the next generation. These companies had something in common: they applied a new project management paradigm. We call it Kaikaku Project Management (KPM).

Kaikaku is the comprehensive term used for a breakthrough program or project which may encompass a framework of the ingredients expressed in the three Japanese concepts of *Kakusin* (innovation), *Kaihatsu* (development) and *Kaizen* (improvement). In fact, these are significant elements for successful performance. The unique context is disclosed in terms of organizational view and platform for knowledge interaction.

Generally, project management has been recognized as a special management technique for engineers who build large, complex technical systems, including man-made creations such as weapons, factories, buildings and information systems. The main features of this project management paradigm are that it is designed to "build closed systems" and that the objectives, basic specifications, and injected resources are the "given conditions". The project manager's job is to hire multiple specialized engineers to integrate different technologies into a single system, while focusing on management by objectives (QCDS: Quality, Cost, Delivery and Scope). Thus, the closed system serves as the basic paradigm for thinking.

Meanwhile, the Japanese-style project management introduces the concept of *kaikaku* (reform). It is a concept based on comprehensive, strategic "destruction and creation". In KPM, the essential power of project management is twofold: the creativity supported by different kinds of knowledge brought together to overcome conservativeness, and the team power across the organization. Society, government and companies are looking in the field of project management for systematic human resource development solutions to train people to be *kaikaku* leaders. To compile a body of knowledge that satisfies such needs, we need to make a paradigm shift from the "closed technical system" to an "open value system". Let us look at an example. Behind a plan to build a factory or an information system, there are strategic intentions and a strong determination to create new businesses or products and achieve organizational growth, while being aware of external changes in the ecosystem, market, clientele, competition, etc.

The traditional role of project management has focused only on the technical aspect, that is, "how we should build" a factory or information system. However, this perspective is only a part of the whole picture. In KPM, we need to consider the overall goal for strategic businesses from a top executive's viewpoint, asking ourselves questions such as, "Why are we building it?" or "When should we recoup the investment?" KPM offers a body of knowledge based on the following concept: taking account of the lifecycle of a project from investment to its recuperation (i.e., planning, systemization and management of the project), the project organization injects the intellectual resources accumulated in the organization into the project to create value for the future.

1   Features of KPM

Some point out that the ideal leaders that KPM is seeking are top executives. Global competition has reduced the lifecycle of an organization to 5–10 years. This makes it difficult for companies to survive without *kaikaku* projects. The question is, can top executives really curtail many reform efforts according to their lifecycles? We have observed that many reform projects have "run out of gas" or "disappeared" in major companies. Accordingly, among rapidly growing companies, there are quite a few bankruptcies because of shortage of reform leaders. Meanwhile, KPM aims at training next-generation leaders who can link company-wide reforms to numerous projects, include such projects in business scenarios, and carry them out.

This book includes the theory and practice of KPM to help your understanding. The following are KPM's main features:

- *KPM is a project management practice which utilizes the perceptive ability that humans are born with.*
  What is the starting point of a reform project? It is the strong desire to become better in the future. We humans are born with the perceptive ability that helps us draw a picture of the future from a comprehensive viewpoint and with a broad perspective. This is an ability that helps us create missions so that we can solve problems as a whole. Creative imagination and wisdom based on experience are integrated into this quality of creating missions, which serves as the key element of the project's success.
- *KPM promotes the creation of future value by utilizing a number of reform projects linked to strategy.*
  Missions for a company's reform can be created not only by the top executives, but also by the entire organization. However, missions tend to be buried within the organization. KPM is designed to create a corporate culture that respects "missions", discover outstanding visions for reform from the entire organization, link such outstanding visions to the company-wide strategy, and use them in the creation of future value that promotes reform projects using project management.
- *KPM provides a body of knowledge to the training of core leaders whose responsibility is to recoup the investment.*
  Core leaders' goal is to achieve the missions. They are also responsible for the management of the entire lifecycle (development, planning and result) of each mission that they are assigned by its creator or owner. The core leaders have the key responsibility for the reform. They play a role in promoting the reform by making the best use of "intellectual resources" that have been accumulated in the organization for the next generation. KPM promotes human resource development by providing a body of knowledge and methodology.
- *KPM proposes a methodology for avoiding risks of failure and resistance in the organization.*
  A reform project tends to generate internal resistance because of conflict of interest, uncertainty, or a result of employee learning, etc., having the risk of failure. This can be solved in two different ways. The first is to introduce a HR system tailored to the project that is

designed to reflect the employees' reform proposals and efforts in their performance reviews. The second is to introduce company-wide human resource development. It is essential to train next-generation core leaders by providing our employees not only with usual organizational experience, but also with multiple career paths that allow us to reassign the employees based on their project experiences.

- *KPM provides a methodology for undertaking the solution of complex issues.*

  In order to solve company-wide issues, it is essential to take an epistemological approach and promote the knowledge of project management. This book describes leading-edge interdisciplinary approaches, theories based on complex system science, and case studies. Agent-Based Simulation (ABS) is useful in explaining the structure, function and behavior of complex phenomena in project modeling based on hypothesizing and testing practices.

2   Structure of This Volume

2.1   *The orthodox, contemporary, and new categories of project management*

This volume consists of six parts for the purpose of introducing the holistic outlook and the most recent papers in applications of project management. A certain guide is implied to readers in terms of what the orthodox, the contemporary, and the new contexts of project management are. The orthodox context is engineering-oriented under closed system thinking. The knowledge is mainly for contractors engaged in the artificial systems. The contemporary context is the value-driven project management in open system paradigm. P2M often appeared in papers as the first Japanese standard developed in 2001 for project and program management belonging to the contemporary type. The knowledge is contrived for either the owner or the contractor for dual usages. Nevertheless, despite its uniqueness, new issues of slowdown and resistance to *Kaikaku* (reform) have emerged.

2.2   *KPM — the new Japanese Project Management*

To overcome the issue, the new context symbolized by KPM (Kaikaku Project Management) has been launched, and its thinking and methodology are being applied. Most papers are written in either the contemporary or the new context or both, because they belong more or less to *Kaikaku*-type project management, which is further segmented to include areas of *Kakusin* (innovation), *Kaihatsu* (development), and *Kaizen* (improvement) solutions. KPM depicts the new knowledge framework improved from P2M by further clarifying the interface and linkage to strategy, role and competency model for mindset change, and knowledge platform in terms of the organizational view. All the papers in this volume cover, relate to, or paraphrase KPM partially or totally. The volume consists of six parts, titled as follows:

Part 1: Framework of Contemporary Japanese Project Management
The history and extensive applications of project management in Japan are overviewed. The paradigm shift from technical to value creation is explained as the birth of KPM version rooted in the first standard of P2M in Japan. In P2M/KPM, a mission-driven approach is adopted, which differs from the orthodox goal-driven approach. A "mission" is defined here as the expectation of realizing a future vision proposed by the owner's initiative for *kaikaku* which is linked to a strategy. In P2M/KPM, the methodology is exhibited in 3S reference project models of scheme, system and service for expanded lifecycle program management. However, conservatism and bureaucracy resulted in frequent slowdowns. The mismatching of human resource allocation had discouraged team motivation in the experiences. In KPM, the new organizational consideration is introduced in 3K thinking of *Kakusin* (innovation), *Kaihatsu* (development), and *Kaizen* (improvement) as aforementioned. KPM thinking and methodology have proved effective and successful so far in improving company-wide learning opportunities, enhancing participation, and motivating consensus and awareness of core leaders.

Part 2: KPM in the Information and Communications Industry
Japan's information industry is a growing industry with a market size of ¥40 trillion combining hardware and software products. In the IT industry, project management has been used for quite a while as a methodology for building technical systems. Nevertheless, it is facing two critical issues. The first issue is the low productivity in the simultaneous management of numerous small to mid-size projects. The second issue refers to development risks and inter-customer relationships. The former is about decision-making on internal authority and its role in a matrix organization. The latter is about mutual understanding of project context between

organizations. Concerning these two issues, KPM suggests from a project governance perspective a framework for information sharing, integration by program managers, project business models, platform design, etc., and explains its own framework.

Part 3: Project Management for Business Reforms Linked to Strategy
Business executives are seeking solutions for resource allocation and overall evaluation in reform projects. There are two issues involved here. One is the resource allocation of project value and the overall evaluation during the planning of reform strategies. The other is the evaluation of the performance of the strategy and its results. KPM proposes "project management that can recoup the investment" as its methodology and suggests an evaluation method using project balance scorecards and a control method using the Key Performance Indicator (KPI). Such control not only serves as a financial indicator, but also aims to establish a management approach that makes the reform successful because of multiple factors including the project owner, high learning ability across the organization, and business growth.

Part 4: Project Management for Knowledge-Based Development Strategy
For many years, project management for development has been used to manage technology development in research institutions, but it has not evolved into an independent PM paradigm. In strategic management of intellectual property and development projects in industry-government-academia collaboration, people are trying to overcome such management trend. While we live in a matured knowledge-based information society, new project management ideas and methodologies are increasingly receiving attention. KPM aims to be a comprehensive management solution while promoting the paradigm shift from the technical system to a "value system" and considering development, execution and implementation as a total lifecycle. Thus, the new KPM is used for the long-term, strategic development of technologies in the public sector, the development of new drugs, and the development of environment-friendly products.

Part 5: Application of KPM for New Value-Creating Activity
To solve a complex social problem, we need to take an interdisciplinary scientific approach because an individual science cannot solve such a problem. In KPM thinking, project management is categorized in the new disciplines as a holistic creative solution. The view is insightful by constructivist

thinking rather than analytical by positivist thinking. Perception has to interact with logic for realizing innovation into reality. The constructivist interpretation is guided by the mission-driven approach and *ba* collaboration platform. To link practice and science, KPM recommends and applies the simulation, agent-based modeling and methodology for hypothesizing, visualizing, and testing practices for logical supports. Here, research on the public project of superhighway and the customized product development of networked team are presented in KPM paradigm. The former research advances the methodology for complex project missions by demonstrating simulation of feasible or optimal toll rate calculation. The latter research deals with a networked project team working on frame boxes for personal computers. The project members in distant locations were obliged to exchange opinions frequently on profiling configuration and specification from design to manufacture stage of the lifecycle. The development process has been traced for project-based learning and modeling. Readers may be interested in media tools of CAD and groupware, and further attracted by progressive description of facts in digital and face-to-face communications.

Part 6: Project Management Infrastructures for Evolving the Standard
The most important elements of the infrastructure for advancing project management are threefold: standardization system, international use and organization-wide education. By strengthening these elements, the cycle of research, implementation and standardization will be ensured. As a result, the infrastructure and the promotion of knowledge become inseparable. Especially in colleges and universities, which have a dual role of research and education, KPM has recently been taught in their programs designed to train future reform leaders. Because of the advancement of global supply chains, more Japanese companies are becoming multinational. To do business in countries whose cultures, customs and languages are different from each other, it is essential to promote KPM so that we can make a complex context of business models adjusted to these countries to speed up business operations.

Volume Editor
Shigenobu Ohara

The Guide of Essential Terminology in KPM

A project

A project is a specific undertaking conducted by a temporary organization, and differentiated by novelty of the job, situation and conditions to be achieved complying with the mission or objectives. In the Japanese way, the essence of a project is underlined to the unique style of its endeavors to organize intellectual resources for problem solutions across and beyond functions.

Project management

Project management is the capability of managing a project(s) based on knowledge, competency, experience, skills, practices and disciplines. It is involved extensively with managing projects or processes efficiently and effectively to achieve missions and goals.

A program

A program is a group of integrated projects designed and conducted under a holistic mission. It is evidently positioned at a higher concept than a project, but is different from multiple projects conducted divergently in an organization. A program is suited to deal with complex missions in need of solutions to diversified purposes like business innovation, environmental problems and social problems.

Program management

Program management is the capability of integrating projects essentially needful to the project owner, who manages the total lifecycle from initiation to the end. In the Japanese way, program management represents the owner's role and view rather than the contractor's. In order to reflect the owner's view, integration management, strategy linkage by way of steering committee, program director, program manager and project office shall be installed and clarified in the organization. In the Japanese way, the 3S reference modeling of Scheme, System and Service is developed and introduced in architecture management.

Kaikaku Project Management (KPM)

Kaikaku is the Japanese word for radical reforms. The word is popularly underlined in turning points for breakthrough. It encompasses awareness of people's mindsets and roles in organizational layers in the three K's of *Kakusin* or innovation at the top, *Kaihatsu* or development at the middle, and *Kaizen* or improvement. Capturing and linking potentials, Japanese project management is described under this major context with its framework.

Mission

Mission is the base statement of launching a project(s) or a program(s) with commitment, which represents the owner's intent of uniqueness. It harnesses objectives, context, contents and requirements during the initial stage. In the Japanese way, the start of a project(s) or a program(s) is defined by the launch of a mission, and this eventually includes the process of its clarification and development if necessary.

Explicit and implicit missions

In general, mission is identified in explicit and implicit types. The explicit type provides the base of full requirements for contractors to assume obligations by specifying the scope and configurations. The implicit type leaves the base for further clarification or development by the owner in collaboration with specialists, and this includes identification of multiple objectives, definitions, requirements, tradeoff solutions, configurations and specifications.

The owner

The owner means an individual or an organized body which holds final decision-making authority and ownership over a project(s) or a program(s) and, accordingly, assumes full responsibility of the total lifecycle of the project(s) or program(s) from its initiation to the end. Therefore, the owner represents the role(s) and position(s) of the client, head office, primary undertaker and/or investor(s).

The contractor

The contractor is a team or an organized body which is assigned to assume a part or all of a project(s) or a program(s) by the owner through a contractual commitment with the owner. This terminology is used occasionally on comprehensive contract(s) between or among organized bodies.

The stakeholder

The stakeholder is a group of people or organized bodies who have more or less vested interests or relations in a project(s) or program(s). The concept is broad, but critical for success in management. It covers in general the owner, customers, end users, consulting bodies, agents, contractors, project managers, project teams, subcontractors, financiers, the community, residents, local or central governments, land owners, etc. In its narrow meaning (dependent upon definition), it includes only major participants, collaborators or related bodies.

Value creation paradigm

Value creation paradigm means the strategic thinking to the value-oriented priority of what could be the target and how limited resources should be allocated to sustain activities for decision making. Enterprises survive and grow by value creation activities engaged in producing products and services. The sustainability of value creation activity depends on requirements in an uncertain environment that values are appreciated and essentially paid as costs or surplus directly by clients or indirectly by stakeholders. That is why *kaikaku* or innovative reform is critical in thinking and actions to be formulated and implemented by project or program management. The paradigm also implies that the pursuit of the framework shall be encouraged to build a body of knowledge, competency and methodology for value creation.

An organizational view

An organization is defined as the collaborative system having social, human, material and information subsystems. It is sustained, controlled and driven by collective goals, willingness of affiliation and communication. Organizations are classified in many ways, but here are simply divided into the operational type in hierarchy and the project type in flat teams.

In the operational organization, routine tasks and duties are performed functionally under principles of specialization, while project organizations are deemed effective to foster creativity under constrained conditions. The advantages of a project organization are that it is suited to innovation, development and improvement, and its hybrid unity for generating dynamic knowledge interaction. Furthermore, leadership, role/competency awareness and team building are essential elements in KPM.

Shikumizukuri view

This term is often used whenever *kaikaku* or reform is launched in Japan. It is a hybrid of *shikumi* and *zukuri*. *Shikumi* means a comprehensive context of the new strategic institution, framework and/or architecture. *Zukuri* means grand design and its implementation complying with the mission. This hybrid term provides a view extremely similar to *Kakusin*-Innovation Program Management's interdisciplinary theories, practices and experiences. In the architecture management, 3S (scheme, system, service) modeling are proposed in terms of lifecycle in value creation paradigm. In KPM, psychological and intelligent aspects are newly introduced, enhanced and guided by organizational view in the form of 3K (*Kakusin, Kaihatsu, Kaizen*) role competency and knowledge platform tool. Evidently, KPM provides the core management for integration and innovation by 3S/3K combined methodology.

P2M

P2M is the acronym for the first Japanese standard of project and program management for enterprise innovation developed in 2001 by a team headed by Professor Shigenobu Ohara and initiated by ENAA (Engineering Advanced Association). The knowledge framework is constituted of entry, project management, program management, and 11 segment management frames.

Acknowledgments

On behalf of the writers, the editors wish to express deep appreciation to Ms. Yvonne Tan of World Scientific Publishing Co. and to Prof. Yasuhiro Monden of Tsukuba University and Mejiro University for giving us the precious chance to publish this book. They have been patient and encouraging throughout the whole course of production. Our thanks is also extended to Ms. Miho Nosaka and Mrs. Yunokawa for their assistance in communicating with the authors.

Contents

Part 2 KPM IN THE INFORMATION AND COMMUNICATIONS INDUSTRY

Part 3 PROJECT MANAGEMENT FOR BUSINESS REFORMS LINKED TO STRATEGY

**Part 4 PROJECT MANAGEMENT FOR KNOWLEDGE-BASED
    DEVELOPMENT STRATEGY**

**Part 5 APPLICATION OF KPM FOR NEW VALUE-CREATING
    ACTIVITY**

Part 1

Framework of Contemporary Japanese Project Management

Abstract

This Part is intended to give an overview of the background and progress of the contemporary and the new project management, to arrive at KPM in Japan. Interpretations of its context and applications are versatile and changing. The paradigm shift from the orthodoxy to the contemporary and the new is essential in the evolution. The heritage of assets in the past is encompassed, engraved and arranged in higher grade. Readers will benefit by reading about the latest research outcomes and practical applications before reading the details in the continuing parts.

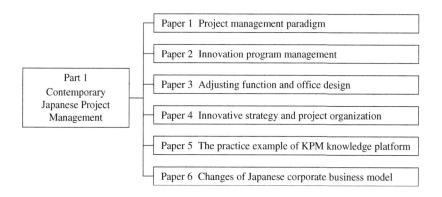

The first and the second papers are contributions written by Professor Shigenobu Ohara at Nippon Institute of Technology. The author is a renowned researcher of project management who pioneered the paradigm and endeavored to develop the first version of the Japanese standard tittled P2M. In the first paper, he explains the historical outlook of the experiences over a half-century in Japan, and launches a new paradigm and knowledge framework of Kaikaku Project Management (KPM). In the second paper, the core part of Innovation Program Management (IPM) is further explained with the new tool of knowledge platform citing applications.

The third paper is written by Tametsugu Taketomi, a business consultant and professor at the Nippon Institute of Technology. The author provides an outline of organizational theories which relate to ordinary operational-type activities, the project-oriented and the interactions. He underlines that the owner's view shall be adopted in the design of project organization for mission achievement. The latest observations are disclosed in his finding that the strategic issue is handled by a united program in lateral form rather than a matrix organization, which is proven and congruent with KPM theory.

The fourth paper is written by Tadamasa Imaguchi, Professor of Management at Keio University. He pays specific attention to the external business environment altered by globalization and computerization, insisting that the organization shall be revamped to be resilient and autonomous to cope with this strategy and business policy rapidly. In line with KPM, the trigger, process and role aspects of organizations are explained clearly from the organizational view in project management.

The fifth paper is prepared by Emi Yunokawa, CEO and President of Humansystem Corporation engaged in the software industry. She is concerned with the new paradigm of KPM and challenges the practical applications of knowledge platform to upgrade products and avoid errors. Factual evidence is exhibited for readers interested in the stiff competition in the industry.

The sixth paper is written by Toshihiko Kinoshita, Visiting Professor of Asia and Pacific Studies at Waseda University. He is well-known in the fields of international economics, management and finance. The author gives a holistic view of the impacts of globalization on the Japanese economy. His unique finding is crystallized in the mission-oriented strong leadership and hybrid business models of the East and the West observed in high performing companies.

Tametsugu Taketomi

President, Corporate Intelligence Corporation
Professor, Graduate School of Management of Technology
Nippon Institute of Technology

Framework of Contemporary Japanese Project Management (1): Project Management Paradigm — Interpretation, Application and Evolution to KPM

Shigenobu Ohara

Professor of Management of Technology
Graduate School of Nippon Institute of Technology

1   Introduction

Orthodox-type project management (hereinafter referred to as PM) has been developed for engineering methodology of building an artificial system. In Japan, the similar context to PM has been spread in the naming of *Shikumizukuri*, which means designing of unique architecture by a team of cross-functional specialists. PM has been widely spread and applied in the engineering arena in Japan. It is deemed an essential skill to ensure steady achievement of project goals under rigid constraints and unique conditions. However, faced with the matured society, business demands are increasing beyond the sole engineering system. This change reflects the potential capability that PM may provide a variety of prospective applications for enhancement of value creation. Nevertheless, it is essential to note that the architecture shall meet requirements to unify reciprocal interaction between business and engineered systems.

This paper starts with a brief context of conventional PM for readers to further extend its application in different areas. The readers may learn its limitations, and expect the new framework of PM to overcome these issues. In 2001, Japan published the new standard and guide under the brand of P2M, which stands for project and program for enterprise innovation. The incentive was driven by METI (the Ministry of Economy, Trade and Industry of the Japanese government) in support of subsidies for the research and development of work represented by the author (Ohara, 2002). In the lapse of seven years, the scheme and thinking of the advanced version is disclosed in the paradigm of Kaikaku Project

Management (KPM). *Kaikaku* signifies the comprehensive contexts of the breakthrough implemented by innovation, development and improvement.

2 Interpretation of Project Management Context and Applications

2.1 *What is project management?*

In general, a project is construed to mean an independent undertaking with a unique purpose and conditions to be managed by a temporary organized body. Most projects are categorized in complex and artificial structure or technical systems. In fact, Japanese people remember monumental constructions like *Tokyo Tower* as a landmark in Tokyo, the dramatic story of *Shinkansen* bullet train railways, and *Aqua Line* expressway under the sea of Tokyo bay. Managing projects, therefore, means the capability to identify the system, control the work, and to capture its output efficiently and effectively under required conditions. Although managing the process of planning, implementing, checking and controlling overlaps with general management, it is more specified to meet the attributes and objectives of the project. Being differentiated from line organization, authority is highly delegated to the leader of a specific team. Undoubtedly, leadership is decisive in teamwork and motivation, which impacts on the success of managing a project (Morris, 1997).

Penetrating the project term in the society, its context is expanding from large to small in scale and long to short in lifecycle. Very occasionally, project success is achieved by team competency in small projects without having specific knowledge. Warning is advisable, however, that fragile competency could hardly comply with complex and large-size type of projects.

Principally, the volume of the task increases relative to size, complexity and difficulty, but the project shares the three common attributes of individuality, time limit and uncertainty. Each project is specific in its job and conditions, which leaves room for creative efforts in individuality. Time limitations vary from a few weeks to a decade, but all projects have a start and an end. Uncertainty is the concept which relates to unpredictable elements beyond human control.

To represent individuality, the lifecycle method is adopted widely as a project management tool. It is also effective to exhibit the S-shape curve as progress by earned value. By comparing actual costs and earned values, the gap is easily figured out for control. The curve helps phased planning for managers by identifying milestones and intermediate outputs in turning points. The Work Break Down (WBS) is another basic and critical tool in managing projects. Primary targets like time, cost, quality and scope are more specified and segmented to the level of tasks and packages for greater control. This is the introductory outline of managing projects. Another requirement for success is related to the human factor in organizations. Though a project team is organized separately, it has to cooperate closely with the mother organization and negotiate to assume full delegation of authority to perform its tasks.

A summary is focused in the following three points:

(a) The term "project" is widely and flexibly used in contemporary society, and so it is likely to convey different messages and pursue individual styles of management.
(b) The orthodox type of PM knowledge is formulated mainly for the construction of a large-size engineering system.
(c) The ordinary methodology of PM is focused on the system construction in terms of lifecycle planning and execution to control time, cost, quality, scope and progress.

2.2 *PM applications in the engineering industry*

The Japanese engineering industry recorded \$11 billion (¥12.7 trillion) of backlog in 2007. The domestic market shares 76.7%, while the remaining 23.3% is covered by the overseas market. Despite the global energy boom, the market for the engineering industry has matured and the firms are looking at the business domain. To grasp applications in the industry, it may be necessary to bear in mind the sharing of capital system. A chemical plant is ranked higher in a share of 18.5% to meet a renovation cycle. Urban development (18.5%) is conducted in big cities, which raises impacts as well as ICT hardware systems (16.1%). The supply capacity of a power station (13.5%) is still short and the construction is sustainable, but industrial plants (11.2%) like steel, cement, environmental system, etc., depend on the market (ENAA, 2008).

As aforementioned in the introduction, project management has developed to cope with the demands of system engineering methodology. A large technical system could be handled only by a group of engineers acquainted with the systems approach rather than those with narrow-depth technological knowledge. The major players of the engineering industry are the capability holders of complex hardware systems. In Japan, they are those engaged in the construction of buildings, integrators of production and environment systems, and heavy machinery suppliers.

The role and responsibility of job sharing is definitely a practice in collaboration. The owner is responsible for producing definite requirements and configurations of the system, while the contractor plays the primary role in engineering, procurement and construction.

In Japan, the lump-sum contract is preferred to cost-plus fee base in the business climate so that risk-sharing is beneficial to either partner. In this Japanese style of contracting system, mutual trust is laid in the foundation of long-term friendly relations. Because they believe that delay destroys the reliability, the Japanese contractors make backtype scheduling from the end to the front. It goes without saying that Japan is the kingdom of quality management.

Thus, long partnership and trust is the strength of the Japanese engineering industry. Though it has the basic paradigm in common with the orthodox PM, it is clear that a delicate difference lies in transaction practice. As reiterated, orthodox PM underlines the role of contractors, in essence, how to construct and deliver a technical system to the owner at the end:

(a) The owner shall give a definite purpose and configurations on the technical system to the contractor, while the system construction is the contractor's full responsibility.
(b) In general, the primary job of the contractor is scoped, and limited maximum in engineering, procurement, and construction in the case of a lump-sum contract.
(c) Communication is the fundamental tool shared by the owner and the contractor to solve conflicts and friction arising on the interface of the system boundary.
(d) An orthodox type of PM knowledge and skill is still dominant in the industry, but some contractors are challenging this to exploit a broader range of business.

2.3 *Project management application in ICT industry*

ICT is an acronym for information and communication technology. Regardless of hardware and software, engineers in the industry have confidence in applying project management. The industry is growing rapidly and widely in Japan — the size of the market is already four times bigger than the engineering industry over several decades. Likewise, the education and training are based on the orthodox PM paradigm (Yamamoto, 2006).

Despite the enthusiasm, it is worth noting that the owner is unable to warrant to provide the definite requirements and configurations to the contractor. The owner has the limitation of specific capability on ICT system offered by the contractor, and vice versa, the contractor may have little knowledge of business processes because of secrecy. There is no choice but to trust the proposed benefits of investment and proceed to the contract.

Meanwhile, the contractor conducts customization of packaged software to apply the business process by learning disclosed to clients, but the efforts are limited in partial coverage. The extra elaboration is more or less similar to developments in exploiting the fitting spot suited to the client. In the digital transcription to computer program from the analogue work, ICT engineering has even more risk of uncertainty. The additional burden of tasks is likely to result in trial and error developments. To avoid this, experience-based specialization is conducted in area segments of finance, logistics, manufacturing, service, etc. Beyond the extra elaboration, the industry is also faced with the issues of ambiguity of requirement definition and hidden risk of development. The controversy is popular and continuing as the issues are undoubtedly major causes of trouble.

The following is the summary:

(a) An institutional gap of information lies between the owner and the contractor.
(b) Although the ICT industry has commonalities with engineering, high hurdles exist in definite job sharing in equal footing.
(c) Project governance is indispensable to control the total lifecycle.
(d) Risk management shall be reviewed and reinforced in project management.

3   Development-Type Project Management and Risk Issues

3.1   *Project risk hazard*

In the late 1990s, Japanese projects in Asia encountered a financial bubble which caused risk hazards. The owner had to reschedule or divest the recovery of capital, while the contractor implemented the payment hedged by insurance or had to agree to the postponement of amortization to be paid for construction. The risk hazard is hardly handled to protect parties by the contract stipulation (Kinoshita and Urata, 2000; Ohara, 2000).

Other types of trouble like the network system was reported in the news inside Japan. The merger of large banks had facilitated an integration of the separate networks, but lack of a holistic view had failed the connectivity of networks. Citizens could neither draw nor transfer cash by cards. The system shutdown of air ticket reservation had delayed or cancelled service operations. The coding trouble of price figures by human errors had generated a huge loss to stock companies. Nobody raised the objection that ICT systems are evidently strong weapons to revive competition as exemplified by business process reengineering (BPR), enterprise resource planning (ERP) and supply chain management (SCM). PM is considered a mandatory education and training for ICT engineers, and qualification programs are provided to reduce failures by approximately 70% as proven in surveys (Nakamura, 2003). Varied from hardware engineering, ICT engineering is based on solution service, which may encompass indefinite client requirements and the accompanying commitments.

In stiff competition, the contractor is likely to accept the desired requirements of the owner over his own capability. Landscape is the new methodology to see the sharing view by way of simulation/gaming (Deguchi, 2004). In the R&D world of manufacturing and assembly, the three-dimensional CAD is already an essential tool in the concurrent-type engineering of complicated hardware like aircraft assembly and the new design of cars. Regardless of hardware and software, the owner's view is essential to see to risks and to make a balanced assessment for control. Figure 1 is the general outlook of an assessment process to clarify the grey zone in so-called "failure". Unless there is critical failure of technology, it shows channels whereby settlements could be reached between the parties by negotiations in the business world. In fact, success or failure varies by the positions and roles in subjective evaluation. The owner has to make maximum effort for recovery of investment, while the contractor has to extend his best service to keep clients' trust in the market. What is critical to the risk issue is summarized by how the project management style shall be formulated.

In the case of the development type of project contract, ambiguity is left in the definition of requirements. That is why project governance is

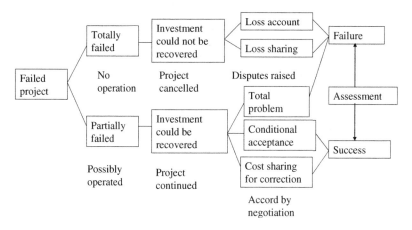

Fig. 1   Assessment threshold of a failed project

critical to improve risk-sharing in the project job. The success rate of a new drug varies between 1 to 1/100,000 orders. Regardless of rating, the owner permits trial and error challenges to projects. In R&D projects in machinery or process system, the success rate for marketable products varies under 20% on average, which is allowed within the range of owner's forecasting. So, projects shall be managed by multidimensional balancing under the project governance framework.

The key points are underlined below:

(a) Project assessment in the development type shall be conducted by the owner's view, because project governance is critical for risk control and decision-making.
(b) Project challenge of the development type is essentially involved with elements of external and internal environments.

3.2   *Inquiry survey for project failure*

In view of the high rate of failure risk, the author intended to find a fact base to give a fair judgment of these issues. The survey had been conducted in the form of questions and answers, and the format was designed to identify elements caused in the three stages of scheme, system and operation. It is evident that the contractor's scope is limited in the system, while the owner is responsible for the total. Table 1 shows the results of implied causes. It is the analytic results from 137 of 794 project managers

Table 1   Causes of failure in stage approach

Scheme Stage	System Stage	Operation Stage
59%	32%	9%

Table 2   Risk elements to failure in stages approach

Scheme Stage	System Stage	Operation Stage
Ambiguity 47.4% (47)	Scope and quality 41.0% (32)	Operating troubles 34.8% (16)
Planning quality 15.2% (15)	Pressed budget 17.9% (14)	Ineffective system 26.1% (12)
Excessive aspiration 14.1% (14)	PMr competency 14.1% (11)	Inconvenient system 21.7% (10)
Scheme quality 9.1% (9)	Organization 12.8% (10)	Bad cost performance 10.9% (5)
Economic visibility 6.1% (6)	Pressed delivery 10.3% (8)	Bad support service 6.5% (3)
Cover ratio 91.9% (91)	Cover ratio 96.1% (75)	Cover ratio 100.0% (46)
Inquired response (99)	Inquired response (78)	Inquired response (46)

(response rate 17.2%) belonging to different affiliations like software systems and network (49%), hardware systems of engineering and machinery (25%), operational improvements (16%) and management consulting (9%). The fact analysis was less in project management, because the scheme and the operation stages had been out of the PM scope. Though most opinions were from the contractors, it is yet surprising that the failure is attributable to the scheme stage, which is almost double that of the system. This shows the lack of deliberate efforts in the upper stream to feed appropriate documents and information to the system stage.

Table 2 exhibits the breakdown of elements, which explains the top five reasons resulting in failures. Apparently, the primary player in the scheme stage is the owner, but open to the contractor, who may make use of the place for dialogue, proposal and negotiations prior to contracting. However, complexity could neither be solved within the issue of definition (Loucopoulos and Karakostas, 1998), nor the scope sharing by parties.

Ambiguity relates to the PM paradigm itself, and it looks like the inter-action of negative impacts in the system step.

Table 2 represents the limitations of the orthodox type of project man-agement, and project management shall be renewed under the owner's par-adigm. In the last decade, R&D projects had been conducted by the technology-push model at large enterprises. Most of the decentralized R&D projects have failed to go over the Death Valley and Darwinian sea. Today, the high-performing enterprises have converted from the technology-push to market-pull models. The implications are summarized as follows:

(a) The primary cause of failure is centralized in the upper stream of project management control.
(b) Project governance shall be reflected to avoid risks uncovered by project management.

4   What is the Difference in Japanese Project Management?

4.1   *Project management standards*

The value of project management has been recognized in the United States. PMI (Project Management Institute) had challenged in 1985 and published the monumental standards of *PMBOK* (*A Guide to Project Management Body of Knowledge*) (Duncan, 1996). The framework guides the project context and then covers the scope of nine knowledge areas for managing time, cost, quality, scope, procurement, human resources, risk, communi-cation and integration.

In 1996, the European professional organization of IPMA (International Project Management Association) subsequently established the *Competence Baseline* (Caupin *et al.*, 1999), and shared it in member countries for the qualification of professionals. This baseline underlines professional compe-tence generated by the fusion of knowledge, experience and attitude. It is worthy to note that the baseline takes consideration of national culture and climate.

A national member association is allowed to design a baseline of 28 core elements plus certain selective options of 14 elements. UK and Australia also have original standards and an accreditation program.

Motivated by movements of PM standards, ENAA (Engineering Advanced Association) started the basic survey in 1998 and METI supported its development funding for original Japanese standards. In 2001, P2M (Project and Program Management for Enterprise Innovation) was launched as the first standard guidebook (Ohara, 2006). Symbolized by the branded title, the unique features exist in program management and enterprise innovation, and its outline of knowledge framework is given in Figure 2. The basic thought behind these features is directed to an open system approach. If the potential power of project management could be applied, the major issue is the interaction of business and technical systems. An insightful idea is indispensable to put the two different systems together. The idea is normally complex, but valuable because it is close

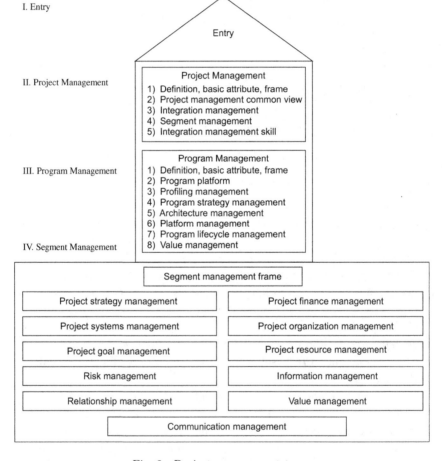

Fig. 2　Project management tower

to innovation. The only solution is to put plural projects together in an open environment. Of more importance is mindful and knowledge innovation driven by PM thinking, and this advanced further from P2M to KPM (Kaikaku Project Management) as outlined hereafter.

To summarize:

(a) There are two sorts of knowledge and competence in PM standards.
(b) The standards and its documents foster professional resources.
(c) P2M is the first guidebook in Japan, and it has been improved to KPM.

4.2   Contemporary paradigm of Japanese project management?

Orthodox-type PM thinkers have endeavored to formulate the knowledge framework for construction of a technical system, placing the contractor as the major player. Their paradigm may be explained in another way: they have been concentrating on "how to build a technical system surely and stably". Here, it is important to note again that the premise of job sharing by the thinkers is that a definite mission shall be given by the owner, while the contractor designs, constructs and delivers the system within the limited lifecycle. Apparently, the role of project manager is imagined as the lead in managing goals and process motivation to acquire a system. The system and major goals are stipulated in the contract and identified in the budget, delivery, performance, progress and specifications.

Contemporary Japanese PM is advocated in this version. Applying the open system thinking where human interaction is dominant, the contemporary PM depends on a "value creation paradigm". What is the value gained by managing projects? This is the basic question. The Japanese answer is the *breakthrough to Kaikaku*. The owner/entrepreneur initiates the innovation to create value in the future and discusses with the contractor. In line with this thinking, the central player is the owner, who is completely responsible for the total lifecycle. Two critical contexts of *mission* and *solution* are introduced in the PM paradigm. Mission is essentially the willingness to commit resources, which is generated by an insightful idea balanced on value. A solution is very occasionally implied

Table 3 Comparison and distinction

PM Version	Orthodox Type of PM Paradigm	Contemporary PM Paradigm
Holistic view	Technical system paradigm	Value creation paradigm
Role and position	The contractor's role and position	The owner's role and position
Mission	Definite mission	Definite and implicit missions
Premises	Solution is given by the owner	Solution is created jointly
Lifecycle	From contract to delivery	From mission to achievement
Managing	Budget, delivery, quality, progress	Value creation
Type	Managing independent projects	Managing compound projects

by the owner, but indefinitely. So the contractor collaborates to jointly achieve value creation, which means the development process is linked to the innovative mission (Ohara, 2006). Table 3 summarizes the comparisons and distinctions of major items between orthodox and contemporary PM in Japan.

4.3   A case study of the introduction of the contemporary PM paradigm

The top management of a printer machine company got a strategic idea to capture the dominant market share in the office segment. To achieve their goal, they formulated a strategic plan to develop a new model of office printer. The strategy intended to establish the dominant advantage by individual differentiation of the office printer against competitors by detailing the novelty of multiple usages with an ecology functionality. It is not unusual for a functional department to not take responsibility when new products go wrong and accuse others instead. So, a unique single responsibility system was adopted. Those who respond to the public announcement inside the company are obliged to explain the justification of their respective development plan to the steering committee for obtaining authority of delegation.

For example, the mission is announced in such a way that the person responsible for the new model development is wanted in closeout of one year for the prospective career path of the challenge, on the condition that $30 million in sales shall be secured for the first six months of production. Compared to the orthodox-type PM, applicants have to plan by themselves not only the total lifecycle plan, but the solution itself guided by instruction. The justifiable scheduling, risk estimate and visibility shall be programmed, while the owner is ready to delegate full authority and desired budget. In effect, what they are doing is creating a solution for business scheme, system model development, assembly test and quantity test production, and giving them accountability.

5   What is Kaikaku Project Management?

5.1   *Kaikaku: Strategy linkage reform*

Kaikaku or innovative reform is a popular and meaningful word in Japan, because it is being pursued in contemporary enterprises of political administration, industry and the company. In particular, project management may be converted to provide dual advantages in dealing with the unique undertaking of creative entrepreneurship and solid implementation of business managers if contrived in the new version. *Kaikaku* is congruent to the strategy context that enterprises have to create and to sustain changes of organizational capability complying with the external environment. In general, corporate strategy is handled to formulate planning by the head office, and implemented to capture outcome by organizations. *Kaikaku* is certainly a challenge and a risk, but value creation sustainability can neither be conscious nor be in hand without it, because it is strategic capability itself in pursuit of uniqueness and novelty at any level. This is why the new version after P2M is named Kaikaku Project Management (hereinafter called KPM).

5.2   *Three layers composition of Kaikaku*

Represented, motivated and encouraged by *Kaikaku,* the versatile challenges of uniqueness have been nominally implemented in Japan. Though the word is widely used in a number of visions at enterprises, the context is not substantially articulated, and its assessment of outcome is varied as well. The comprehensive context is engraved in many ways, and so *kaikaku* differs in what it means to stakeholders. Some use it as radical innovation, while others use it as small innovation. Likewise, some emphasize digital business development, while others give priority to marketing development. To avoid confusion, KPM is defined here as encompassing the 3 K's of *Kakusin* (innovation), *Kaihatsu* (development) and *Kaizen* (improvement), or more specifically, the synergetic unity to be challenged and linked to corporate-level strategy.

Table 4 shows a brief outline of 3 K's components with the detailed explanation hereafter.

(a) *Kakusin* (innovation) means the radical type of comprehensive breakthrough by uniting all layers of a new combination of knowledge and wisdom. With the objective of dramatic upgrade in performance, the top managers shall be conscious of the decisive will to play the primary role of leadership in initiating strategic uniqueness, big changes and high impacts.

(b) *Kaihatsu* (development) means the challenges to acquire new knowledge and information. It is intended to enhance competitive advantage. Development does not necessarily refer to technology, but covers more extensively business, product, process and even market as well. Nevertheless, it has risks and uncertainties in common and is linked more or less with innovation.

In today's competitive environment, the lead-time speed is also detrimental. It ranges from short to long terms, and from small to large scales and scopes. Impacts are extremely variable.

Table 4   The three components of *Kaikaku*

Components	Methodology	Targeting and Organizational Impact
Kakusin (innovation)	Breakthrough by a new knowledge combination	Targeting to upgrade dramatic performance on the whole
Kaihatsu (development)	Acquiring front-edge knowledge and information	Intending to capture competitive advantages in specific fields
Kaizen (improvement)	Incremental and continuing efforts in proactive work life	Implanting project-based thinking to link to the whole

(c) *Kaizen* (improvement) means the incremental and continuing efforts for improvement at work-floor level. The *Kaizen* activity in the Toyota group is renowned as one of the best practices. It is an autonomously driven small group activity, which is initiated for a discovered issue solution. A typical example of the agenda is related to the efforts in proactive work life where a clean, well-ordered environment is preferred as represented in 5S (*Seiri, Seiton, Seisou, Seiketsu, Sitsuke*) symbols.

Kaizen is positioned between routine and project activities, including the quality control activity, but the incremental efforts have borne far bigger outcomes in corporate performance. The 3 M's (*Muri, Muda, Mura*) also need to be overcome. *Muri* means enforced styling work where good quality is hardly produced. *Muda* is symbolic of non-valuable junks or wastes, where people are not aware that they are producing more stocks of parts than needed. *Mura* means deviations or variations from a certain standard, which might result in lack of control or improper handling of process. KPM implants project-based thinking in *Kaizen* and links the work floor and market front efforts of knowledge.

5.3 *KPM knowledge framework*

The strategic capability of human resources is designed to be congruent with the organizational hierarchy and functions, because it is fostered by awareness of roles and learning by doing work in the organization. Though cross-functionality of teams has been emphasized in project management, the lateral phase of collaboration may be significant, with room for further practice. KPM intends to explore the framework of enhanced methodology of strategy implementation in the form of the hybrid of lateral and cross-functional collaborations (see Figure 3).

In the value creation paradigm, there exists *Kakusin* (innovation), the intent process of entrepreneurship, and *Kaihatsu* (development) of the creative process in the upper stream. *Kaizen,* relating closely to implementation of project(s), is the subsequent process thereafter, which the contractor may collaborate with as a partner. The final process is the operation and maintenance, which is occasionally taken over by divisional organizations, after which the project is deemed to be terminated.

The sophisticated distinction arises in project termination, because the true end is the recovery of invested capital in terms of the owner's view.

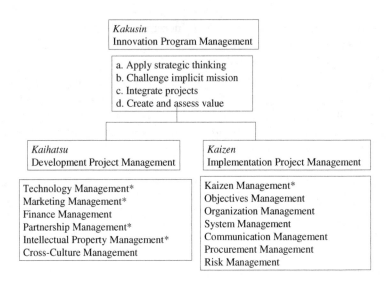

Fig. 3   KPM knowledge framework

Note: P2M version has no classification by 3 K's. Asterisk mark has been newly included in the KPM version.

Kakusin Innovation Program Management (IPM): Being seriously conscious of innovation, the program manager has to perform critical roles on behalf of the owner. To accomplish the job, it is needless to reiterate that higher and broader knowledge has to be covered. In addition to this competency, innovation links and interacts further with plural development projects. Accordingly, organic managing of projects is demanded in the form of integration of horizontal models and lateral projects.

Kaihatsu Development Project Management (DPM): Research and development is a specific form of acquiring new knowledge, system or information. In managing these projects, risk and return are the principal issues of concern. Depending on the project types, probability and lead time are also important parameters to manage. Since development itself is a creative activity, team formation, partnership, collaboration, communication channels and frequency of contacts among members are essential points for managers to control. Some of this knowledge was insufficient in the orthodox type of project management.

KPM supplements the comprehensive knowledge framework hitherto rarely compiled.

Kaizen Implementation Project Management (KIPM): The orthodox type of project management is still dominant, and its scope of knowledge is more or less the same in its intent. Nevertheless, it shall be noted that smaller sizes of software projects in the short-term are increasing in numbers rather than the large, long-term ones of hardware. In KPM, *kaizen* management, thinking and its attitudes have been newly included in the framework to cope with demands for success. In particular, incremental efforts of knowledge stock is extremely useful.

To summarize:

(a) KPM is the advanced version of P2M, linked to corporate strategy and positioned as practical implementation methodology in terms of the owner's view.
(b) KPM intends to explore the framework of enhanced methodology of strategy implementation in the form of the hybrid of lateral and cross-functional collaborations.
(c) KPM may encompass the 3 K's of *Kakusin* (innovation), *Kaihatsu* (development) and *Kaizen* (improvement), the synergetic unity to be challenged.

6   Conclusion

In project management paradigm, systems thinking is in the background. In particular, the large complex of the technical system had been the first choice since system engineering took part of the domain. As repeatedly explained, the orthodox project management had been colored by closed system thinking. Unless the value premise is given, the contractor and system engineers would be at a loss as to where to go.

Emerging technology has changed the environment. Technology has penetrated and become essential engines for productivity and digital transformation, resulting in the interaction among open systems. Undoubtedly, paradigm shift is mandatory whenever technical system is used for business purposes.

P2M had steered the first step in Japan by publishing the first standard guidebook in 2001. In the lapse of eight years, the orthodox type is still dominant, but high-performing enterprises have started shifting from the contractor's view to the owner's view. The knowledge framework of the newest version has been presented and the subsequent applications further detailed in this paper.

Acknowledgments

The author is delighted to thank World Scientific Publishing, Yasuhiro Monden (Professor Emeritus at Tsukuba University and Professor at Mejiro University) and Takayuki Asada (Professor at Osaka University) for the opportunity to publish on contemporary Japanese project management. My appreciation is also extended to Professor Yamamoto of Hitotsubashi University for his precious advice.

References

Caupin, G., Knopfel, H., Morris, P., Motzel, E., and Pannenbacker, O. (1999). *IPMA Competence Baseline*, IPMA.

Deguchi, H. (2004). Organizational failure assessment and landscape learning, *Organizational Science* 38, pp. 29–39 (in Japanese).

Duncan, W. R. (1996). *A Guide to the Project Management Body of Knowledge*, PMI.

ENAA (Engineering Advancement Association Japan) (2008). *Engineering Industry Fact Survey* (in Japanese).

Kinoshita, T. and Urata, S. (2000). Asian economy — Challenge to risk, in *Economic Development of East Asia and International Capital Flow*, Keiso Shobo, pp. 17–72 (in Japanese).

Loucopoulos, P. and Karakostas, V. (1998). "System Requirements Engineering" Wilhelm Scheer "Aris Business Process Framework" "Aris Business Process Modeling" Springer Verlag Heidelber.

Morris, P. (1997). *The Management of Projects*, London: Thomas Telford.

Nakamura, K. (2003). *Unoperatable Computor, Research on Information System Failure*, Nikkei BP Computor (in Japanese).

Ohara, S. (2000). Reform of Asian economy and roles of entrepreneurs, in *Economic Development of East Asia and International Capital Flow*, Keiso Shobo, pp. 109–148 (in Japanese).

Ohara, S. (2002). *P2M, Project and Program Management for Enterprise Innovation*, ENAA (Engineering Advancement Association Japan)/PMCC (Project Management Certification Center Japan).

Ohara, S. (2006). Mission-driven approach (MDA) of managing complex projects — Demystifying the new framework and its background, *Journal of International Association of Project & Program Management* 1(1), pp. 61–70.

Yamamoto, H. (2006). Methods of sharing information about IT system construction in strategic program management, *Journal of the International Asssociation of Project & Program Management* 1(1), pp. 11–20.

Framework of Contemporary Japanese Project Management (2): *Kakusin*-Innovation Program Management (IPM) — Organizational Acceptance and Dynamic Intellectual Cycle

Shigenobu Ohara

Professor of Management of Technology
Graduate School of Nippon Institute of Technology

1 Introduction

Program management is a rational methodology based on the owner's view or thinking. It is more suited to deal with the implicit mission by dividing into plural projects for partnership collaborations. Integration is the aspect of program management that controls these partnerships under a single policy or strategic innovation. Should the program manager be less interested, the owner might lose the big benefits of strategic collaborations and suffer risks. Therefore, the essential points for success of innovation are closely related to raising awareness of organizational roles so that a dynamic intellectual cycle is generated to upgrade added value.

2 Organization and Value Creation

2.1 *Corporate strategy and organization*

High-performing companies in Japan (Monden *et al.*, 2006) recognize that strategic management thinking underlines the unification of both formulation and implementation. Basically, the head office formulates corporate strategy composed of business and *Kaikaku* policies. Business policy is related to the strategic planning of goals and methods to be conducted by the routine organization. *Kaikaku* policy, on the other hand, clarifies the investment program to be achieved by project organizations.

Different from the business policy, apparently specific capabilities and skills are demanded to cope with *Kaikaku* programs where the owner's view is required.

In large corporations, a steering committee is installed as the top organization to monitor and review the program's progress. A program office is also installed at headquarters in cases where plural programs or numerous projects are organized. However, in small corporations, a core team could replace the program office, and the program manager could act like the program director. Figure 1 is the typical type of large high-performing corporations where policy management is introduced. What is essentially significant to note lies in the awareness and capabilities of critical positions of the *Kaikaku* program.

As shown in Figure 1, three significant improvements are devised in the organization:

(a) The steering committee periodically monitors and directs the whole program.
(b) The program director coordinates the head office and program implementation.
(c) The program manager controls the project manager.

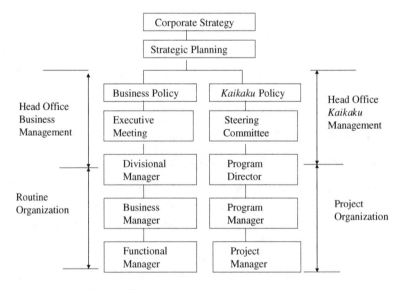

Fig. 1   Corporate strategy and organization

2.2 *Value creation view*

The current value creation is achieved by the routine organization, while the future value is accomplished by project organizations. The project is firstly envisioned and determined according to why it should be and what should be done. To accomplish this, the activity has to be recognized deeply in each layer of the organization. Without this awareness, it is only an illusion written in scenario, similar to a car without an engine.

Innovation program management (IPM) is based on the strategic thinking as explained in the previous chapter. The principal objectives are the adaptation to the external environment which causes the obsolescence in capabilities, business and value chains. To simplify this thinking of innovation program management (Ohara, 2007), the several concepts used in project or program management are exhibited in the following formula:

$$\frac{\text{Outcome}}{\text{Investment}} = \frac{\text{Deliverable}}{\text{Investment}} \times \frac{\text{Outcome}}{\text{Deliverable}}$$

Scheme	System	Service

The intent of the formula is summarized in the following three points:

(a) Innovative mission involves developing to the total scheme committed by the investment.
(b) Once the decision is made, the system is designed and built to put in service for value-making.
(c) Service is the recovery of investment, and needs know-how for capital recovery.

3 Innovation Program Management (IPM)

3.1 *Program lifecycle and integration of plural projects*

IPM plays the two central roles of vertical and horizontal control. First, it controls the long span of lead time from the mission formulation to achievement, being aware of the owner's view.

Second, close channels of communications are opened here so that the three layers of *Kakusin, Kaihatsu* and *Kaizen* are densely united. This new

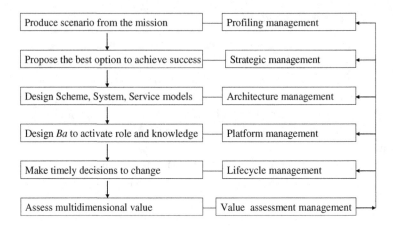

Fig. 2   Innovation program management

consideration has been conducted from the fact that vertical projects are scarcely communicated, compared to the horizontally designed projects (Ohara and Arai, 2004a).

Figure 2 shows the whole outlook of IPM. The six types of management are further explained below.

3.1.1   *Profiling management*

Mission is the descriptive requirements of the expected outcome together with implications of policy and commitments of implementation from the owner to the contractor (Ohara, 2006). There are two types of missions — explicit and implicit. The former is definitely described in its intent, objectives and solution, while the latter leaves room for further development of its definition, since it leaves room for exploitations of its innovative ideas to which the contractor's efforts are desired for complete solution. An excellent manager in general has such multiple talents as an innovator, manager and assessor, and so innovation thrives. Profiling management deals with the process of clarifying, justifying, assuring and documenting the mission intents to stakeholders so that the mission shall be converted to a business scheme, and planning to be ready for practical undertaking.

3.1.2   *Strategic management*

Though strategic thinking is introduced, it is within the scope and to the level of program management. Being aware of this, however, it is critical to have sufficient knowledge to coordinate with corporate strategy. Numerous methods are available like portfolio, SWOT (Strength, Weakness, Opportunity, Threats) and CSF (Critical Success Factor) analyses. Simple analysis like risk-return positioning is surely helpful, but a multidimensional approach is also needed. To be more specific, the major role here is to produce appropriate plural options and then select the best by assessment suited to the program for success.

3.1.3 *Architecture management*

Architecture is frequently used in buildings and system designs. It refers to the grand design, rather than the detailed one, to put the holistic plan forward in the three aspects of structuring, functionality and behavioral expressions (Ohara, 1999). To further clarify the architecture, KPM offers a 3S modeling of Scheme, System and Service. Scheme means the business plan which overlaps with the profiling management, but also encompasses the large scope from scenario, justifications and feasibility to the master plan. System is a very comprehensive concept applicable to technical, business and social domains, but here, in program lifecycle, it comes second to scheme with an intent of more or less technical systems of hardware and software to be applied for the scheme intent. The Service model handles the service of operating and maintaining the system to get capital recovery. This is out of the scope of the orthodox type of project management, but the model is critical in other aspects of extended service to capture knowledge for and from clients. In short, the architecture aims at holistic harmony, optimization and satisfactions of stakeholders in the owner's view.

3.1.4 *Platform management*

The platform covers principally such human areas as communications, culture, intellectual interactions and human relations. It means the common place and infrastructure to be formed under certain conditions in the coverage aforementioned. In trust of the significance of human intellectual activities, platform management provides and maintains the best suited platform by which participant communication, team activation, dynamic intellectual cycles, and finally knowledge, could be stored. In relation to the theory and methodology, the Japanese have contributed a lot in *Ba* theory and knowledge management.

3.1.5   Lifecycle management

This lifecycle shall be construed in the role and position of the owner. In this view, the internal and external uncertainties are the major issues of concern. Uncertainty depends on the length of lead-time and limitation of the capability of the owner. The economy, market, competitors, price and technology are variables of the external environment that affect the process of achieving the mission. Probability, capabilities and critical information related to development are parameters of the internal environment. Lifecycle management is involved largely with such risk mitigation and aversion. Cost-benefit analysis, econometric methods, Monte Carlo simulations and agent-based modeling are available as effective methods.

KPM recommends the concurrent engineering methods. Very occasionally, they are used for curtailing lead-time and for clarifying interfaces, by which risk controls are far advanced. Here in KPM, the risk option approach is also recommended to apply to the architecture modeling basis for making fair decisions in selecting options of downsizing, expansion, postponement and cancellation over the long range of the lifecycle.

3.1.6   Value assessment management

Assessment means the diagnostic method of a specific object for intended purposes by using certain criteria, and it is indispensable for program navigation. It is also effective as a driving force for programs. In order to put assessment into practice, systematic framework design, measurement methods and process documentation have to be prepared in advance to assure reliability. In the owner's view, a multidimensional assessment is required. Though numerous methods are available in economics, system analysis and accounting, it is recommended that a balanced scorecard is one of the most practical (Asada *et al.*, 2004).

3.2   *A case study of electronic components innovation*

A Japanese company had been producing a print circuit board (PCB) since the late 1980s. Because of stiff competition in the market, the firm had struggled to secure 2%–3% profit to US$3.5 million in sales. Taking note of the potential growth of PCB, the new president had introduced program management linked to corporate strategy in 1995, and amazingly, the firm had attained 20% profit to sales of US$36 million in 2008.

Since PCB is a basic electronic component used universally, market pricing is controlled by the cost leader. Facing the slowdown of business performance in 1995, the new president looked into profiling of the market and converted to the differentiation strategy of "*Kaikaku* to high-performing company". Complying with differentiation, he advocated *Kaikaku* policy expressing "the front-edge PCB developer at the fastest speed". Applying innovation program management, he had transformed R&D divergently conducted in laboratories, merchandizing and production to a centralized form. The president also installed a steering committee and took the leadership role of program director until the new form was in orbit to identify its outcome. At the office, the program director organized plural unified teams for the compound development projects composed of product, process and market.

Clients at the front-edge demand of PCB are mobile phones, personal computers and digital cameras of which the average lifecycle is 12 months. To catch up on the clients' lifecycle, six months is the fastest possible estimate for the component supplies, even though this could be very difficult. Under the uncertainty of development, the program director had placed several product teams in competition, and monitored the progress from time to time. Though variation was taken into account, the process lifecycle was two years with depreciation as well. Thus, the room for test production is extremely short.

What were the secrets nobody could achieve in other projects? The secret lies in *Kaizen* and team collaboration. Knowledge, data and information have been stored in the *Kaizen* data warehouse. Managed under a single strategy, it was proven that IPM offers the synergetic benefits of speedy delivery, dominant share in the new market, and quick recovery of capital cash flow.

3.3 *Analytic interpretation*

Figure 3 explains the essence of innovation program management. The horizontal axis is the time horizon of the program lifecycle which is also expressed in 3S model's exhibit of Scheme, System and Service.

The vertical axis is the program value or cumulative cash flow. The dotted lines show the inflow of cash generated at the service model stage in two separate cases. One case represents the "plus" side of program value beyond the horizontal bar, while the other case is the "minus" side under the horizontal bar.

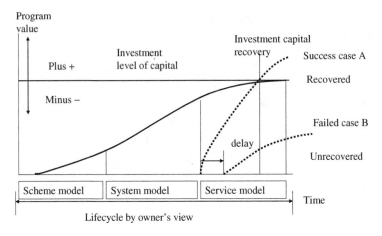

Fig. 3   Analytic interpretations in threshold of success and failure

The horizontal bar is the investment level of program capital, which may intersect some time within the service model to be deemed a successful case like A. However, should the program be delayed, it could cause failure due to market chance loss with exposure of higher risks like case B.

In terms of analytic interpretations by models, the success case A corresponding to the PCB producer may be summarized in the following points:

(a) The paradigm shift of differentiation and its mission is the most effective point.
(b) The quality of the Scheme model is refined in the process of profiling scenarios.
(c) Product and process are united concurrently in the System models.
(d) The Service model is supported by an intelligent *Kaizen* platform proven by facts.

4   The Threshold of Success and Failure

4.1   *Inquiry research survey by organizational approach*

There is no guarantee an organization's *Kaikaku* program will be successful. Success and failure are both influenced by leadership style, collaboration with the mother organization, team activation and dynamic intellectual cycles.

Table 1 shows the analytic results of project failures based on an inquiry research survey of 137 project managers conducted in 2004 (Ohara and Arai, 2004b). The left side of the column is related to the

Table 1   Organizational and human resource factors causing failures

Organizational Factors	Human Resource Factors
(a) Disregarding attitudes towards systematic heritage of empirical knowledge 26.4% (69)	(h) Insufficient capabilities, lack of empirical knowledge and its heritage 54.7% (64)
(b) Rigidity of organization to environmental change 16.1% (42)	(i) Poor support for PM education 12.0% (14)
(c) Dissatisfaction of rewards for endeavors to outcome 13.8% (36)	(j) Excessive estimation of individual competency of skills and experience 7.7% (9)
(d) Dissatisfaction of priority to jobs in line routine organization 12.3% (32)	(k) Shortage of competency/actions/ attitude of core human resources 6.8% (8)
(e) Weak linkage of projects to corporate strategy 10.3% (27)	
(f) Insufficient awareness, education and training of PM 10.3% (27)	(l) Dissatisfaction of incentives and rewards for efforts 6.0% (7)
(g) Weak availability of information system and tools 3.8% (10)	(m) Adverse effect of bad human relations 5.1% (6)
	(n) Difficulty of securing competent staff 4.3% (5)
Cover ratio 93.0% (243)	Cover ratio 96.6% (113)
Inquiry number of recovery (261)	Inquiry number of recovery (117)

organizational factors causing failures, while the right is human resource factors. Looking at the left column, the top factor of failure (a) is the disregarding attitudes towards the systematic heritage of empirical knowledge (26.4%). It is surprising how often projects are organized in *ad hoc* styles and without weapons of past experience. The second response (b) is the rigidity of the organization to environmental change (16.1%). This response implies isolation of the project from the mother corporation, and the organization itself is neither flexible in mind nor action. The remaining factors (c)–(g) relate to causes of dissatisfaction. It is clear that the project is deemed as something auxiliary and *ad hoc*, which anyone might do by oneself. Once it is organized, the team is isolated and efforts are little respected.

Concerning human resource factors, the top factor (h) of failure is insufficient capabilities and a lack of empirical knowledge and its heritage (54.7%). This in turn is related to the second response (i) of poor support for PM education. In short, relative weakness is engraved in project management training in mind, skill, knowledge, and in particular, institutional training.

5   Upgrading Success Rate by Human Platform

5.1   *What is Ba or platform?*

In view of the several implications observed from the inquiry survey, the success factor shall be further explored. Though the organizational approach was adopted in the survey, here, for the countermeasure, the action approach is better to look into small team plays and designs. Whenever collaboration work is performed, a community is formed, which Japanese call *Ba*. *Ba* gives a mental impact to interactions of program members. The author believes that *Ba* is an essential element of human relations and its activities. According to Itami *et al.* (2000), *Ba* means a formation of collaborative minds when a specific agenda is acquired by a certain informative media. Whenever *Ba* rises, human interaction of high density communications are accelerated continuously.

The similar word in English is used in two ways. One is an organizational base or platform for producing product, and the other is collaboration, though the context for platform insofar as it is used is mixed with organizational and action approaches. What is critical here is summarized into two essential points — one is definition, and the other is its application in mind consciousness and knowledge interaction:

(a) *Definition*: *Ba* platform (hereinafter referred to as platform) refers to facilitating a program or a project of collaborative work essential for building on, acquiring and sharing information and knowledge of human, information and cultural aspects.

(b) *Application*: Here, two applications of platform are presented. The action approach is based on the individual manner, and by conjoint use with the climate survey method, a platform could be applied for team activation and vertical channel communications. The second intent is the new challenge to dive deep into knowledge dynamism by which a stock of knowledge could flow into the process as resources (Nonaka and Takeuchi, 1996). Figure 4 is the platform tool exhibits for program use. This platform tool is composed of the further smaller nine platform cells. In practical use, these could be broken down to proper size according to application purposes.

5.2   *Application to human system for success*

Organizations tend to remain as is. As *Kaikaku* program changes and requires new efforts for adaptation, a variety of anxieties are unavoidable

Position	RC/Model	Scheme	System	Service
Senior middle	Innovation	K11	K12	K13
Middle	Development	K21	K22	K23
Workplace	*Kaizen*	K31	K32	K33

Fig. 4   Platform tool

in the workplace. For example, if the company applies the new business reengineering system, excess staff shall be shifted to other jobs or restructured. Thus, people tend to dislike and resist *kaikaku*, unless their anxieties are resolved and *kaikaku* is justifiable for them to accept it. Considerable efforts are required to relieve such factors of organizational resistance as psychology, participation and vested interests.

At least six options are available as modern countermeasures for success. These are participative climate, climate survey, motivation, organizational development, democratic leadership and top commitment (Imaguchi, 2001, pp. 121–146). In addition to these, the new platform option is introduced. It is critical to apply the proper combination of options rather than disregard the resistance.

Figure 5 shows the application example of how to raise role awareness and competency matching by the platform tool. Another way is the stepwise expansion of team design. To relieve the organizational stress, the first step is limited in small scale, and subsequently, makes the action

Role

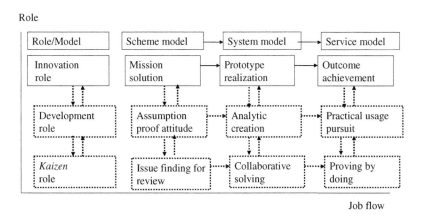

Job flow

Fig. 5   Platform type of role model competency for human system

research method to assess the climate in advance of the expansion. By this, the participative mood is penetrated. The platform can also be used to expand the priority teams in matrix cell numbering. Thus, this tool serves to help visibility and control.

To summarize:

(a) Organizational resistance should be considered seriously to avoid conflict.
(b) It is critical to apply the proper combination of options rather than disregard the resistance.
(c) The platform tool provides such two ways of application as role competency congruence and stepwise expansion priority mapping of team design.

5.3   *Organizational climate survey*

Many *Kaikaku* are stuck in trouble or fail due to its careless styles. Figure 6 is the climate survey of a small company of 250 staff for comparisons between using a platform and not using a platform. It shows the results of two different projects in the same company.

Case A in white color bars in the figure refers to the business process reengineering project in which a platform was not used, while case B in grey color bars has to do with client satisfaction project in which a platform was used.

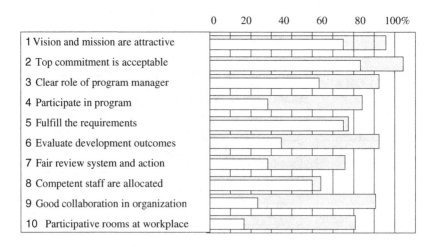

Fig. 6   Comparative climate analysis

Now, it is apparent that case A without platform use was inferior to case B with platform use in all the inquiries. These results are summarized as follows:

(a) Organizational resistance exists, but by applying the platform use, outcomes will improve.
(b) Success depends on how to improve the participatory climate at all levels.
(c) Success depends on the evaluation of development outcomes.

6   Knowledge Platform for Success

6.1   *Knowledge base*

In terms of knowledge, the success of the *Kaikaku* program could be hampered by access rights of intellectual property and flow of intellectual resources if the program manager wishes to ensure success by upgrading added value. Intellectual property is managed by the routine organization and not by the program organization. Even though specialists are dispatched to the program, they have no rights of access unless they are permitted by the routine organization. So, KPM has determined to allocate program directors and program managers to such K11, K12 and K13 positions with the intent that their influence and power may enable access to intellectual stock without conflicts.

Sharp Company is famous for this type of experience called *Kinkyu* (urgent) project, which produces only one product like liquid panel (Miyamoto, 2007, pp. 175–222). The special feature of the *Kinkyu* project is the development from prospective technology to proven technology for merchandizing in 12 months. Under this system, the project office is permitted the power to pick up any talented men from the routine organization at its will, and nobody could be denied by presidential instruction. Sharp has 30 years of history under this system and 260 cases are recorded from liquid panel application of calculator, television and mobile phone.

6.2   *Interpretation of intellectual resources: Dynamic flow*

It is well-known that Nonaka and Takeuchi advocated the SECI model of cyclics for dynamism of explicit and tacit knowledge in the form of socialization, externalization, combination and internalization (Nonaka and Takeuchi, 1996). In fact, an intangible asset like knowledge is 2.5 times bigger than a tangible asset (Konno, 1998, pp. 73–102). Figure 7 shows the application of the reference flow of knowledge cycle.

As Figure 7 illustrates, innovation of the new combination of knowledge shall be initiated by the top layer of the organization, while the development shall be led by the middle layer so that innovation could be put in possible practice by acquiring new knowledge. Improvement at the workplace is indispensable to convert and assist the new knowledge to become a usable one. This is based on the idea that program knowledge shall be identified and stored proactively in each cell, and challenges to it will flow to program process as resources.

To summarize:

(a) Platform may contribute by systematically supplying knowledge resources to the process.

(b) Platform provides the bases to supply reusable package resource, and upgrades productivity by shortening lead time, reducing costs and improving quality assurance.

(c) By introduction of a platform, access rights shall be well-identified and maintained to give a basis for intellectual property in program management.

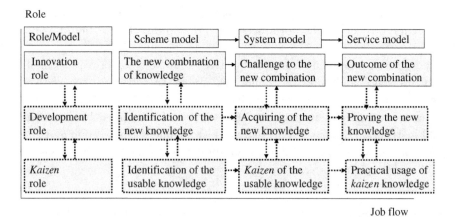

Fig. 7   Knowledge platform and dynamic cycle

6.3 *Case reference of knowledge innovation*

6.3.1 *Outline of the S company*

The principal business of S company had been providing the traditional dyeing services of silk fabrics by skilful craft. It boasted US$4 million in sales with large textile companies as clients. Nevertheless, after it opened a supply chain network in Asia, global competition caused its transactions to gradually decrease, sending the company into crisis. Faced with *Kaikaku*, the company transformed entirely the high-performing enterprise by utilizing knowledge of silk chemistry and dyeing stored in the organization. For instance, non-allergy-type cosmetics and artificial blood tube made of fiblin protein are high-tech products in the biomedical domain. By applying impregnation technology used in dyeing, barrier filter to electromagnetic beam and inflammable housing material have been developed. The company has since diversified to biomedical, electronics, housing, fashion and automotive domains of business from single silk fabrics dyeing. Here, focusing on the fashion business, we explain how the knowledge platform is applied to cause knowledge dynamic cycle in the whole organization.

6.3.2 *The old paradigm of textile industry*

Because of the long processing chain, the textile industry had been generally classified into upper, middle and down stream. The upper stream manufacturer dealing with materials of yarn now produces synthetic fibers, chemicals and medicines. The down stream has been modernized to an apparel or fashion industry, while the middle has remained unchanged for a century. This middle process encompasses spinning, refining, knitting of yarn and textile dying. For a century, production processes as well as business practices have been maintained in the traditional manner, because this traditional mode had depended on conventional wisdom to survive. The skill, expertise, and know-how embodied in the human resources had been believed to be the competitive edge of the company. This old paradigm had been solid in the mindset of the management. Now, however, a set of batch processing and business customs has been shackled due to modernization, and the manual mode of operation has been exposed to the ups and downs of trade and even climate change.

Knowledge stock

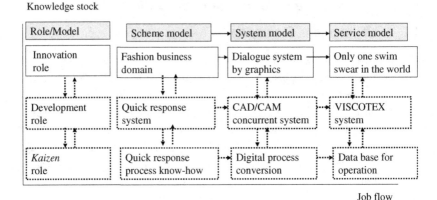

Job flow

Fig. 8   VISCOTEX development platform

6.3.3   *The paradigm shift of Kaikaku*

The scheme process of quick response is an essential point (see Figure 8). Conventional dyeing of silk business was high in cost with delivery of more than six months, and in line with the response paradigm, the delivery shall be 7–10 days at a reasonable cost that the end user approves. CAD (computer-aided design) system is an effective tool to convert manual work of three months to digital work of a few days.

The original design given by the customer was of a variety which included pictures, design sheets or photos. The hand-made sophistication of the original designs had been replaced by digital scanning into a computer. Subsequent innovation of detailing was attempted, but it was extremely time consuming to convert expertise processes to a digital design system. The third dimension of CAD was introduced to store the data digitally and to build a profile of the final product. The combination of high precision scanning and CAD had given the designer considerable freedom in conducting work of expansion, reduction, deformation and synthesis from the original form. In customizing the profile, the featuring function is indispensable to fixing position, pattern and volume.

6.3.4   *A step towards a virtual factory*

In the fashion business, another technological obstacle is the delicate difference perceived between actual and luminescent colors on a computer screen. It happens occasionally that the human eye and sensitivity have turned out to be a shackle. The company had organized a project team to further develop a calibration method of mapping colors exactly on patterns. Finally, it was connected with a database of 17.6 million colors. At this stage, the lead-time was shortened by only four months. The dyeing process was key to accomplishing the seamless digital conversion from data feeding to manufacturing. An ink-jet type textile printer was finally invented. A customized design data is transmitted to the computer connected with the automated printer. Today, CAM (computer-aided manufacturing) control is either programmed by drawing or solid configuration data.

6.3.5 *CAD/CAM integrated system*

This system is composed of the seamless digital manufacturing from the client terminal, to CAD and CAM. It has achieved virtual reality by VISCOTEX — visual communication for textiles — and the client can identify it on the computer (see Figure 9). The simulation mode has become critical for the ultimate success of business. The profile and its

Fig. 9   Fashion business by VISCOTEX

subtle feeling have to be visualized until the client is satisfied with an image. The terminal is placed at a shop in Tokyo, and the factories coupled with network are located 400 miles westward from there. Customers have access to computer graphic interface at any place where the terminal is installed. Profiling, mapping colors and tailoring services can be provided. Customers enjoy creating their originality of patterns. The digital message is transmitted by EDI Internet to several virtual factories in Fukui where CAD-linked CAM is working.

7 Conclusion

For problem solution in the modern society, the proactive approach shall be challenged by the implicit-type mission, in which the insightful method is indispensable to look into the problem in a comprehensive way. Innovation Program Management (IPM) complies with this thinking of the owner's view that multidimensional assessment is vital. For this, knowledge framework, auxiliary practice breakdown and standard documentations are the essential points. To summarize:

(a) IPM is ready to contribute to those who promote *Kaikaku* effectively.
(b) It is recommended that the enterprise apply IPM to foster leaders by education.
(c) IPM helps integrate divergent intellectual properties in a systematic manner.
(d) By putting IPM into practice, the enterprise may organize career paths and give incentives to potential human resources.

Acknowledgments

The author is delighted to thank World Scientific Publishing, Yasuhiro Monden (Professor Emeritus at Tsukuba University and Professor at Mejiro University) and Takayuki Asada (Professor at Osaka University) for the opportunity to publish on contemporary Japanese project management.

References

Asada, T., Ohara, S., and Suzuki, K. (2004). *Project Balanced Score Card*, Seisansei Syuppan.
Imaguchi, T. (2001). *Strategy Formulation and Organizational Design Management*, Chuou Keizai Sya Publishing (in Japanese).

Itami, T., Nishiguchi, T., and Nonaka, I. (2000). *Dynamism of Ba,* Touyoukeizai Syuppan (in Japanese).

Konno, N. (1998). *Management of Knowledge Asset,* Nihon Keizai Shinbun Sya Press (in Japanese).

Miyamoto, A. (2007). *Sharp Company — The Secrets of Uniqueness,* Jitsugyo No Nippon Sya Publishing (in Japanese).

Monden, Y., Miyamoto, K., Hamada, K., Lee, G., and Asada, T. (2006). *Value-Based Management of the Rising Sun,* World Scientific.

Nonaka, I. and Takeuchi, H. (1996). *Knowledge Creation Enterprise,* Touyoukeizai Syuppansya (in Japanese).

Ohara, S. (1999). Linking mission with value creation activities, in *Proceedings of International Conference on Project Management (ICPM),* 8–9 September, Kuala Lumpur.

Ohara, S. (2006). Mission-driven approach (MDA) of managing complex projects — Demystifying the new framework and its background, *Journal of International Association of Project & Program Management* 1(1), pp. 61–70.

Ohara, S. (2007). The fourth generation-type Japanese project management — Synergetic integration of innovation, development and improvement, in *Proceedings of the Second National Conference of International Association of Project & Program Management,* Tokyo.

Ohara, S. and Arai, K. (2004a). Complex project management and gaming simulations methodology: Enriching interfaces between the mission and performance, in *Gaming, Simulations and Society,* edited by Shiratori, R., Springer, pp. 259–268.

Ohara, S. and Arai, K. (2004b). Incongruent assessment of complex project management and organizational development, *Organizational Science* 38, pp. 40–50 (in Japanese).

Adjusting Function and Office Design in Japanese-Style Project Management Organizations — Applying the Idea of KPM

Tametsugu Taketomi

President, Corporate Intelligence Corporation
Professor, Graduate School of Management of Technology
Nippon Institute of Technology

1   Introduction

Various devices for organization design are introduced in *Kaikaku*, a Japanese-style project management paradigm (hereafter, KPM), so that it can be applied to innovations, development projects and programs. Above all, KPM has originality in two areas: its thorough responsibility for quality control in the world's leading *monozukuri* (the art of making things), and in its backward operation process planning system with focus on securing the delivery. In large-scale and long-range developments, judgments on whether to continue or stop them or on how to make prioritizations are necessary. In addition, organizations need to be designed to meet global market needs. KPM office design has devices and evaluation systems that correspond to the needs mentioned above.

2   Establishing a Project Management Organization

2.1   *Matrix organization design and its issues*

The idea of a matrix organization is introduced to a good number of companies that adopt a project management system. In a matrix organization, a functional division that performs ordinary operations is set up as part of a vertical line organization, while a division that carries out projects is set up as part of an *ad hoc* organization (horizontal line) crossing over an organization. A project manager with an independent responsibility runs this division. Here, one can see the intent to operate the organization by clarifying the responsibility and the authority of the vertical and horizontal lines and ensuring operations are run based on instruction and reporting. In this type of organization, know-how is accumulated in the functional division, in line with the characteristic of traditional organization which focuses on a functional division, while the mobility and the profit control are kept in project divisions, in line with the characteristics of project-centered model which crosses functional divisions. For example, in functional divisional organizations, it is not clear where responsibility for profits rests, but in a matrix organization, it rests with the project manager in the project division. Vertical functional divisions add costs to each project, clarifying where the responsibility for costs lie. Below are the characteristics for each of these organizations:

(a) Functional-type organization (a structure that achieves maximum functions)

- Accumulation and development of technological skills are easy
- It is not clear where profit responsibility lies
- There is a clear division of roles among divisions
- E.g., a large number of manufacturers

(b) Project-type organization (project-centered structure)

- Authority is vested in the project manager, and it is clear where profit responsibility lies
- Accumulation and development of technological skills require much time
- Resources tend to be wasted
- The company-wide strategy tends to be unclear
- E.g., contract service industries that handle systems developments

(c) Matrix-type organization (matrix structure)

- It is clear where profit and cost responsibility lie
- Scrambling for resources among projects occurs
- It tends to not function well due to the two-boss system
- E.g., contract service industries that handle design development and construction, construction companies, etc.

A functional-style organization is often seen in conventional manufacturers, and is well-suited for carrying out ordinary operations. In manufacturers, production division, research & development division, procurement division, sales division, etc., are each composed as an independent organization. Knowledge and know-how obtained through business activities are accumulated in these functional divisions. However, these functional divisions work under the directions and orders of a vertical organization. Each division has cost and sales responsibilities according to its respective role, but the overall profit responsibility can be borne only by organizations in upper positions. Furthermore, the roles of adjusting each functional division's strategy and its planning are left to an upper organization that bundles together functional divisions.

On the other hand, a project-style organization is most often seen in system integrators that handle contract business. Strategic Business Units (hereafter, SBUs) are set up according to each customer's market including financial, service and manufacturing. Each unit has a structure fit for carrying out respective contract work activities and project activities following the receipt of orders. More emphasis is placed on carrying out each project than on pursuing the strategy of the whole company. When a project is over, the members in charge disperse. Profit responsibility is borne by each project. Organizations such as technical design or procurement that cover various SBUs corresponding to vertical functional division do not exist. This makes it difficult to convey and accumulate technique or know-how.

The matrix-style organization was introduced as an organization that assimilates this project-style organization and functional-style organization. Today, this organization form is mainly seen in construction companies that handle design or engineering companies. In this organization form, designing divisions, procurement divisions, etc., are arranged as vertical functional style divisions, while projects are set horizontally across the organization for dealing with customers. This organization has merits of both the project-style and functional-style organization; the former is able to better meet customers' needs and bear profit responsibility, while the latter easily conveys technique and know-how. But this organization has an inherent issue that is always pointed out. It is called the two-boss problem; members of the organization face the situation of having to receive instructions from and report to two bosses in vertical function line and horizontal project. In a company that has developed centering on a functional division, setting up a new project organization horizontally covering the organization does not necessarily work. The main reason for this is that the project members place priority on following instructions from the existing functional division's boss over the ones from the project division's boss. This is caused not only because the project members are unaccustomed to the project management system, but also because the company has not set up a structure in which a project manager can exercise his or her leadership. The main part of this problem consists of factors such as unclear division of roles between project division and functional division, and dependence of members' personnel evaluation on the conventional evaluation of functional divisions.

Especially in the manufacturer, new products that reflect market needs must be developed and introduced to the market in a timely manner. In the case of a functional-style organization, the barriers among functional divisions are so high that they cannot reflect market needs to development, nor can they develop and produce new products timely. As a result, efforts are made to develop products in a project system that covers the organization horizontally, as this system enables instructions and orders to be given consistently to sales, development, production and procurement. However, in many cases, this system does not work because of the two-boss problem mentioned above.

2.2 *Devices for Kaikaku project organizations in Japan*

As a measure to solve the problem mentioned above, in KPM carried out in Japan, a matrix-style organization is not utilized. Rather, a project organization is set up as a task force under the direct control of top management, and personnel are picked from functional divisions to form a full-time team that works under instructions from top management. There are a number of successful examples in new product development and company innovations. A certain domestic electronic manufacturer successively introduces new products to the market using this structure. *Kaikaku* project organization is structured in such a way so as to convey missions of top management directly to project members, aiming at not only managing a project smoothly, but also at changing the company culture. Figure 1 shows this structure.

2.3 *Devices for Kaihatsu (development) project organizations in Japan*

The manufacturers that originally operated with functional model organizations have adopted a project management system as a promoter of the

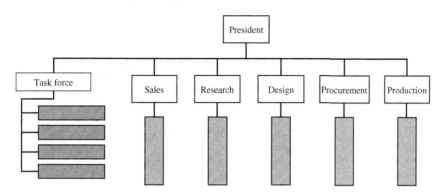

Fig. 1 Organization of *kaikaku* project

whole development, to more directly reflect market needs on new product development. In particular, automobile manufacturers, which develop new models concurrently, have adopted a matrix system called *shukan* or *shusa* (both mean "in charge") system for products in which the *shukan* or *shusa* holds the responsibility for the overall development of new models. But this system also faces the two-boss problem in the same way as other matrix organizations.

Thus, *kaihatsu* "development" project organization tries to function by defining which section should bear responsibilities for Quality, Cost, and Delivery (schedule), the basic management items of a project. Here, the traditional functional division bears the responsibility for Quality, while the project manager is responsible for cost and schedule. As a project is a cross-organizational system, a project manager does not necessarily excel in specific skills. In the case of a *kaihatsu*-style project organization, the quality of certain techniques often greatly influences the success of the whole project. Thus, the division of roles for the project is defined by having a person in charge of a functional division take responsibility for quality, while having the project manager take responsibility for the overall project quality. Examples of this are development of new automobile models and electronic products like TV. By defining in this way the role sharing of QCD, the basic management items of project management in a matrix organization, where each responsibility lies becomes clear. At the same time, the system tries to function by defining the role of a functional division as a cost center, placing priority on ideas of the project in terms of profits and schedule. Figure 2 shows this system.

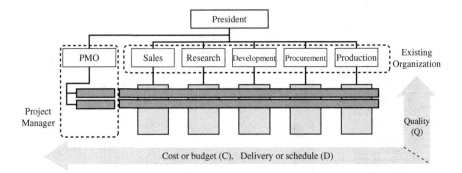

Fig. 2   Role sharing of management items for a project (e.g., automobile company)

In spite of this, there are cases in *kaihatsu*-style project where priority is placed on quality. In such cases, prioritization is performed as a whole by making a structure in which governance functions in upper organizations where program managers and others belong.

3   Two Models of a Project Management Office (PMO)

3.1   *Development-style office design to which the idea of KPM is applied*

When a project system is introduced to a functional-style organization, authority and ability of a project manager alone is not enough to manage a project to success. Therefore, a Project Management Office (hereafter, PMO) is constructed as an organization to ensure the project functions and to support the project manager. The positioning and role of PMO depends on how the company positions the project management system strategically.

PMO has a Program Management Office (hereafter, PgMO), which supports program management, and a Project Management Office (hereafter, PjMO), which supports the project. Figure 3 shows the hierarchical placement of PgMO and PjMO.

PgMO is positioned on the very top, so as to link the practices of corporate strategy and those of each project. Research and development-style companies, where many "development"-style projects are carried out, establish PgMO. In "development"-style program management, judgment on which projects should be given priority or the amount of investment that should be made on each project is consistently required. Moreover, in

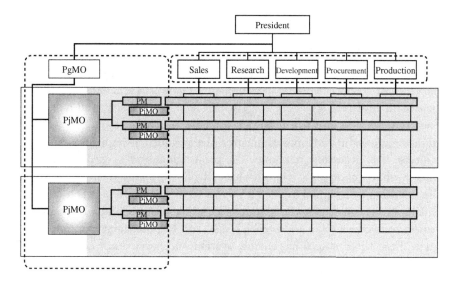

Fig. 3   A hierarchical placement of the project management office

managing high-risk and high-return *kaihatsu*-style projects, judgment on whether to continue with them or abandon them is sought. A project manager cannot be requested to make such judgments on prioritization of investment or on continuance or abandonment of the project. In the development project, the project manager is requested to carry out a management that would maximize the value of the business on the assumption that the project should be successfully led to the end of the development. Since it is a warring concept to request the project manager to decide on the priority of investment or judge whether to reduce the amount of investment or abandon looking at the total balance, it is common to entrust the judgment to a higher decision-making body, a PgMO.

It is especially important to establish this program management office in the field of medical supplies development. Since it requires as long as ten years to develop new medical supplies and many projects are called off during this process, it is necessary to have a program management organization and a function for supporting the development. They should be established separately from the project management office that helps the project management develop new products. Recently, the number of companies that establish program management office as a product strategy department has been increasing. This department prioritizes development projects, selects, or evaluates and judges on continuation or abandonment of projects according to the portfolio, in line with the overall company strategy.

Moreover, in projects for developing medical supplies, the required core skills for project management change according to the three different types of stages during its development. There is a scheme stage which focuses on research, a system stage which focuses on study, and a service stage that focuses on work from development to market launch as well as market expansion and operation after the product is launched. In such projects, it is necessary to change the project manager according to each stage, while managing the project itself throughout its lifecycle. Organization is designed in such a way as to differentiate between a high-ranking project manager who manages the whole lifecycle and a low-ranking project manager who oversees each stage, and to post them hierarchically when these three stages of scheme, system and service are continuously managed. And the project management office is established to provide overall support.

3.2   *The office design for global development of products applying the idea of KPM*

In companies that develop products globally and concurrently, there are some cases where a program manager who supervises the whole project is posted and manages the program during scheme stage, and an area project manager is posted for each area once it reaches system stage, to manage synchronization of the developments. Because the investment amount for development is increasing and product lifecycles in the global market are becoming shorter compared with before, timely return of investment is not possible if a product is launched to other markets at a proper time after launching it to a certain market. Therefore, the program manager is requested to carry out the project, aiming at synchronization of different areas.

The companies that are aiming at global development of automobiles, electric appliances and medical products, are all demanded to display similar global responsiveness. In such companies, management system utilizing PgMO is established. Figure 4 shows this situation in the form of a chart. Recently, the construction of a program management system covering the whole lifecycle and a global program management system which extends across many areas is becoming very important. Here, PgMO plays an important role as an organization that supports program management.

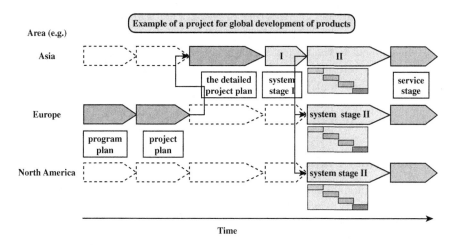

Fig. 4 How to lead a project for the global development of products

The project management office (PjMO) is positioned in a lower rank of PgMO. As mentioned above, several forms of PjMO can be considered according to characteristics of each project: for example, an organization that is established to support a project manager at each stage of the life-cycle, or one that is installed in each area to support the global project. In large-scale projects, it is common to have many project management staff under the project manager, besides personnel in charge of development and design. In this way, several forms can be considered for PMO, and considering the characteristics of projects, they can be built flexibly according to the environment at the time of their planning.

4 The Various Roles and Functions of a New Project Management Office (PMO) in Applying the Idea of KPM

Similarly, in Europe and America, many PMOs have been introduced to projects for technical system introduction and research & development. However, in Japan, new management system innovations applying the idea of KPM are introduced. Thus, in Japan, PMOs have been assigned various roles and functions. Many types of roles and positioning for PMOs can be considered according to the background of the project system in each company. For example, PMOs can assume roles and functions assumed by PgMO mentioned above, where judgment on start, continuation and termination are made, strategically putting together projects. They can also include providing such lateral support as maintaining tools and data concerning the project management to the project manager as a supporting organization for the project. PMO can be organized considering the character of the company's business and how mature the existing project system is. Since there is no decisive rule, constructing the organization in a way that enables projects to be managed smoothly becomes important.

5   Personnel Evaluation System

The project management system does not function merely by constructing an organization with such supporting function as PMO. There are companies that make projects function by adopting a personnel evaluation system that puts emphasis on project manager evaluating project members. In the case of KPM in which reporting is made directly to top management, project members are motivated to work for the project simply by belonging to the project. However, in *kaihatsu*-style projects where a matrix organization is constructed by newly introducing a project system to existing functional-style organization structure, role sharing structure is not enough to have project members always give priority to instructions by the project manager. It becomes necessary to incorporate an evaluation of project activities into a personnel evaluation system and to have clear instructions. If one wants to have the project system function well in a matrix organization, it is necessary to clearly define roles in the project and to match them well with the personnel evaluation system.

Also, in companies that position not only project managers but also project management specialists by establishing a project profession and having professionals belong to PMO, there are some that are separating those who are evaluated by his or her position in functional division from those who are evaluated by his or her position in the project division. These are often found in companies that are reinforcing project management by treating it as a source of the company's competitive power. The project system can be established across the company by setting the career route in project positions for those who wish to pursue a career in project management. The career route can be set not only for the project managers, but also for assistants and others.

In a matrix organization, when conflicting instructions come from both bosses, a project member who works for the project under the one man–two boss style decides which instruction to put priority on and acts differently, depending on whether the project member's evaluation is made with emphasis on the project or on functional division. As a result, even if a matrix organization is introduced, in many cases, it does not function well if an evaluation of functional division has priority over an evaluation of project division. Therefore, a mechanism is established which makes the project system function better by making clear how much weight is placed on evaluating each. In this case, ingenuity can be exercised to enable the project manager to manage the person in functional division who is posted to the project, by putting a bigger weight on evaluation of a project than on evaluation of a functional division. Moreover, by making the weight on evaluation of a project bigger than evaluation of a functional division as the position becomes higher, it is possible to have a mechanism through which the higher the position, the bigger the weight placed on making the project successful becomes. Thus, there is more incentive to collaborate with the project manager. Figure 5 shows this relation in the form of a chart.

Especially in companies that emphasize teamwork, measures are often devised to place emphasis on evaluating the success and failure of the whole team than on evaluating the good or poor results of individuals.

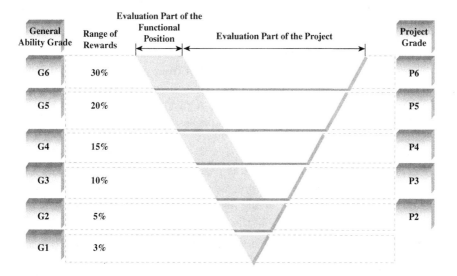

Fig. 5   Example of a project evaluation system

In companies where the success and failure of the project directly influences business results of the company, efforts are made to design the evaluation system so that the project can function as a team with its members thinking more about the whole project than about the work and evaluation of individuals, which is also an important element.

5.1 *Parallel adjustment planning system using a process from delivery date in KPM*

The basic way to proceed with a project is to complete work in upstream and input the results or output as requirements of downstream. The WBS is displayed with the individual tasks. The critical path is identified, and the whole schedule is decided.

In KPM and a *kaihatsu*-style project, "target management" is carried out. Time limit for each milestone is set and the starting date is decided counting backward from that deadline. In this case, even if work in the upstream process is not complete, work in the downstream process needs to be started. This method in which work in the downstream is started before work in the upstream process is finished is called the parallel development system. Using this method, shortening the duration of the whole project becomes possible. This approach is taken in many projects from *kaihatsu* projects of automobiles, electronic products to construction projects for designing in construction and engineering industries. To summarize:

(a) *Sequential Development*: As soon as work is finished, a task is passed on to a division in downstream process from a division in upstream process.

(b) *Simultaneous Parallel Development*: A task in downstream process is started before a task in upstream process is finished, shortening the development period.

In carrying out projects using this parallel approach, it is necessary for those handling work in the lower process to bear the risk of proceeding with design development without having all the conditions in the upper process established. Also, as conditions of the upstream process become established, changes and adjustments become necessary in the downstream process. On the other hand, retrogressions sometimes occur through having to change design in the upstream process according to the already decided conditions of the downstream process or other causes.

5.2 The role of the middle manager in coordinating between the top and bottom and making suggestions, as well as the characteristic of utilizing the function of "Ba" (place) in Japan

In order to have this method function, KPM and *kaihatsu*-style projects need to meet the following conditions:

(1) Project managers and PMO staff have roles as coordinators.
(2) *Ba* is provided to encourage good work communication between those in upper stream and those in lower stream.
(3) Personnel evaluation system which lets people take risks in starting work of lower stream process is introduced.
(4) Flexible work hours are set and changes are dealt with.

Condition 1 enables the project manager and PMO members to give instructions to those in downstream to work based on rough estimates or undetermined conditions in order to proceed with work in downstream process when conditions in upstream process are undetermined. Then they make necessary adjustments following these instructions. According to the needs, they provide *Ba*, where those specified in condition 2 can have a meeting to discuss the details. This *Ba* is used not only as a place for a meeting, but also as a place where all the members can work together for a long period. At any one given point in time, as the need arises, all those related to the project gather to adjust and discuss specifications and designs. This is partly because when there are multiple parties involved in upper and lower stream processes, enabling all involved parties to discuss issues in the same place whenever the need arises is important for efficient operation.

In addition, depending on the issue, sometimes a strategic decision is requested. In this case, the project manager coordinates with top management and decides on the communication with project members and coordinates with the members.

Furthermore, as specified in condition 3, because people in the downstream process take the risk of starting the task with undetermined conditions, group responsibility system and personnel evaluation mechanism that ensure responsibilities do not go only to the person that started the task or his or her superior, are provided. Moreover, there is a necessity to allocate a considerable amount of time to make adjustments in a short period of time. It is possible to shorten the time and reduce personnel cost for the whole project, but in the short-term, this puts a considerable burden in terms of time on the person in charge. Thus, it becomes imperative to flexibly allocate time among project members to enable them to withstand the time pressure. *Kaihatsu* and *kaikaku*-style simultaneous parallel development projects are processed, fulfilling these conditions.

6 Conclusion

In KPM, a project management system that fits well with the needs for "innovation", "development" and "reform" is set up. Building an organization while being aware of each character in scheme, system and service stage is also important in KPM. Companies that construct organizations in such a way have project management systems that function well and many cases of successful projects.

Acknowledgments

In writing this paper, I would like to express my appreciation to Professor Shigenobu Ohara of Graduate School of Management of Technology, Nippon Institute of Technology, for his substantial guidance and advice. I would also like to thank Dr. Hideo Yamamoto, Professor of Graduate School of Hitotsubashi University, for his advice on the structure of my writing.

References

Ohara, S. (2001). *Project & Program Management Standard Guide Book,* Project Management Certification Center.

Ohara, S. (2007). P2M program management, in *Management of Technology in Small- and Medium-Sized Companies,* Kougakutosho, Chapter 13 (in Japanese).

Taketomi, T. (2005). Challenges of program management in contributing to the new society, in *Solution and Value Creation of Project & Program Management*, International Association of Project and Program Management.

Taketomi, T. (2007). Fundamentals of project management, in *Management of Technology in Small- and Medium-Sized Companies*, Kougakutosho, Chapter 14 (in Japanese).

Yoshida, K. (2004). *Industry Big Bang,* Maruzen.

Innovative Strategy and Project Organization

Tadamasa Imaguchi

Professor of Management, Faculty of Business and Commerce
Keio University

1   Introduction

Recent developments in globalization and computerization has altered the business environment for Japanese companies dramatically and facilitated their rapid structural change. They created new business, developed new products at a high speed, and expedited progress, either revolutionary or incremental, as a way to adapt to the changing environment. They revamped their motivational system by stimulating their employees' strategic thinking, and created mechanisms to integrate their autonomic behaviors with perspicuity. In other words, top management was in search for, first, a clear vision to direct autonomous behavior to a desired end, and second, an organizational structure to realize the vision.

The purpose of this paper is to present a working hypothesis to realize an autonomous organization to survive the challenging economic situations by creating new business. Project organization is one such resilient organization that can solve complex business problems with speed, flexibility and resourcefulness. This organizational model manifests itself variously as virtual enterprises in the cyberspace, horizontal organizations, knowledge creation firms, and networked enterprises that the progress in the information technology has made possible.

2   *Kaikaku*: Its Trigger and Its Process

2.1   *Trigger of the Kaikaku*

Kaikaku (Organization Development) stands for radical reforms in Japanese, which encompasses awareness of people's mindsets and roles in organizational layers in the three K's of *Kakusin* or innovation at the top, *Kaihatsu* or development at the middle, and *Kaizen* or improvement.[1]

Stagnant firms manifest several tell-tale symptoms. Their manpower, market share and property shrink, and they lose the ability to recognize and address the problems when their sustainable competitiveness is endangered (Cameron, Kim and Whetten, 1987). Their power structure is diffuse, and they are unable to make long-range planning, innovation or turnover, and are forced to cut costs in such fields as personnel, production, sales and R&D (Imaguchi, 1993). Their organizations often resist *kaikaku* due to the low morale, criticism towards leaders and conflict among the employees, more specifically, the problems caused by special interest groups (Lorange and Nelson, 1987). As a result, they cannot embrace the innovations that are necessary for adapting to environmental changes.

Stagnation manifests itself in the immediate decline of performance as well as in the change of power in the top management. Managers' unfairness and tolerance to incompetence, and cumbersome administration characterize the initial stage of corporate stagnation. Other symptoms of stagnation include uneven distribution of staff, unproductive formalism, outdated organizational structure, and lack of open exchange of ideas among employees, of clear goals and decision benchmarks, of effective communication (Lorange and Nelson, 1987). Decline is accelerated when the managers overlook or defer acknowledgment of these symptoms, as the insensitivity to environmental change will delay technological innovation. Their business behavior is inconsistent with their own target, and often compromises the faiths and values of the organization.

As the decline accelerates, drastic and risky measures for recovery become mandatory (Weitzel and Jonsson, 1989). According to the stage theory of decline, stagnation can be divided into the stages of Blindness, Non-activity, Wrong action, Crisis and Death. For instance, "Good information" is needed to recover from the "Blindness" stage, but "Prompt action" is necessary to recover from the "Non-activity" stage. When the decline enters the "Wrong action" stage, a "Correct action" is needed for recovery. Unless some drastic reorganization is implemented at the "Crisis" stage, recovery becomes very difficult and the risk of bankruptcy looms large. Decline or drop in business performance triggers *kaikaku*, and a larger-scale, drastic *kaikaku* will be needed once the decline accelerates (Imaguchi, 1993).

---

[1] Ohara, S., *The Guides of Essential Terminology in KPM* (distribution sheet).

2.2 *Process of Kaikaku*

Kaikaku follows four steps (O'Reilly, 1989). The first step is to clarify strategic targets. After setting a short-term target to achieve the strategic target, we need to draw up an action plan for its realization. The second step is to analyze the current organizational characteristics such as values and norms. The third step is to clarify the difference between the ideal standard norm and the present standard norm. Disruptive norms and effective norms must be differentiated clearly at this stage. The fourth step is to design a suitable norm for the organization.

To plan and accomplish *kaikaku* effectively, we need to establish four conditions (Schein, 1970). The first condition requires the ability to take in and communicate information reliability and validity. The second requires internal flexibility and creativity to make the change. The third requires integration and commitment to the goal of the organization. And the fourth requires an internal climate of support and freedom from threat. The processes to accomplish these conditions consist of three stages of freeze, change and freeze again (Schein, 1980). Freeze stage creates the willingness to change, and change stage develops new attitudes and behaviors based on new information and knowledge. Freeze again stage establishes a new frame of reference in the organization.

First, it is necessary to create motivation to overcome the current behavioral problems. Change is accomplished by examining the environment closely, learning new behavioral patterns and attitudes from a role model, and establishing new information and concepts. Finally, other members of the organization have to accept these changes and internalize new attitudes in their own personality. Otherwise, the situation will revert to the former condition.

Organizational culture is defined as shared values or norms in the organization (Imaguchi, 2001). It controls the behavior of the members of the organization at various levels and is quite difficult to change. It is particularly difficult for successful organizations to change their organizational culture, owing to their tendency to maintain the status quo. In 2003, Matsushita Electric Industrial Co. Ltd.[2] reorganized their business into 14 business domains including semiconductor, mobile communication, electronic parts and home appliance (Nihon Keizai Shimbun, 2002).

---

[2] Founded in March 1918. Net sales was ¥9,108.2 billion. Number of employees is 328,645 (31 March 2007).

"AVC network" field was subdivided into AVC (sound, image and computer), AVC Network (fixed communication, mobile communication, car electronics), Appliance System (domestic electrification, house equipment and lighting), Industrial Equipment (FA, healthy system, environment system) and Device (semiconductor, electron, parts, motor battery, display). Because of the slowing down of business performance, Matsushita Electric Industrial Co. Ltd. restructured their group firms into a system centering on Matsushita. This example shows a *kaikaku* activity that successfully changed the corporate culture of a consumer electronic enterprise into that of an industrial electronics manufacturer.

3   The Role of Mission

3.1   *What is the meaning of mission?*

A mission describes a company's present and future prospects of products, market, technology, and so on. It clarifies the values of the management that is responsible for the organization's strategic decision making (Pearce, 1982). Missions also include information on the product, service, market, technology, goal, and the social identity of the firm or the image of the company as perceived by outsiders. More concretely, it can be defined in terms of six dimensions (Aeker, 1984): (1) definition of the product; (2) general customers' needs; (3) definition of the market; (4) technologies; (5) stages of production and distribution; and (6) particular capabilities or properties. This six-dimension description clarifies the scope and extent of the corporate activities along with the organizations' future prospects and targets, and effectively informs stakeholders of the conditions of the firm.

When a company plans to develop a new product, market or business, or when it changes domain, a mission serves to define its future strategies. It is important to clarify the fundamental targets of the change in terms of the corporation's strategies, features and management. Moreover, a mission helps to inform both the employees and customers of the identity and objectives of the enterprise, and to promote mutual understanding.

3.2   *Mission and organizational Kaikaku*

As the market rapidly changed and fragmented in recent years, firms acquired the growth-oriented ability to change dynamically according to the situation, and to secure earnings (Goldman, Nagel and Preiss, 1995). A mission has an important role to play in the realization of the business concept. The organization begins to: (1) deploy expertise, leadership and power; (2) design structure to concentrate on core competence; (3) combine several flexible organizational structures; and (4) manage with strong leadership, motivation and trust. The organizational *kaikaku* moves from rule protection to goal formation, from product orientation to market orientation, from hierarchical structure to network structure, and from dependence structure to alliance relation (Imaguchi, 1998).

A bureaucratic organization is unable to decide and act promptly, and does not serve as a model for business organizations. When an organization does away with strict rules to control its behavior and shifts from rule protection to goal formation, it needs to set a very clear objective to guide its progress towards the goal it has set. Moreover, when the emphasis shifts from product to market, managers learn to focus less on efficiency and productivity of the organization than on the external market. Change to network from hierarchy means that the layered structure is efficient when the condition is stable but is not responsive to drastic changes, while a horizontal network organization is more agile and creative. As the economic environment is changing rapidly, it becomes important for organizations to construct alliances such as joint venture and partnership.

4 Management of Project Organization

4.1 *Project organization*

The project organization consists of multiple project teams, which enables the organization's operational mechanism to address various problems simultaneously. To adapt to the rapid environmental change and diversification, multiple project teams solve problems promptly, as the management team entrusts their decision making authority to project managers and makes them solve individual project problems. Therefore, project organization solves multiple problems with speed, flexibility and resourcefulness. A project organization consists of project teams, and is similar to a decentralized autonomous organization in its structure.

Project organization is proximate to the concept of "Dialogue organization model" (NRI , 2001). This model emphasizes the creation of new business through dialogue with customers and encouragement of autonomous behavior among the staff of the organization. This type of organization is customer-oriented and aims to satisfy customers' needs. Dialogue with customers spawns new business models, and the decentralization and autonomous behaviors among the employees facilitate the process. The decentralized organization is designed to observe the behavior of customers, as it enables small autonomous teams to respond to customers' needs immediately. The make-up of this organization is task-based, and is highly adaptable to changing environments. Moreover, the platform, which supports the decentralized organization, embraces information sharing system, dialogue promotion system and self-management system through information disclosure. The role of top management is to build the fundamental architectures which indicate frame of reference, policy and code of value.

In Japan, Kyocera's ameba-type organization is a good example. This organization consists of many small groups and each group acts under a self-support accounting system, which is comparable to ameba. An ameba transacts with other amebas autonomously with innovative ideas and the transaction is judged according to simple profitability. This autonomous organization involves its individual members in the decision making, encourages human resource development and builds alliances between production department and sales department to efficiently respond to market demand (Asada, 2005).

The Mita Industrial Co.[3] has rebuilt its traditional photocopier business by introducing this ameba system. Mita failed to ride the wave of digitalization of the photocopier industry, and due to the poor performance at its overseas production bases, went under the Corporate Reorganization Law in August 1998. However, their ten-year reorganization target was accomplished in just three and a half years as it became a subsidiary of Kyocera Co.[4] Mita Industrial Co. was known for its family-oriented or group (as against competitive) corporate culture. After the introduction of Kyocera's ameba management method, Mita Industrial Co. changed its culture and improved its organization, thanks obviously to the ameba's small group flexibility. Through this development, employees learned to respond to their customers' needs promptly, and authority was entrusted to them, increasing the degree of their discretion. Managers became

---

[3] Kyocera Mita Co. at present.

[4] Established on 1 April 1959. Consolidated net sales was ¥1,181,489 million. Group employees are 61,468 (31 March 2006).

responsible for personnel development and improvement of their subordi-
nates' job performance.

4.2 *Matrix organization*

Matrix organization is designed to address conflicting requirements such as
efficiency and creativity. For example, in the defense and construction industries, various projects progress simultaneously and concurrently. In these
cases, an organization to enhance both project performance and functional
efficiency is needed. This organization resembles the matrix structure.

Matrix organization is characterized by the cross-chain of communication,
which contributes to both project and functional performance. Though
matrix organization can accomplish particular functions and *ad hoc* projects
at the same time, it has strengths and weaknesses. This system realizes the
possibility to: (1) apply the wide-ranging project-oriented business activities;
(2) train managers to execute the strategy; (3) make use of the managers
effectively; (4) make use of the diversified resources; and (5) show the strategic issues concerning various businesses to middle managers. The weaknesses
are: (1) possible confusion and contradiction due to the double responsibility, and (2) the necessity to adjust row and column authority (Pearce and
Robinson, 1985). Therefore, it is important to nurture a cooperative organizational climate and mechanism to resolve confrontations in the organization.

Murata Manufacturing Co.[5] in Kyoto is well-known in Japan for prac-
tising the matrix management. Its manufacturing division is divided
according to the processes of "Mixture", "Temporary scorch" and "Mold",
as well as to the products such as capacitors and piezoelectric parts. Each
unit of the matrix is managed by a self-support accounting. Murata
Manufacturing Co. established an efficient management system, increased
the intangible assets by revamping the production and decision making
system, and greatly increased competitiveness (Nikkei, 2001).

4.3 *Organizational ability of project organization*

What kind of organizational abilities are needed for a project organization to
function as *Ba* (Itami, 1992) of persuasion and inducement? Organizational
ability or capability forms intangible assets constitutive of organizational

---

[5] Established in October 1944. Consolidated net sales was ¥566,805 million.
Number of employees is 29,392 (31 March 2007).

competitiveness. In an extremely volatile business environment such as the IT industry of Silicon Valley, organizational architecture of prompt and appropriate information processing is mandatory. Such architecture is characterized by: (1) elimination of excessive information; (2) decentralization of decision making authority; (3) effective transmission of information and knowledge; (4) focus on core activities; and (5) networking with outside partners.

Organizational IQ is an index to measure the organizational ability to process information promptly and effectively (Mendelson and Pillai, 1999). Organizational IQ consists of five indexes: (1) recognition of external information (make the organization acquire external information promptly and accurately); (2) organizational architecture (decisions are made by those who have most effective information and who have superior ability to understand whole condition of organization); (3) knowledge sharing in the whole organization (horizontal and vertical communication in the organization and high accessibility to the needed information); (4) focus on core activities (restriction of the range of business and simplification of structure and process, and avoidance of excessive information and complexity); and (5) network with outside partners (alliance and value creation with outside partners).

RIETI (Research Institute of Economy, Trade and Industry) in Japanese METI (Ministry of Economy, Trade and Industry) compared the organization IQ index of 17 high-tech firms in Japan with IT enterprises in Silicon Valley (Ando and Motohashi, 2002), and found that Japanese high-tech companies have an aptitude for strong task accomplishment and incremental innovation. According to the organizational IQ index, their focus on core activity and innovation through networking with outside partners ranked higher than the IT firms in Silicon Valley. Moreover, sensitivity to the outside information and decision making in the organization scored almost the same value as the average Silicon Valley firm. But they scored extremely low in sharing information. This shows the strength and weakness of Japanese enterprises. Japanese enterprises tend to permit suboptimal behavior in which partial interest is prioritized over the overall performance of the organization. But in the belonging division or project, cohesion with colleagues is strong and shows highly task-oriented behavior. It is important for a particular project team to share its new created knowledge with other project teams, and put the common information to practical use. The top management team has to lead *kaikaku* to construct an effective information sharing system.

References

Aeker, D. A. (1984). *Strategic Market Management*, Wiley & Sons.

Ando, H. and Motohashi, K. (2002). Concept of competitiveness of Japanese economy, *Nihon Keizai Shimbun* (in Japanese).

Asada, E. (2005). Ameba management, *Nikkei Biz Tech* 7, pp. 116–121 (in Japanese).

Cameron, K. S., Kim, M. U., and Whetten, D. A. (1987). Organizational effect of decline and turbulence, *Administrative Science Quarterly* 32(2), pp. 222–240.

Goldman, S. L., Nagel, R. N., and Preiss, K. (1995). *Agile Competitors and Virtual Organizations: Strategies for Enriching the Customer*, Van Nostrand Reinhold.

Imaguchi, T. (1993). *Organizational Growth and Decline*, Hakuto Shobo Co. (in Japanese).

Imaguchi, T. (1998). Management of network organization, in *Management Paradigm in the Age of Cyber Space*, edited by Tonegawa, K., Dobunkan Pub. Co. (in Japanese).

Imaguchi, T. (2001). *Management of Formulation of Strategy and Organizational Design*, Chuo Keizai Co. (in Japanese).

Itami, H. (1992). Introduction of the management of Ba, *Organization Science* 26(1), pp. 78–88 (in Japanese).

Lorange, P. and Nelson, R. T. (1987). How to recognize and avoid organizational decline, *Sloan Management Review* 28(3), pp. 41–48.

Mendelson, H. and Pillai, R. R. (1999). Information age organizations, dynamics and performance, *Journal of Economic Behavior & Organization* 38(3), pp. 253–281.

Nihon Keizai Shimbun (2002). Matsushita: Wager towards recovery, Nihon Keizai Shimbun Inc. (in Japanese).

Nikkei (2001). Innovative company: MURATA Manufacturing Company, *Nikkei Information Strategy*, pp. 52–53 (in Japanese).

NRI (2001). Dialogue-type business creation, *NRI Reports (Intellectual Property Creation)*, February (in Japanese).

O'Reilly, C. (1989). Managing organizational culture, in *The Management of Organizations: Strategies, Tactics, Analysis*, edited by Tushman, M. L., O'Reilly, C., and Nadler, D. A., Ballinger Pub. Co.

Pearce, J. A. (1982). The company mission as a strategic tool, *Sloan Management Review* 23(3), pp. 15–24.

Pearce, J. A. and Robinson, R. B. (1985). *Strategic Management*, 2nd ed., Irwin.

Schein, E. H. (1970). *Organizational Psychology*, 2nd ed., Prentice-Hall.

Schein, E. H. (1980). *Organizational Psychology*, 3rd ed., Prentice-Hall.

Weitzel, W. and Jonsson, E. (1989). Decline in organizations: A literature integration and extension, *Administrative Science Quarterly* 34(1), pp. 91–109.

The Practice Examples of KPM Knowledge Platform

Emi Yunokawa

President, Humansystem Corporation

1 Introduction

The characteristics of IT projects vary in the fields of its adaptation, how to carry the development forward, contracts, development ranges, development period, budgets, the systems of the client side and so on. Certain characteristics sometimes make it difficult to manage IT projects by the orthodox project management alone. Recently, IT has been applied in a wide range, and many systems have already been introduced to the customer side. Therefore, it is getting more and more difficult to clarify the "demand" which the customer used to have definitely in the traditional IT system development. To lead the problematic IT projects which have short delivery dates or very changeable specifications to success, it is important to "visualize" a design and a plan of the whole project by the project management and promote them. Our company, as an SI (System Integrator), has begun to take action to circulate innovation, development and improvement using KPM in order to solve the various problems mentioned above. It is extremely important for SIs to save the project knowledge as intellectual resources and reuse the experiences which have solved various problems and issues by "visualization" of projects.

In this paper, I describe how to build the structure that practises the knowledge stock and the flow of knowledge circulation concretely to improve success rates. This is also discussed in Section 6 ("Knowledge Platform for Success") of the second paper on *"Kakusin*-Innovation Program Management (IPM)". Furthermore, I report the results obtained when I applied this technique to the actual IT projects to implement reduction of delivery dates, costs and risks in the projects.

2 Visualization and Circulation of Knowledge of IT Projects

It is said that the Japanese are good at working as a team. However, in today's project information management, there are various elements depending on technologies and information of specifications; so the progress management becomes really complicated. Many problematic projects reach the construction of the system model without defining the clear mission in the owner's viewpoint proposed by KPM. In these projects, basic specifications of the system are often changed in the middle of the development, hence big problems are caused as to the project management. If an experienced super engineer good at technology, communication and management is in charge of such a project, he can manage it well without any big problems. Nevertheless, this know-how has much information depending on implicit knowledge and is difficult to be visualized. Besides, there are few project managers good at such ability. Therefore, it is necessary to utilize the knowledge platform proposed by KPM, drive the "visualization" of projects, and practice the "circulation of knowledge" with the knowledge stock. I show four important points for the KPM activity in the following:

(1) Stocking experience knowledge on nine platforms, reinforcing it and raising the knowledge equipment degree;
(2) Supplying knowledge resource from a platform to a process and raising the success rate;
(3) Accumulating the reusable package knowledge and reducing the delivery date/cost/risk;
(4) Deciding the access privileges by the platform and offering the management base of intellectual assets.

In this paper, I aim to carry out the third point — "Accumulating the reusable package knowledge and reducing the delivery date/cost/ risk" — which is the most effective activity of KPM practically. Even a project manager with little experience can acquire project management information with the results by utilizing this knowledge stock and can draw up a detailed plan quickly. By this "circulation of knowledge", how were we able to raise the success rate of the project? I concretely describe how to save the knowledge of IT projects as intellectual resources, practise it and achieve effects.

3 The Knowledge Base for the Visualization of Projects

In IT projects, there are more and more chances to "visualize" the responsibilities shared and work scopes, and the ordering sides also have more chances to confirm and approve them. WBS (Work Breakdown Structure) is often used to investigate all the work items in the development range. Both WBS and EVM (Earned Value Management system) methods are firmly established to manage large-scale IT projects. WBS is also included in the *Guideline for Operation/System Optimization* settled by the Chief Information Officer (CIO) liaison conference in March 2006, which has the purpose to improve optimization and the cost effectiveness of whole government information systems.

However, we cannot utilize WBS and EVM as the knowledge base of IT project management because they are only used to manage costs and schedules of projects. Therefore, I introduce a new management package called IWCP (Intellectual Work Component Package), which can accumulate the information that is not included in WBS, such as results time, deliverables, quality, functional added value, information for reuse and devices carried out in projects. Hence, I newly define the following items for elements of WP (Work Package) to manage the information for a knowledge base:

- *Elemental items of traditional WP*: large item, middle item, small item, task, status, charge, plan man-hour, schedule man-hour, beginning expected date, end expected date, beginning date, end date.
- *Elemental items added in IWCP*: reason for change, branch number, time increase and decrease to high rank layer, cost increase and decrease to high rank layer, increase and decrease of deliverables, updated by, approved by, approved day, expense burden division, reflection day, etc.

In addition, there is a difference between the activities of traditional WP and those provided by breaking down IWCP as the following:

- *Elemental items in activities of traditional WP*: large item, middle item, small item, task/work item, status, charge, plan man-hour, schedule man-hour, beginning expected date, end expected date.
- *Elemental items added in activities of IWCP*: beginning date, end date, results man-hour, delay, development difference, remarks, outbreak

division, standard division, AC division, reason for change, deliverables, work order, planner, new making day, updated by, approved by, approval, etc.

WBS consists of WP, which is an effective minimum unit of management costs and schedules. In KPM, I use not only the information of costs/schedules, but also a new management unit called IWCP as a package of knowledge base. Furthermore, this IWCP is divided into many activities, and the activities themselves can manage their own priority, reusability, results, times and bidirectional information in a project management. Because IWCP contains information of WBS, we can extract the information of costs and schedules for information sharing with the customer, and moreover, we can manage various information which is to be used as a knowledge base of the project. I define the knowledge of a project accumulated in these IWCPs as CTKS (Common Template for Knowledge Stock) (see Figure 1).

This CTKS manages the information of the system model of knowledge stock defined in the knowledge platform of Section 6.2 ("Interpretation of intellectual resources: Dynamic flow") in the second paper on "*Kakusin-*Innovation Program Management (IPM)". Because this CTKS manages the on-site information of the project and its progress, the information sharing between the vertical innovation roll/development roll/improvement roll of the system model can be realized bidirectionally. In addition, we can reuse project management information as a template while maintaining a

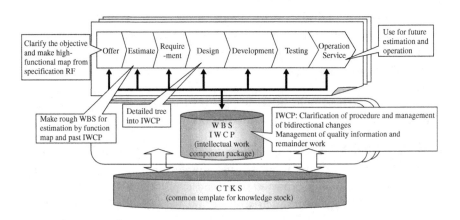

Fig. 1   Concept of project knowledge base

relationship between functions and the real operations in future similar IT projects.

4 An Example of a Project Management That Applied a Project Knowledge Base

As an example, I applied the knowledge base to a web development project and performed the project management. In this case, I used a development framework which the enterprise offered in multiple projects for the same customers and constructed different websites. Table 1 shows information of six projects including development periods, costs, the number of IWCP, development scales and the number of failures after operational tests.

Projects A–E were the projects undertaken from the basic design to production release, and whose requirements were in a clear state when they started and their delivery dates were short. In our company's past case of small scale and short delivery date projects, we used to encounter problems where their profitability worsened and their quality decreased.

4.1 The advantages obtained by using knowledge base in projects

In Projects A–F, their customer base was the same, but there was not relevance at each. In Projects C and D, developments were carried out for almost the same period. Project A was the first one and its productivity was not high enough since it was a project of the new customer and there was no concept of IWCP: it took 24.5 men per month (11.9 men per month, 194% cost excess) for 12.6 men per month estimates. In Project B, which was totally different from A, we performed project management by IWCP for the first time. The same project leader was in charge of Projects A and B, and B had a result of the cost excess of 1.4 men per month as it was a small project. Even if its requirement was decided definitely, 33 item numbers of IWCP increased at the end of this project in comparison with the beginning. The oversight of the work items at the time of the plan led to the excess of the cost for 1.4 men per month. Each project leader of Projects C–E was a different young person and big cost excess was not observed in these projects. Project F was managed by one total project manager, who was also Project A's leader, and five sub-leaders, three of

Table 1   An example of IWCP in development projects for the same customers

PJ	Period	Mon-month			No. of IWCP		Development Scale			Operation
	Month	Estimated	Result	Difference	Beginning	End	No. of Screens	No. of Reports	No. of Modules	Failure
A	3	12.6	24.5	−11.9	—	—	17	9	20	20
B	1.5	4.4	5.8	−1.4	125	158	5	14	0	0
C	2.5	4.7	4.9	−0.1	239	237	21	15	1	1
D	2	3.75	3.8	−0.3	186	206	5	20	1	1
E	1.5	1.5	1.4	0.1	56	57	58	0	0	0
F	4.5	73	69.2	3.8	563	3230*	234	12	108	7*

* All items of IWCP in Project F were not clear at the beginning because its scope was from requirement to production release. (The number of failures is similar, too.)

whom were project leaders of Projects C–E. The work range of this project was from requirement to product release and this project was completed with a man-hour to be less than an estimate (reduction of 3.8 men per month; 94%). Below are the advantages that the CTKS knowledge base gave in the management of five projects (except Project A):

(1) It was possible to use the past project information, prevent reversion and raise productivity and quality of the projects.
(2) It was possible to prevent cost excess because the differences of estimates were reduced and information sharing with the customer was good.
(3) New project leaders were able to acquire experience without losing productivity greatly in small projects.
(4) Based on the knowledge gained in basic design and development phases, it was possible to succeed the project from requirement phase.
(5) We were able to carry out the projects from requirement concurrently for a short period.

4.2 *Utilization of past project information*

Projects in Table 1 were different in the sites of the objects, development period, range and scale. However, we could think that frameworks of the development, infrastructures, procedure of the release work, and how to lead work were basically the same because the projects had the same customer. Although the record was not left in proper form in Project A, the past project information was succeeded personally because the same leader was in charge of the next projects. In Project B, we decided to make IWCP and determine work ranges of projects, hence, there was an overhead of preparations for registration of project information and registration procedures itself first. However, we did not expect that there were 33 oversights of the IWCP work items (there were 7 items to succeed them to other leaders), even if a leader was a veteran with the experience of the same project. Because most developments were for reports, this project hardly had the problem of uncertain specifications. As a result of analysis, oversights caused by a change and the addition of specifications were only 8 cases, and most others were the small work items such as 12 common items or 6 procedures, which were experienced in Project A. It was clear that there were many works of which the project leader was not conscious at the estimate phase, and accumulation of slight works became reversion of the big man-hour.

We recognized that it was difficult to record detailed rules in a form that anyone could understand and that man-hour excess by reversion held the ratio bigger than excess by the real specifications change.

IWCP managed not only the schedule and the information of the cost, but also shared information of the procedure note at a detailed work level. An actual figure did not show the improvement of the productivity clearly, but it was good in reducing reversions in the concurrent development with small scale and short delivery date (for example, 5 screens/14 reports for 1.5 months). As a result, we raised reliability of estimates and project plans. This enabled us to remove impossibility and waste in two points — we could eliminate detailed work, and plans were made based on the results. Therefore, we could shorten the time for set-up of the projects, compress the cost and improve the quality. In addition, as for small projects from C to E, existing project leaders did not manage the projects; those who were members in former projects became leaders in Projects C and E, and another new member was able to play the role of leader in Project D. It is thought that IWCP is an effective tool from the educational viewpoint of the young leader and members.

4.3   *Visualization of project information and information sharing with customers*

In the projects after Project B, it was possible to share the work level between people in charge and their customers through the WBS derived from IWCP. This was quite effective because we could cope with oversights of works early. We were able to remove vagueness as much as possible because we could confirm the total work with the customer. By showing the work items to the customer definitely, we can recognize oversights of the work later mutually, manage costs and time of the project, and make their influence to the project and responsibility of them clear. Oversights of work assignment can be investigated to some extent at the prior meeting, even if a customer does not have deep knowledge of IT. Also, in the case using advanced IT skills, we can put the schedule in the proper situation as much as possible by sharing progress information with the customer.

One of the important reasons why differences in the estimates became smaller from Project B to C and D was that the recognition difference between the customer and the vendor was decreased by sharing the implicit work contents and concrete information including time, which they agreed in advance. With this customer, a number of other vendors carried out similar developments concurrently. However, we were able to get the customer's trust and then finally get the order of Project F, whose range and quantity of development were large, since we had such a framework of project visualization and information sharing, and provided the estimate derived from the framework. Thus, the result eventually depended on the knowledge base of projects.

4.4 Measures to perform concurrent development at the stage of requirement phase

Project F was more difficult than other existing projects because it had a short delivery date; furthermore, we pushed forward the project with the customer from its requirement phase. Its development scale was also large, but the customer demanded a development period of only 3.5 months at the time of ordering the project. When we extended the development period for one month on the last estimate at the contract, we were able to show the work items and productivity/problem list which we investigated from past project information concretely. In addition, we measured a development scale at the beginning of the requirement phase, and divided a function group into five major groups (a common development and four function groups). By this grouping, we were able to carry out the works from the requirement in the short period concurrently. There were many cases where concurrent requirement phase failed, but in this case, temporary man-hour based on the past information at the planning of the project was very helpful as well as detailed work items.

It was easy to investigate the same functions and create the plan for the IWCP package of project knowledge base because it had the reusable structure of the template form. On the basis of this information, it was possible to visualize the project with high precision from functions assumed at the planning and prediction time of changed works. As a result, we improved precision of planning for costs/schedules and clarified basis of estimates for the customer. In Project F, we succeeded in delaying the delivery date for approximately one month by negotiating with the customer while getting the order of the project. As for the total cost excess issue, which should be considered most carefully while multiple groups concurrently discuss requirement definitions, when we had problems we contacted each other in all big functional groups to solve them in real time. We also coordinated the messages among the leaders and reported the message to the customer by this project information sharing.

5   The Effectiveness of the Knowledge Base of the Project Management Information

A project is defined as time-limited individual activities which have a specific mission at the beginning, not limited to only IT. Thus, it has been doubted whether the information of past projects saved as knowledge could be utilized from a point of individuality. In the case of the IT project with short delivery date, the delay found out after a half month can become the fatal problem. Projects which are driven by the hour need close plans and information sharing, but the project management also often depends on personal skills. It is also important to share the progress and delay information and its prediction. Since there are many variables defined in the requirement definition phase of IT projects, it is difficult to conduct the requirement definition concurrently.

This is a major difference between the IT industry and the engineering industry, which assembles special hardware to build production lines. To solve the problem and share the information in real time, we need to keep the project management information as the form of knowledge base and provide the latest project information to anyone if necessary. Some changes under certain functions may influence others. In the project management, it is always important for us to report the impact of revisions to the customer as soon as possible and share its risk. Therefore, it is more and more effective to accumulate the experience of the project into the knowledge base and utilize it. Our problem is how to clarify the circulation of knowledge, explain it and practise it.

6   Conclusion

With commoditization of the IT technology, the profitability of the projects in the entrusted developments gets worse. The original major prime constructors take the plan to reduce cost by offshoring or lowering the amount of orders in domestic developments, and the customers hold down the volume of developments for non-routine tasks and manage various existing tools. Under such an environment, the developments which have short delivery dates, frequent changes of specifications and small scales increase in domestic development projects. To raise profitability of IT projects, it is essential to create the framework which visualizes the processes, finds similarity of each project, and improves their quality and productivity.

This CTKS manages the information that is necessary to carry out a project effectively described as a management object by the conventional "objective management". Besides, CTKS can practise and manage not only the experience of a project organization, but also the technology, information and know-how that are used as the knowledge. This IWCP package is the information infrastructure for the purpose of creating and operating practical project management, and we are able to realize the "circulation of knowledge" by extracting reusable information from the management information base and utilizing it.

In this paper, I described the framework to accumulate the project knowledge, share the change information in real time, understand their influence, and store and circulate the IT project knowledge effectively. I also described its example in practice. The circulation of knowledge of KPM — Kaizen Project Management (eliminating impossibility/waste/ unevenness) — is the effective method that can change the various negative elements which are imposed on SIs into positive ones. In the future, I would like to spread *kaizen* as the on-site wisdom in the whole office as one style of lateral collaboration.

Acknowledgments

I really appreciate those who taught and guided this study to the end of this paper. I express sincere appreciation for Professor Shigenobu Ohara who gave me the opportunity to write this thesis, and Professor Tametsugu Taketomi from the Graduate School of Nippon Institute of Technology who taught me kindly. I also thank Professor Hideo Yamamoto from the Graduate School of Hitotsubashi University, who gave careful advice heartily.

References

Chief Information Officer (CIO) liaison conference (2006). *Guideline for Operation/System Optimization*, http://www.e-gov.go.jp/doc/060331/doc2.pdf (in Japanese).

Ohara, S. (2003). *Project & Program Management Standard Guidebook: The Second Volume*, PHP Institute Co. (in Japanese).

Changes of Japanese Corporate Business Model under Global Pressure: Evidence Justifying KPM

Toshihiko Kinoshita

Visiting Professor, Graduate School of Asian Pacific Studies
Waseda University

> "It is not the crisis that Japan is facing. The world has completely changed. It may take 30 years until we regain new stability. Japan should tackle to respond to the unprecedented change. Never refuse to change."
>
> — Peter Drucker

1　Introduction

This paper reviews the changes of the business model of big Japanese firms[1] over the past 20 years from a perspective that the basic energies of these changes are the vectors for how to pursue total optimization from multiple partial optimizations, equipped with individual missions in firms under a quickly changing domestic and external business environment. It shows that they need further changes in more innovative ways and how the missions of firms and their education and training should be toward the future.

The business world or that of an individual country is not the same with the natural world. In the business world, governments intervene in various ways by legalizing how to compete, charging taxes, supporting the socially weak and setting up lots of artificial barriers which prevent free movement of resources among countries/areas, for instance.

---

[1] I omit to write on some 4.6 million small and medium-sized enterprises in Japan (number-wise, it shares 99% of the total firms), only due to the space restraint. Some 1,500 Tokyo Stock Exchange-enlisted companies are by far influential in shaping the Japanese economy and in the relations with the rest of the world.

But still, similar phenomenon are observed in the globalizing business world as we see in the natural world. Charles Darwin once stated that the winners of the natural world are not the strongest nor the wisest, but those that most flexibly adapt to the changes. It appears most distinctively when the natural environment undergoes dramatic changes, such as the advent of the Ice Age. It may be a bit exaggerated to compare the business conditions when Japanese firms tackled the socioeconomic difficulties for over ten years with the Ice Age of the earth. But, for those who had recorded the best performance for over 30 years after World War II, the "lost decade" looked literally like the Ice Age. They have become slim and reinvigorated in recent years through "sweat and tears" over a long time. What was Japan's "lost decade" like? Is there some similarity in Japan's economic recovery process with that of the US in the 1980s and 1990s?

Wrong financial and fiscal policies on too quick appreciation of the yen-US dollar exchange rate in the latter half of the 1980s,[2] the subsequent collapse of the "bubble economy" and the delay of the policy change by Japanese government for "small government" brought about an unprecedented miserable macroeconomic performance. Japan recorded a historically low annual averaged growth rate of only 1% in the 1990s, with continued deflation. Simultaneously, such changes in international politico-economic environment as follows gave the Japanese government, firms and individuals sightless challenges:

(a) Japan's strategic (military) importance to the western world, the US in particular, was suddenly gone when the Cold War ended. In addition to asking for "managing trade" of semiconductors, etc., the US government aggravated negotiations with the Japanese government by asking for a complete structural change[3] to realize a "common playing field" by the US standard.

(b) European Union (EU) and North American Free Trade Area (NAFTA), two trading blocs comprising majority of OECD countries, were set up in the early 1990s, leaving only Japan, South Korea,

---

[2] Japanese yen rate per US dollar was appreciated from ¥250 just before the Plaza Accord in September 1985, and reached ¥120 (yen's value doubled) within two and a half years. No other country has experienced such a drastic appreciation.

[3] The US-Japan negotiation named Structural Impediments Initiatives (SII) was convened from 1989 to 1990. This SII was aimed at reforming structural problems of both sides, but the US has never completed its promise, to increase domestic savings, for example.

Australia and New Zealand outside. As the business model of Australia and New Zealand is more or less of the Anglo-American type, Japan and South Korea became "stray sheep". Free and open multilateralism gave a seat to a new type of "global regionalism", though one cannot compare it to the pre-WWII "bloc economy". Japan has had to conclude FTAs with ASEAN countries, Mexico, Chile and others.

(c) The Big Bang of capital market had to be done from 1996 to 2001 under the severest recession as scheduled, as Japan wished to keep its capital market internationally competitive.

(d) Japan has had to reform its industrial structure dramatically as China, the most energetic newly emerging country with a population of 1.3 billion, is Japan's neighbor, whose averaged per capita income has been 3% to 5% of Japan's, and the transportation cost from Japan and China is one of the lowest in the world. Although China has offered its expanding domestic market over time to the world including Japan, the pressure for factor cost equalization in labor-intensive and resource-oriented industries in Japan is still amazingly strong. Another neighbor, Korea, also emerged as one of the strongest manufacturers of electronics and cars in the world.

How have Japanese firms survived under such severe conditions? Briefly, they made every effort to restructure and reform (*kaikaku*), particularly amid the financial fiasco at home as well as the Asian financial crisis from 1997–1998 and the "IT bubble" burst in the US in the early 21st century. It was just the time when the newly-born Koizumi Cabinet began to undergo drastic institutional reform. Japan was lucky in that the world trade has grown fast, which helped its recovery as a state and firms. Now, most of Japan's macroeconomic indicators show that the economy has revived and is entering the normal orbit of business cycle, except still-increasing fiscal debts. GDP growth rates of FYs 2004, 2005 and 2006 were 2.0%, 2.4% and 2.4% respectively. Ratio of current profits of major Japanese firms (some 20,000 firms) *vis-à-vis* total sales recorded the highest level of 4.5% in the second quarter of 2006 since 1960. Outstanding of the total aggregated value of Tokyo Stock Exchange (TSE)-listed firms as of the end of March 2007 reached ¥556 trillion, almost 100% of the current GDP, nearing to the past peak figure in 1989, which showed a big jump from ¥297 trillion or the corresponding figure of some 60% in 2002, the lowest level after the bubble economy collapsed. The unemployment ratio, which was 5.5% at the worst period in 2002, fell to 3.6% in July 2007. The growth rates of Japan in 2007 and

2008 estimated by OECD as of May 2007 are 2.4% and 2.1% respectively, which are almost equal to those of the Euro Area and the US, if not higher. On top of that, the Japanese economy, which had long grown fast assisted by strong public policy, has been transformed to the private sector-led economy.

It was not the deterioration of their technologies in most cases, but the economic model and corporate business model of Japan simply did not fit with the changed environment that needed drastic reform (*kaikaku*). Our Project & Program management (P2M) was conceptualized circa 2000 under such a basic question — why many Japanese firms equipped with excellent technologies could not raise enough profits.[4] Now, a new question is raised in the extension of P2M: how have Japanese firms transformed themselves under harsher global and domestic pressures and continued to raise higher profits? Is there some similarity with the recovery of the US economy and firms in the 1980s and 1990s? And what is the relation between the new corporate business model of Japan and KPM (Kaikaku Project Management),[5] the 4th generation phase of P2M?[6] Clarifying these questions is the main subject of this chapter.

2 Japanese Business Model Evolved under Long-Term Recession and Global Pressure

The new mainstream business model of Japanese firms in the 21st century is not the conventional model lasting for half a century, but evidently an

---

[4] Many arguments were made for why Japanese manufacturers or engineering firms could not win in many biddings in BRICs, for instance. It proved to be due to so-called "over-specification". Most importers in BRICs tended to put more emphasis on price as lower-priced products did not incur serious problems often. We cannot simply conclude in such cases that Japanese firms' competitiveness is gone.

[5] The concept was initiated by Prof. Shigenobu Ohara. His paper is included in this book (Part 1, Papers 1 and 2).

[6] P2M was also developed with the initiative of Prof. Ohara. This concept has been crucial in Japan, where more than 95% of business leaders are not "professionally" educated in business schools or law schools. In the US, the business norm is different from Japan, as business leaders, many of whom are "professionally" educated or sent from outside the firm, would aim at targeting total optimization for shareholders as a matter of course though temptations by stock options; ignorance on foreign market/practices and overconfidence sometimes distort their decision making. While many US executives have been given stock options, few Japanese executives in the "old economy" have been given stock options.

evolutional one. I define it as a hybrid model,[7] mixing its own organizational competitiveness with new ingredients derived from the Anglo-American, "Shareholder Wealth Maximization" (SWM) model[8] (Eiteman *et al.*, 2007).

What was Japan's conventional model which had enabled Japanese firms to be global winners for decades? First, the shareholder's interest was not prioritized like in SWM model. Second, the so-called Japanese way of management was adopted; namely, the seniority system, the lifelong employment system (until the retiring age, say 60 years old) and the in-house trade union, associated with the "main bank system". Cross-sharing of a firm's stock with banks used to be very popular and it was regarded normal, as the deal was legal and they could expect utmost stability in managing firms. There were some exceptions, though, such as venture businesses or some sorts of service industries like IT software industries whose business model has a similarity with the Anglo-American model. Japan's conventional model facilitated the teamwork leading smooth OJT and better quality control, and reduced labor disputes like strikes, through acquiring high loyalty of the employees to the firm and better human relations or mutual trust from the viewpoint of corporate discipline, though it may not be the best model for innovation.

Kaizen has been a child of the Japanese way of management based on the model. It was supported by the main stakeholders of a Japanese firm, or the management and employees. The following three conditions supported such a system: (a) continuous high growth of Japanese economy under the relatively free, open and ever-expanding international trading system; (b) majority of their shareholders, which largely consisted of banks, insurance companies and many *keiretsu* companies in Japan with smaller share of Japanese individuals and foreign investors, preferred stability of

---

[7] Few Japanese top executives admit, however, that they have adopted part of the Anglo-American model for revival. Sure, they did not induce it willingly, but were forced to do so together with others. In the same context, many of them dislike the phrase "a hybrid business model" which I am using in this paper. Some of them told me in the summer of 2006 that what they were targeting is neither a traditional Japanese way of management nor an Anglo-American's, but "good management". No one can expect that their perception would change. My analysis is conducted by more objective cross-border comparisons over a long period to forecast the future.

[8] Some use the phrase "stockholder capitalism", not "shareholder capitalism".

transactions with firms to high dividends; and (c) it fitted with the traditional sense of value of the common, local people, or of the vertically rooted society. One is promoted slowly but steadily over time through competition and cooperation, and one's basic salary/wage rises basically in accordance to the gradual promotion, which matches one's lifestyle, namely, one that is married, with children and owns a house requires more money in aging. It is interesting that many people have regarded it as "the most successful socialistic system in the world" or "a one-country capitalism".

With the advent of the post-Cold War period, such conditions had to change, which eventually forced the Japanese conventional business model to reform to a new one. The biggest pressure originated from overseas, a thrust of globalization. The other pressure arose from a burst of the bubble economy, though it was related to changes in the international business environment. How so?

Until the middle of the 1990s, the US economy and the competitiveness of US firms seemingly continued to fall in the world standard. The US initiated the Plaza Accord in 1985, devaluing the US dollar substantially against major currencies, the Japanese yen in particular. Then, the US government advocated the imminent need to strengthen the competitive power of its private sector, in such ways as: (a) conducting good macroeconomic policies; (b) adopting new science and technology policies, among others, promoting information technology (IT); (c) encouraging better education in schools and intra-firm education and training; and (d) adopting effective international economic policies such as "modernizing" the GATT to the WTO to include services and investments, and to protect intellectual property rights (IPR) (Dertouzos *et al.*, 1989). The US-led IT age began to blossom internationally in a few years under such a strategy.

It should also be noted that the US eventually won the 40-year-long Cold War. Then, the former Eastern Bloc began to move towards the market economy. Thus, US-led "globalization" began to prevail at all corners of the world.

However, countries in Western Europe founded the EU and created the regional currency Euro, to insulate their socioeconomic models to a large extent from the US-led globalization model. The UK has walked at its own fashion, with relatively strong sympathy for the US-led globalization though the two models are not completely identical. The US responded to the emergence of the EU by forming NAFTA with its neighbors, Canada and Mexico, soon afterwards. The new *Zeit-geist* of the world became regionalism — open in a region but not totally open to the rest of the world — as many trials of Doha Round have resulted in complete failure. Multilateralism, whose biggest beneficiary used to be Japan in the post-WWII period, has waned, and Japan could not take initiative to break through pending problems of the WTO mainly due to its own agricultural problem.

Japan, with the US as its biggest trading partner until now and the largest direct investment destination, was tossed about by such paradigm shift to global neoclassical-type capitalism from the end of the Cold War. Unluckily, the Japanese government had mishandled the economic policy in the late 1980s, when the Japanese yen-rate *vis-à-vis* US dollar overshot to less than 100 yen after the Plaza Accord. Both monetary and fiscal policies were overly eased in order to absorb the negative shock and to move its export-led economy to a domestic demand-led one, thereby reducing the trade conflict with the US. These policies invited the unprecedented "bubble economy". The government and the private sector did not concern themselves with the asset inflation for years, due to overconfidence from past success stories as well as the relatively low-level rise of consumer price index.

When the USSR was broken up, the global politico-economic environment changed dramatically. It was then when the Japanese bubble economy collapsed and uncertainty for the future brought about a vicious circle. On the political front in Japan, the one-party rule of the Liberal Democratic Party came to an end, and the era ruled by a coalition cabinet started. The politician's role increased in the national economy, and the age when the bureaucrats virtually ruled the important decisions in the Diet ended.

Japan's averaged annual real GDP growth rate dropped to only 1% in the 1990s and the expression of the "lost decade" caught on. Firms were subjected to an unprecedented and severe struggle for the fittest, but their painstaking efforts to transform their business model for the new age achieved high profits and created many winners for 10 years at maximum. New senses of value such as higher shareholder's value, global environmental consideration, respect for intellectual property rights (IPR) and corporate social responsibility (CSR) have also been stressed.

The newly set-up Japanese model seeking total optimization for the stakeholders is stronger in its competitiveness compared with the conventional model, but has weak points due to the same reason. The shareholder's status has risen, and, conversely, the employees' status has sunk to a certain degree. But their managers still believe that their human resources are the indispensable fountain of the new value added. The number of firms in many fields of the industry has decreased through competition, changing industrial structure substantially. Most of the successful companies changed their business model, not necessarily because they believed that was the best way to go, but because there seemed no other choice left. It has some similarity with their process to become multinationals. Figure 1 shows that their efforts resulted in high profits and a fall of debts in these several years, and stock prices jumped up as a whole since 2002.

Let me introduce two interesting figures to show this fact. Averaged return on equity (ROE) of the 1,424 Tokyo Stock Exchange (TSE)-listed companies reached 9.5% as of FY 2006, showing increases for five consecutive years, though not high enough in the international standard. Share of the stocks of the same TSE companies owned by foreign investors continued to rise to an all-time high 28% as of the end of FY 2006, while those owned by Japanese financial institutions, firms and individuals continued to fall for several years. This verifies the foreign investors' expectation on the improvement of the Japanese corporate performance (Shipley, 2007)

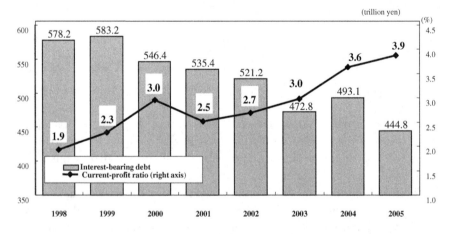

Fig. 1   Performance of Japanese firms: Profits up and debts down

Note: Interest-bearing debt includes short- and long-term loans, corporate bonds and notes receivable discounted; calculations of current-profit ratio are based on annualized aggregates of released quarterly figures.

Sources: Ministry of Finance of Japan statistics.

and the success of financial big ban taken by the Japanese government in the late 1990s.

3 Features of Economic Recovery in Comparison to the US's

The Japanese macroeconomic economic recovery has some features contrasting with the US's recovery since the middle of the 1990s, in particular:

3.1 *Private sector-led economy*

The recent revitalization of Japan has been led obviously by the private sector. Americans would say that the US economy was always led by the private sector. This is true in comparison with the case of Japan. But historically, the "big government" had been the main stream in the US until President Reagan changed the model completely in the early 1980s. Japan followed the reform, albeit not completely, after 20 years.

The traditional method of Japan to avoid recessions was to increase fiscal expenditures and to reduce interest rates. The Japanese government and the Bank of Japan began to take these measures in the early 1990s. Initially, mainstream economists and media in Japan and overseas said that the increasing fiscal expenditures were "too small and too slow". After a few years, many of them began to say that increase of fiscal expenditures at that time proved to be nonsense. However, the Japanese economy would have triggered a world depression if this policy had not been taken for some time as Japan's financial position was considerably high in the world at that time. Capital loss due to the bursting of the bubble economy was incredibly big. Hindsight teaches us that the monetary policy should have been thoroughly eased, however. The Bank feared the return of the bubble economy.

Japanese firms were ailed by the so-called "three excesses", namely, over-investment, over-employed and over-indebted, since the land and stock prices precipitated and the monetary system was half-paralyzed until the early 21st century. Sure, investments in real estate, some retail business and big projects by banks and their financial subsidiaries for housing had been evidently overheated. But, few had pointed out "excesses" of the firms in terms of human resources and borrowing,

The scale of asset losses *vis-à-vis* GDP during the period exceeded more than double of the current annual GDP. The US has never experienced big capital loss in the post-WWII period. Japan's bubble economy stemmed mainly from the following four factors, though it was evidently a financial phenomenon boosted by the main banking system, over-money supply by the central bank, and debt financing by the government for fiscal expansion: (a) the Japanese kept a strong belief in the ever-fast-growing GDP and the ability to manage the macroeconomy by the government-private sector complex; (b) likewise, the Japanese believed in the mythology that local real estate prices in urban areas would never fall, as the density of population *vis-à-vis* national land space is one of the highest in the world, the land space where people can physically live is very limited, and everybody seemingly has strong perennial aspirations to acquire land for housing, etc., especially when the Japanese economy was said to move to a "domestic demand-led one"; (c) firms had made too much equipment investment "for rationalization", by the wishful prospects of many business units within firms, namely, aiming at partial optimizations, while shareholders had weak voices. Ironically, the recovery of Japanese firms has been possible in most cases by inducing a part of the "global standard" derived from the Anglo-American business model, while keeping their own organizational competitive edge. In other words, one can say that they could flexibly respond to the dramatic changes both at home and outside; (d) Japanese firms depended on the banking system, or more precisely on the main bank system, for their financing. Local banks used to loan to their clients with real estate and stock as main collaterals. Excellent firms could raise funds whenever necessary cheaply from the international market in the 1980s, but they also borrowed much short-term money cheaply from local banks to use it virtually as long-term funds by rolling it over (repay-and-borrow simultaneously). So, once the banking system was half-paralyzed, even excellent firms were affected negatively and became generally bearish in making new investments.

Most Japanese firms initially expected that the economy would recover sooner or later, say in a few years. Many of them, manufacturers in particular, even thought that the bursting of the bubble economy should be celebrated for their sound future. While profits shrank, they continued to pay wages/salaries in accordance with their contracts with their in-house trade unions. Unbelievably, the averaged ratio of wages/salaries continued to rise until the end of the 1990s or throughout the "lost decade". They had hidden pockets — unrecorded net assets stemming from the difference between the current stock values and the acquired stock prices on record, usually very cheap. The Japanese accounting system then had not asked them to use real time evaluation of net assets.

Hence, it was natural that dramatic structural policy change of firms began to be implemented after the financial fiasco and the burst of the US IT bubble and further drop of their stock prices circa 2000. The Koizumi reform began around that time. Most Japanese people willingly accepted it, for they had recognized that the crisis this time was not cyclical but deeply structurally rooted. Deregulations to a "small government" looked inescapable for most of the people due to the widening gap between the expected fiscal revenue and expected financial needs for the quickly aging society. Firms now recognized that nobody but themselves would assist them amid high risks and high uncertainty.

3.2 Revitalization centered on manufacturing sector or "old economy"

By reviewing the economic revival in detail, one can see that revitalization of the manufacturing sector (*Monozukuri*)[9] led non-manufacturing industries (Table 1).

Indeed, sales amounts, current profits, net profits and the ratio of current profits *vis-à-vis* total sales of listed firms in the manufacturing sector, especially steel manufacturers, chemical firms and machinery makers, have been higher than those of non-manufacturing industries. In the US in the 1980s and 1990s, however, the total productivity of aggregated industry, not that of manufacturing productivity, was targeted. Many Japanese service industries have been more or less insulated from global competition by regulations, practices, people's tastes, language, etc. Take the peculiar services of IT software firms, many of the region's hospitals, traditional publications, universities as well as much of government jobs, for instance. Nevertheless, it is also true that they have been negatively affected by the sluggish growth of the Japanese economy. Healthcare institutions are a few exceptions.

Japanese big and medium-sized firms, however, have had to quickly commit themselves to the "logic of capital" to a certain extent in recent years irrespective of their industry and size. They have generally adopted the new

---

[9] *Monozukuri* originally meant to make a product politely by artisans. If one gets profit by selling a product by way of outsourcing, it would be out of *Monozukuri*. It implies that key technologies and main production processes have to be kept by a manufacturer.

Table 1   Sales amount and profits of Japanese TSE-listed firms (trillion yen, %)

	As of End of March	Sales Amount	Current Profits	Net Profits
All Industries	2002	410.8 (−1.9)	9.5 (−40.3)	−0.1 (−)
	2003	412.8 (1.3)	16.0 (71.7)	5.3 (−)
	2004	420.4 (1.8)	20.3 (26.8)	9.3 (76.8)
	2005	406.8 (6.1)	25.0 (25.4)	11.5 (20.9)
	2006	446.6 (8.1)	28.2 (13.2)	15.9 (38.6)
Mfg.	2002	218.8 (−1.6)	4.8 (−56.4)	0.1 (−96.6)
	2003	223.4 (2.8)	9.5 (102.4)	3.6 (4683.0)
	2004	231.2 (3.3)	12.5 (31.3)	5.8 (62.3)
	2005	248.4 (6.0)	15.6 (24.6)	8.1 (32.2)
	2006	274.5 (8.6)	18.5 (16.8)	10.1 (24.5)
Non-Mfg.	2002	192.0 (−1)	4.7 (−25.7)	−0.2 (−)
	2003	189.2 (−0.5)	6.5 (38.6)	1.7 (−)
	2004	192.3 (0.0)	7.8 (20.2)	3.5 (107.1)
	2005	157.6 (5.1)	9.4 (26.7)	3.4 (0.8)
	2006	171.2 (7.1)	10.1 (7.0)	5.7 (73.6)

Note: Figures in parentheses show the percentage of increase/decrease compared with the corresponding figures in the previous fiscal year. Numbers of firms in each year are not the same, as M&As and newly listed firms changed them. See details in Kinoshita (2007).
Sources: *Nihon Keizai Shimbun*, dated 9 June 2003, 3 June 2004, 22 March 2006 and 4 April 2007.

capital efficiency measure as ROE/ROA/EVA, market-value accounting, combined balance sheet and individual's performance-based evaluation. They have depended on outsourcing of human resources more than ever, and have largely abolished traditional "automatic" adjustment (increase) practice on annual wage/salary base, usually conducted every spring period.

Many of the people that praise revitalizations of Japanese management centering on *Monozukuri* tend to overlook this trend. Even the Toyota group that enjoyed Japan's largest amount of current profit amounting to ¥2.2 trillion for the term FY 2006, ending March 2007, has largely made revisions to its conventional "seniority-based payment system" and "life-long employment" and has embarked on accepting contract workers and temporary employees extensively. Overseas production ratio, or the ratio of overseas production amount (OPA) *vis-à-vis* (OPA + domestic production amount), has been on a continuous rise. Hence, failures of foreign operations are not allowed. Japanese technical systems can be brought in, but localization of human resources, materials and parts, money, design and engineering are unavoidable to reduce cost and to satisfy the local community. Amid this situation, mistakes in production are gradually increasing. A new issue of how to cover such unprecedented risks is being produced.

Furthermore, the product lifecycle (PLC) has become shorter and shorter. With such changes taking place, the number of good manufacturing firms that could set with confidence long-term targets such as new investment, which has been considered a characteristic of Japanese firms, must be decreasing. A limited number of excellent firms still have the luxury to continue with it, but pressures from foreign shareholders and individuals that put emphasis on "logic of capital" relatively in the shorter-term have intensified. Not all foreign investors have asked Japanese firms for the same thing, though. A teachers union's fund in the US, for instance, wishes to see better CSR than high ROE. So, international investor relations (IR) has become vital for top executives in Japanese firms to find good foreign investors who would sympathize with the firm's mission and its own way of management rather than higher yield.

3.3   Hybrid Japanese-style management system: Similarity and dissimilarity in the recovery of the US

It took a number of years before Japanese big firms became slim and recovered. Many small and medium-sized firms in the region have been left behind. It is not likely that many of them could restructure themselves to become competitive by assuming a hybrid management system under the global pressures and severe domestic economic situation and that the government, ruling parties and opposition parties could compromise in continuing policies to support many of them by fiscal measures, etc., although some of them have been successful and could seek global and domestic niche markets with their high-level technologies and wisdom.

It is notable that Japanese firms learned a lot from the US experts and firms in the post-WWII period — for instance, from W. E. Deming, a statistician proficient in quality control, and Jack Welch, former CEO of General Electric — in the same way that the US firms including Welch himself had studied good practices of Japanese firms. Motorola was said to be the first American firm which had begun to study Total Quality Control (TQC), which Americans could evolve to Total Quality Management (TQM), from Japanese manufacturers and its market, followed by GE. Japan established the Deming Award, dating back to the early 1950s. The US firms also studied good practices of Japanese style of management such as *kaizen* through good teamwork, Toyota's Lean Production System, client-oriented marketing and reduction of lead time for creating a new product in the 1980s. The US government followed the private sector by promulgating new government policy aiming at higher productivity and better quality control, setting up the Malcom Baldridge National Quality Award in 1987, for instance.

Despite mutual learning, the US economic recovery was conducted in a revolutionary way through business process reengineering (BPR) (Hammer and Champy, 1993) of uncompetitive firms, which most Japanese firms would hesitate to emulate with a few exceptions such as Matsushita and Toshiba (though not completely the same). The US-based investment funds, investment banks and management firms, however, have encouraged the losers in Japan in various fields to conduct BPRs with their assistance and money, if necessary.

Hence, conversions of ideas and methods for reform between the US and Japanese individual firms have been widely observed, but how to realize them has been different in principle. In Japan, the thought that "human resources in a firm are the biggest assets of the firm" still remains steadfast, and a number of firms still hate to simply layoff their employees just to raise profits, which is commonplace in the Anglo-American model. Mr. Fujio Mitarai, then President of Canon and currently Chairman of Keidanren, for instance, unveiled a plan in November 2004 to build the most automated printer-making plant in Kyushu and to have it assume different roles from its subsidiary's plants in China. He clearly stated that "Canon will assure employment for life, but will conduct severe evaluation on each individual staff and worker, and may transfer positions whenever necessary".

True, there were not a small number of Japanese firms that reduced personnel by encouraging voluntary retirement with special bonus-added systems in the last 10 years. However, we have seldom observed cases in big firms where full-time employees were forced to retire on short notice, say within a week. Japan's social norm is apparently different from the US's. The difference basically originates from the fact that an American firm can generally employ competitive human resources, even management executives, in the market whenever necessary, and that wages/salaries are to be set equal to the marginal productivity of an employee. So, if one does not wish for someone to be recruited by rival firms, one should raise wage/salary up to his/her potential capacity. This may be natural for firms equipped with the individualistic Anglo-American type model.

Japanese manufacturing firms equipped with a hybrid model, however, have tried to unite the conventional model comprising 5S, teamwork for *kaizen* and other *monozukuri* cultures with the modified version of logic of capital such as "Selection and Focus", an evaluation system on employees, and rationalization by M&As. For instance, more than half of big firms have adopted the so-called performance-related evaluation method, but it is still not completely fixed as it is logically against "teamwork" and OJT which those firms have emphasized. Yes, the shareholders' voice became bigger and the management and their staff began to listen more carefully to them. But, the basic Japanese way of management is still unchanged in the organizational decision-making process and in human relations among stakeholders. In essence, Japan's hybrid model still reflects the stakeholder's capitalism, not the Anglo-American capitalism or the SWM model.

4 How Japanese Firms Could Regain Profits

Japanese macroeconomic recovery had been accomplished when the virtuous cycle began in 2002–2003. Firms had been slim with increased competitiveness. Corporate profits rose. Foreign investors never overlooked the improvement and continued to buy stocks. Stock prices rose. Then, both corporate debts and banks' bad loans reduced significantly. Banks began to take risks. Firms began to expand their activities and make new equipment investment, while keeping their cost relatively low. Thus, corporate profits continued to increase.

Hence, if one wishes to know how the Japanese economy has revived, one has to know how Japanese firms could manage themselves to regain profits. Taking up manufacturing firms as typical examples, I wish to point out the following four factors/strategies as answers.

4.1 *Lasting efforts to reduce costs and risks*

(a) *"Rationalization" of labor cost or from fixed wage/salary formula to elastic wage/salary formula, and outsourcing of human resources.* Due to the continued deflation, increased risk and uncertainty, the high growth of the sales amount was not easily expected. But for the need to keep an incentive for high employee morale for profit-making, labor contracts for most firms were amended from the conventional type of (wage/salary base + seniority factor + annual inflation adjustment + bonus [reflecting company's profit but relatively fixed]) to the new one (wage/salary base + bonus [reflecting employee's contribution to the company's profit] + other adjustment), apart from fringe benefits. Reward calculation scheme for executives also changed in most of the firms, with the bonus portion which reflects corporate profits being increased. Now, yearly inflation adjustment in most companies is virtually abolished and the seniority factor reduced, even to zero in some extreme cases, though the family factor of employees and other fringe benefits are generally left. Evaluation on the individual's contribution to the company's profit has become harsher. Besides, most firms have severely administered the number of their employees, for instance, by "voluntary retirement" and by recruiting only a very limited number of fresh university graduates, increasing the usage of part-timers and outsourcing human resources for non-core business. Thus, the annual average ratio of labor cost *vis-à-vis* value-added peaked just before 2000 and went down to the similar level of the US's in 2004, which was still higher than those in the 1980s (Figure 2).

(b) *Reduction of number of firms and closures/sales of idle assets.* Before the "lost decade", the number of M&As of Japanese big firms made by foreign firms as well as other Japanese firms was extremely low in comparison with other OECD countries. In fact, the number of firms in a certain area of the industry tended to be unchanged for a long time, because: (i) most of the big firms could grow at status quo; (ii) the cross-sharing of stocks barred M&As; (iii) the post-WWII anti-monopoly law prohibited firms to have holding companies except for specific purposes, like PFI; and (iv) most firms, regardless of their

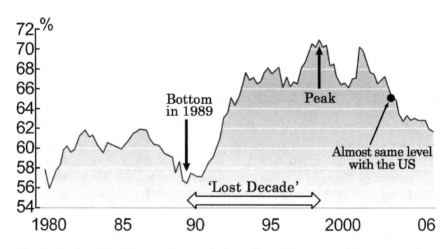

Fig. 2   Ratio of Japan's annual wage/salary *vis-à-vis* aggregated corporate value-added (from 1980 to 2006)

Source: Ministry of Finance statistics.

size, could get necessary financing from their main banks or government-owned financial institutions, while commercial banks were protected by the government's "convoy-fleet system" of the banking industry until the financial fiasco in 1997–1998. When the anti-monopoly law was amended in 1997, firms could establish holding companies for general purposes. Since then, M&As became popular over time at home as well as overseas to make active firms internationally competitive. This move has accelerated the integration of firms in certain areas. Typical cases of integration are shown as follows: 14 pulp companies were reduced to only 4; 14 oil companies to 4; 7 large-scale cement companies to 3; and 7 industrial gas companies to 3. Banking was no exception — 15 big banks were reduced to only 3 mega-bank groups (Mitsubishi-Tokyo-UFJ Group, Sumitomo-Mitsui Group, Mizuho Group) plus one (Risona Bank Group).

(c) *Expansion of outsourcing at home and from overseas of intermediate products and materials.* While the selection and focus strategy was widely adopted by firms, cost management, speed of change and flexibility became more important. Hence, outsourcing of intermediate products, parts and materials became popular. They outsource those items to either domestic firms and overseas, using independent firms, group companies or foreign OEM/ODM/EMS factories in consideration of the expected cost reduction, expected PLC, and possibility of leakage of technology and know-how, thereby increasing rivals, possibility of managing quality control in terms of product liability and the effect on existing employees.

(d) *Produce new production materials.* High-tech industries need better quality production materials which tend to create high value-added. If new good material is developed by a firm, the company's competitiveness would be strengthened, its IPR value would rise and the possibility to innovate in the next round would be high. Japanese manufacturing firms keep a strong position in this field through the past R&D investment and accumulated experiences as well as technologies. This needs not only brain work for innovation, but also experiments to be realized by good teamwork. To copy the whole process to produce new materials is difficult compared with that of assembly of new products. To name a few, specially strengthened stainless steel, carbon fiber for aircrafts, solar battery materials, materials for digital cameras and chemical materials for LCD panels.

(e) *Reduce interest-bearing borrowing.* As the cash flow positions of firms improved, they continued to repay past debts to be free from the financial fiasco as well as to reduce borrowing costs.

(f) *To reduce inventory to minimal, idealistically to zero.* Toyota's lean production system including *kamban* system, for instance, is aimed at targeting this.

4.2 *Change of corporate targets and clarification of firm's mission*

Firms used to adopt the sales amount and the share of their product line rather than profit indicators as corporate targets and tried to realize full-set-type product line, although they generally stressed the importance of contributing to a better society. Currently, most of them adopt capital efficiency indicators, namely, ROE, ROA or EVA to measure their performance. The reason for this has already been mentioned. This change naturally has been related to the "selection and focus" strategies. Firms tended to alter their missions accordingly, to transform them from a "problem solution"-type firm to a mission-oriented one, stressing "fair" distribution of their "fruits" among all stakeholders, high efficiency with CSR, etc. Slogans of "Only one rather than Number One" and "Product Innovation" rather than "Process Innovation" are widely known. Some firms have tried to establish cross-functional teams for this purpose. "Selection and Focus" strategy is crucially important for them to establish and maintain the strong image of the company and of their products (branding). This is what P2M and KPM has emphasized among others.

4.3 *Increase in overseas income*

Many Japanese firms have made relatively large amounts of direct investment since the 1970s, mainly: (a) to enter local markets in the US, Europe and Asia, half positively and half by being forced by trade conflicts; (b) to procure products cheaply to Japan or export to other areas; and (c) to procure energy and natural resources for import to Japan. Their subsidiaries in Europe and East Asia had to be restructured in the past decade as their subsidiaries had generally deteriorated in competitiveness. Now, net incomes of their subsidiaries have increased, particularly the auto sector in the US and in East Asia. For instance, the ratio of net profits of subsidiaries (except those related to direct export from Japan) out of combined profits of TSE-listed 427 firms rose from 20% in FY 2000 to 30% in FY 2004.

4.4 *Keeping one of the highest R&D ratios in the world, honoring the IPR seriously, producing environment-friendly products, and activating IR in the world*

These activities are interrelated. There will be no need to detail these as they become a kind of common sense. The only thing to be noted is that all manufacturing firms try to keep their IPR by patents, to "black box" a certain/whole process to produce high-value products and avoid being copied by others, or legal suits in the worst case scenario.

It is difficult to know how much each factor has contributed to the increase of profits. Many factors are interrelated, and there is no detailed breakdown showing contributions to profits in the financial statements of the firms (the same with those of the rest of the world). But it is clear that the improvement in efficiency has been done not by an increased number of human resources, but in most cases by a reduced number, and that the revision of wage/salary calculation scheme has given not a small influence on the profit expansion, at least during the initial stage of recovery.[10]

5 Concluding Remarks: Strong Leadership in Many Success Stories and P2M/KPM

We could conclude that all these efforts of Japanese firms have been more mission-oriented and that they have endeavored to realize total optimization by adopting a hybrid model, integrating their competitive corporate DNA with newly absorbed genuine profit-seeking methods derived from the SWM model. How was this possible while they experienced the "lost decade"? In one word, they never slept — efforts made in comprehensive partial

---

[10] Dore (2006) argues in his book that most of the newly created value-added in Japan from 2001 to 2004 was distributed, first, to shareholders as dividends, and secondly, to salaries and bonuses of big firms, not small firms, at the sacrifice of employees. He insisted, together with Ito (2006), that Japan's conventional-type stakeholder capitalism, the fairest to all stakeholders, should not give seats to the Anglo-American model. However, Japan cannot survive alone as most big firms and some small firms are multinationals seeking a freer and open international trading system and work under ever-updating international orders. Many employees have supported changes of Japanese firms, though not willingly. Most of them already have vested interests. An ideal society for Dore and Ito is continental Europe, not the US. But what about Europe-based multinationals? They are more oligopolistic than Japan's and tend to behave as largely as the US-based ones outside Europe.

optimization by major business units continued until the last moment, the real crisis circa 2000. Then, most of them changed their behavior toward total optimization by changing labor contracts, selling idle assets or unprofitable business units and focusing their investments on the highest potential area(s). This could be done in most cases by strong leadership. A limited number of firms which continued to grow profits regardless of the recession and crisis were led by superior leaders. Those leaders took advantage of the worst corporate environment for their evolution to become slim and more competitive firms. They clearly knew what to do. But without this critical situation, even the best leaders could hardly restructure their firms with high-level technologies and create many success stories where important decision-making had been done largely on consensus and bottom-up.

The direction they should go and how was well-discussed in P2M. Actual processes of their restructuring to meet the new round of global competition have proven that the P2M's argument and the related educational system are completely correct.

Historically, Japan took a similar reformation, a flexible response to the new reality of the world, by leaving its own strength and absorbing a new competitive edge from the outside world. The Meiji Restoration and the "modernization" after the defeat in WWII were the typical examples. Not all countries take a similar process when a dramatic change of a society or firm is necessary. The US, for instance, tries to take more dramatic ways as per Schumpeter's "destruction to innovation".

The revitalization of Japanese firms this time has given their management, and to a lesser extent, employees, confidence in their evolutionary behavior. Japan's mainstream business model still keeps the basic employment system and in-house trade union, bearing respect to the elderly. However, exceptions are observed in many IT software houses and venture businesses. Simply put, it is not easy for Japanese firms to assume a flat organization with a strong leadership suitable for complete use of IT software. This is a cost of the new Japanese version of management. This trend is interpreted by many critics as the reason for halfway utilization of IT software in the field of important decision-making processes and global networking. This is by no means due to the weaknesses of IT software infrastructure. According to the recent survey by *Washington Post*,[11] Japan is far ahead of the US in its IT infrastructure in communication

---

[11] An article of *Washington Post*, 29 August 2007. The original date is from ITU.

speed, the usage ratio per population, and the unit price (far cheaper, regardless of the speed). This may be due to the same reason many Japanese firms that had begun overseas operations some 20 to 30 years ago are still struggling with "localization" of management, i.e., the difficulty in flattening the organization.

To sum up, we have witnessed that firms have generally attained the primary target of P2M with some exceptions, and that we need more mission-oriented innovation not only in the manufacturing sector but in all industries in the next round of global competition, which is a core concept of KPM. A similar approach may be effective for firms in the rest of the world. In fact, there seemingly exist many concrete ways for exodus, not just one, for smart firms around the world, with "excellent" Japanese firms as one of the good examples (Mintzberg, 2003; Berger *et al.*, 2006).

The Japanese economy, plagued by a rapidly growing proportion of elderly people, will be more handicapped in decades to come. Hence, not only companies, but' also central and local governments, universities and individuals will need more severe scrutiny with regard to what kind of missions they will have and how they will do in the future. However, not only existing firms, but also most Japanese people, bound by many current agendas, tend to forget true entrepreneurship — a mother for innovation. They have been influenced by conventional education, training and grading system in Japan that has been overly segmentalized. How we will break through such a situation under systemic fatigue of the politico-economic society in Japan is another important agenda for us. However, this is beyond our study of KPM.

References

Berger, S. *et al.* (2006). *How to Compete*, New York: MIT Press.

Dertouzos, M. *et al.* (1989). *Made in America — Regaining the Productive Edge*, Cambridge, MA: Harper perennial, The MIT Press.

Dore, R. (2006). *Dare no Tameno Kaisha ni Suruka (To Make a Firm for Whom?)*, Tokyo: Iwanami Press (in Japanese).

Eiteman, D. K. *et al.* (2007). *Multinational Business Finance*, Peason International Edition, 11th ed., San Francisco and New York.

Hammer, M. and Champy, J. A. (1993). *Reengineering the Corporation — A Manifesto for Business Revolution*, New York: Harper Business Book.

Ito, M. (2006). *Nihon Keizai wo Tou (Questions over Japanese Economy)*, Tokyo: Iwanami Press (in Japanese).

Kinoshita, T. (2007). *Business Model of Japanese Firms and Sino-Japan Relations*, Tokyo: Iwanami Press, Chapter 2 (in Japanese), for a COE project of Waseda University.

Mintzberg, H. (2003). *Calculated Chaos*, Cambridge, MA: Harvard Business School Press.

Shipley, A. H. (2007). *The Japanese Money Tree*, NY: FT Press.

Part 2

KPM in the Information and Communications Industry

Abstract

The Japanese information and communications industry, including related manufacturing, has a market scale of about $440 million (¥48 trillion) as of 2005.[1] It will continue to grow. Information and communications technology (ICT) is utilized not only in enterprise strategic systems, but also as an information-sharing platform common to the entire business world. The ICT industry has made a remarkable contribution to all industries and to the entire Japanese market.

From the viewpoint of business administration, it is important to plan and carry out projects that enhance corporate value in order to beat the global competition, despite a rapidly changing environment.

The management of system construction in a way closely connected to the business strategy is necessary for an enterprise that introduces an ICT system to improve its business value. On the other hand, the system integrators, who contract to build the ICT systems, should be able to ascertain a client's needs precisely, right from the stage of system design. Though the importance of strategic ICT system construction is increasing, integrated project management methods that promote the enhancement of business value simply do not exist.

In Part 2, Kaikaku project management (fourth-generation project management) is explained for the stakeholders of an ICT system, such as the project owner, system planner, contractor, system user, etc., expressing the essence of Japanese *kaikaku* projects in sophisticated companies which plan and carry out their program in order to enhance corporate value.

As mentioned in Part 1, *kaikaku* project management consists of three models: a scheme model, a system model and a service model. A management that supports the free circulation of specialist knowledge among people working on a project will be systemized in each model.

The management skills required of the owner who asks for system construction based on a corporate strategy are different from those needed by contractors who receive the order for ICT system construction.

---

[1] *2007 White Book Information and Communications in Japan,* compiled by Ministry of International Affairs and Communications, p. 342 (in Japanese).

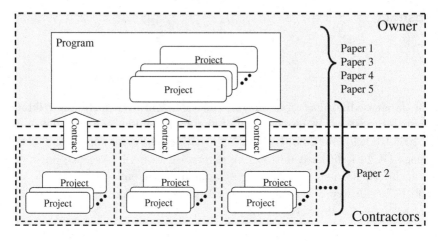

Fig. 1   Viewpoint of each paper

The viewpoint of the description of each paper in Part 2 is shown in Figure 1. The first, third, fourth and fifth papers are described mainly from the viewpoint of the owner. The second paper is described from the viewpoint of the contractors. An essential guide is presented here together with profiles of the authors for compact access to grasp the outline and the respective paper contents.

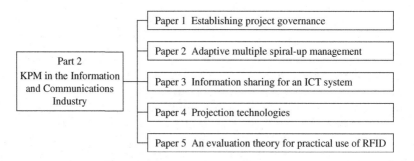

Tametsugu Taketomi is CEO of Corporate Intelligence Corporation and professor at the Nippon Institute of Technology. Based on his consulting career, he asserts that the lifecycle controls of a program be conducted according to the owner's view. The first paper focuses on how project governance copes with system development projects at high risk. Each of the three models in KPM indicates the essential governance for the lifecycle of the projects.

Shoei Komatsu was director of a large engineering company in Japan, and moved to academia where he had lectured on information systems and project management. He continues his research work at institutions and as visiting professors at universities. In the second paper, after analyzing the factors of success and failure of previous projects, the importance of the views of the owner and collaborative organization are emphasized. The program is classified into three parts: the initial stage, the construction stage and the operational stage. Not only is the lifecycle management of the construction stage necessary, but also the multiplex spiral management of the lifecycle that includes all three stages.

Hideo Yamamoto, the author of the third paper, is a professor at the Graduate School of Commerce and Management at Hitotsubashi University. His research career in the field of information technology has been highly esteemed in education and research as being effective by his interdisciplinary approach for problem solution in ICT management. The method for sharing common information to improve an organization's level of knowledge for the lifecycle of the program is shown in the third paper. An evaluation function is proposed that is related to the effect and risk of the investment for stakeholders, such as the ICT system owner, system planner, contractors, system users and operations people. Probability distributions are applied to the evaluation function, and the shapes of the probability distributions of the investment effects are determined by the Monte Carlo simulation method.

Naokoto Kogo and Atsushi Miyagawa, the authors of the fourth paper, are affiliated at the Graduate School of Economics at Osaka University. Their research is evaluated to cast light on the field of complexity of project profiling in upper stream. Projection technology used in the project management, such as 3D imaging and image simulation, is featured in this paper. Communications using the ICT media can facilitate agreement between the ordering company and contractors. Using the road construction project in Kochi city as an example, a decision-making process using projection technology is presented.

Takashi Katayama is an engineer at Unichika Corporation, and Takayuki Asada is a professor at the Graduate School of Economics at Osaka University. They are the authors of the fifth paper. Here, a method for measuring investment is discussed, using the process of introducing an RFID system. When we have to decide on investing in the development of a new technology, the project should be evaluated not only by financial value, but also by non-financial factors. The evaluation continues from the stage of the feasibility study to a trial introduction and then the real operational stage.

Hideo Yamamoto
Professor, Graduate School of Commerce and Management
Hitotsubashi University

Toward Establishing Project Governance

Tametsugu Taketomi

President, Corporate Intelligence Corporation
Professor, Graduate School for Management of Technology
Nippon Institute of Technology

1 Introduction

Governance is needed to lead a project to success, achieve the original mission, and bring the expected return to the project owner (hereafter, owner). In the engineering industry where project management has traditionally been applied, return on investment is sufficiently considered before starting a project, and in most cases, an experienced engineering company is selected to perform the project. Should a project not be accomplished as scheduled, the owner would suffer losses without the expected earning after project completion. Therefore, a compensation regulation is specified in the contract for indemnification for damages in quality and delay. It can be said that governance need not be emphasized for this industry since sufficient elements are there to make the project successful.

On the other hand, in system development projects, this governance often does not work. Research has revealed that in more than half of the cases, system projects do not meet the due date or are over the budget. Some people view delivery delay as inevitable, citing the difficulty associated with system development projects. The biggest difference between a system development project and other projects is that the former consists mainly of work to replace existing operations by computers under the existent circumstances. Such planning and execution of a project under the existent circumstances encompass many factors of uncertainty. Furthermore, from an investment perspective, evaluating return on investment is extremely difficult. The purpose of the investment and how it is justified are not very visible. The existence of many failed projects shows that there is an extremely big risk. In spite of this, investment for a system is increasing year after year. Thus, the establishment of IT governance is a pressing issue today.

This paper intends to define characteristic issues that system development projects face, and to suggest a way of establishing the project governance over the whole lifecycle of a project in line with three reference models as an approach to overcome these issues. An approach to governance will be suggested through introducing cases of how an investor or a system owner should manage the system development.

2 Project Governance from the Viewpoint of Project Lifecycle

Let us first go back to the definition of a project and discuss project governance. In KPM, project is defined as "a business of creating value for the future aiming at accomplishing within a specified period with a beginning and an end, a certain mission that is assigned under certain restrictions such as resources and a given situation". Program is defined as "a business in which several projects are organically combined to realize the whole mission". A project is an element constituting a program.

Generally, an organization that conducts business tries to make changes to correspond to changes in the environment, reinforce its competitiveness or start a new business. Programs and projects are non-stationary activities for making such changes.

Thus, programs and projects are activities that are performed for a limited time only, until they are settled down as the next stationary activities. They have missions and purposes to create changes, and are considered to be finished when a particular mission or a purpose is accomplished. Managing this non-stationary situation that exists at a stage with characteristics different from those of a stationary situation is called Project and Program management. A period of non-stationary situation becomes the lifecycle of Project and Program management. Figure 1 shows this relation.

Many contractors that start the business from an activity to receive orders can see neither the first scheme stage (framework) at the beginning of this lifecycle, nor the service (operation) stage at the end. Moreover, the inflow and outflow of money and the comings and goings of personnel are most frequent during the stage of system (realization) at mid-stream. Therefore, managing this system stage is difficult and entails a high management risk. For this reason, a traditional project management system has developed, focusing on the management of the system stage from the contractors' viewpoint.

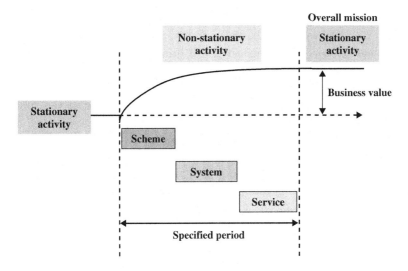

Fig. 1   Lifecycle of a project and program

In this traditional project management, there appears to have been no room for discussion about the governance from the project owner's viewpoint. Furthermore, it can be considered that in traditional projects, adoption of project management was limited to the management of matters that had already been decided, and a situation requiring governance did not surface in project operation.

The owner's viewpoint enters the project lifecycle at the initial scheme stage when the project plan is elaborated. This is because the type of project that can be newly started is based on how much investment can be justified. At this stage, it becomes necessary to consider the expected effect (investment profitability) from the project. Thus, governance at the scheme stage becomes a process toward justification of investment, evaluation of risks, and realization of a system project worth that investment.

From the owner's viewpoint, governance means selecting members and organizations that would evaluate the validity of investment, checking what the realistic investment is for accomplishing the owner's wishes through the project, and surely realizing it. In other words, this involves devising a project plan and examining its feasibility considering technical and market risks, and at the same time, selecting members and organizations that would manage the project according to the plan and realize the original plan. It suffices for the owner to manage this process.

The system stage entails carrying out governance to check whether the selected members and organizations are managing the project according to the original plan and whether they will bring the project to completion. In exercising governance, the important point is not to manage the project itself, but to ensure that project risks are managed. Thus, the owner should manage and monitor whether or not risks assumed at the time of planning are within the permissible range.

Finally, at the last service stage, confirmation on the following is made: that the business is operated as per the original plan, that the management is carried out to ensure the business is maintained and operates smoothly, that the performance expected in the original plan is attained, and that expected effects are realized by the new system.

The governance structure can be established by incorporating this series of processes in the operation of project management.

3   Issues of Governance

Many of the system development projects replace existing work such as manual work, collection of data and transactions by computers. Systematization in recent open network environment is increasingly seen as investment in infrastructure for business operation, since connecting to the network constitutes the foundation for reinforcing the company's competitiveness. Investing in systems poses some problems from the governance viewpoint.

(1)   Firstly, it is difficult to evaluate the validity of investment in terms of expected return at the scheme stage. This is because in most cases, the extent of sales increase and cost reduction resulting from introducing a new system is not clear, and as a result, the criteria for how much should be invested tends to become unclear. Even if an investment worth several hundred million dollars is made, one cannot expect to be able to see any visible return. Yet, there are many cases of clear disadvantage compared with other companies if system is not made. Such situations make it difficult to justify the investment amount. Since the effect cannot be measured clearly, it is difficult to decide on the criteria for evaluating if the investment is viable. As a result, even in the case of similar infrastructure, investment amount differs greatly depending on the situation at the start of the project.

An example of this can be seen in two competing companies of the author's acquaintance, with similar sales size and number of personnel that introduced very similar ERP packages. One company invested ¥10 billion to introduce ERP, while the other invested ¥4 billion. Although the original expected effects are not completely clear, as far as tangible effect is concerned, the company with the smaller investment has achieved better results. The company that invested ¥10 billion has seen improvements in service-level quality, decrease in the burden of employees, and acceleration in the speed of handling work, but whether these improvements were worth the investment is not clear. It is not easy to verify that more than twice an expected return has been obtained, big enough to match the difference of over twice in investment. The major difference lies in an approach for selecting a contractor and a project management structure. The company that made a smaller investment for introducing ERP had clearly established a defined governance structure. Here, the difference in governance can be observed and the importance of governance from the investment viewpoint is recognized.

(2) Secondly, many risks exist during the scheme stage associated with project planning. Since it is the replacement of existing work, even if the range of system development project is decided, there is an extremely high risk of fluctuation in cost in interfacing with the existing system and in fixing the specification to meet existing work. As a result, in interfacing with the existing system and in designing work processes for smooth work performance, there arises a problem that the estimated original budget will fall short. Normally, research and preparatory designing work are conducted prior to execution of a project. Those research and preparatory designing work cannot always reflect existing specifications properly and therefore hold high risks.

From the viewpoint of governance, it is sufficient to allocate risk money, but as the necessary risk evaluation method is not yet established, uncertainty remains even after risk money is allocated. Since in many cases, how much risk should be assumed at the time of budget planning depends on the existing situation, it tends to become obscure. From the owner's viewpoint, this causes the problem that because of the high uncertainty, how much should be invested in is not clear at the starting point, yet a considerable amount of risk money needs to be allocated. This influences greatly an investment return.

(3) In the system stage, generally in many cases, orders are made separately in each phase to a contractor starting from a phase for defining requirements, a phase for a basic design, and a phase for detail design and development. In this situation, from the owner's viewpoint, since changing a contractor for a phase for detail design and development from a phase for basic design means a high switching cost, in most cases, orders are given to the same contractor. This means an extremely advantageous contract form to the contractor for development work. Even if the order price is low for a phase for basic design, as there is hardly any competition in a phase for detail design and development, the contractor is able to pass on the risk of bearing the cost to the ordering party, or to the owner. The owner is obliged to bear the risk of cost increase during a phase for detail design and development, while the receiver of the order has no incentive to keep within the budget set by the owner. Thus, the risk of exceeding the original budget for development is very high. At the very least, the risk of not being able to fix the budget at a phase for a basic design is included.

In the engineering industry, Japanese companies have established a style undertaking the fixed lump-sum contract which reduces the owner's risk-taking. However, this style has not been employed in the system industry. Moreover, as a common practice, a process is established through which the owner is made to aggressively bear the risk. Introducing a system in which the contractor is made to bear this risk leads to reinforcement of governance.

(4) In addition, as most of the system development projects correspond to conversion projects that replace existing business processes, they have many risks peculiar to conversion. For instance, there are many cases in which whether to adapt the new system to existing business processes or to unify existing business processes into the standard specifications prepared by the new system cannot be specified until the time of detail design. If the business process specification is different, the cost for connection sometimes becomes about ten times different. Thus, such a development project not only faces the problem of an insufficient risk judgment at the planning phase, but also the difficulty in fixing technical skills and design risk due to immaturity of project team members in charge. This can be regarded as immaturity in the team's project management competencies. Furthermore, such risks peculiar to conversion as mismatching of existing data at the time of testing, or changeover limitations due to

existing business process at the time of transfer, exist. Since these kinds of risk are difficult to detect completely in advance study, they are likely to become evident during the later stages of development, and when they do so, they show up in the form of schedule delay. These risks peculiar to conversion work are significantly high in system development projects compared with projects in other industries.

(5) Even if the project for the system stage is successfully completed at the end, the expected return is often not achieved merely by introducing a system. How to manage business processes with the new system after introduction is a key to success. Management following the introduction and monitoring the effect with appropriate measurement that are defined in the service stage has significant meaning. For instance, even if introduction of a system is planned with the aim to reduce inventory, and its validity is evaluated, the actual effect of reducing inventory cannot be realized for one year after introduction. In addition to showing actual effect of reducing inventory, operating a new system and appropriately performing business are required, aiming to reduce inventory. Otherwise, the expected return at the start of the project cannot be achieved. Whether this proper management can be realized remains as risk after a system introduction.

In the engineering industry and construction industry where project management is already established and matured, governance works in another way without specially introducing a new governance system. For example, in plant construction industry, investment risk is grasped and covered to a large extent through a determination of financing eligibility made by the bank at the time of financing. Moreover, by selecting contractors with experience and having them construct plants under a fixed lump-sum contract, the responsibility of bearing the risk of investment increasing during construction is to some extent transferred to the contractor, and the risk of project management failing is also reduced. In addition, also for such operations and return of investments as securing buyers of products after plants are constructed and attracting of tenants, a well-thought-out planning and review is usually carried out in the initial stages of making the framework and conducting a feasibility study. In this way, a solid system is established for the whole lifecycle to enable effective governance. Also, in business reform and management innovation projects that consist largely of projects by top management initiative, it is easier for governance to function.

To make governance function, the procedure of what to do and how to do them should be clear, and the work of monitoring and checking the progress of the project should be put in place. In the industries mentioned above and restructuring projects, how to make governance work is clear, or it can be interpreted that governance functions because of the character of the projects. Compared with these projects, in system development projects, risk items exist throughout the project's lifecycle and management methods for them are not clear. Hence, the owner's governance often does not function, displaying a characteristic of system development projects.

Here, to make governance function, risks specified in each of the five problems discussed above are defined in order as follows:

(1) Risk at the time of planning an investment;
(2) Risk at the time of planning for integration with an existing system;
(3) Risk of the project at the time of development;
(4) Risk at the time of development for integration with an existing system; and
(5) Risk in achieving the expected return.

Risks (1) and (2) are in the scheme stage, risks (3) and (4) are in the system stage, and risk (5) is in the service stage. Recognition of the existence of these risks and managing them along the lifecycle of the project leads to making governance function.

A structure will be suggested in the following pages that will make governance function by managing the risks along the lifecycle of the project to deal with such high-risk system development projects.

4   Governance in the Scheme Stage

4.1   *Risk management and governance at the time of planning an investment*

Usually, during the stage of designing a systematization plan, investment for systematization is budgeted in some form. In calculating return on investment for budgeting, generally for cases of investment aiming at improving business processes, several reductions in expense can be considered:

- Reduction in expense by extracting room for cost reduction through improvement of supply chain efficiency;

- Improvement of cash flow by reducing inventory;
- Reduction in personnel cost by speed-up and streamlining of accounting works;
- Reduction in personnel cost by introducing shared services;
- Reduction in purchasing unit price by streamlining of procurement works and purchasing electronically.

All the methods mentioned above require the assumption that work is carried out rationally in accordance with the new system after its introduction. Therefore, to secure the investment return estimated at the initial planning stage, introduction of measurement to monitor effects at the service stage after the system starts operating and the governance that secures its execution are needed. Furthermore, in the case of investment in infrastructure, calculation of effective investment return is difficult. For example, measurable effects on investment that can be reflected in financial figures cannot be obtained in such cases as upgrading of infrastructure by providing PCs to all staff, enabling them to use the mailing function.

Such difficulties in calculating investment profitability in many cases become one of the causes of exceeding the budget for systematization without clear standards. It is natural for a person in charge of systematization to want to purchase the most expensive system possible, whilst allocating much money to cope with the development risk. Similarly, for a development contractor, the bigger the budget, the better it is. As just described, a system development has the characteristic that the interests of people in charge of ordering and receipt coincide, and that the investor's viewpoint tends to fall out. Under such circumstances, it is not possible for owner's governance to function.

In addition, to formulate the investment budget, an approach of obtaining an estimate from a development vendor, fixing specifications with the vendor, and then proceeding to make a contract at discretion is apt to be taken. In so doing, both the ordering and order-receiving party tend to assign sufficient money to deal with the risk.

In such cases, cost effectiveness perspective falls out, and governance for investment does not function. Therefore, the approach of making governance function by having different contractors for the phase of preparing estimates and inquiry papers, and for the development phase by having them check one another, is needed. Figure 2 shows this approach.

As in case (A) in Figure 2, if a development contractor is selected at an early stage of defining requirements when advancing from systematization

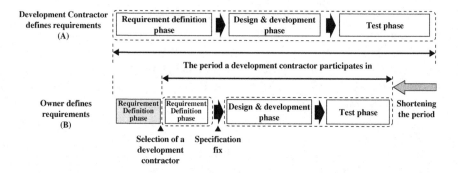

Fig. 2   Preparation of request for proposal (RFP) by owner

plan to development, it becomes almost a contract at discretion, and governance for development amount does not function. On the other hand, in case (B) in Figure 2, an early stage of defining requirements is conducted by the owner, including this specification document for requirements in RFP (Request for Proposal), and then selecting a development vendor through competitive bidding. In this way, this method tries to make owner's governance function. In this case, at this stage of defining requirements, it is important to make clear to some extent the range of risk a development vendor takes by clarifying the risks that accompany the development. By taking this measure and through competitive bidding, it becomes possible to request a development vendor to conclude a lump-sum contract that covers until completion. Risk money can then be allocated at the time of planning, and shifting to the contractor the risk of increased expense burden accompanying development can take place. This form of contract is the same as the lump-sum contract used in plant construction.

By completing this series of processes from defining requirements, making RFP and selecting a development vendor, governance for contract amount for development can be made to function. Naturally, to make owner's governance function during the process from making RFP to selecting a development vendor, it is necessary to appoint an expert who can manage the process. A certain domestic manufacturer that adopted this approach was able to reduce development costs to 60% and shorten development period to 60% compared with development by contract at discretion. The company was also able to keep risk at the time of development to a minimum.

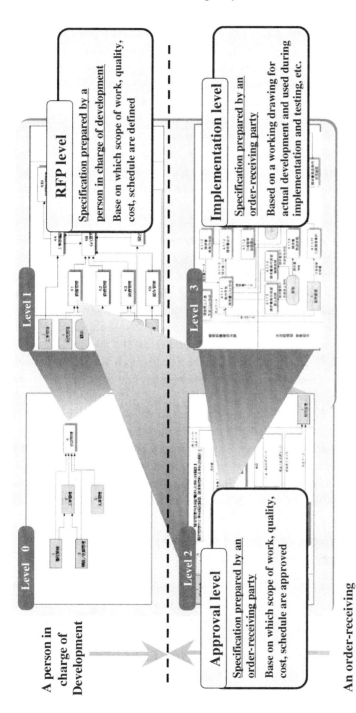

Fig. 3 Design level to carry out system development

Now, to proceed with this process, it is assumed that the specification document for requirements is included in RFP. By standardizing the level of specification for requirements prepared by the owner and the level of development specifications prepared by the developer at a detailed design stage after the contract is concluded, this approach becomes possible. If RFP does not include a minimum required specification, the bidding contractor cannot submit an estimate that includes an allowance for risk. In order for the owner to exercise governance at this point, it is necessary to incorporate a method that puts a brake on increasing development cost. That is the standardization for each level of design specification. Figure 3 shows the level of this specification.

In the case of the above-mentioned manufacturer, the company takes this approach in selecting a development contractor, and presents RFP with a solid design specification to bidders.

In addition, in system development, as specialization of functions is immature, if an order for the whole work is placed with a certain contractor on a lump-sum basis, there are cases in which development risks increase in areas where the contractor has little experience. In order to avoid this situation and put risks within a permissible range at the system stage, it is important to select an experienced contractor for each field. At the same time, this approach reduces the risk of development failure or distributes the risk of the owner having to bear an increase in cost in reasonably large-scale projects. By playing contractors off against each other, it also leads to decrease or avoidance of the risk that governance does not function.

This signifies the importance of designing a project structure considering governance in the scheme stage. Figure 4 shows an example of such a structure. A certain manufacturing company has successfully completed a system development project, reducing risks by applying this framework.

4.2 Risk management and governance in integration with existing systems

In interfacing with existing systems, it is necessary to evaluate technical risks in interfacing and risks in integrating business processes simultaneously. There are many cases in which, because specification sheets and design documents for existing systems are not preserved, neither technical specifications nor appropriate estimates for schedule and cost are known for interfacing. Moreover, there are also cases in which the extent of consistency in business processes between existing systems and a new

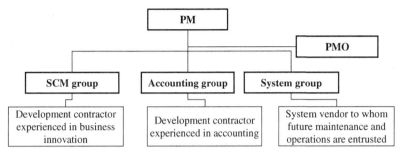

Fig. 4   A development project organization that considers governance

system is not clear enough to withstand the decision on how much to invest.

The first step for managing risks and governance is to clearly pick out interface items with existing systems and consistency items for work as risk factors at the time of planning. Then, on that basis, it is necessary to define risks at the time of planning by taking such steps as mentioned in issue (1) of Section 3 and to establish a structure that enables these risks to be incorporated into investment as risk money before selecting a development contractor. Steps to be taken include the following:

- Adhere to the series of processes from the defining of requirements to making RFP, followed by selection of a development contractor;
- Keep the same level for specification sheets at the time of making RFP;
- Select a development contractor who makes governance function.

If, at this planning stage, risk money increases and the original investment return cannot be expected, then the original plan should be given a hard look, or withdrawal from the project can be an option. As the sum of investment until the scheme stage is small compared with that for later stages, risks can be minimized. In this way, governance can function in the scheme stage.

5   Governance During the System Stage

5.1   *Risk management of a project and governance at the time of development*

What kind of structure should be introduced, after having chosen a development contractor, to function governance during development?

Even if a development contractor is selected according to an owner's plan, unless it really functions and the development is completed, it will be of no practical use. In this sense, governance at the time of development is extremely important. Once a development contractor is actually selected, governance functions if an organization or a meeting structure that leads a project manager is established, making the progress of a project or issue management and a structure for risk management visible. Project audit can be executed according to the needs. Figure 5 shows this organization structure of governance.

In Figure 5, a steering committee is established subordinate to the owner to monitor the progress and direction of the project. Furthermore, a structure for managing the project efficiently is realized by establishing a project management office (PMO) as a structure for assisting a project manager.

A way to secure project quality and construction of an organization that monitors its progress as discussed here is necessary to exercise project governance. In order to make governance function in a practical sense, it is also possible to organize a specialist group that is able to monitor whether a project manager or a project manager of a development contractor is properly managing a project itself.

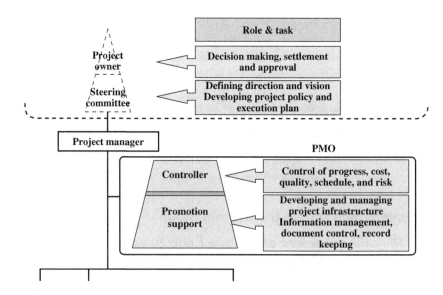

Fig. 5   Organization structure for governance

The focus of project management at this development stage is as follows:

- To manage tradeoff among quality, cost and delivery;
- To organize and manage a project;
- To control risks;
- To manage communication system.

Here, the focus is on how to organize a project and successfully manage it efficiently under already decided requested specifications, budget and delivery deadline. This is a kind of management that aims at properly achieving with precision the goal set by the owner. The owner governs to ensure this management is performed properly, within the organization structure shown in Figure 5. From the viewpoint of governance, it is important to manage whether quality not being achieved, cost increase or schedule delay during the system stage, come in under risk money projected at the start of a project.

5.2 *Risk management and governance in integrating with existing system at the time of development*

If the governance functions during the scheme stage and risk projected in integrating at the time of development is managed, then risk from the viewpoint of investment can be dealt with by providing risk money. What then remains is how to manage the risk of connection with the existing system and migration to a new system, peculiar to conversions. This accomplishment of development and smooth migration has the highest risks in the development stage. It means the owner is confronted here by whether the development has succeeded or failed in a visible manner. From the viewpoint of governance, making some kind of schedule adjustments besides providing risk money is important. This is because migration is usually on a critical path, and its delay leads to delay of the whole project.

To avoid this delay, it is necessary to enumerate from the beginning test items related to the migration as items of project activity, and properly put them on the schedule. Items that should be put on the schedule are as follows:

- Unit test
- System test
- System integration test

- User acceptance test
- Rehearsal for migration
- Migration.

It is important to define these items precisely and to put them on a schedule.

Of course, if the overall project schedule is not expected to produce expected return at the time of planning in the scheme stage, the schedule needs to be reviewed at that point in time.

Developing a plan in line with the above-mentioned items and managing to ensure that it is properly executed will enable risk management and governance to function.

6 Governance in a Service Stage

6.1 *The risk management and governance in realizing the expected return*

After moving to the service stage, it is necessary to manage whether it can be operated within a maintenance expense estimated at the time of planning, or whether there is not a defect in the structure of the operating organization that would greatly influence additional development going forward. Furthermore, managing whether the expected return projected at the time of planning can be realized is required.

In system development projects, the initially expected return cannot be necessarily realized merely by completing a new system. For example, even if a system is developed aiming to reduce inventory and the system is indeed successfully introduced, it does not mean inventory will be reduced. Even if a shared service is realized with a new system, it does not mean personnel cost will be reduced. In reducing inventory, work needs to be operated in such a way as to reduce inventory while using a new system. In the case of a shared service, the number of personnel needs to be reduced in line with actual improvement in work efficiency. This should be realized together with implementing training for the staff members who are actually in charge. In addition, measures to reduce the number of personnel will be greeted with predictable resistance from those who are laid off as well as from such groups as the labor union. There are cases in which these human elements become risks in realizing expected return, incurring unexpected expenses.

As presented in issue (1) of Section 3, it is difficult to expect many system developments projects to yield investment return in a visible manner. Even if similar systems are introduced, in cases where the business had been managed efficiently to begin with, return from a new system may be small. This is because returns that can be realized depend not only on the way business is managed, but also on the organization and quality of people that work there. Conversely speaking, even if expected return is large, it will not produce a return if the quality does not change. This is similar to a case in which no matter how good a machine is prepared, performance differs according to an operator. Moreover, technical risk during the system stage becomes high in cases where a design is made during the system stage to change the way business is managed, with an expectation that transfer to the new way will be made automatically to some extent. It is difficult to make an effective structure, appropriately deciding at which point to incorporate this expected return to be realized. This factor remains a risk in governance.

In this way, in system developments, management of human resources during the system stage becomes important for realizing return. In addition, since the output from the system stage is invisible, defining return measurements in advance and properly managing them is also important. In order to measure expected return from the system stage, it is necessary to define effect measurement items during the scheme stage, and to embed from the system stage the mechanism to measure return.

7   In Search of Effective Project Governance

In comparison with other projects, it is often the case in system development projects that a structure for making governance function is not in place. Therefore, there are many failed system development projects. The reason for this is not only because of issues peculiar to system development projects that are found in the system stage, but also in large part, because governance does not function in line with the lifecycle of the project. In order to make governance function, do away with failures and make investment effective, it is necessary to recognize and identify the risks in each stage of scheme, system and service, to check the permissible range, and to establish the structure of governance that corresponds with them.

In constructing a structure, designing of the governance structure during the scheme stage influences the system stage and the service stage, and the relative merits of the governance at the system stage influences the governance at the service stage. In this way, since it is necessary to design and exercise governance with consistency in a series of flows for each stage, it is important to establish a management structure that spans the whole lifecycle. Moreover, it is necessary to not only appoint a program manager for each stage, but also, as the need arises, to appoint a program manager for the whole lifecycle, and to construct a structure that makes governance function accordingly.

Governance does not mean the project manager constructs a structure that enables his or her project to be managed smoothly. Rather, it means to make a structure that enables the owner to minimize investment risk that comes from managing a project and to complete the project smoothly. Merely making a structure of surveillance is not enough for this governance to function in a practical sense. Standardization of project execution processes and its management are required. KPM provides a method and an approach for making this structure.

References

Ohara, S. (2001). *Project & Program Management Standard Guide Book*, Project Management Certification Center.

Personnel Training Program Development Project Survey & Study Report (2005). *IT Project & Program Management*, Project Management Certification Center.

Personnel Training Program Development Project Survey & Study Report (2005). *Real Option Tool Development Project Research Study*, Project Management Certification Center.

Taketomi, T. (2005). Challenges of program management in contributing to the new society, in *Solution and Value Creation of Project & Program Management*, International Association of Project and Program Management.

Taketomi, T. (2007). Fundamentals of project management, in *Management of Technology in Small- and Medium-Sized Companies*, Kogakutosho.

Management Model of Information Development Program — Adaptive Multiple Spiral-Up Management

Shoei Komatsu

Senior Researcher, Advanced Planning and Scheduling Organization for Manufacturing

1 Introduction

Society in the 21st century is forming a network of intertwined information systems. Enterprises are trying to win clients not as a group or groups, but as "a guest" individually. They are also trying to differentiate themselves by services as well as products, which makes information systems increasingly important for enterprises.

Although various development process models have been developed and carried out, only about 25% of information systems are successful. Business process modeling notation such as UML or BPMN reduces the distances and differences in business knowledge between owner and contractor, as well as excluding the unclear from the requirements. This recently resulted in the definition of "Work Breakdown Structure dictionary" in PMI/PMBOK (PMI, 2004).

Management models, however, have been seldom discussed. For example, it is stated that the necessary functions of management, such as reporting on, monitoring and controlling a project, must be appropriate for the actual circumstances of the software engineering process, although management should select the most suitable software engineering process models for the project.

Furthermore, few papers describe project management by the owner and the collaboration between owner and contractor, although project management by the contractor is described in various standards for project management, with the exception of PMCC/P2M (PMCC, 2003).

Recently, PMI published standards for portfolio management and for program management, which owners may find useful. Japan's Ministry of Economy, Trade and Industry (METI) has enacted Users' Information Systems Skill Standards (UISS) (METI, 2006a), in addition to Skill Standards for IT Professionals (ITSS) (METI, 2006b).

On the other hand, many studies have examined *ex ante* evaluation of information systems projects, while few have looked at *ex post* evaluation.

2   Status Quo of Project Management

2.1   *Causes of project failure or success*

Many reports have been published about failed projects. The Japan Users' Association of Information Systems (JUAS) published a survey on trends in enterprise IT (JUAS, 2006), which pointed to unclear and incompletely defined requirements, and organizations with inadequate staff and members.

The Union of Japanese Scientists and Engineers (JUSE) published a survey on project success (JUSE, 2005), which pointed out project member motivation as vital to a project's success. The report stated that motivation comes from clearly defining the work or task, forming an adequate organization and having good communications between owner and contractor as well as among members of the project team.

In short, project failure is due mostly to a lack of management proficiency.

2.2   *The cost of maintaining information systems*

According to various surveys, maintenance costs comprise about 80% of the yearly budget for information systems, although new project costs are sometimes included in maintenance costs, when top management does not approve the budget for a new information project.

Compared to the approximate 3% maintenance costs for process plants, maintenance costs for information systems are very high, so it is unrealistic to consider an information system project completed when the immediate requirements have been fulfilled, as they are in the case of an engineering project for a process plant. In other words, achieving the functional requirements may be more important than achieving the cost and time schedule targets.

2.3   *Defining requirements*

In the case of a hardware project such as a process plant, the target is visible and immutable. The target of an information systems project, however, is invisible and deeply entwined with the owner's business process. Moreover, part of the current business process (AS-IS) is converted into a more appropriate and computerized process (TO-BE).

Knowledge workers, however, have differing understandings of the current AS-IS process and may not easily come to a common understanding of the TO-BE process, because of conflicts of interest among the concerned individuals and organizations.

Furthermore, changes in the environment surrounding an enterprise may force fundamental changes in the business process during the lifecycle of the information systems or even during the building stage of business process. A survey (Larman, 2004) of projects showed that 45% of the functions are not fully used and 19% rarely used. Moreover, 25% of requirements change in medium-scale projects and over 35% change in large-scale projects.

2.4   *Software metrics*

Regarding the work volume estimation of software development, Putnam and Myers (2003) say that person-day requirements for software development depend upon software size, development duration, process productivity, etc. They see process productivity as a key problem, since the estimated productivity ranges from 1 to 100 even for the same scale of software development.

This is a statistical numerical value. A specific project may not have this degree of uncertainty. However, productivity is an inherent uncertainty that project managers must consider.

3   Project Breakdown Structure

3.1   *Visualizing the project*

In the case of an engineering project, the planned process plant is visualized from the initial feasibility study by means of various types of drawings. All machinery, equipment and piping are fully illustrated on papers and/or computers. These drawings are the basis of communication between owner and contractors as well as between contractors and sub-contractors.

Such visualization is not easy in the case of information systems projects. As noted in the JUSE survey, project members must clearly understand their roles and be motivated to work autonomously for a project's success.

Up to the present time, work and organization breakdown structures have served as useful means of visualization. Information systems projects, however, have not been structured to the same extent that engineering projects have been, as can be seen by the fact that arguments have been made both for and against the need for documentation for project management.

3.2   *Work breakdown structure*

Work breakdown structure (WBS) has been widely recognized as necessary for project management. JUSE (2004) says that the unit job size of a work package or task at the lowest layer should be somewhere between five to ten person-days, while O'Connell (2001) says that the unit job size should be somewhere between one to five person-days.

The work package or task itself, however, is not necessarily defined in detail. Furthermore, in many cases, WBS is defined as the coexistence of software product and management work, since the word "work" encompasses both products and works.

WBS should be defined first on software product. In other words, the software architecture should be defined after data modeling and business process modeling are completed. Next, the works relating directly to software development, such as system design, coding/testing and integration tests, should be broken down into the work units.

This should be done according to some kind of standard, such as the ontology and business rules of the relevant business domain (Harman, 2006), for example PSLX (Advanced Planning and Scheduling Organization for Manufacturing, 2006/2007), in order to minimize personal discretion. Moreover, the project members in charge of the work should develop the details of the WBS, because such tasks provide them with intrinsic motivation (Deci, 1985; Deci and Flaste, 1995).

Next, the project leader, project control staff and persons in charge of the work should, together, estimate the volume of works needed for software development and management based on the details of the software architecture. By defining the details of WBS in this way, management can more easily mobilize adequate members at an early stage, to monitor progress in detail and improve process productivity.

3.3 *Organizational breakdown structure*

Under both PMBOK and P2M, the organizational breakdown structure (OBS) generally relates the work package at the lowest layer to the unit organization. A Responsibility Assignment Matrix is used to define the OBS in more detail. The basic concept of the organizational structure in an engineering project differs greatly from that in an information systems project. Specifically, the organization of any engineering project is based on functional groups, as shown in Figure 1.

A software project, however, is organized around a small group of people (Wiegers, 1996; Royce, 1998). Moreover, while an engineering project manager has full responsibility for the project, a software project manager shares responsibility with the development process manager, project review manager, and the others in a typical case. Because the project team is small, project control staff are not exclusively appointed to a specific project. In Japan, a software project manager has no general

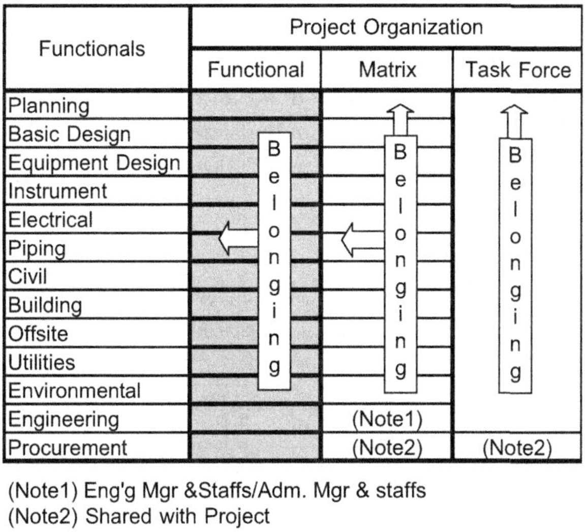

Functionals	Project Organization		
	Functional	Matrix	Task Force
Planning	Belonging	Belonging	Belonging
Basic Design			
Equipment Design			
Instrument			
Electrical			
Piping			
Civil			
Building			
Offsite			
Utilities			
Environmental			
Engineering		(Note1)	
Procurement		(Note2)	(Note2)

(Note1) Eng'g Mgr &Staffs/Adm. Mgr & staffs
(Note2) Shared with Project

Fig. 1   Project organization — Engineering

authority or responsibility, although a cross-functional team is frequently organized. Moreover, as in the ITSS framework but unlike in engineering firms, software projects have no backup functional groups composed of people with specific skills, so a project manager has to do by himself the human resource management, such as improving skills of team members and accumulating and standardizing lessons learned during project execution.

Owners must find the proper means of organizational correspondence with contractors at each development stage of planning/definition and design/building. Figure 2 shows a collaboration framework for organizations collaborating on multiple medium-scale engineering projects.

In this figure, a major function of the owner's program management office (PgMO) is to provide support for project portfolio management, while a major function of the contractor's project management office (PjMO) is to provide support for executing multi-projects. In the case of a large-scale project, the project control staff belong to neither the PgMO nor PjMO. Rather, they are appointed exclusively to a specific project team.

3.4   *Communication breakdown structure*

Meetings, both formal and informal, are vital for communications between organizations and members. Documents, including minutes of meetings, are powerful and important means of communication within and among organizations. Systems should be defined and established respectively for meetings (Itakura, 2003) and documents. Figure 3 shows a communication breakdown structure (CBS) (Komatsu, 2006) for documentation. In this

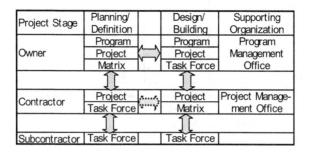

Project Stage	Planning/ Definition		Design/ Building	Supporting Organization
Owner	Program Project Matrix	⟺	Program Project Task Force	Program Management Office
	⇕		⇕	
Contractor	Project Task Force	⋯	Project Matrix	Project Management Office
	⇕		⇕	
Subcontractor	Task Force		Task Force	

Fig. 2   Collaboration framework of organizations concerned

			A	B	C	D	E	F
			Lifecycle					
			Scope	Business Model	System Model	Technology Model	Detailed Expression	Monitor -ing
			Process Scouting	Process Model	Architec -ture	System Design	Coding/ Testing	Perform -ance
1	Owner	Program	A-1	B-1	C-1	D-1	E-1	F-1
2		Project	A-2	B-2	C-2	D-2	E-2	F-2
3	Contractor	Multi- Project		B-3	C-3	D-3	E-3	
4		Project		B-4	C-4	D-4	E-4	
5	Sub- Contractor	Project				D-5	E-5	

Fig. 3   Project document system

system, all documents, both formal and informal, are registered and numbered in order to track the project's progress.

3.5   *Project breakdown structure*

Based on the above, the project breakdown structure could be formulated as Eq. (1) and applied to projects of both owner and contractor within the collaboration framework described above:

$$PBS = F\,[\text{WBS}, \text{OBS(WBS)}, \text{CBS(WBS}, \text{OBS(WBS)}, \text{DPM}, \text{Ct})], \qquad (1)$$

where
  PBS: Project Breakdown Structure
  WBS: Work Breakdown Structure
  OBS: Organizational Breakdown Structure
  CBS: Communication Breakdown Structure
  DPM: Development Process Model
    Ct: Contract Type (ex. Cost Plus — Fee, Lump — Sum, etc.).

The development process model is included in this equation as an independent variable, since such models will affect the CBS, especially the system of documents relating to project execution. The contract type will also affect documents relating to project execution, especially documents exchanged between owner and contractors, and between contractors and subcontractors. For example, a cost plus-fee contract requires more documents than a lump-sum contract.

4   Program Management Model

4.1   *Requirements of management model*

First, an information system should be able to adapt to the rapidly changing environment around the enterprise. Second, the owner should manage both the new investment in the information system and the cost for maintenance, which is a large part of the yearly budget for an information system. Third, data about the actual performance of information system should be fed back to the design/building and planning/definition stages.

Moreover, when repetitive process models such as the prototyping model are adopted instead of straightforward models such as the waterfall model, a feedback loop is automatically formed in the design/building stage. When the feedback control loop has a timebox (Highsmith, 2004), some lower priority requirements may be postponed.

Program management of multiple lifecycles must encompass the planning/definition, design/building and trial/operation stages.

4.2   *Program management model*

As mentioned above, the lifecycle of an information system is divided into three stages. These are further broken down into scope-business model, architecture-system design-coding/test, and integration test-monitoring/analysis, as shown in Figure 4.

Based on project breakdown structure described previously, iterative system development is managed under the timebox in the design/building stage. Information system performance is managed in such a way that it spirals upwards in a repeated PDCA cycle under the economy box, which covers all three stages.

4.3   *Timebox and economy box*

The timebox method is usually used in iterative processes, which complete the information system project, being in a stable state, up to the scheduled date, by reducing the scope of the project and postponing lower priority requirements.

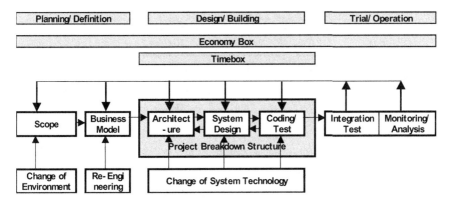

Fig. 4   Adaptive spiral-up program management model

Similarly, in economy box, the project is evaluated by using an economic evaluation index such as the net present value (NPV) or the sum of NPV and real options (Komatsu, 2004) for *ex ante* evaluation in the earlier stage, and again NPV for *ex post* evaluation in the operation stage.

The NPV as *ex post* evaluation index is calculated based on the realized cash flow up to the present and the expected cash flow over the planned lifecycle. *Ex post* evaluation is used to determine the feasibility of the next project.

Spiral-up development is performed not only in the design/building stage, but also in the PDCA cycle across all three stages. The next project in the series, including the requirements postponed in the timebox, is planned in the front part of the economy box. This is the adaptive multiple spiral-up program management model.

4.4   *Ex post evaluation of software investment*

NPV is widely used as an economic evaluation index. The index can be used by itself or augmented with other indices such as real options. NPV has the ability to evaluate multiple projects in series or also in parallel. In this study, NPV is used as an *ex post* evaluation index.

For example, using EDINET data (Financial Service Agency, 2007), simple rates of returns can be simultaneously calculated for machinery and software investments, using Eq. (2) and the least squares method, while optimized rates of returns and the NPV can be calculated for both investments (Komatsu, forthcoming).

Table 1   *Ex post* evaluation of software investment

Basis		Results			
Data	EDINET	Industry	Chemical	Machine	Electric
Record Years	2002–2006	Enterprise	Showa Denko	Brothers	Sony
Capital Cost	0.050	Evaluation Years	2002–2014	2002–2014	2002–2014
Legal Lifetime		Enterprise NPV*	33,776	29,895	197,643
Machinery	8	*Rate of Return*			
Software	5	Machinery Inv.	0.160	0.095	0.004
Time Lag (Years)		Software Inv.	0.103	0.546	0.473
Mach. — Chem.	2	*Individual NPV**			
Mach. — Mach.	3	Machinery	34,488	(3,375)	(213,539)
Mach. — Elec.	1	Software	(712)	33,270	411,182
Software — All	1	Total	33,776	29,895	197,643

* Unit: mm\en.

Table 1 shows a result calculated using a spreadsheet model based on Eq. (2), which optimizes the rates of return on machinery and software investments. The time lags in the table are estimated by statistical analysis of EDINET data, using Cobb–Douglas production function (Brynjolfsson and Hitt, 2003). As Table 1 shows, the NPV values for software investment sometimes exceed those for machinery investment.

$$
\bar{S} = \min_{\alpha, \beta} \left[\sum_{t=-T}^{0} \frac{(1-\tau)(P_{t+1}-P_t)}{(1+c)^{(t+1)}} + \sum_{t=1}^{Y} \delta \frac{\left\{ \sum_{t=-T}^{0} \frac{(1-\tau)(P_{t+1}-P_t)}{T} \right\}}{(1+c)^t} \right.
$$

$$
+ \sum_{t=-T+1}^{0} \left\{ \sum_{t=-T+1}^{-T+Dm} \frac{\left(\frac{Im_{-T+1}}{Dm} \right)}{(1+c)^t} \right\} + \sum_{t=-T+1}^{0} \left\{ \sum_{t=-T+1}^{-T+Ds} \frac{\left(\frac{Is_{-T+1}}{Ds} \right)}{(1+c)^t} \right\}
$$

$$
\left. - \sum_{t=-T+Lm}^{Y} \frac{\alpha\, Im}{(1+c)^t} - \sum_{t=-T+Ds}^{Y} \frac{\beta Is}{(1+c)^t} \right]^2 ,
$$

(2)

where

    S: Least squares

    α: Rate of return on machinery investment

    β: Rate of return on software investment

    t: Fiscal year

    T: Years of performance record–1

    τ: Tax rate

    P: Consolidated ordinary profit

    c: Capital cost

    Y: Years of evaluation (=Legal life of machinery)

Dm: Legal life of machinery

  Im: Machinery investment (=Increased amount of machinery assets)

  Ds: Legal life of software

   Is: Software investment (=Increased amount of software assets).

5 Conclusions

Information systems projects have low rates of success due to incomplete specifications, inadequate organizations and imperfect communications. All of these problems originate in the management of the project.

Management, however, especially owner's management, has been rarely studied. Moreover, while many studies have examined *ex ante* evaluation of information systems economics, few have looked at *ex post* evaluation.

In this study, the scope of management is extended to encompass all stages from planning/definition to trial/operation, as well as multiple projects in a series. This is the adaptive spiral-up development program. To make the development program successful, it is necessary to define the project breakdown structure. The project breakdown structure is defined by the breakdown structures of work, organization and communication, and is applied to management by both owner and contractors.

The management model of the adaptive spiral-up program has two core drivers — the time box and the economy box. The requirements postponed in the timebox are examined later together with any new requirements, and take into consideration the economic evaluation results of the actual performance of the information system. *Ex post* economic evaluation is one of the core functions of the economy box. The method and examples of *ex post* evaluation are described in this paper.

Acknowledgments

This paper is based on the research activities of the following special interest groups: the International Association of Project and Program Management, "Fusion of Management and IT System", Chair: Tametsugu Taketomi (Professor, Nippon Institute of Technology); the Japan Society for Management Information, "Information Investment and Management Performance", Chair: Masafumi Hirano (Professor, Waseda University); and the Society of Project Management, "Communication Management", Chair: Keiju Matsushima (Professor, Musashi University). The author wishes to thank all people concerned for their contributions to this paper.

References

Advanced Planning and Scheduling Organization for Manufacturing (2006/2007). *PSLX Standard Specifications,* Ver. 2 (in Japanese).

Brynjolfsson, E. and Hitt, L. M. (2003). Computing productivity: Firm-level evidence, *The Review of Economics and Statistics* 85(4), pp. 793–908.

Deci, E. L. (1985). *Intrinsic Motivation,* Plenum Press.

Deci, E. L. and Flaste, R. (1995). *Why We Do What We Do: The Dynamics of Personal Autonomy,* G. P. Putnam's Sons.

Financial Service Agency (2007). *Electronic Disclosure for Investor's NETwork* (http://info.edinet.go.jp/EdiHtml/main.htm), June (in Japanese).

Harman, P. (2006). Business process standards, *Business Process Trends* 4(20).

Highsmith, III, J. A. (2004). *Agile Project Management — Creating Innovative Products,* Addison-Wesley.

Itakura, M. (2003). *Elucidating Project by Super S.E.,* JUSE (in Japanese).

Japan Users' Association of Information Systems (JUAS) (2006). *Trends of Enterprise IT* (in Japanese).

Komatsu, S. (2004). The economic evaluation framework of enterprise information systems — Applying real options, *Journal of Japan Society for Management Information* 13(1), pp. 95–118 (in Japanese).

Komatsu, S. (2006). Aiming to the success of information system project, *Journal of International Association of Project & Program Management* 1(1), pp. 1–10 (in Japanese).

Komatsu, S. (forthcoming). Statistical analysis of securities report data and measurement of return on software investment, *Journal of Japan Society for Management Information* (in Japanese).

Larman, C. (2004). *Agile and Iterative Development — A Manager's Guide,* Pearson Education.

Ministry of Economy, Trade and Industry (METI) (2006a). *Users' Information Systems Skill Standards* (in Japanese).

Ministry of Economy, Trade and Industry (METI) (2006b). *Skill Standards for IT Professionals*, Version 2.0 (in Japanese).

O'Connell, F. (2001). *How to Run Successful Projects in Web Time*, Artech House.

Project Management Institute (PMI) (2004). *A Guide to the Project Management Body of Knowledge*, 3rd ed.

Project Management Professionals Certification Center (PMCC) (2003). *Project & Program Management for Enterprise Innovation* (in Japanese).

Putnam, L. H. and Myers, W. (2003). *Five Core Metrics: The Intelligence Behind Successful Software Management*, Dorset House.

Royce, W. (1998). *Software Project Management: A Unified Framework*, Addison Wesley Longman.

Union of Japanese Scientists and Engineers (JUSE) (2004). No. 2 subcommittee, *WBS Group Report* (in Japanese).

Union of Japanese Scientists and Engineers (JUSE) (2005). *Consideration about Key Successful Factors for a Project* (in Japanese).

Wiegers, K. E. (1996). *Creating a Software Engineering Culture*, Dorset House Publishing.

Information Sharing for an ICT System for Strategic Program Management

Hideo Yamamoto
Professor, Graduate School of Commerce and Management
Hitotsubashi University

1   Introduction

As information and communications technology (ICT) become increasingly widespread in society and the importance of ICT is recognized, the volume of investment in ICT is increasing. Many studies on the effects of ICT investment have been carried out (Weill and Broadbent, 1998; Rapp, 2002; Brynjolfsson, 2004). There are two typical opinions concerning the effects of ICT investment on business. One opinion is that "The core function of ICT — data storage, data processing, and data transport — has become available and affordable to all. Their very power and presence have begun to transform them from potentially strategic resources into commodity factors of production" (Carr, 2003, 2004). On the other hand, "ICT is inherently strategic because of its indirect effects — it creates possibilities and options that did not exist before" (Brown and Hagel, 2003).

As the ICT system consumes a larger portion of total plant investment, it becomes important to introduce an ICT system that adjusts the business strategy of the enterprise and to make efficient use of it. Therefore, we focus on efficient system construction techniques that can be achieved by using a computer system design framework such as enterprise architecture (EA) (Zachman, 1987; Sowa and Zachman, 1992). At present, EA is used for ICT system construction not only in business, but also in government. The strategic management of ICT systems is also described for executives of corporations (Nolan and McFarlan, 2005). The efficient usage of ICT systems has also been investigated in Japan (Kokury, 2004; METI, 2006).

Today, the rapid progress in ICT is changing the business environment quickly. Therefore, it becomes more important for stakeholders, such as the ICT system owner, system planner, contractors, system users and operations people, to share information relevant to both the business environment and the risk in organization, not only at the planning stage of system introduction, but also throughout the lifecycle of the practical use of the ICT system.

This paper discusses how information about the outcomes and risks of ICT investment can be shared easily between ICT system stakeholders. An "evaluation function" for evaluating the results of ICT investment will be proposed. The evaluation function can qualitatively describe the features of the ICT system, which depend on the purpose of the investment, including such aspects as business application needs, cost reduction or infrastructure maintenance. A procedure for decision-making is explained in order to incorporate the evaluation function in the Kaikaku project management (KPM) process (Ohara, 2007). Probability distributions are applied to the parameters of the evaluation function, and the shapes of the probability distributions of the investment effects are determined by a Monte Carlo simulation method.

2   The Information Sharing to Make Use of an ICT System

When the purpose of introducing an ICT system is to create new corporate business value, we should focus on three kinds of risk management — traditional business risk management, project risk management, and assessment of effect on investment — according to the business stage shown in Figure 1. Traditional business risk management should be undertaken to guard against specific mishaps in business circumstances. In addition, project risk management is essential while carrying out system construction, and after system construction, an assessment of its effect on investment must be considered. This paper focuses on the value-creation activities where KPM covers the items shown in Figure 1, and then shows how information about the outcomes and risks of ICT investment can be shared easily between ICT system stakeholders, considering both project risk management and assessment of the effect on investment.

3   The Evaluation Function of the ICT System

Various stakeholders have different roles in business, such as the owner who is concerned about the return on investment of an ICT system, the system designer who is interested in planning the building of the system with limited time and money, contractors who are to perform their jobs according

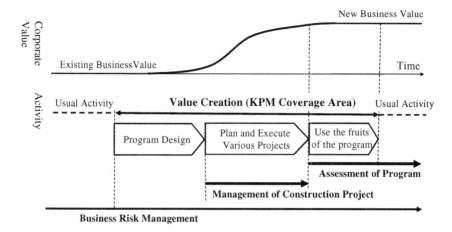

Fig. 1   Three kinds of risk management in business activity

to their agreements with the owner, and system users who are committed to making a profit by using the ICT system. Therefore, it is difficult for each person to share a common viewpoint about values, because each party's responsibility is quite different. The big issue is to develop a method to share the value and risk information of the ICT system investment in such a way that each stakeholder can appreciate the others' positions.

In the case of a profit-making company, however, the evaluation of the basic cash flow is easy to understand, because people in the company can easily recognize the benefit of cash flow to the company.

Furthermore, the evaluation function should be connected to the business record for which each person is responsible, and to the business risk due to the change in competitive environment. An intuitively clear visual expression of the risk is more desirable for stakeholders than simple numerical expressions, in order to establish a collective awareness of the risk potential.

An evaluation function *Be* which shows the effects of the ICT system introduction can be represented by:

$$Be = -I + \sum_{t=1}^{T} [-Cope(t) + CR(t) + CG(t)]f(r,t) + Opb + Opi], \tag{1}$$

where

   I: Estimated initial installation cost
  Cope(*t*): Estimated operating cost of ICT system

CR(t): Expected cost reduction from ICT system use
CG(t): Expected sales increase due to ICT investment
   T: System lifetime
Opb: Added benefit from improving prior investment
Opi: Added benefit in terms of social responsibility.

A function to convert to present value $f(r, t)$ is:

$$f(r, t) = 1/(1 + r)^t. \tag{2}$$

Figure 2 shows the relations between cost and profit in Eq. (1). Positive factors of the evaluation function Be are estimated as the present value of each year's profit and cost reduction during the lifetime of the system, added business benefits Opb (such as improved customer satisfaction), and the added benefit Opi, that considers the loss of business opportunity which would occur in the absence of the ICT investment.

The purpose of building an ICT system can be subdivided into three categories: strategic investment, business process improvement, and infrastructure. Equation (1) can throw light on each of those with the size of the parameters.

The main factors in Eq. (1) regarding strategic investment are the estimated increase in sales $CG(t)$ and the added benefit for prior investment Opb. For business process improvement, the estimated value of the cost reduction $CR(t)$ is dominant, therefore $CG(t)$ and Opb in Eq. (1) tend to be ignored. With respect to infrastructure, we cannot expect cost reduction by improving the business process or increasing sales. In other words, the actual cost factors, $-I$ and $-Cope$, should be considered to obtain additional benefits, Opb and Opi, which are difficult to estimate numerically at the planning stage because they depend on uncertain features in the business environment. The purpose of ICT system investment will vary

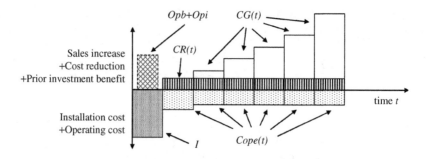

Fig. 2   Cost and profit in Eq. (1)

according to the financial condition of the enterprise and the competitive environment. What was a useful infrastructure system at the beginning may become a strategic system in the future. Therefore, information sharing as in Eq. (1), which includes all the effects and risks surrounding the ICT system during its lifetime, should be regarded as essential from the viewpoint of business management.

4 The Value Propagation Chain Caused by the ICT System

In order to maximize the benefit of a newly introduced ICT system, we need to introduce systematic innovation, *kaikaku*, in the company, as well as the sophisticated ICT system.

First, there must be a business strategy that sets a clear goal corresponding to the corporate vision. Second, an ICT system is built that actualizes functions based on the strategy, and then business policies and process innovations must be formulated that make use of the ICT system. Furthermore, the person in charge must formulate an action plan corresponding to the business policy. When all of these processes work well, the full beneficial effect of the ICT system will be achieved.

The mechanism of producing actual effects with the ICT system described above can be shown in the form of a value propagation chain, which is similar to the strategy maps in Kaplan and Norton (2004). A value propagation chain contains both financial and non-financial values of the ICT system, together with the business process design and the organization's capabilities.

An example of a value propagation chain map with an ICT system is shown in Figure 3. The evaluation function Be, which is represented by Eq. (1), corresponds to the value items at the top of Figure 3.

In actual management, to get the value of the newly introduced ICT system, the following process should be carried out. First, the factors of business performance essential to attaining higher customer satisfaction and increased sales are extracted, and Key Success Factors (KSFs) which tie each person's activities to the essential factors of the business are selected. Next, KSFs are broken down to a numerical expression easily managed in terms of realization of the business goal. KSFs are set for each organizational capability, corresponding to the action plans of people working for the company, as indicated from (a) to (f) in the second column from the top in Figure 3.

Considering the actual management procedure described above, the expected value of the ICT system Be depends on both the expected values at the beginning and the level of KSF realization along the way.

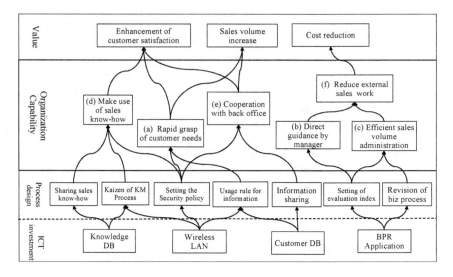

Fig. 3   Example of the value propagation chain with an ICT system

Table 1   Relations between the KSF and the parameters in Eq. (1)

	(a) Rapid grasp of customer needs	(b) Direct guidance by manager	(c) Efficient sales volume administration	(d) Make use of sales know-how	(e) Cooperation with back office	(f) Reduce external sales work
Sales increase (*CG*)	✓				✓	
Cost reduction (*CR*)		✓	✓			✓
Added value (*Opb*)	✓			✓	✓	

The level of KSF realization is the ratio of the numerical value of KSF set at the beginning to that of the observed KSF realization at the time of evaluation. The relations between KSF indicating the realization of the value chain in Figure 3 and the parameters in Eq. (1) are shown in Table 1. We must consider that there will be deviation in the realization of KSF from the expected figure because business activity depends on management skill coping with internal control risks and external competitive conditions that change day by day. If the effects on the evaluation function caused by deviation in the realization of KSFs are estimated, it will be easy for people to manage to utilize the ICT system to achieve the business goal from the viewpoint of risk management and assessment of the investment.

5 Active Use of the Evaluation Function in KPM

In KPM, the stakeholders in an ICT system are able to share effect and risk information, and then use the ICT system efficiently. The management process of KPM is shown in Figure 4.

(1) According to the corporate vision and the mission for the division, a plan of ICT system introduction is initiated, taking social responsibility into account.

(2) The functions of the system to build are decided based on the business goals selected.

(3) When value evaluation of the infrastructure investment is difficult, the amount of investment is decided from the viewpoint of corporate policy, for example, some percent of the preceding fiscal year's profit.

(4) Expected $CR(t)$ and $CG(t)$ are determined from the expected value established with process (2). Opb and Opi are assigned values. If Be is positive, implementation proceeds to process (5).

(5) The probability distribution for risk is assumed, and $CR(t)$ and $CG(t)$ are determined from the conditions inside the organization and the outside business environment, based on management judgment.

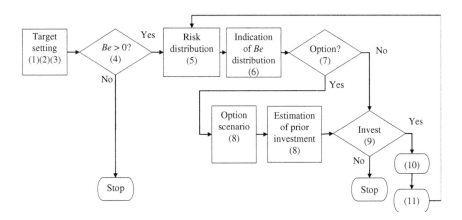

Fig. 4   Information sharing procedure in KPM

(6) The distribution of the evaluation function *Be* is illustrated by a technique such as a Monte Carlo simulation.

(7) If there are any alternative scenarios corresponding to changing circumstances in the future, implementation proceeds to process (8) or (9).

(8) For each scenario along the way, investment value is calculated by a mathematical technique such as a real option simulation.

(9) The appropriateness of the investment yielded by process (8) is evaluated from the viewpoint of business strategy. If the decision for investment is yes, the program proceeds to process (10); if not, it stops.

(10) The program for achieving the business strategy is subdivided into more than one project, and within each project planning is settled on.

(11) If changes in the external environment require it, a modified plan is settled on at a scheduled progress evaluation point. The distribution of the evaluation function is revised and fed back into process (5).

Know-how, such as the best way to examine time and management methods that meet the progress conditions of the program, can be accumulated by carrying out the above process with more than one project.

6 An Example of Visualizing the Effect of Risk Distribution on Investment

6.1 *Sample calculation*

The cost conditions shown in Table 2 are assumed. A mid-scale system is introduced (building cost: ¥1 billion, maintenance fee: ¥150 million per year), with an expected ¥300 million cost reduction effect per year, or 30% of the initial investment, and a ¥200 million sales increase per year. In addition, ¥100 million of added value due to improvement in customer satisfaction is expected.

Table 2 Calculation conditions

Intial investment I (million yen)	1,000
Operation cost $Cope$ (million yen/year)	150
Cost reduction CR (million yen/year)	300
Sales increase CG (million yen/year)	200
Risk free rate (%)	5
Additional value Opb (million yen/year)	100

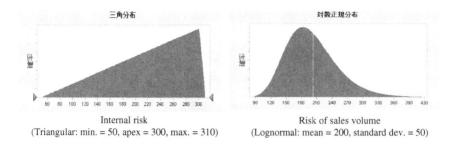

Internal risk
(Triangular: min. = 50, apex = 300, max. = 310)

Risk of sales volume
(Lognormal: mean = 200, standard dev. = 50)

Fig. 5   Distribution of parameters

The evaluation function Be of the investment is calculated as ¥1.125 billion when the lifetime of the ICT system is assumed to be seven years, and any deviation of the assumed numbers is not taken into consideration.

This numerical value, ¥1.125 billion, may give the initial impression that there is no question about the benefit from the ICT system introduction. But how much risk is involved in this investment? Uncertainty in the expected value in Figure 5 is introduced as a probability distribution.

Lognormal distribution is assumed as the probability distribution of the increase of sales, and the triangular distribution of the ¥300 million apex with a minimum value of ¥50 million and a maximum value of ¥310 million show the cost reduction effect.

Figure 6 shows the probability distribution of the evaluation function by a 5,000-repeats Monte Carlo simulation, where the mean of the lognormal distribution is ¥2,000 million and the standard deviation is ¥500 million.

At the same time that the probability of a positive result from the investment appears to be 91.7% (more than 90%), we have to be cognizant of the approximately 8% negative effect level and the dominant factor that causes the negative. The negative effect level increases to 15% if the standard deviation is ¥1,000 million, which means the uncertainty in the market is larger than the calculated conditions in the description above. Furthermore, if Opb is supposed to be 0, the negative effect level increases to 25%. If an added benefit due to social responsibility Opi in Eq. (1) is taken into consideration, the negative effect of the investment will decrease.

6.2 *Discussion*

After Japanese SOX Law becomes effective in 2008, both the risk decrease effect of an ICT system and the assessment of ICT investment will be vital

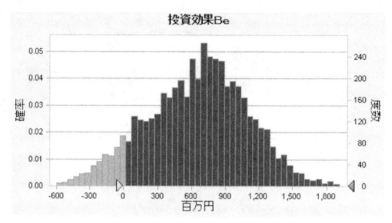

Sales increase = 200, Std. Dev. = 50, Opb = 100, $P(Be > 0)$ = 91.7%

Fig. 6   Distribution of Be

for managing a company. The importance of risk control that relates to the information and communications system has increased in the financial and securities industry since the system failure incident at the Tokyo Stock Exchange in November 2005.

Therefore, risk is characterized as negative risk that connects directly to loss of profits, and as positive risk that can be changed into a business opportunity. We should always consider both features of risk as connected to the total corporate value.

Typically, the strength of a Japanese company comes from a combination of risk control in each component of corporate activity and risk management from the top in terms of corporate value enhancement. When the relationship is clear between each job related to an ICT system and corporate value enhancement, and the realization of KSF is evaluated at every milestone, the stakeholders will share a common viewpoint and find it easy to carry out their jobs proactively.

7   Conclusion

If ICT systems are constructed with a top-down approach and their evaluation throughout their lifecycle is treated lightly, appropriate value evaluation of ICT system investment is not possible because quantification of the ICT system investment is difficult. Moreover, if there is little information exchange between the stakeholders, it becomes difficult to draw out and use the real-world capability of the workers — the source of the company's strength.

As the proportion of business processes that depend on ICT systems increases, the productivity of the company will increase, but the reliability of the organization is apt to decline. Therefore, the total control of risk, as described in this paper, is essential for corporate management, including ordinary risk management, system building, project management and assessment of investment.

References

Brown, J. S. and Hagel, III, J. (2003). Does IT matter? Letters to the editor, *Harvard Business Review* July, pp. 109–112.

Brynjolfsson, E. (2004). *Intangible Assets*, Diamond, Inc. (in Japanese).

Carr, N. G. (2003). IT doesn't matter, *Harvard Business Review* May, pp. 41–49.

Carr, N. G. (2004). *Does IT Matter?*, Harvard Business School Press.

Kaplan, R. and Norton, D. (2004). *Strategy MAPS*, Harvard Business School Press.

Kokury, J. (2004). *IT Capability*, Nikkei BP (in Japanese).

METI (2006). (http://www.meti.go.jp/press/20051221001/2-cio-set.pdf), 27 March (in Japanese).

Nolan, R. and McFarlan, F. W. (2005). Information technology and the board of directors, *Harvard Business Review* October, pp. 96–106.

Ohara, S. (2007). The fourth generation type Japanese project management — Synergetic integration of innovation, development and improvement, in *Proceedings of the Second National Conference 2007*, International Association of Project & Management, pp. 204–215 (in Japanese).

Rapp, W. V. (2002). *Information Technology Strategies*, Oxford University Press.

Sowa, J. F. and Zachman, J. A. (1992). Extending and formalizing the framework for information systems architecture, *IBM System Journal* 31(3), pp. 590–616.

Weill, P. and Broadbent, M. (1998). *Leveraging the New Infrastructure*, Harvard Business School Press.

Zachman, J. A. (1987). A framework for information systems architecture, *IBM System Journal* 26(3), pp. 276–292.

Project Management from the Viewpoint of Projection Technologies

Naokoto Kogo
Associate Professor, Graduate School of Economics
Osaka University

Atsushi Miyagawa
A Master of Graduate School of Economics
Osaka University

1 Introduction

In this paper, we consider a project management (PM) which enables a good circulation of understanding between the interested parties, using an example of a road improvement project. Generally in PM, required knowledge and skills and motives are different between the person who orders construction based on corporate strategy, and the person who contracts its work (a contractor). This makes it difficult for both parties to come to an agreement. Using the grounds that IT moderates this difficulty and supports both to come to an agreement, we show that KPM (Kaikaku PM) is expectable as the project promotion technique. Simultaneously, we discuss that it is very important to examine the effect of IT (here, it takes up only projection technologies) as an information-sharing means in KPM.

However, first, we will reexamine the original meaning of the word "project". Then, we will consider the role of IT in PM again. Not jokingly, we are focusing on "the projection technology utilized for a project" and on reaching an agreement between the interested parties.

2 A Workshop-Type Project

We will introduce a project which utilized the latest IT (Miyagawa, 2006). The road improvement project in Kochi prefecture, as a measure to improve the traffic congestion and traffic safety, is a plan in the range of about 1 km from Sanbashi-Dori crossing to Hitsuzan-Tunnel along Route 56 in Kochi city. Since a public open space is generated along with road space, the construction plan was able to ask for practical use of road space. Furthermore, the city must look into disaster prevention on the occasion of the reoccurrence probability of the Nankai big earthquake. With this in mind, the residents who live in the area jointly with experts have started a workshop-type project for future community improvement. In order to reach understanding and agreement of local residents to the plan proposal, a workshop will be held four times with no less than a total of 127 local residents participating in it.

In the first workshop, the present condition and the problem of the area were mainly explained by the experts. For instance, if there is a possibility of the Nankai big earthquake occuring, there is a danger of a 5-meter-high tsunami. But it was learned that there are almost no preparations in place to face floods. For residents, the contents of the report handed out were too technical to be understood. Therefore, a special form of explanation was required. Holding the meeting and vocally explaining to local residents the main point several times and reaching an agreement has been the normal procedure until now. If explanatory meetings are held faithfully, a model or/and a stereogram will be offered. However, if implementation of a plan is a matter closely concerned with the life of residents, the situation usually gets entangled and produces emotional friction and conviction, and agreement cannot be easily obtained due to the huge difference between them.

However, the project introduced here did not take the conventional manner. The plan proposal which is going to be implemented from now on will be carried out as a virtual projection which can be understood by anyone. Based on the projection in which members can view and listen, they can propose corrections and improvements and retry on a new model immediately. The project will be repeated until it is satisfactory. From the viewpoint of PM, the "projection" will just be positioned as the "mainstay of the project". Omitting the details, only the main points will be shown here.

Computer Graphic (CG) was used to make the proposed construction visible from all viewpoints. As a plan, experts proposed a pedestrian deck at the Hyakkoku crossing (refer to Figures 1 and 2; really animations). The community deck can cope with a height of 5 m of "tsunami" which is currently assumed. As a link to the locally divided community,

Fig. 1   Present state at Hyakkoku crossing

Fig. 2   Future plan at Hyakkoku crossing

the community deck is also used for a flea market, etc. (not only functioning as a road). In the following sections, the meaning and the role of using a projection technology for PM is reevaluated using this example as a reference.

3   What is Projection?

3.1   *J. J. Gibson's perception theory*

From the Latin origin of the word, project means "pro + ject" (throw in front), and is also used metaphysically of projecting the idea of an inside, the feeling and the subjectivity. Imagination or anticipation has a derivative meaning that projection is reflected in the self. Thus, there is a long history in the handling of the word of projection in the West, and there are many points which should be noted in it, but at the same time carefulness is also required.

Special cautions are required when it is projected on a two-dimensional flat surface. As one grows, in addition to recognition of the external world which is obtained by self-perception, human beings have an opportunity to acquire the "knowledge that comes from parents, teachers, pictures, and books" (Gibson, 1979, p. 253). Since this is too natural for adults, it seems not special for their perceptional activity (Gregory, 1970). The meaning of being special is widely different at first-hand natural perception. It is easy to forget that "A picture is a record of what its creator has seen or imagined, made available for others to see or imagine" (Gibson, 1979, p. 291).

A house and an animal drawn on a piece of paper in two-dimensional form also look three-dimensional to us. Furthermore, it is a miracle that a sketch, a mark, a notation and a word drawn on two-dimensional surfaces can express a certain object. However, the explanation of a two-dimensional image (which is tied to the external world) through an eye, is easy to be entrapped into a certain mistake. That is to say, the information included in a picture (having color and form) projected on the retina of an eye, sent to the brain as a signal, and constituted by the thing which we know and falls into the knowing, can be a mistake.

Many may think as follows. By processing what only entered as a stimulus, a sense data forms perception, and more is sent into a higher mental process. In this process, functions such as memory, thinking, imagining, reasoning, judging, expecting, recognizing, meaning, etc., called variously, are carried out.

In the same way, we think that an expert will be able to perform advanced cognitive expertise, or have its capacity. On the contrary, non-experts (include experts of different fields of study) will find their capacity missing or weak. Therefore, since the same understanding is not obtained among both, it can be concluded that the cause of difficulty to agree comes from an inner ability gap.

If this ability gap is accepted, and since cognitive processing is made deep inside oneself, individual understanding formed differs greatly, even if it is prepared with projection media among both. Furthermore, since the means to cancel the variance of mutual mental understanding does not exist in principle, it remains to be seen whether it is made very difficult for experts (even when a non-expert is included) to reach a certain agreement by communication, or doubt the possibility of communication itself (Ryle, 1949).

3.2 *Projection as artifact*

Now, I will recall again a phrase of Gibson: "A picture is a record of what its creator has seen or imagined, made available for others to see or imagine". The method which human beings use in order "to facilitate knowing, to aid perceiving, or to extend the limits of comprehension" are "the use of instruments, the use of verbal descriptions, and the use of pictures" (Gibson, 1979, p. 258). Unlike instruments, the characteristic of pictures and verbal descriptions is that information given is acquired at second-hand. "Any picture, then, preserves what its creator has noticed and considers worth noticing" (Gibson, 1979, p. 274).

One ought to be deeply impressed with the fact that most projection media requires understanding at second-hand. We will pay attention to facilitate, to aid, or to extend the knowing and comprehension, by using projection media. The place of cooperative work must be regarded as a place of lapping each other's understanding by the projection of the information to the others, rather than asking for direct sharing of an understanding. In PM, it must not depend on a common base of inner understanding among project participants, but rather, it must concentrate all efforts on "the (pro + jected) artifact that its creator has seen or imagined, made available for others to see or imagine". It is impossible to copy a certain creator's idea directly to others. More than one can imagine, the medium used by cooperative work is subtle and delicate. It does not suppose that the people who were concerned in a project fully understand the important role of this medium.

4 Use of Media in Project

4.1 *Display*

"What it (picture) records, registers, or consolidates is information, not sense data" (Gibson, 1979, p. 280). It should not focus on what is composed in a brain, but should take further notice of the picture projected outside: "Pictures convey knowledge at second hand and thus are efficient methods of teaching the young" (Gibson, 1979, p. 274). Also, the created image (continuous image) is "... an array that makes information available to a viewer at the point of observation.... The information in the display can specify the turning of one's head, the act of approaching or withdrawing, and the adopting of a new point of observation ..." (Gibson, 1979, p. 302). To those who are watching the movie, video can give information which easily exceeds the perceptual experience of the object contained in the event which has actually happened in the movie, by using edit techniques (zoom, dolly, panning, cut, fade, wipe, dissolve, split screen, flashback, etc.).

For those who freely look at a movement of projector virtually, they will possibly try moving around and looking at the environment. Thus, the width of their understanding is expanded and understanding is deepened more. This essentially leads to carrying out possible cooperative work.

This technique is mainly observed in this paper. But, before that, I will inquire about the media used for the projection so far. For that purpose, it is necessary to give a little account of the role of an artificial medium.

4.2 Role of an artificial medium

A human being's property in comparison with an animal's is that he can touch the world at second-hand (as shown by Section 3.2). This newly added dimension is not prepared automatically; it is artificial. As a result, language, various instruments, working environment and culture are offered to the special environment for human beings' development, and a human's activity can be guided for them. If this point is emphasized further, a human being can make an artificial change himself to his surroundings, and impose a settlement and control his actions using this change.

All technology can also be called media. These media are the by-products of the history of our cultural practice. A medium produces or controls interaction of humans. According to Vygotsky (1930), one's intellectual activity is carried with the artifact (i.e., comprehensive name of an instrument, a notation, a language, an organization, rules, etc.), and one's usefulness is demonstrated by using of an artifact, and it is completely meaningless to consider the mental faculties of The Naked Man without having an artifact. That is, when we do a certain activity, it always passes a medium, and if the medium changes, one's domain of activity itself will change (Vygotsky, 1930).

It should be observed that the capacity of human beings is extended by the use of media. McLuhan explains this as "the extensions of man" (McLuhan, 1964). Thus, although the topic that media extend one's capacity is a view which is easy to be accepted by IT-promoting groups, it will tend to overlook other important roles of a medium. Two are raised in the following.

The first one supports individual thinking. It can be realized that media and technologies carry out "externalization of our thinking activities". Using a drawing and a memo deepens the understanding of a problem, and at the same time, a solution is gradually formed. Rather than exertion of direct capacity of mankind, this asks for the way of work to change, and supports intermediate creation of thinking and understanding (Yamamoto and Nakakoji, 2005; Brown *et al.*, 1989; Hutchins, 1995).

The other one supports group activity. Ordinarily, the project is undertaken by the cooperation of experts from various special fields of study. Therefore, for performing the collaborative activities between different experts, it processes the media which it has so far treated in the cultural sphere of the same context, or the new media corresponding to it are needed (Boujut and Blanco, 2003; Bodker and Grondak, 1996).

What kind of media did we use to carry out externalization of the thinking and how far did it extend the range of understanding among project participants? The following section will describe the property from old projection technologies to the latest ones. From what is explained so far, one will notice that the following projection technology is only a part of many media (Norman, 1993; Gregory, 1981; Dennett, 1996).

5   Old and New Projection Technology

5.1   *From old to new*

(1) *Sketch*

First, I reaffirm that a sketch is not an artifact on which a mental image is projected. A new sketch is a representation expressed by one, which investigates further the intention which was not explicit and is used as a means to repeat polishing. Although there are also many dissatisfied with the result, by having been expressed first, one may become aware of what was intended to be done in the first place.

(2) *Drawing*

The big difference between a sketch and a drawing is that the drawing can perform its production somewhat mechanically. Although free design for an idea is not allowed, there is an advantage that individual differences do not appear.

(3) *Perspective and photograph*

The perspective was developed in the early Renaissance period and had a big influence on subsequent European pictures. If artistry alone is not desired, the appearance of photography brings innovation to the method of the exact projection. Looking at photographs of things and people helps guide us "to visualize what is in the head" and justify its existence. In other words, there is an effectiveness of making experience as "I feel as though I am actually looking".

(4) *Model of an object*

One advantage of a model is that one can observe the reduced or expanded state. We can look at a model in a hand, or observe it in detail from all viewpoints. Everyone can have experiences in which understanding is deepened by a model. If that model is close to a three-dimensional object, then it is special. It can be said that the latest projection technologies are aiming to approach a model. But, in many cases, making a model requires considerable time and skill.

(5) *Computer graphics*

Computer graphics is a software which enables a photograph taken from one view to be viewed from all other angles. Since CG is pursuing reality, although there is nothing in hand, it supplies a part of information which a model has. Since an image has reality, special training is not needed in order to observe it like in the case of a model.

(6) *QuickTimeVR*

QTVR (QuickTimeVR) is a virtual reality technique using Quick Time, which is a moving-image-reproduction technique of Apple. One can read easily three-dimensional images from one's desired directions, by operating a mouse on the screen.

In the progress of a project, it is very common in an everyday cooperative work environment that an argument and a task advance toward a direction which is not the prepared scenario. Therefore, it becomes impossible to correspond with the scenario prepared like animation beforehand, when the interest of the persons concerned moves from the whole design to each detail. The appearance of QTVR exercises its power at the time of these phases and supports those desires.

(7) *Real-time simulation*

The real-time simulation can operate a model in real time, by applying VR technique to reproduce a design proposal on the screen. In addition, it has the feature which enables a user to check according to an interactive operating environment, and to compare a design proposal done in real time.

The existing media were insufficient in terms of the interactivity corresponding to the spots, such as availability of free view motions and modification of a plan proposal. The real-time simulation which can express realistic high-speed drawing and can use an interactive function emerged. The road improvement project introduced in Section 2 performs cooperative work using this technology.

5.2   *Contribution of new projection technology towards PM*

PM can expand the application area, when the ideal of the projection is such that "since you can see naturally, you can examine easily" is developed technically. The project can achieve better outcomes (when many opinions must be considered), using the projection positively. What kinds of effectiveness does the latest projection have, really? They can be summarized into three:

(1) *Making things visible (visualizing)*

In a drawing, you have to make an effort to synthesize two-dimensional information and complete the image of a three-dimensional body cognitively. However, the already visualized three-dimensional image (a still picture and an animation) is expressed in a form near to what is being seen usually. Therefore, the media to which it appeals in a visual sense make it easy to understand the contents of a design, and make divergence of the recalled image from media decrease. The latest remarkable trend of using IT for visualization is regarded as a development in the same direction.

(2) *Reacting quickly to operation (prompt answering)*

Since the non-experts forced to defend a proposal can listen to explanations of an expert skeptically, a deep understanding is obtained. And since the positive relation of a non-expert to media with prompt answering becomes possible, he changes his attitude such that he makes another proposal.

(3) *Carrying out on the spot (interactive playing)*

The most unique point of CG still pictures and animation is their dynamic nature. For us, this dynamic nature makes it possible to improve our understanding of an object by moving it around. Since the user can observe an object by direct manipulation, he can check the object from all directions satisfactorily. In a meeting, since opinion is tried at real time on the spot, agreement is easy to be attained.

However, more fundamental innovations will be brought about such that the projection is asking PM for change. Until now, the amateur was an obstacle; but since the range of understanding has been expanded by the projection technique, participants' frontage has become large.

The same is said in the case of ordinary companies. When there is a big risk such as a product's development by experts only, it is necessary to consider the opinion of many non-experts. It will also become possible to start a new project. It is the property of "visualizing, prompt answering and interactive playing" which makes it possible as discussed above.

6 A Concluding Remark

The framework of KPM suggests that for the common understanding of the project's context between organizations and individuals, a challenge to the participated-type agreement and information sharing is very important. There is one way which aims at the advancement of communication processes utilizing IT or ICT, such as exchange and/or accumulation of information. However, there is also another path in which agreement is formed by the gradually developed media via history, as suggested in this paper.

New media gave people a new *modus operandi*, and since it had the influence of transforming our society, it is important to consider the method of deciding which media is to be used as a way of cooperation and how to obtain agreement. In the road improvement project of Kochi prefecture, it is introduced that the artifact externalized by an expert (real-time simulation of a plan in an example) supported the understanding of a participant, and what was missing or expected was taken for discussion. Since it is easy to understand the visualized projection image, it was easy to obtain the opinion of residents. Using these efforts, the comparison with a plan proposal and the status quo becomes clear, and convincing decision-making can be made.

The technology of the projection was developed from a real static image to a free change of the view, and at the present, it could also give an output of dynamic virtual motion picture. However, originally "we ought to treat the motion picture as the basic form of depiction and the painting or photograph as a special form of it" (Gibson, 1979, p. 293). The human being who acquired the technology of the motion picture easily got the fundamental tool (media) of the project at last. Literally, isn't it overstating if it is said that human beings stand on the starting position? Furthermore, if a series of flows called analysis of a problem and reexamination of a plan proposal can be projected in the continuing design process by using proper media, it will become possible to offer a convincing decision-making process for many concerned. In order for people with various backgrounds to reach a certain agreement in a project, media is suitable as it has the three properties of visualizing, prompt answering and interactive playing.

However, future matters or the affair of the imagination holds various risks, such that it may either fail or include an error. It is important to extend the range of an understanding as much as possible so that such a risk can also be shared. This is the responsibility imposed on KPM.

References

Bodker, S. and Grondak, K. (1996). Users and designers in mutual activity: An analysis of cooperative activities in systems design, in *Cognition and Communication at Work*, edited by Engestrom, Y. and Middleton, D., Cambridge University Press.

Boujut, J. F. and Blanco, E. (2003). Intermediary objects as a means to foster cooperation in engineering design, *Computer Supported Cooperative Work* 12, pp. 205–219.

Brown, J. S., Collins, A. and Duguid, P. (1989). Situated cognition and the culture of learning, *Educational Researcher* 18, pp. 32–42.

Dennett, D. C. (1996). *Kinds of Minds*, BasicBooks.

Gibson, J. J. (1979). *The Ecological Approach to Visual Perception*, Lawrence Erlbaum Associates.

Gregory, R. L. (1970). *The Intelligent Eye*, Weidenfield & Nicolson.

Gregory, R. L. (1981). *Mind in Science*, Cambridge University Press.

Hutchins, E. (1995). *Cognition in the Wild*, MIT Press.

McLuhan, M. (1964). *Understanding Media: The Extensions of Man*, McGraw Hill.

Miyagawa, A. (2006). 3D area information acquisition support system, Master Thesis, Graduate School of Engineering, Osaka University (in Japanese).

Norman, D. A. (1993). *Things That Make Us Smart*, Addison-Wesley.

Ryle, G. (1949). *The Concept of Mind*, Hutchinson.

Vygotsky, L. S. (1930). *The Genesis of Higher Psychological Function*, Gakubunsha (in Japanese).

Yamamoto, Y. and Nakakoji, K. (2005). Interaction design of tools for fostering creativity in the early stages of information design, *International Journal of Human-Computer Studies* 63, pp. 513–535.

An Evaluation Theory for Practical Use of RFID under Supply Chain Project Management

Takashi Katayama
Engineer, Unichika Corporation

Takayuki Asada
Professor of Accounting, Graduate School of Economics
Osaka University

1 Introduction

These days, RFID and its applications are given a lot of attention and some trials of testing practical applications are done with an alliance between a national laboratory and the private sector. However, there are still a number of problems for applying this innovation in practice, for example, "technical problem at actual tasks, tag price, the investment evaluation problems of RFID systems, and privacy problems under this application".

First of all, all firms are at the trial stage for establishing "how to measure the effectiveness of the investment of RFID", and many companies have hesitated to introduce this innovation into practical problems because there are no clear rules about such investment performance. No establishment of methodology for the evaluation is thought to be one factor preventing this application into practice. The goal of this paper is to discuss effective evaluation methods for RFID's investment.

We think that many application effects depend on the function of information systems. By considering RFID as a part of information systems, the evaluation methods in the investment for traditional information systems might be applicable to RFID systems investment.

Thus, in Section 2, we review evaluation methods of traditional information systems investment, and in Section 3, we consider the applicability of such systems for RFID investments. After such arguments, we propose a new model for an evaluation of RFID systems investment. In Section 4, we discuss a case study of Company A.

2 An Investment Evaluation of Information Systems

2.1 *Status quo of the investment evaluation of information systems*

After the latter half of the 1990s, we could not have done appropriate evaluation on information systems investment using only the following methods — ROI, IRR and NPV — because information systems have became more complex. Owing to this situation, all research institutions, information technology vendors and consulting firms over the world often try to repeat such research about evaluating and measuring the management value of information technology or the investment effects of it. However, there is no established methodology called the "common way" (Uchiyama, 2003).

2.2 *Cost measurement*

2.2.1 *Status quo of cost measurement*

Following on the advancement in downsizing or networking of information technology with an increasing number of end-users, not only the operations and maintenance costs of computers but also further costs concerned with outsourcing some services, the education and supporting for general users have became accruing in business. Management could not have measured or controlled such operation costs of IT because invisible costs are increased in addition to visible costs of information hardware and software. Under such reasons, "TCO" is produced to put hidden costs into visible ones.

2.2.2 *TCO (total cost of ownership)*

TCO is a measurement method to help managers grasp lifecycle costs of IT when a firm has owned information technology, put it into practice, and managed it. It is a methodology for measuring the costs including outside outlay costs which mean cost of software and of hardware to be developed and operated by outsourcers, as well as expenses of employees who manage an information systems department, and also opportunity costs, i.e., hidden costs (Management Research Institute of Nippon Telephone and Telegraph, 2004).

There are no formal models or standards in TCO theory. Thus, there are several kinds of models presented by some research companies, and the

Table 1   TCO's model elements and average costs proposed from TCO Consortium

An Element of Each Component	General Summary of Costs	Average Costs[*] (JPNYEN:¥)
End-user's operation costs	End user's opportunity time used for IT operation management or colleagues' support or lost time caused by system down to be counted as labor costs	1,106,000 (62%)
Technology support costs	Some labor costs of employees who belong to Information Systems department are counted as supporting end-user smoothly to use IT systems	185,000 (10%)
Management costs	Some labor costs of employees who belong to IS department are counted as doing control activities for planning, implementation and auditing of IT system, monitoring and IT network control	443,000 (25%)
Investment and maintenance costs	Acquisition and maintenance costs for IT resources which consist of hardware, software and distributed network systems	73,000 (4%)

* These costs are calculated from yearly average expenses per one client machine from 13 companies' total data about TCO performances.
Source: Adapted from Management Research Institute of Nippon Telephone and Telegraph (2004).

differences in these models depend on some assumptions to be designed and on the categorical conditions (Uchiyama and Endoh, 1998). In Japan, the TCO Consortium established a TCO model shown in Table 1, into which Japanese practices are added to Gartner's TCO model.

TCO is a method applicable in three phases of information technology — *ex ante* evaluation, on-sight evaluation and *ex post* evaluation — from the viewpoint of lifecycle of IT investment and performance. At the time of *ex ante* evaluation, TCO can be applied into total lifecycle costs incurred under the information technology project, and also, by using benchmark of best practices, it will become a kind of framework for evaluating and managing information technology investment projects. When we apply this model in the intra-period evaluation phase, we will manage sub-projects of the total IT program or option management of the project. In the phase of *ex post* evaluation, by using the same framework model we can grasp the detailed differences of variances between *ex ante* plan and *ex post* results (Management Research Institute of Nippon Telephone and Telegraph, 2004).

In addition to the results of TCO analysis, the process whereby we realize the concept of TCO and decide whether a company's TCO is appropriate or not will provide an opportunity for improving cost consciousness in managers and users, which in turn is good for the company (Uchiyama and Endoh, 1998).

2.3 *Measuring effectiveness*

2.3.1 *The status quo of effective measurement*

When we try to measure information investment effectiveness, there are many characteristics not measurable by a simple method. In general, we distinguish the effectiveness of IT investment into "Quantitative Effects", "Qualitative Effects" and "Strategic Effects". If the investment is to be made for realizing quantitative effects, we could easily measure the effectiveness of such project relatively. However, as the goals of IT investment become qualitative or strategic, measuring the effectiveness of investment in monetary units becomes difficult. Furthermore, there are increasing numbers of information technology investment projects achieving strategic goals lately (Kogure, 2000). Thus, we discuss KPI as one means for solving such a problem.

2.3.2 *KPI (key performance indicator)*

KPI is an indicator to measure and evaluate the progress of qualitative strategic goals that are difficult to measure. Therefore, the merit of introducing KPI is to be able to measure the degree of success even if the objectives of such investment are qualitative. According to this argument, a practitioner has a tendency to put emphasis on using KPI for evaluating IT investment (Japanese Information Systems Users Association, 2005).

In trying to set up KPI definitely, we can connect corporate strategy to information technology investment and evaluate whether IT investment contributes to the extent of KPI's realization or improvement at the time of planning, on process or on *ex post* (Hiyoshi, 2002). Also, we could induce the agreement formulation through KPI setting and evaluating the processes between operations department and information systems department (Suita *et al.*, 2005).

2.4 Section summary

In measuring IT investment amounts and effectiveness, we think multiple evaluation measurements would be effective with KPI, which can measure qualitative effects and strategic effects. With TCO framework, we can evaluate IT investment's monetary performance by ROI measures. But these ROI scores only indicate break-even judgment for financial bottom-line. Yuasa (2003) issued the merits of both financial and KPI measurement.

3 IC-Tag Investment Evaluation

In this section we discuss how to use some applications of the traditional evaluation methods of information systems projects for IC-Tag systems.

3.1 Arguments about IC-Tag investment evaluation models

An introduction of IC-Tag into intra-organizations is enlarged into the total supply chain, which means the inter-organizational network's monitoring systems, and after such enlarged application of IC-Tag into various business processes is realized, we predict that costs after introduction of IC-Tag into business are larger than the introduction cost for traditional information systems. This is because IC-Tag investment needs a lot of additional monitoring instruments due to tremendous amounts of transaction volume based on increasing business activities.

The effects from the application of IC-Tag into business not only include direct monetary effects to be translated from reducing inventory volume or reducing expenses, but also include the non-quantitative results such as improved customers' satisfaction or non-monetary effects owing to information sharing and good traceability by IC-Tag. We can indicate many such systems applications to realize the indirect effects or non-monetary effects as the main objectives.

Following such arguments above, for IC-Tag investments, it is important to not only measure initial costs but also operating costs as well as non-monetary effects under such operations. Thus, we think that both financial evaluation and KPI's qualitative evaluation from the viewpoint of TCO can be applied into IC-Tag investment evaluation.

However, there are some alternative methods in economic evaluation, namely ROI, IRR or NPV. It is necessary to draw a line on the use of such methods depending on the kinds of investment projects. Generally, we try to use the ROI technique because of the following reasons:

- ROI is clear on the basic concepts and we can explain the effects from the viewpoint of accountability.
- In the practice of IC-Tag investment projects, IT vendors or IT consultants as well as managers in corporations often try to use ROI as an evaluation method.
- According to Yokozawa (1999), information systems' ROI = profit/costs (TCO) is a useful evaluation measure for new information systems' projects or the evaluation of the status quo of such systems.
- ROI is simple but comparable between alternative projects' evaluation.

3.2   *TCO model in IC-Tag projects*

We try to measure the denominator of ROI in the TCO approach, and discuss the measurement methodology and the classification of costs. As indicated previously, there is no standard model in TCO and there are a lot of classifications for cost elements. There are many cases using Gartner's model in information systems' evaluation.

However, as the implementation of IC-Tag systems are very large in scale, and when we try to apply IC-Tag systems into inter-firms' SCM (Supply Chain Management), the cost volume for IC-Tag systems increases either before introduction or after introduction of such systems.

Thus, throughout the system's lifecycle, we need to control costs under each phase of system construction. Gartner's model is not enough for classification of costs. We refer to three phased cost classifications for IC-Tag systems costs, namely "Pre-transaction costs, Transaction costs and Post-transaction costs" as argued by Ellram (1993). The reason we refer to Ellram's model is because it is easily applicable to measure time-series costs, easily manageable and covers all cost elements thoroughly. Also, Ellram's

Ellram's classification	TCO's application for IC-Tag systems
Pre-transaction ------ →	Before introduction of IC-Tag systems (systems building)
Transaction --------- →	Introduction (systems development)
Post-transaction ----- →	After introduction (systems application)

Fig. 1   Our TCO classification based on Ellram's model (1993)

model is concerned with purchasing activities, not with information systems, and can be a good framework for transaction-based cost measurement.

Referring to Ellram's three costs classification, we try to apply such framework of TCO into IC-Tag systems. First, we try to redefine Ellram's model into the three phases shown in Figure 1.

Before we try to consider the full applications of IC-Tag, at the phase of verification test studies, we need to consider these three stages, i.e., "system construction, introduction and implementation", and we need to allocate total verification phase costs into each stage. Therefore, we can allocate the exact cost assignment of total ownership costs into each phase, i.e., verification test, full-scale project and also into each stage of a phase. Additionally, when this assignment of costs into each stage is completed, we can use such cost data in each stage as the basis for the next stage's cost estimate (see Figure 2).

We show the elements of costs based on each stage in Figure 2. However, cost elements to be included as Total Cost Ownership approach are different in the field of IC-Tag application, so we should uniquely define the elements of costs and items for costs. Table 2 shows the general cost items or elements in an IC-Tag application project with total cost ownership approach, and this classification should not be fixed.

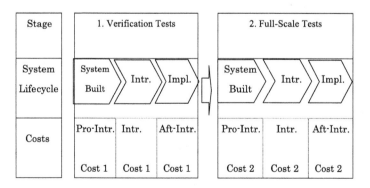

Fig. 2   IC-Tag systems and lifecycle model of TCO

Note: Figure 2 leaves out stage 0, which means Experimental Tests.

Table 2   Cost elements for IC-Tag project

	Cost Examples
Pre-introduction costs	On-the-spot investigation, consulting fees, system construction
Introduction costs	1. Resource costs: (i) IC-Tag, (ii) reader/writer, (iii) antenna for reader, (iv) PC and server, etc.
	2. System introduction costs: integration, installment, tuning, writer, firm-ware, etc.
	3. End-user tutoring costs, radio-wave fee, consulting fee, etc.
After-introduction costs	1. Asset use: (i) IC-Tag, (ii) reader/writer, (iii) antenna for reader, (iv) PC and server, etc.
	2. Operation costs: (i) asset management costs, (ii) security management costs, (iii) operation costs of IT systems
	3. Technology support costs: (i) help desk support expense, (ii) end-user education expense, (iii) expense for hindrance
	4. End-user costs: (i) formal training costs (costs for in-house seminar or seminar initiated by information systems department), (ii) voluntary training costs (costs for learning systems by means of a reference on systems manual or help desk), (iii) end-user-based development costs (costs of small-scale development or maintenance activities by end-user), (iv) peer or self-support expenses (expense occurred from prevented primary work caused by supporting colleagues' works), (v) opportunity expenses by down-time of system operations

As indicated above, the TCO model in an IC-Tag system project will evaluate both financial and non-financial measurements. However, Eq. (1) is the synthesis of both financial and non-financial measures, so this kind of scorecard is necessary for integrating both dimensions. Equation (2) is generally used for this project evaluation:

$$\mathrm{ROI}\left(= \frac{profit}{costs(\mathrm{TCO})}\right) + \mathrm{KPI} \tag{1}$$

$$\mathrm{F(ROI)} + \mathrm{G(KPI)} \tag{2}$$

Equation (2) means two things. First, this function will translate numeric numbers into point numbers. So, ROI = 10.5% and the F(ROI) = 3 points; also, KPI = 80% (about achievement level of specified KPI's measure) is achieved from this project, G(KPI) = 5 points. So, the sum of numbers is to show the IC-Tag investment project evaluation scores. Of course, these kinds of summation from different measures may have some problems such as the balance between measures, objectivity of evaluation from such measures, etc. However, we try to make clear the significance of such measures by case studies.

4   A Case Study of Company A

The business segment of Company A is electronics-related goods and tools and home electronic appliances (development, production, sales and exports).

4.1   *IC-Tag projects*

Company A has set reform projects by making full use of IT technology to realize company-wide innovation controlled under a department of headquarters. IC-Tag application system project is one such IT project.

In particular, concerning IC-Tag systems for controlling supply chain processes, it is positioned as a kind of incubation project. Thus, the manager of Company A thinks we need to have three processes before introducing IC-Tag full systems, which consist of desk works, experimental tests and verification tests for IC-Tag systems.

In 2004, Company A tried to examine how to use this system in the field of intra-company supply-chain process, and in 2005, he tested this process with the following fields, i.e., production process, logistics and overseas' mass-production by the desk work.

The manager of Company A tries to grasp all IT investment expenses including IC-Tag project costs from the viewpoint of TCO approach. We can understand total IT investment cost as two cost categories — initial investment costs and operation costs. Let us discuss this classification model now along the following three different stages of projects: experimental test project, verification project and full-scale project.

4.1.1   *Experimental project*

In this stage, project leaders try to check the performance of IC-Tag technology under the real task environment with various kinds of constraints and to succeed after several attempts at fixing the maximum effects of this system.

Costs: Experimental tests are very small in scale, so the total cost is also small. After-introduction costs are especially thought to be very small as the ratio of this cost to total cost and total amount of such cost is also small.

Effects: Controlling IC-Tag introduction in the manufacturing process has the following dramatic effects: "the period for account settlement works is shortened from four days to one day", "invoices become paperless from 10,000 volume of invoice papers" and "the number of employees for material controls becomes less than half".

Evaluation: The goal in this stage is to verify the expected effect as discussed on desk work on a real project. Thus, in order to evaluate whether we should go to the next stage of this experimental project or not, the main point for evaluation is not on the "degree of an effect to some investment" but on the "degree of effectiveness". Given the dramatic effects indicated above in the example, we can go on to the next stage. To grasp the costs for this project is to do budgetary control, and we usually do not recognize such aspects as important for this strategic project's evaluation.

4.1.2   Verification test project

In the stage of verification test, we try to confirm the true effects for such same kind of "manufacturing supply-chain" project and to verify whether the target "ROI" is achieved or not.

Costs: "Before-introduction costs" do not change so much in the amount of costs or the amount of invested money as compared with experimental test project. "After-introduction costs", however, are not changed in the cost categories but are very huge in the amount of cost due to scale-up of the project. Also, "after-introduction costs", are not incurred as much in the experimental test project, but are in the verification test project as part of "end-user costs".

Effectiveness: We can count the effectiveness of this scale project by means of KPI indicators, which are "manufacturing lead-time", "the ratio of meeting the deadline", "ratio of inventory amount's reduction" and "efficiency of office work". If possible, we can count the effectiveness based on the monetary performance transferred from such KPI numbers.

Evaluation: We evaluate the profitability by ROI as the criteria for going into the next stage at the stage of verification test project. The numerator of ROI is the cash-based number translated from the KPI effectiveness measures as shown above, and the denominator costs consist of "investment expenses as primary costs" and "operating expenses". Managers use this ROI to prioritize investment projects, i.e., determine the ratio between the KPI effectiveness measure and the approximation to assets and make decisions for project selections.

4.1.3 Full-scale project

Manufacturing projects do not advance into a full-scale project, but the evaluation methodology is done with basically the same manner as in IT investment projects.

Costs: There are large differences between partial and full-scale projects in cost. In the case of full-scale IC-Tag systems projects, we need to integrate or control various devices, arrangements between some standards or protocol, and softwares or applications. After doing such activities, costs increase or the cost structure is changed compared to verification test projects.

Considering end-users' costs, Company A formally counts the costs accrued like formal training costs, but cannot count other costs such as voluntary training costs or peer self-support costs, because they are difficult to assign into each product.

Evaluation: Managers try to measure effectiveness using the combination of G(KPI) and F(ROI) measures based on corporate strategy. According to Company A's case, managers try to make a "strategy map" and set KPI consistent with corporate strategy, and also show top management and other departments this target ROI. After implementation of the systems, managers try to analyze whether costs or effective goals are achieved or not and make it clear what the problems are, and finally they try to evaluate this systems by the target ROI fixed in advance.

Figure 3 shows the evaluation process of IC-Tag project in Company A.

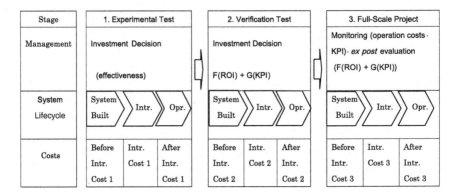

Fig. 3   IC-Tag project investment of Company A

4.2 Summary

Finally, we try to put together Company A's case from the viewpoint of costs and effectiveness.

4.2.1 Costs

IC-Tag systems have several kinds of practical problems to be grasped and solved by engineers through several rounds of experimental tests during which the problems are occurred, such as the rate of exactly reading data or careless operational problems. Managers and engineers need to solve such problems using a step-by-step approach. Thus, such experimental or verification tests take a long time and require significant costs.

Based on the classification of the three stages of "pro-introduction, introduction and after-introduction", our being able to measure the costs using the theory of "Total Cost Ownership" is very effective for cost allocation or cost management. We can also make more precise investment decisions about this IC-Tag investment.

Furthermore, in this case of IC-Tag systems, we need such systems enlargement after the introduction of such systems, but it is very difficult to estimate such costs before introduction of such systems. However, by using the TCO approach and estimating after-introduction costs, we can translate the "not-seeing costs" into "seeing costs".

Company A has enough organization to do a phase-review after systems introduction. So, grasping costs by TCO theory is thought to be very effective for measuring or managing such costs in the operation stage. As the total volume of costs or the percentage of cost element is changeable based on the degree of active use along the system's lifecycle, we try to distinguish the stage of such systems lifecycle, and we can approach the reasonable cost volume and cost structures with the TCO theory.

However, Company A cannot measure end-user costs precisely. We think the possibility of the cost increasing is very high because IC-Tag influences many more departments than the usual systems, and familiarizing managers with this system needs more time. Also, even if measuring end-user costs is very difficult, such costs are one of the most controllable in the after-introduction costs category. We consider it important to measure such costs and to make end-users conscious of such cost data.

4.2.2 Effectiveness

Company A thought that the reason for low ROI of IT investments was the lack of integration between management innovation and IT investment. Thus, they tried to systematically connect corporate strategy with IC-Tag investment KPI by the cause-effect relationship and the strategy map. According to these methods, they have made the evaluation of ROI clearer, and they have reached an agreement among top management, user departments and information systems departments.

This type of investment, such as IC-Tag project, has a large influence on many departments' activities, and it can be reasonably judged according to the cooperation from these departments in a company.

In conclusion, both ROI and KPI along the TCO approach are very operational and effective evaluation measures for IT projects or IC-Tag systems projects.

5 Conclusions

We discuss whether the evaluation method effective in traditional information systems investment can be applicable into IC-Tag investment projects, with reference to the case of Company A. We can confirm the "composite measures of the ROI and KPI" to be effective in IC-Tag investment, and also the "TCO" model in IC-Tag project proposed by the authors.

There are two problems not discussed in this paper. One is how to evaluate investment projects of "Closed-Type" like the case of Company A, and also how to make investment evaluations in the "Open-Type" IC-Tag introduction project like inter-firm projects. We also need more studies on how to apply our model into a practical case.

References

Ellram, L. M. (1993). Total cost of ownership: Elements and implementation, *International Journal of Purchasing and Materials Management* 29(4), pp. 3–10.

Hiyoshi, J. (2002). IT investment is truly effective? — IT investment evaluation under e-government   (http://japan.internet.com/public/report/20020410/1.html), (in Japanese).

Japanese Information Systems Users Association (2005). *JUAS Systems Reference Manual (SRM)*, Japanese Information Systems Users Association (in Japanese).

Kogure, H. (2000). A thought on cost vs. effectiveness of information investment, *Research Paper of Tokyo Management College (Tokyo Keiei Tanki Daigaku)* 8, pp. 137–149 (in Japanese).

Management Research Institute of Nippon Telephone and Telegraph (2004). Information platform planning in 2003: Studies report on IT investment vs. effectiveness, in *Research Report of NTT Data*, pp. 60–64 (in Japanese).

Suita, N., Misuno, H. and Akatsu, M. (2005). *Business Information Systems: Information/Management of Technology Series*, Corona Publisher (in Japanese).

Uchiyama, S. (2003). A new approach to IT evaluation: Information value chain model, *CIO Online* (http://www.ciojp.com/contents/?id=00001421;t=11), (in Japanese).

Uchiyama, S. and Endoh, G. (1998). *TCO Management Innovation: Make a Question on Management Value for Information Investment*, Seisansei Publishers (in Japanese).

Yokozawa, M. (1999). ROI evaluation on information systems investment, *Knowledge Assets Creation* 7, pp. 8–9 (in Japanese).

Yuasa, T. (2003). Information system evolution and economic evaluation, *Kuwansei Gakuin Management Review* 2, pp. 341–375.

Part 3

Project Management for Business Reforms Linked to Strategy

Abstract

The theme of Part 3 is "Value Creation through Project Management for Business Innovation". A number of firms are to do both business process innovation and management innovation with an introduction of information technology. In Parts 1 and 2, we proposed the fourth generation of Project Management. The same points of view reflected in KPM were considered and such business development or *kaihatsu* was advanced in the Japanese manufacturing sector. We report that there are some services industries, e.g., information technology services and hotel services, where managers use a "project balanced scorecard" as a value creation methodology. Also, renewal of business in the construction industry is shown as a business case of *kaikaku* project service.

All these cases in the services business have the same problems, i.e., "capacity management problem", "the timing problem in manufacturing and consumption", "difficulty of standardization" and the cost for market promotion to establish "Brands" vs. Effectiveness. Such problems are not easy for productivity improvement. For example, the productivity score of the Japanese service industry is 75–85 in comparison with the 100 point scores of American service industries as shown in Figures 1 and 2. Owing to more aging Japanese and more population decrease, such industries need more productivity improvement.

Looking at international comparative studies in labor productivity, Japanese productivity in 2005 was 71 compared to 100 in USA, and is also lower than the average score of OECD. This is said to be due to the low productivity of service sectors, which made up 44% of all industries in 1990. Those industries of such low productivity are attributed with retail, distribution, and "Gas or Electric Power industry". Wholesale industry and retail industry show an opposite performance in productivity. But only retail industry is not good in such indicators. Manufacturing industries are said to be high in productivity, but only those three industries — automobile, other transportation vehicles, and chemical and construction industries in Japan — are higher in productivity than those in the USA.

This Part's contents are given in the following, together with the author's profiles. The first paper of this Part explains value management

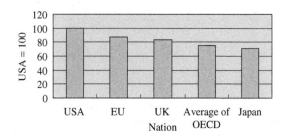

Fig. 1   International comparison of labor productivity

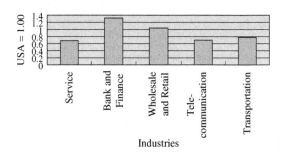

Fig. 2   Japanese service industries' productivity (1990 statistics; the score of America is 1.0)

and program management under an example of the manufacturing sector. We explain a technical application of PBSC (project balanced scorecard), to be applied into a *kaikaku* project for a "777" airplane product development by Boeing.

Fumihiko Isada is the author of the second paper. He is an active and well-known scholar in the field of strategic management theory. His paper makes a theoretical development where the modularization of parts' or products' interface would develop into an industrial platform standard, when business value chain would connect vertically or horizontally by means of parts' or products' interface modularization, with some examples such as the alliance between Intel and Microsoft. The alliance on virtual projects about interface between parts is argued as one producing a large competitive advantage.

Hiroshi Sasaki is well-known as a distinguished scholar in IT strategy. In the third paper, he discusses three problems of business portfolios from

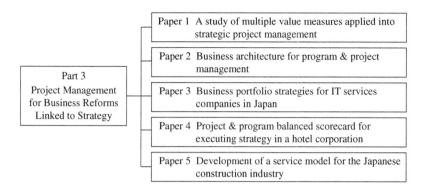

product or service characteristics in information technology service firms. He indicates that there are different problems in different industrial firms, for example software companies, network companies and system integrators. These indications would suggest that there are different firms' tasks or value drivers, and as an example we could find a hybrid firm whose main function is product development and sales, and also service sales.

Kenichi Suzuki is a well-known professor in management accounting. His paper explains the concrete application of PBSC in the hotel business. According to this case, PBSC is explained as a strong tool for team members in a company to be conscious of strategic consensus or agreements among them under complex or non-clear goals.

Finally, Kazuo Tanaka and Masaru Tamaki are distinguished engineers and management staff at Taisei Corporation in Japan. Their paper deals with the importance of knowledge management at the time of trying to do *kaikaku* or *kaizen* projects in a construction business. Concretely, construction businesses need more than 60 years to manage, and this is called lifecycle management. So, scheme management, system management and service management need to be reoccurred roundly.

Takayuki Asada

Professor of Accounting, Graduate School of Economics
Osaka University

A Study of Multiple Value Measures Applied into Strategic Project Management

Takayuki Asada

Professor, Graduate School of Economics
Osaka University

1   Introduction

What contents of "project management" would you mean? Generally speaking, "project management" is often used as the usual management terminology in any situation of the business works. Managers often use this terminology in business cases without knowing its exact meaning. Here, we define "project management" as "process management to realize certain goals and missions under a certain condition of finite period, specific tasks and certain resource constraints". Examples of this project management are recognized in several kinds of assignments in a firm. Generally, specific individual business affairs are recognized as "projects" in engineering or construction business. However, today's projects are recognized as more enlarged concepts which include complex management affairs to realize the specific missions or values. The former definition of "project" is recognized as the first generation of a project's concept, and the latter definition of "project" is recognized as the second or third concepts. We shall use the latter concepts in this paper.

We think that the new significant meaning for "project management" is assigned in this business world. If we try to grasp several kinds of enterprise problems as projects, we could solve such enterprise problems effectively. For example, it would be necessary for us to solve the problem between enterprises as a kind of project. Secondly, the framework of project management would be useful for realizing corporate strategy. Thirdly, project management would be useful for solving certain complex problems to realize a kind of social significance.

Thus, we have two objectives in this paper. The first is to make clear the significance of modern project management. The second is to show the contribution of management accounting to this modern project management.

2   The Function of Management Accounting in a Project Management

We try to discuss the function of management accounting concerned with project management. In this paper, we insist that a management accounting has a kind of linkage role between management strategy and operations management. This function has two sides. One of these functions is to translate management strategy into a concrete action or a series of actions if a management strategy is recognized as a kind of business concept. This entails the breakdown of a strategy into a series of actions, and we think that a kind of project concept and value indicator is very important for this translating process. This planning and development of value indicators should be done in management accounting. One other function of management accounting is as a feedback process from the results of operations into strategic process. In order to make such management accounting function effective, we must define what "an operation" is — we consider "an operation" to be an operational control of line activities.

In looking back into old management accounting topics related to project management by means of textbooks or cases (Anthony, 1965), we think that there was a strong relationship between them in a series of various phases. The typical examples are PPBS (Planning Programming and Budgeting Systems) and Capital Budgeting, which are applied into management accounting as an evaluation among several exclusive projects or a kind of ordering between them (Bierman and Smidt, 1984).

These days, management accountants and researchers are researching programs or projects as important planning tools that are connected with budgetary planning (Anthony and Govindarajan, 2000, Chap. 7). Another recent trend of strategic management is said to be a resource-based view approach (Andrews, 1991). Strategic superior management focuses on "which kinds of cooperation or alliances between some organizations with a core competitive advantage should be built up?", and "How to make a project" is discussed in such a context (Contractor and Lorange, 2002).

In this paper, we discuss both the function of management accounting concerned with the transferring phase of strategic planning into strategic projects and also of such strategic projects into the operation process. Thus, the first feedback loop of operational process into project planning phase or an open feedback loop from operational process into strategic planning is not discussed. Instead, we focus on the two kinds of feed forward process.

3   Project Management and PBSC

The significance of management accounting is as a linkage function between management strategy and operational planning or operational control process. A strategic plan is a plan by means of top management or executives' initiatives, and to put it into practice, a series of scenarios or concrete means must be prepared or linked into such strategic plans. As the operations for putting a plan into practice are diverse, an evaluation of which operation activity will realize value creation must be prepared. Thus, a specific project choice among alternative projects must be made, and management methodology through management accounting for some evaluation of strategic projects should be necessary at the middle stage between an operation process and a strategy formulation.

This is shown in Figure 1 as a management accounting function where a strategy is developed into strategic evaluation measures. Let us call this the "Strategic Program and Project Balanced Scorecard" (PBSC). Another function of management accounting is evaluating specific projects through a choice of a specific scenario and project formulation.

This PBSC makes clear strategic value measures, and the role of strategic process is to determine what kind of means should be used to realize a strategy in advance, what kind of value should be realized, and finally, to evaluate a project relevance for a goal or mission. Thus, we are not evaluating a project or means in advance by means of accounting measures, but evaluating some projects with multiple value measures. According to Figure 1, firstly we use a SWOT analysis and we try to make a concrete action plan, necessary resource and ability planning, and to introduce necessary KPI (Key Performance Indicators). We try to introduce strategic KPI during the strategic planning phase.

This PBSC develops the strategic plan into a kind of scenario along the fourth dimension. It is similar to the strategic management tools referred to by Kaplan and Norton (1996) as a balanced scorecard (BSC). But, the function of PBSC is very different from Kaplan and Norton's BSC. The function of our strategic PBSC is to evaluate a "strategic program" from the multiple value perspectives for strategy implementation, and it is a methodology for developing strategic projects. Thus, four measures — financial measures,

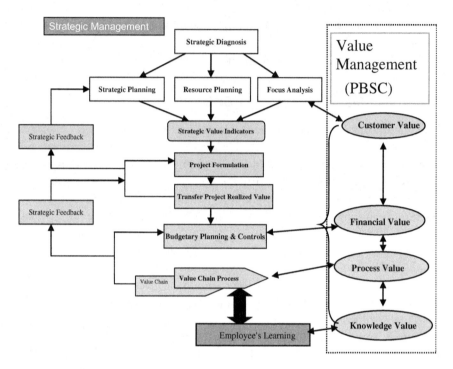

Fig. 1 Management strategy and value management

Source: Adapted from Futagami (1984, p. 34).

customer's measures, process measures and knowledge measures — are applied into a specific program. By applying Program-BSC into program evaluation, some programs are broached, following which some specific projects broken down from the program are also evaluated by project-BSC. Finally, such projects and program are translated into a project-based budget, and the business unit budget is associated with such project budgets.

4 Three Generations of Project Management

We have already indicated that there are several definitions of project management. The transition in the definition of "project management" is explained by several researchers (Ohara, 2002; Shibao, 2003). According to their explanations of this transition, there are three generations of project management.

The first generation of project management was from the 1940s to 1960s, and a typical example of such project management was a large-scale project management such as the Manhattan Project and Apollo Project. The main theme of such project management was the specific performance by a definite date under some specific quality and specific delivery date. Project managers must manage the project cycle of planning, implementation and seeing for realizing such specialized targets. The main goals of project managers were to carry out quality management, cost management and delivery management, and managers for each project must build a project organization and conduct progress management by controlling some risks (manufacturing risk and resource consumptions) under a definite level. The representative means for project management was called "earned value systems". Also, work breakdown method (WBS) was developed as a smoothing task progress method. Summing up the first generation of project management, we can highlight the following eight points: (1) task process management, (2) field conscious management, (3) the appointed date of delivery management, (4) technology conscious management, (5) a management neglecting the mission of a project, (6) a job order production-type management, (7) a management neglecting strategy, and (8) a management neglecting project values.

The most important problem for the first generation of project management was its neglect of project values. This type of project management was managed by managers from the engineering sector, who were not aware of the significance of management. Thus, the task of project managers was to faithfully realize the work assigned by top management. This type of project management was applied to various kinds of business, for example plant engineering and government-sponsored large-scale facility buildings. However, around 1970 to 1980, the main customer of a project management changed from military business or engineering business to information technology business. The typical example of "a project management" methodology was a guidebook of "a project management", i.e., PMBOK (Project Management Body of Knowledge) published in 1987. The revised edition was published in 1996, with additional revisions done in 2000. This knowledge standard consisted of nine areas of knowledge, including an "integration management" area and an "individual management" area.[1]

---

[1] PMBOK was produced by PMI (Project Management Institute) in 1987. Individual Knowledge Area consists of Time Management, Cost Management, Quality Management, Purchasing Management, Scope Management, Organization Management, Risk Management and Communication Management.

The main characteristic of PMBOK is "to obtain an expected performance consistent with stakeholder needs by considering operational process". This knowledge body along the lines of "Business Process Reengineering" was paid attention to by information technology business people who wanted to promote business speed or productivity and satisfy customers' needs. A typical case using this methodology is Boeing Aerospace Company's development of the Boeing "777" jet-plane. According to a manager of Boeing, they used a new cost management methodology — ABC and ABM — for cost management in this new project management. The management style in assembly organization changed from functional management to process management.

When some projects are complicatedly interrelated with each other and we must look at the totality of the project, we must consider strategic problems and business values. However, the second generation's PM is not enough as a methodology to solve more complex management problems. This second generation of PM does not have a strategic point of view and there are some differences between engineering management and strategic management. For example, we could not consider program management or value management, except for earned value management.

Let us look at the third generation of "Project Management".[2] This methodology has three characteristics relevant to "Integration Management". The first is "Project Lifecycle Management" and the second is "Value Management", which must be considered in advance of project implementation. The third is a methodology for dealing with complex problems, and this is called "Program Management". This body of knowledge was announced in 1992 as "P2M" with the support of the Ministry of Economy and Industry in Japan, and this standard is managed by PMCC (Project Management Certification Center).

The main value of this third generation of PM is to realize business value or enterprise value through PM rather than problem-solving tasks and satisfying stakeholder needs. A number of companies these days need PM activities for enterprise value realization, and the third generation of PM is thought to be necessary for managers and employees of a company to do cooperative work for value creation.

---

[2] The third generation of PM was established as "P2M (Program and Project Management)" in 2002 in Japan. The main contributions of this methodology are on "program management, value management and lifecycle management process".

Thus, we consider a management accounting's role under the value creation through the third generation of project management. This new role is a kind of linkage between business strategy and business operations.

5   Program Management

One of the main characteristics of the third generation of PM is to focus on multiple project management as opposed to single project management. This is shown in Figure 2 and it shows the transformation of PM from single PM to complex management. This PM simplifies more complex problems by organic integration of multiple projects and by designing business value rather than designing business. This is called program management. The main difference between program management and project management (management for a single project) is the discrimination between designing business and designing value creation. Single PM obtains results through implementing an individual or a specific process, whereas complex PM realizes a value or mission through a series of projects to achieve specified objectives.

This discrimination is relative, and considering designing business, we must naturally regard a value to be produced. However, under the second

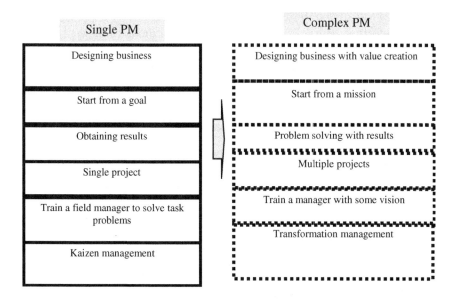

Fig. 2   Single PM to complex PM

or first generation of PM, value management is only done by executive managers as part of the strategic formulation process, since a field manager of PM is not related to such process; rather, such goals are assigned by executive managers. However, when we consider program management, a leader of program management needs to consider the project's value along the basic mission of the program from the beginning, and prioritize among multiple projects.

For example, a firm must change its business domain in line with the changing environment. If the firm cannot change its business domain, it must face default in no later than five years. Most employees who belong to the R&D, production, finance, human resource and marketing departments face this high risk. But, there is no sharing of how to overcome such risk between them. They are aware of the need for cross-functional teams in transformation projects. But, in what order should they set up the series of projects?

Evolutionary CEOs try to make the following scenario and strategic program. First of all, by listing their business problems and setting up a new business vision against today's environment and threats, they cease all useless activities. After such series of action, they keep or collect the necessary resources to build a new business design and then transfer the new business design into action by means of project management. Making this kind of schedule of business design in developing a new strategic trend is very important. However, this process — which includes first extracting an important issue, setting up a concrete vision, making a concrete new business design and making a strategy map for arranging multiple projects as a program — is rarely done in many large-scale projects.[3]

6   An Introduction to Value Management

Here, we introduce value management for developing program management as explained above. What kind of value would we produce by projects? We need a value-based evaluation phase with a strategy and mission management for a bundle of projects at the *ex ante*, in process and *ex post* of project management.

---

[3] In Japan, Nissan had a number of strategic projects initiated by some CEOs before Karlos Goone took over. However, these projects did not succeed and were only achieved by Goone with a program management philosophy under strong business commitment.

This depends on the introduction of management accounting into program management. We have already indicated the position of management accounting in this paper; once again, "the linkage function between business strategy and operation process" is necessary for program management. This linkage is equal to the application of BSC (issued by Kaplan and Norton) into "program and project management". We can consider two types of applications of BSC. The first is as a program value indicator, as exhibited in Figure 1. The second is as a project value indicator. We try to explain them further.

The basic BSC proposed by Kaplan and Norton is an extension of performance evaluation measures into today's business environment. Their BSC is developed to support the management cycle and as a strategic communication tool for supporting strategy. However, according to this theory, there is no clear relationship between the breakdown from strategic plans with the performance measures from the operational control process in the financial planning phase. Although multiple performance evaluation measures are emphasized in the plan and policy of top management under BSC, the linkage between strategic plans and operational plans depends on the same structure of Hoshin Management. Also, in the financial terms of the planning phase, they also use traditional budgeting.

However, we issue a new structure and process of strategic management. This new structure is shown in Figure 3, using program and project management and also PBSC (program and project balanced scorecard).

The firm shown in Figure 3 has multiple business units and must produce business plans or a program. This program is equal to strategic action plans including multiple projects. If we try to classify programs into two types, one would be a transformation program and the other would be a regular or current program. The difference between transformation and regular programs is the following: the former is a new action plan to change the total structure of value chains, whereas the latter is to change task contents or structures. This radical change is related to new markets or new products.

These two types of programs are interrelated and can change business units' management cycle or improve such cycles. Individual planning for such a change depends on the contents of a project. However, there are usually many projects in each program, so we must use the project portfolio to evaluate project ordering. This portfolio is constructed by X and Y axes; the X-axis indicates "project risk" and the Y-axis indicates "financial performance". We can put each project into this map and evaluate the total program.

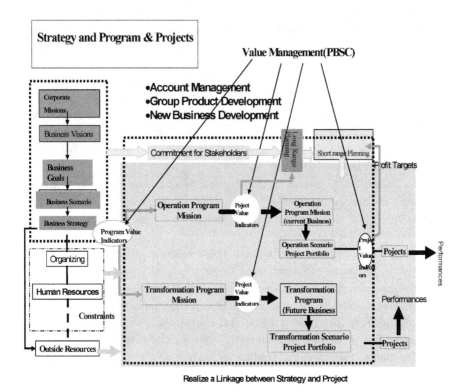

Fig. 3   Operation program mission

We present budgetary control as a box, and traditional financial control which includes current program or transformation program is made at an incremental cash flow basis as a long-period budget. By translating it into a short-period budget, this short-period budget becomes the implementation plan or performance measures. Thus, we translate from cash basis budget into accrual basis budget.

What relations in such PBSC are recognized in this company? Basic BSC is explained in Figure 4. This figure shows a strategic program-BSC. This BSC is similar to the one proposed by Kaplan and Norton, and four perspectives or goals (financial, customer, internal process, and learning and growth) are explained.

This basic BSC does not make clear how to keep the implementation of business line projects and it does not explain the concrete action from such BSC. The action plans or action goals are explained through a strategic map, also proposed by Kaplan and Norton. We divide this

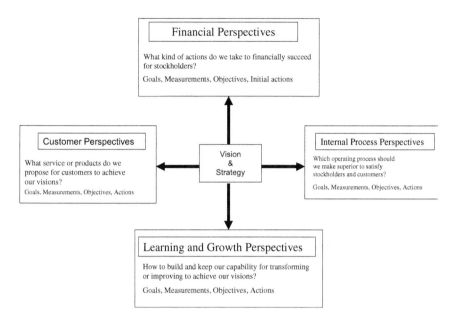

Fig. 4   Basic balanced scorecard

Source: Kaplan and Norton (1996).

strategy map-making process into three stages as a strategy scenario. Thus, there are three maps. The first map is concerned with strategic scenarios to produce value goals; the second map is concerned with the relationship between strategic program and projects; and the third map is related to project-BSC for evaluating projects in multi-measures. Figure 5 shows the three kinds of strategy maps. Each map has a unique function, and the content of each map is shown in Figure 6 as an example of the first map.

Figure 5 also shows the relationship between strategic management and management accounting. Management accounting introduces implementation management and serves as a linkage function between management and implementation.

Strategic success factors are chosen from key factors in each value indicator. The customer's perspective is to obtain a customer's satisfaction; a process perspective is to obtain and keep an excellent operation process; and a growth and learning perspective is to educate excellent engineers. To transfer such goals into specific measures, PBSC needs to set up a customer ratio, option ratio, efficiency of production process, and

Strategic Management

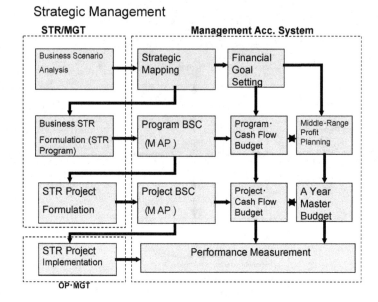

Fig. 5   PBSC and strategy

Source: Ohara *et al.* (2004).

From Strategy, Budgeting, Process Management, to Learning Management

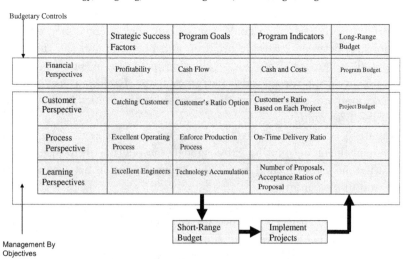

Fig. 6   A development of strategic management goals and measures

a degree of the use and accumulation of technologies as specific objectives. These goals or objectives are ultimately connected to cash flow goals or financial goals.

7 Making a Strategic Map

Let us take an example of PBSC from Boeing Company, using the case of the Boeing 777 airplane development program. Figure 7 shows the strategic map of PBSC of Boeing Company. There are two large-scale strategic programs for achieving specific financial goals yet to be described. Operational projects for achieving these programs are also not explained.

These strategic programs consist of a new airplane development program and a strategic alliance program. The former focuses on new airplane development and puts into practice the "PJ1" program, which is concerned with constructing virtual development systems and developing the new body's material resources.

The strategic alliance program consists of "PJ2" and "PJ3", and each project is related to the global SCM project, development and production

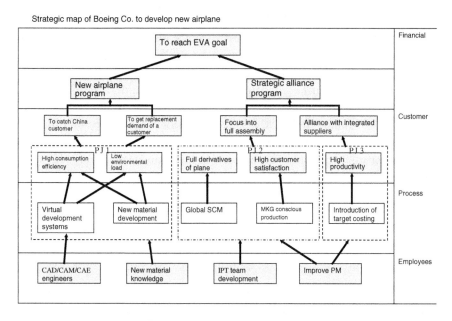

Fig. 7 A strategic map to create program-BSC

with customer consciousness, and a new cost management called Target Costing. To promote such process management, what kind of knowledge or technology should be kept or reinforced in engineers or marketers? These are shown in the bottom line of the figure. IPT in this figure means "Integrated Production Team" which involves marketing personnel, customers and development engineers who share various kinds of information.

Making a strategic map using PBSC methodology helps create scenarios relating various kinds of projects to an organization, its technology and people, whereby all employees share tasks, functions and other information. This PBSC is a communication tool linking all projects. It is not an accounting tool to calculate money, but a management linkage tool from a strategy to each specific project. That is to say, PBSC achieves a direct communication function from strategists to engineers of program and projects.

8 Conclusions

PBSC and a linkage function between value management and a strategic program is thought to show today's management problems. What kind of linkage to management projects from a strategy or mission could be made? We recognize that PBSC supplies us with one solution to such problem. However, this methodology has a lot of issues. One such issue is whose work is it to do this breakdown from a scenario analysis to strategy maps? Also, we do not need an accumulation-type budget, but an incremental budget based on detailed cash estimation to solve a problem. Thirdly, this PBSC needs multiple-based criteria, and traditional management accounting measures such as EVA and MVA are de-emphasized.

Lastly, we cannot discuss the post-evaluation for projects or program by means of PBSC. But, business is done along the specific mission or program as a cross-functional team and not as line management, and the work of managers and line staffs is increasingly being shifted from current work to transformation work. Naturally, the big problem is how to evaluate their collective and individual performance and how to link such performance to rewards or penalties.

References

Andrews, K. (1991). *The Concept of Corporate Strategy*, 3rd ed., Irwin.

Anthony, R. N. (1965). *Planning and Control Systems: A Framework for Analysis*, Harvard University.

Anthony, R. N. and Govindarajan, V. (2000). *Management Control Systems*, 10th ed., McGraw-Hill Irwin.

Bierman, Jr., H. and Smidt, S. (1984). *The Capital Budgeting Decision — Economic Analysis of Investment Projects*, 6th ed., Macmillan Publishing Company.

Contractor, F. J. and Lorange, P. (2002). *Cooperative Strategies and Alliances*, Pergamon.

Futagami, K. (1984). *Strategic Management and Management Policy*, Chuo Keizai Sha (in Japanese).

Kaplan, R. S. and Norton, D. P. (1996). *The Balanced Scorecard — Translating Strategy into Action*, Boston: Harvard Business School Press.

Ohara, S. (2002). *An Introduction to P2M*, H&I (in Japanese).

Ohara, S., Asada, T., and Suzuki, K. (2004). *Project Balanced Scorecard*, Seisan-Sei Publisher (in Japanese).

Shibao, Y. (2003). The age of program management, *Diamond Harvard Business Review* February, pp. 38–53 (in Japanese).

Business Architecture for Program and Project Management

Fumihiko Isada

Professor, Business School
Nagoya University of Commerce and Business

1　Introduction

In this paper, the business architecture is explained, which is requisite in considering Program and Project Management. The business architecture is the fundamental plan for the whole business, and shows the blueprint of business drawn by many organizations. The business architecture focuses especially on the relationships between business activities, and how to design the interfaces between them. In this paper, prior research about business architecture is surveyed first. Then, the dynamic angle of the business architecture is considered by introducing the concept of business platform, which considers how to control the relationships and how to reconstruct the business architecture.

2　Change of the Relationship between Companies by Modularization

2.1　*Evolution of information and communication technology, and modularization*

Various indications are made about the effects that the evolution of today's information and communication technologies have had on companies' competitive environments. They are as follows.

First, it is the velocity of the change of the competitive environment. This comes from the velocity of evolution of information and communication technologies. Innovations have been made one after another, especially in the IT and associated industries; further, various players have entered and various products and services have come to be offered. Through these changes, the lifecycles of products and/or services have become shorter, and it has become difficult for companies to remain in the existing technologies.

Also, the advances of information and communication technologies bring global competition. Competitors who were not anticipated appeared from all over the world. Prices of products and services are shifting toward the global prices. Even the rules of competition may change to the global ones, which are different from the domestic ones.

Moreover, various players, especially in electronic communication and related industries, compete together based on Internet protocol — by the evolution of digitization, which is one of the keywords in the advance of today's information and communication technology. Generally, digitization has caused the following changes: copy and transfer of information has become easy; information has moved and become common earlier; and the competitive advantages of holding information are now lost easier due to imitation, as are the advantages of enterprises by asymmetry of information, which are lost due to consumers' easier access to information.

As the impact of these changes in the competitive environment — such as speed-zing, globalization and digitization — the technologies and market have changed faster, are highly developed and are increasingly complicated. Further, the amount of information which companies should take into consideration, such as rivalry, has expanded, and it has become difficult to complete the offering of products or services within one's own and group companies only. Since companies prefer selecting and centralizing their domains, they have tried to plan strategic alliances with various external companies. The new strategy — to open the architectures and interface rules about products or services and cooperate with various external companies — has become more desirable than a closed strategy. Companies now narrow down products and services to the specific areas of the value chain and try to standardize the interfaces of products and services so that they can be used by many other companies. Companies try to make their products and services module (components using standardized interfaces).

Figure 1 shows that the interfaces between the parts are customized for each finished product, and the parts used for a certain finished product do not suit other finished products in the vertical integration-type architecture.

Also, the interfaces between the parts are standardized, and they suit different finished products in the module-type architecture. It becomes easy by such modularization to internalize the parts in which a company has an advantage and make them to be sources of profit, and cooperate with other companies for the parts in which they have an advantage.

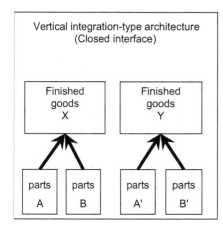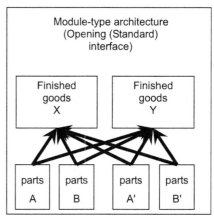

Fig. 1   Product architecture and interface

Moreover, by the modularization of products and services, modularization of organization — in other words, modularization of business architecture — becomes easy to progress (Fujimoto *et al.*, 2001). By standardizing interfaces and modularizing, performances in one's own module parts can be raised without adjusting specifications between the products and services of the other companies to each other. Then, communication — like transferring information and negotiating specifications — is completed in one's own company, making calibrations between companies unnecessary. Since the merit of communication is not fundamentally obtained even if the company internalizes over the scope of the module as long as the architecture itself is not improved, it is thought that differentiation of organizations tends to progress so that the scope of each organization coincides with the architecture of products and services.

Moreover, the evolution of communications technology, such as the Internet, has brought about the rise of the end to consumers' data collection capability and information dispatch capability. Very many kinds of companies are required to position such end consumers as one player on a value chain and create new related structures, and such skill has been a subject in connection with the success or failure of businesses.

2.2   *Modularization of supply chain*

The viewpoint of the modularization discussed previously is about the architecture of the product echelon. If the interfaces between two or more parts which constitute one finished goods become standardized and modularized, the necessity to internalize many products in one organization decreases. Then, the organization tends to specialize for each moduled product. However, modularization of business architecture is advancing not only in the product echelon, but also in the whole supply chain from suppliers to the end consumers.

In the relationships between the companies on the supply chain, the same kind contest change of the business environment as products accelerate modularization on the echelon of those business processes. Outsourcing business processes is one example of how the series of activities of the value chain — such as research and development, purchasing, production and distribution — in one company dissolves, cooperating with external companies. Then, there can be two types of external companies providing parts of the business process — one of which is to provide the standard interfaces, while the other is to provide the customized interfaces for each company. The former case can be called modularization of the business processes on a supply chain (Figure 2).

Through modularization, the business processes can be connected with many companies, including materials flows, money flows and information flows, and the scale merit and externality of network can work strongly.

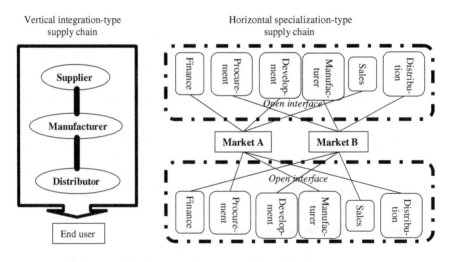

Fig. 2   Modularization of supply chain

3   Modularization and the Change of Competition Structure

Progressing openness and modularization of the products and inter-organizational relationships have merits for companies, such as entry of various players and exploitation of the network externality.

On the other hand, if open and standardization of interfaces progresses, differentiation by internalizing the sources of the competitive advantages become difficult. Convergence of competition, lapsing into a price competition, tends to take place.

This is especially so regarding information resources, and it becomes impossible to consider gaining the competition advantage as before. It becomes difficult for information resources to be the source of differentiation and competitive advantage. Because the organization becomes open and modularized, information becomes easily spread by the evolution of information and communication technology and digitization.

Under the status of progress for both openness and modularization, each company can internalize the source of the competitive advantage and create profit by the performance of each module, or combine modules. That means blackboxizing technologies in the module that are difficult to be copied by other companies, or grasping the leadership to build the rule to combine each module and build the product architecture to the convenience of the company, i.e., using the modules or technologies of its company.

Thus, information which can be the source of competition advantage is information which is difficult to spread openly and information which is hard to be digitized. For example, this includes such information that is kept by the inferential property rights, personal- and knowledge-level information, primary and scarcity information obtained by a consumer's exploitation experience, etc.

4   Required Ideal Model of the Relationship between Companies

In this section, the ideal model is discussed to reconstruct the new or existing business, to build and evolve relationships with the players of 4C (Customer, Competitor, Company and Complementor) through the whole supply chain against the background of the modularization accompanying the evolution of information and communication technology. The evolution of information and communication technologies especially do not allow companies to remain in an existing business domain, requiring them to innovate one after another. The subject here is how the business's dynamic methodologies continue to evolve with such innovations, how to cooperate with other complement companies, how to compete, and how to keep the customers.

Regarding these issues, it is imperative to obtain the competitive advantage to compete and then expand the business domain horizontally through the competitive advantage of each module (platform), and/or to compete and then expand the business domain vertically through the competitive advantages of the ways of integration of modules (integration). Also, when expanding the horizontal business platform, it is necessary to build complementary relationships with the various players on the value chain vertically.

In this paper, the ideal model to build complementary relationships with the various companies vertically, evolve the whole value chain, and continue expanding the values of the whole business industry for the customers is named as the virtual project type of the supply chain. The virtual project type of supply chain is defined as the cooperation with the players of other layers in the value chain based on its own business platform, which specifies the horizontal and vertical business architecture.

If the virtual project type of supply chain functions well, business platform is expanded, and the benefits of the players on the business platform are expanded. For that purpose, however, the difficult subject occurs: to progress the innovations of whole players on the supply chain one after another toward the desirable direction and by the desirable pace for the leader of the virtual project type of supply chain, by cooperating with the various players, who may not have any capital relation, whose profits or losses may be opposed to each other, and enter and leave one after another. Hereafter, such subjects are examined by the viewpoints of horizontal and vertical cooperation of the ideal model.

5   Platform Zing of the Relationships between Companies

First, the business platform, which is a component of the ideal model of the virtual project type of supply chain, is defined.

"Platform" means a base or a basic skeleton literally, and also the language of computer systems, operation system, etc., which offers the interface various software and hardware uses in common. Furthermore, the common part used as the base which opts for architecture of the body of a car, etc., is also called a platform.

The business platform in this paper does not mean the platform in one product, such as a personal computer or car, but the platform in a business process. Platforms like a personal computer mean the basic parts which two or more finished parts use in common; a business platform is the activities in the business process that two or more companies use in common. Therefore, the object of a business platform is not a business process in one company, but it is the whole processes on the supply chain. It offers not only the interface peculiar to *keiretsu* or customized products or services, but also the common interfaces. By standardizing the interfaces, the business platform offers the functions available for two or more companies in common.

Functions that the business platform here offers are not the entirety of the series of a value chain, such as development, procurement, production and distribution. There is significance in specializing in some specific activities, and providing them to many companies in common. It decides the method of concentrated modules and specifications of interfaces in modularization of an organization. While industrial structure specializes in horizontal-international, it can be called by what raised the degree of integration by specific functions.

The significance of offering the standard interfaces is deeply related with modularity as shown. They are mutually connected such that if modularization progresses, standardization of the interfaces between modules also progresses. Here, progressing standardization means that the players using the specifications of the interfaces between modules increase. As the business environment changes to the modularization, the necessity for standardizing the interfaces between modules increases, and business platform is what realizes this.

The business platform is premised not on the vertical integration model but on the horizontal specialization model, and the interfaces are both for vertical and horizontal. The viewpoint of the business platform in this paper is to offer a standard which specifies the architecture of the whole supply chain, specializing in specific functions on a supply chain. That is, relationships between various players on the supply chain, from suppliers to the end consumers, are specified based on the business platform. Through the business platform, various players cooperate, and materials flow, cash flow and the information flow are produced (Figure 3).

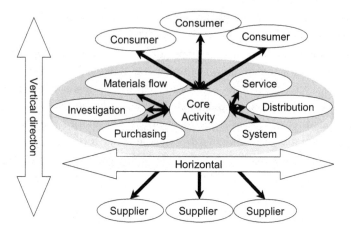

Fig. 3   Concept of business platform

The interfaces of the business platform are also divided into the following two types:

(a) *Vertical interface*: The interfaces between the players of vertical direction like supplier-maker-wholesale-retail-consumer; and   ·
(b) *Horizontal interface*: The relationship with other players in the same
layer of the horizontal direction.

Here, the more modularization progresses in a supply chain (namely,
as the trends to select and concentrate the business domain to some of the
activities constituting the value chain become strong), the more important
the subject of how to set up the interfaces becomes.

Horizontal cooperation is the complementary relationship whereby
companies concentrate resources on their competitive activities — such as
research and development, production and distribution — which constitute
the value chain, and depending on other activities for the other companies.
It is the business platform which specializes in specific activities and standardizes the interfaces by its own rule.

The business platform expands its activities of the value chain horizontally and vertically, by reorganizing the supply chain. It expands horizontally by making complementary relationships with other companies, or
by competing with other companies' business platforms which specialize in

the same activities in the same layer. It also expands vertically by reorganizing the layers of the supply chain, from suppliers to the last consumers, exceeding the layer of itself, and becomes a complementary relationship with or to compete with other companies in the other layers of the supply chain.

A business platform is the place at which information of two or more companies on a supply chain gathers, and also where innovations begin. Information on more players can be collected by offering the standard interfaces. The business platform is the mechanism to collect such information.

In order to collect many players, it is required for the business platform itself to have an inducement. It is required for the business platform to have many competitive advantages itself, and offer common interfaces of some activities of the value chain to two or more value chains.

6 Conclusion

In order to consider business architecture under the situation where modularization progresses, it is necessary to see 4C (Customer, Competitor, Company and Complementor). Complementors are products and/or services companies that have complementary relations.

If modularization of products and services of the company progresses and differentiation of the whole value chain progresses, it will be more important to analyze what kind of other companies will cooperate, as well as how to be offered the complementary products and services by the other companies. The idea of a business platform is useful to manage such kind of inter-organizational relationships.

References

Baldwin, C. Y. and Clark, K. B. (2000). *Design Rules: The Power of Modularity*, London: The MIT Press.

Chesbrough, H. W. (2003). *Open Innovation: The New Imperative for Creating and Profiting from Technology*, Harvard Business School Press.

Christensen, C. M. *et al.* (2001). Skate to where the money will be, *Harvard Business Review* Nov-Dec, pp. 73–81.

Fujimoto, T., Takeishi, A., and Aoshima, Y. (2001). *Business Architecture*, Yuhikaku Publishing (in Japanese).

Gawer, A. and Cusumano, M. A. (2002). *Platform Leadership*, Harvard Business School Press.

Isada, F. and Kobayashi, T. (2002). C2C4B as ideal business model in distribution industry, *Osaka University Economics* 52(2), pp. 278–293 (in Japanese).

Kobayashi, T. (1999). Foresight of electric commerce & management issue, *Int'lecowk* 890, pp. 7–16 (in Japanese).

Kokuryo, J. (1999). *Open Architecture Strategy*, Diamond Corp. (in Japanese).

Business Portfolio Strategies for IT Services Companies in Japan: IS Strategy, Governance and Management*

Hiroshi Sasaki

Professor, Department of Business, College of Business
Rikkyo University

1 Introduction

Michael Cusumano divides software businesses into three types — services companies, products companies and hybrid solutions companies — and insists that the hybrid type is the most realistic strategy. This paper investigates all the listed IT services companies in Japan, and seeks desirable business portfolio strategies that fit the tough business environment.

2 IT Services Industry in Japan

Various kinds of e-businesses have changed the structure of the IT services industry in Japan. E-business leaders such as Yahoo Japan or Rakuten have gained a dominant position instead of traditional mainframe manufacturers such as Fujitsu, NEC or Hitachi. As Hamel and Prahalad (1994, p. 5) state, "Any company that succeeds at restructuring and reengineering, but fails to create the markets of the future, will find itself on a treadmill, trying to keep one step ahead of the steadily declining margins and profits of yesterday's business". Executives should continue to find new, innovative areas and invest in opportunities to develop technology, goods and services for the future. At the same time, they should reduce business risk and allocate all resources in an appropriate way with the viewpoint of business portfolio.

---

* This paper was originally published by the author in Japanese, in the proceedings of the Second National Conference 2007, International Association of Project & Program Management.

Business portfolio theory holds that companies should develop more attractive and profitable segments called "stars" (high-growth business with high relative market share). This is also true for the IT services industry. What then are suitable business portfolio strategies for IT services companies? This is the main theme of this research.

When we think about the business portfolio strategy of the industry, Michael Cusumano's (2004) book, *The Business of Software*, gives us a good suggestion. He divides software companies into three groups, and points out:

- There are products companies at one end of the strategy spectrum, services companies at the other end, and hybrid solutions companies in between. Products companies in enterprise software also tend to evolve into hybrid solutions providers and even into primarily services and maintenance companies (p. 272).
- Although I have called this a separate business model, many enterprise software companies will pass through the hybrid solutions stage on the journey from being a products company to becoming a services and maintenance company, like it or not (pp. 273–274).
- The hybrid type is the most realistic goal for a software company that does not have a hit product or a dominant platform to sell (pp. 279–280).

He also mentions Japanese software firms as follows:

- The Japanese, for much of their history, have followed IBM and a few other American companies in designing and building mainframe computer systems.
- Japan's computer manufacturers and software firms have shown significant skill in writing programs for all sorts of applications, ranging from real-time banking systems, to fault-free bullet train control and reservation systems, to video game software. But most of these systems are custom-built for specific customers in Japan and contain relatively few innovative features by design (p. 11).
- With some exceptions, such as game software and some more creative consumer electronics applications, the big Japanese companies I know well have tackled large-scale systems development with heuristics (engineering rules of thumb), process discipline, some capital (e.g., computer-aided tools) and manpower. Hence, we have *software factories* (p. 11).

From a Japanese point of view, some of Cusumano's points are true but some are false, because his research on Japanese firms was conducted before 2004, and the industry has been dramatically changed since then by new entrants, for example SNS providers and/or e-business vendors. We have to study Japanese IT services companies more comprehensively and make clear the desirable portfolio strategies.

3 Business Portfolio and Maturity Process

3.1 *IT services and business categories*

In January 2007, I collected the consolidated statements of all listed IT services companies in Japan, and analyzed business segment information. The Japanese companies are separated into three groups, according to their primary segments:

(1) *SI services (System Integration: S-services)*

This category corresponds to Cusumano's services companies. As he states, "services range from consulting and systems integration to product customization and maintenance of custom systems. Services companies may also derive part of their revenues from software products that drive some or all of their services" (p. 273). As this research mainly focuses on the internal structure of IT-related services, we will exclude hardware vendors such as IBM, Hitachi, Fujitsu, NEC and so on. This is because hardware vendors bundle integration services and product services into one segment in their consolidated statements, and we cannot grasp the internal structure in detail. For the same reason, we omit internet cable or cellphone carriers.

(2) *Product services (P-services)*

This category corresponds to Cusumano's products companies. He defined the product company as having well over half its revenues (around 60%) coming from new sales of software products (software license fees, excluding product upgrade fees included as maintenance or product support) (p. 36). However, we define products companies as companies whose primary segment is software products, even if the segment is less than 60%. In this category, two types of products, B2B (business-to-business) type and B2C (business-to-consumers) are included.

(3) *Net services (N-services)*

This is the new category. Various kinds of web-based services such as electronic commerce, ASP, net portal services and SNS are all included.

3.2 *Business portfolio and maturity process*

We will customize the traditional Boston Consulting Group's (BCG) business portfolio matrix. The BCG matrix has two dimensions: one is relative market share on the horizontal axis, and the other is market growth rate on the vertical axis. But we will change each axis as follows:

(a) *The horizontal axis*: the internal business share according to sales volume of each business segment;
(b) *The vertical axis*: the sales growth rate of the same business segment of the company.

Through this modification, we can suppose the general maturity process of a company's diversification and compare the difference between business portfolios easily. In the first maturity stage, the company has only one segment and very few start-up segments. The internal sales share of the main business is 70% or above (see Figure 1). As the start-up segments grow (they are called "stars"), the share of the main segment will be relatively small (less than 70%). This is the second stage. When those segments

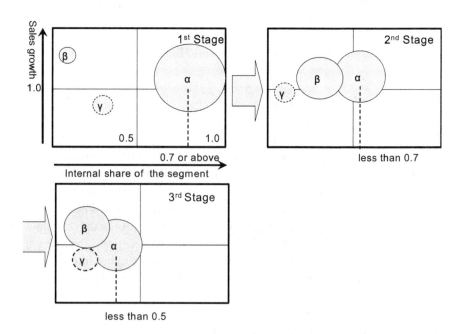

Fig. 1   The maturity process of the business portfolio

are more matured (they are called "cash cows"), the share of each segment will be less than 50%. This is defined as the final third stage.

4 Data Collection and Analysis

4.1 *Data collection and overview*

I extracted listed companies from the Japanese stock market (TSE: Tokyo Stock Exchange, OSE: Osaka Securities Exchange, and JASDAQ), in the IT services industry with the following conditions, and found 83 companies with 285 segments as a whole:

(a) Main business of the company relates to S-services, P-services or N-services;
(b) The company has more than one segment and discloses its consolidated statement and segment information for the last two years.

The number of companies in the three categories was 42 S-services, 15 P-services and 26 N-services. The number of segments in the three categories was 128 in S-services, 54 in P-services and 101 in N-services. On average, one company had 3.4 segments [(128 + 54 + 101)/(42 + 15 + 26)].

Figure 2 shows the comparison of the average maturity stage of each category. I conducted the *t*-test method to investigate whether the maturity level of each category was different or not, and found that N-services

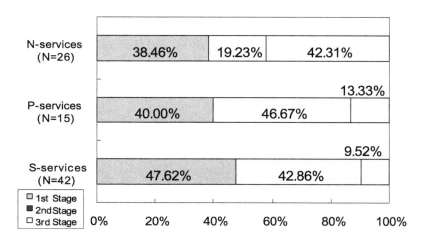

Fig. 2   The comparison of the maturity stage

Table 1   Cross-table of the three categories and the profit ranks on a company basis

Type of Business	Maturity Stage	Profit Rank				
		0–Under	0–10%	10%–20%	20% or Above	Total
S-services	1	0	12	7	1	20
	2	2	15	0	1	18
	3	1	3	0	0	4
P-services	1	2	1	1	2	6
	2	1	4	1	1	7
	3	0	1	1	0	2
N-services	1	1	3	3	3	10
	2	0	4	0	1	5
	3	3	2	4	2	11

companies (the maturity level being 1.62) are more matured than S-services companies (the maturity level being 2.04). On the other hand, P-services companies were in between (the maturity level being 1.73) and had no significant difference statistically.

4.2   Business portfolio analysis

We classify each segment into four ranks according to the operating income rate (operating income/sales). They are 0–under, 0–10%, 10%–20%, and 20% or above, and we call this the "profit rank". Table 1 shows the cross-table of the three categories and the profit ranks.

4.2.1   Business portfolio of the high profit rank companies (20% or above)

11 companies are included here (see Table 1). The two S-services companies have B2B software products. One of them has popular ERP modules that adjust to Japanese domestic business operations and customs, and the other has industry-specific software for medical institutions (Figure 3). Both companies have secondary or third segments which are related to the main segment (i.e., systems support, maintenance and so on). At this point, the two are categorized as the hybrid solutions companies.

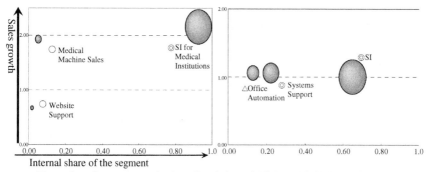

Fig. 3   Business portfolio of the high profit rank companies (S-services)

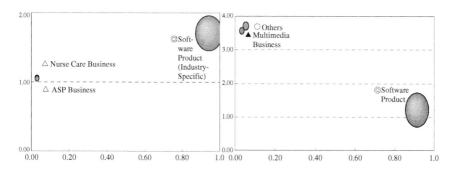

Fig. 4   Business portfolio of the high profit rank companies (product services)

Next, Figure 4 indicates the business portfolio of typical P-services companies. They sell B2C software or games and their primary segments have very high market share without exception. They try to build new "stars" in various fields, but sales and market share are relatively small.

Third, Figure 5 shows the business portfolio of three N-services companies out of the six. They have very attractive websites and provide many types of services on the internet. In their portfolio, we can say that they all have some sub-segments with high growth and achievement.

4.2.2   Business portfolio of large-scale companies

The three biggest firms from each category are examined. They are chosen on the basis of revenue. One company out of the three in S-services companies

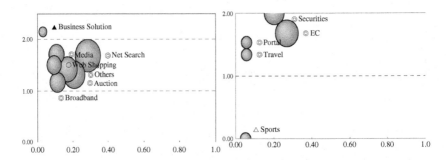

Fig. 5 Business portfolio of the high profit rank companies (net services)

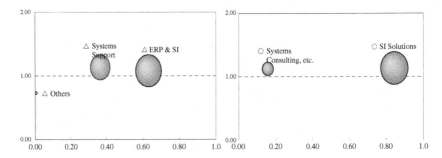

Fig. 6 Business portfolio of large-scale companies (S-services: Hybrid and non-hybrid)

is the typical "hybrid solution" company. It has the original ERP software, and the portfolio is composed of the ERP-related maintenance/support. The other two are pure system integrators (see Figure 6). The operating income rate of these three companies is not so high (they are ranked at 0–20%). On the other hand, the big three of N-services companies are also high on the list in the profit rank, and both companies of Figure 5 are included. As for P-services companies, they are all game providers, but not PC software sellers (see Figure 7).

4.2.3   The deficit operation companies

There are three types of companies which fall under deficit operation. One type is due to the loss of the attractiveness of its primary services. The second type is due to the increase of overhead costs (administrative costs or advertisements, etc.). The last type is due to the failure of new investments.

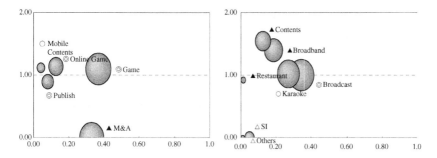

Fig. 7   Business portfolio of large-scale companies (left: P-services; right: N-services)

5   Discussion

IT-related business practices in Japan are changing, and game providers or web-based services have arisen. The notable features of the two are as follows:

- Game providers show excellent performance in terms of revenue and profitability.
- Net services companies are distinguished from high growth rate and many "star" segments.

On the contrary, the success of traditional S-services companies is not so easy. There are several reasons for this. One reason is that it is not easy to provide new B2B software as US firms or European firms try to penetrate the Japanese market with their cutting-edge software products. The best solution is to provide industry-specific or Japanese custom-specific software in niche markets to survive. The second reason is that the B2B market is already matured in Japan, and we have so many "pure" SIers (non-hardware vendors). Now, SIers have lapsed into cost-based competition. The third reason is that SI providers have rigid hierarchies with a few oligopolistic contractors, many second-tier contractors, and many more third- or fourth-tier contractors.

In this case, each company's profit (service margin) is relatively thin. The business environment brings about deflation of the services, and Japanese firms cannot escape from factory-type business. Peter Drucker (1974) said, "Doing the right things and doing the things right" are both important. But Japanese SIers are deadlocked and cannot find a new innovative way. Figure 8 shows a typical example of a deadlocked situation,

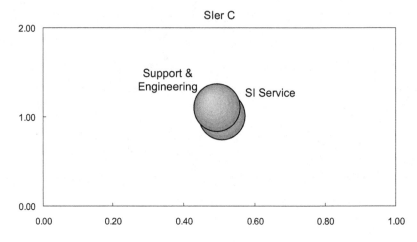

Fig. 8   Deadlocked situation of a SIer

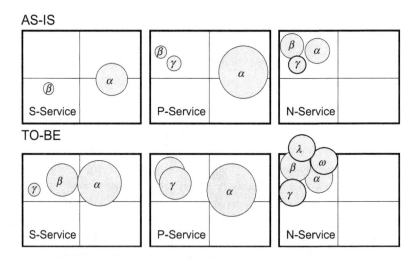

Fig. 9   "As-is" and "To-be" portfolio of the three types of business

where the SIer has only two related segments and cannot easily find a new "star" segment. In this case, internal organizational restructuring or reengineering practices do not make sense. Instead of these endeavors, new business portfolio strategies are needed.

Then, what are suitable business portfolio strategies that fit the business environment? Figure 9 (upper side) shows the typical "as-is" business portfolio of the three groups, while the lower side indicates the "to-be" portfolio. Desirable strategies are:

- S-services: The scale is large, but the growth is stable whether the company is a hybrid type or not. Activating each segment and creating new segments are critical. For the real hybrid strategy, going into P-services/N-services is another option.
- P-services: Risk sharing is essential to grow new "star" segments and to get a well-balanced portfolio.
- N-services: Continually creating new web-based services and building a scattered portfolio with many "stars" is the best strategy.

6 Conclusion

This paper investigated consolidated statements of all the listed IT services companies in Japan, leading to desirable strategies in terms of their business portfolios. Japanese IT services were classified into three groups (S-service, P-service and N-service), and preferable strategies were different for each group.

There are some limitations in this research. First, this research could not cover all the IT services companies. The number of the listed IT services firms was nearly 300, but only 83 companies were studied. This was because:

- A substantial number of the companies do not divide their services into individual segments, even though they have different types of services;
- Even if companies disclose segment information on their consolidated statements, some of them have changed the structure of their segments so often under the so-called "dog year" economy. If we cannot get the same segment information for at least two years, we cannot draw business portfolio charts.

The second limitation to be mentioned is whether the results can apply to different countries or not. Further research is needed to generalize business portfolio strategies in IT services companies.

References

Cusumano, M. A. (1991). *Japan's Software Factories: A Challenge to US Management*, Oxford University Press.

Cusumano, M. A. (2004). *The Business of Software*, The Free Press.

Cusumano, M. A. and Kemerer, C. F. (1990). A quantitive analysis of US and Japanese practice and performance in software development, *Management Science* 36(11), pp. 1384–1406.

Drucker, P. (1974). *Management: Tasks, Responsibilities, Practices*, Harper & Row.

Gawer, A. and Cusumano, M. A. (2002). *Platform Leadership: How Intel, Microsoft, and Cisco Drive Industry Innovation*, Harvard Business School Press.

Hamel, G. and Prahalad, C. K. (1994). *Competing for the Future*, Harvard Business School Press.

Ito, Y. (2005). *Net Industry and Companies (Net Gyoukai & Kigyou)*, Shoseisya (in Japanese).

Project & Program Balanced Scorecard for Executing Strategy in a Hotel Corporation

Kenichi Suzuki

Professor, Faculty of Business Administration
Meiji University

1   Introduction

A Project & Program Balanced Scorecard (PBSC) comes from the concept of strategic planning and control of projects. The purpose of this paper is to explain the PBSC as well as to examine the effectiveness of the PBSC by describing a Japanese hotel corporation case. The hotel corporation (HC) operates 12 luxury hotels in Japan. Its sales amounted to about US$3 billion and it employed about 5,000 people in 2003.

This research will show what PBSC is, and the strategy of the HC. Then, the purposes for using the PBSC and the procedures of the PBSC will be provided. After pointing out the effectiveness of the PBSC, a conclusion will be drawn.

2   What is the PBSC?

The PBSC, a strategic planning and control concept for projects, was established by the Japanese study group (Ohara *et al.*, 2004). The basic idea of the PBSC is to use a Balanced Scorecard (BSC) for planning and control of projects, which are managed through the framework of Project & Program Management for Enterprise Innovation (P2M). Developed by Kaplan and Norton (1996, 2000, 2004), the BSC is a strategic planning and control concept focusing not only on the financial perspective but also on the non-financial perspectives, while the P2M is the project management body of knowledge developed by Ohara with the support of the Ministry of Economy and Industry in Japan (Ohara, 2003a,b).

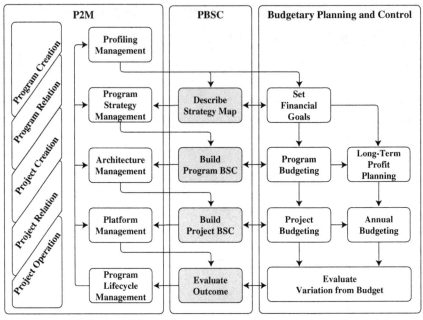

Suzuki, K. and K. Matsuoka, *Chapter 1: PBSC Framework* (Ohara, Asada and Suzuki, 2004, p. 18; Japanese)

Fig. 1   The conceptual workflow of the PBSC

Figure 1 shows the conceptual workflow of the PBSC combined with one of P2M as well as Budgetary Planning and Control for reference. The meaning of each step will be explained in the hotel corporation case.

3   The Strategy of the HC

The HC experienced a slow but certain three years of one point a year decrease in its capacity utilization ratio. To lighten the negative impact on profitability, top management had been cutting costs. However, they soon recognized the limited effectiveness of cost-cutting on their financial performance, and embarked on an aggressive course to increase the capacity utilization ratio in January 2003.

The new strategy was called Customer Intimacy. The Customer Intimacy strategy forced the HC to reform its business model for increasing the loyal customers, who have used its hotels repeatedly and contributed to the HC's bottom line, by providing services which offer these customers value.

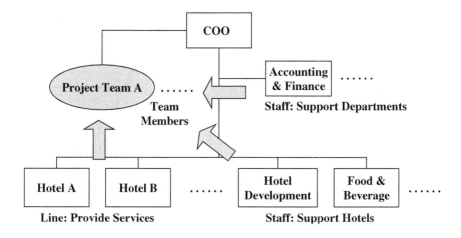

Fig. 2 The cross-department project team of the HC

4 The Purposes for Using the PBSC

To change the exiting business model from the viewpoint of the loyal customers who valued the provided services as a whole, the COO of the HC needed cross-department project teams, arranged across the spectrum of the HC departments, such as the hotel development department, the food and beverage department, and each hotel operated as one department (see Figure 2). However, the COO worried that these teams would not work well due to the contradictory interests of the team members.

In fact, the HC had experienced a dozen failures with the cross-department team's activity in its history because individual team members had given more priority to the profit of their own departments than that of the whole company. To avoid repeating the past failures, the COO decided to introduce the PBSC for maintaining goal congruence among the cross-department project team members.

5 Four Procedures of the PBSC

5.1 *Describe strategy map*

Looking back, the first step of the PBSC in Figure 1 is to "Describe Strategy Map". The strategy map, formulated in the BSC concept (Kaplan and Norton, 2000, 2004) and drawn before building the BSC itself, is a cause-and-effect relationship diagram, demonstrating paths to reach the strategic objectives. In the framework of the PBSC, each path, called a program, is

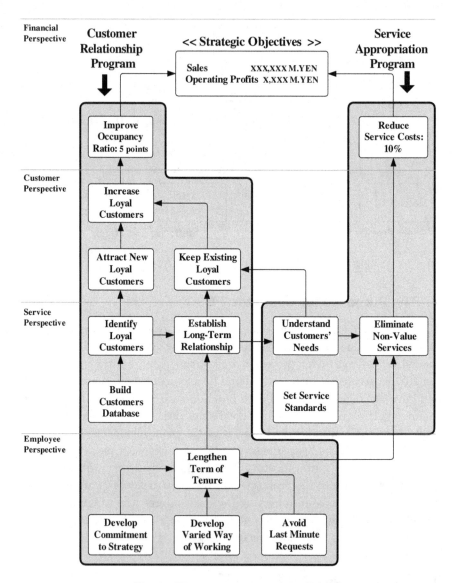

Fig. 3   The strategy map of the HC

divided into several sub-paths, called projects. That is, the strategy map in the PBSC is to identify the programs required to accomplish the strategic objectives as well as the projects needed to execute each program.

In conference for two days, the HC top management and all department heads except the three hotel department heads drew the strategy map, proposing two programs as shown in Figure 3, namely Customer Relationship

Program and Service Appropriation Program. The Customer Relationship Program aims to improve the hotel occupancy ratio by increasing the loyal customers, while the Service Appropriation Program endeavors to reduce costs by eliminating the non-value services for the loyal customers.

After establishing the programs, the COO's staff broke each program down into projects. For example, the Customer Relationship Program was separated into three major projects: Increasing Loyal Customers Project,

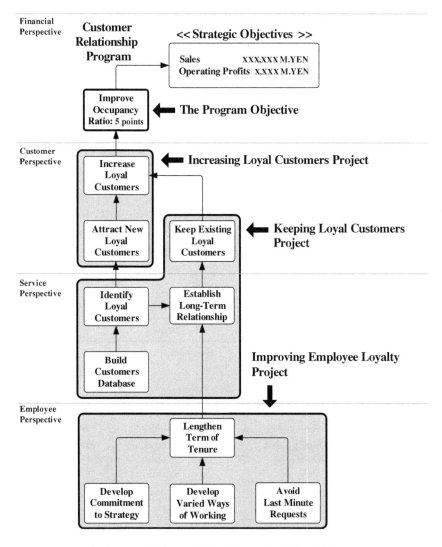

Fig. 4   The projects for the Customer Relationship Program

Keeping Loyal Customers Project and Improving Employee Loyalty Project, as highlighted in Figure 4.

5.2 *Build program BSC*

After the strategy map is drawn, the "Build Program BSC" for each program begins (see Figure 1). The program BSC provides measurements and targets for evaluating each project outcome to maintain the goal congruence among the project team members.

To build the program BSC, the HC top management, the projects leaders and the core project members had one-day meetings once every two weeks over three months' time. In the meetings, the top management defined their expectations for each project leader, who clarified the expectations, and together they came to a consensus on the project leader's responsibility. As an example, Table 1 shows the essence of the Customer Relationship Program BSC, in which the project measurements and targets were set to meet the program target of improving 5 points occupancy ratio.

5.3 *Build project BSC*

The "Build Project BSC" comes after the program BSC is made (see Figure 1). The project BSC defines activities for executing the project with measurements and targets to evaluate the outcome of the activities. Thus,

Table 1   The program BSC for the Customer Relationship Program

Perspective	Program	Measurement	Target
Financial	Customer Relationship	Occupancy Ratio	Up 5 Points (3 years from now)

Perspective	Project	Measurement	Target
Customer	Increasing Loyal Customers	Ratio of Loyal Customers	More than 30% (3 years from now)
Service	Keeping Loyal Customers	Ratio of Maintaining Loyal Customers (year to year)	More than 80% (2 years from now)
Employee	Improving Employees' Loyalty	Average Tenure Term	More than 5 years (2 years from now)

the project BSC emphasizes project planning and control at the activity level. This feature distinguishes the project BSC from Earned Value Management, a well-known project planning and control technique at the task level, a specific element of the activity.

In the Japanese hotel corporation (HC), each project leader built the project BSC, thinking together with his/her project team members. Table 2, an example of the corporation's result, shows the essence of Keeping Loyal Customers Project BSC, which was designed to hit the project target of increasing the ratio of loyal customers to more than 80% of the ratio of maintaining loyal customers. It generated three major activities with a measurement and target for each.

5.4 *Evaluate outcome*

The final step of the PBSC in Figure 1 is to "Evaluate Outcome" by comparing the targets and the results in the program BSC and the project BSC. Comparison of them first motivates the project team members to accomplish the targets. Secondly, the comparison indicates to the project leaders the changes in the activities needed to improve the projects' performance, and to the top management the changes in the projects to improve the programs' performance more importantly.

Table 2   The project BSC for Keeping Loyal Customers Project

Perspective	Project	Measurement	Target
Customer	Keeping Loyal Customers	Ratio of Loyal Customers (year to year)	More than 80% (2 years from now)
Perspective	Activity	Measurement	Target
Service	Establish Long-Term Relationship	Evaluation from Loyal Customers	Score of 5, Well-Known Evaluation, from More than 90% of Loyal Customers
	Identify Loyal Customers	Accumulated Sales & Customer Share of Identified Loyal Customers	70% of Sales Share & 35% of Customer Share of Identified Loyal Customers (1 year from now)
	Build Customers Database	Evaluation from Front & Reservation Staff	Full-Satisfied Evaluation from More than 70% of the Staff (8 months from now)

The HC project leaders had meetings to evaluate the project outcomes and to revise the project activities' designs monthly, while the top management held Project & Program Review Conferences to scrap unneeded projects and build new ones quarterly.

6 The Effectiveness of the PBSC

In fiscal year 2006, the HC reached its strategic objectives for sales and operating profits, improving occupancy ratio to 5.4 points and reducing service costs by 6.8%. The COO summarized the effectiveness of the PBSC, saying, "Though the Japanese economic recovery aided us in our challenge, this satisfactory result shows the effectiveness of the PBSC. The PBSC process forced me to take a lot of time to communicate with the executives, the department heads and the project leaders, but it helped to create the strategy consensus". He continued, "It also encouraged individual team members to give more priority to the profit of the whole company rather than that of their own departments. I knew this with a certainty when a young project team member said, 'We have just one company wallet'".

The COO concluded, "I highly appreciated the PBSC's documentation outputs, especially the strategy map, as the agenda and interpretation code for executing the strategy. This agenda and interpretation code helped every project team member to understand the meanings of his/her project and also the co-relationships among the projects to accomplish their mission collaboratively".

7 Conclusion

As demonstrated in the HC case, the PBSC can be used to make a strategy consensus, providing the agenda and interpretation code. This consensual strategy motivates the strategic project team members, facing the uncertainty and challenges of executing the strategy, to work collaboratively for the objectives of the whole organization.

To improve the PBSC's effectiveness, cross-departmental and two-way vertical communication is absolutely required prior to starting the strategic projects. The HC realized the PBSC's potential by taking a lot of time for these communications, which is one characteristic of Japanese management practices.

References

Kaplan, R. S. and Norton, D. P. (1996). *Balanced Scorecard: Translating Strategy into Action*, Harvard Business School Press.

Kaplan, R. S. and Norton, D. P. (2000). *The Strategy-Focused Organization: How Balanced Scorecard Companies Thrive in the New Business Environment*, Harvard Business School Press.

Kaplan, R. S. and Norton, D. P. (2004). *Strategy Maps: Converting Intangible Assets into Tangible Outcomes*, Harvard Business School Press.

Ohara, S. (ed.) (2003a). *Project & Program Management for Enterprise Innovation: The Standard Guidebook I*, PHP Press (in Japanese).

Ohara, S. (ed.) (2003b). *Project & Program Management for Enterprise Innovation: The Standard Guidebook II*, PHP Press (in Japanese).

Ohara, S., Asada, T. and Suzuki, K. (2004). *Project Balance Scorecard*, Seisansei Press (in Japanese).

Development of a Service Model for the Japanese Construction Industry — Application to Business Innovation and Improvement Activities for Building Renewal

Kazuo Tanaka

Manager of CS Center, Building Construction Division
Yokohama Branch, Taisei Corporation

Masaru Tamaki
Manager of Engineering Planning Department, Engineering Division
Taisei Corporation

1   Introduction

The building renewal business is an activity in the building construction industry that supports the business innovation activities of companies. However, at the same time, it includes activities that create new values that contribute to business management and projects. In other words, because the lifespan of a building is long, there is always an inevitable search to improve values as a result of exposure to the changes in the time environment and the sense of values. However, here, the strategically carried out activities are the innovation and improvement activities of companies, as a result of building renewal. In this paper, examples are examined to find the emerging future service model. However, this model is a prototype of a practical concept that allows innovation activities to be continuously developed.

2   The Value Created by Building Renewal Activities

It is necessary to consider the relationship and meaning of the building value throughout the period of time that is the lifecycle of the building.

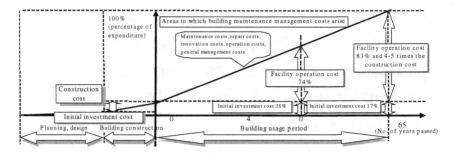

Fig. 1   Concept diagram of building lifecycle costs (LCC)

Figure 1 shows the lifecycle cost (LCC) of a normal building from construction to final demolition. This shows that according to the model of the facilities maintenance department of the former Ministry of Construction, the initial investment, which includes the planning, design and construction costs, is about 17% of the LCC of a building over 65 years. The facility operating cost amounts to between 4 or 5 times the construction cost, which illustrates how large the costs are after the building has been constructed (Japan Facility Management Promotion Society, 1998, pp. 215, 219). This large LCC corresponds to the repair, renovation and improvement activities shown in Figure 2. However, the "repair" in these activities corresponds to

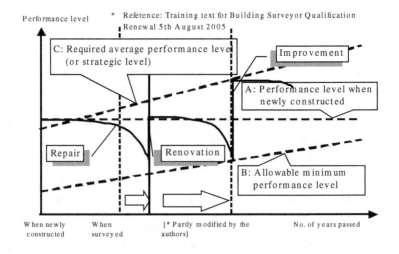

Fig. 2   Repair, renovation and improvement management activities

repair and maintenance activities to maintain the function and appearance at the performance level at the time of new construction as shown by the line A. In other words, looking from the viewpoint of the asset value, this can be said to be an expenditure cost approach activity with awareness of asset maintenance, as a result of the building procurement cost and the subsequent series of costs. Also, in terms of facilities management, these are conventional after-the-fact maintenance activities.

As time passes, a building approaches its time for "renovation", generally referred to as its physical life. However, renovation is an activity that restores the performance of a building to its level at the time that it was originally constructed. Resources are allocated from the total LCC, and the time for implementation of renovation is decided. In other words, this is a management method that emphasizes preventing the reduction in the building asset value, viewing the building planning and management from a viewpoint of the future costs approach. However, for this evaluation method, an LCC future prediction model is necessary, such as that shown in Figure 3, but these models are not yet common.

Then the time approaches for "improvement", which is a big turning point for the LCC. Whether to proceed with this improvement is a big management decision for businesses, to assess the "allowable minimum performance level" indicated by line B and the "required average performance level/strategic level" indicated by line C in Figure 2. This work is determining the level by reference to the social environment, which is

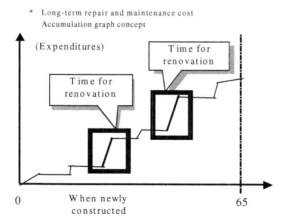

Fig. 3   LCC future prediction model

the environment outside the building, and differs fundamentally from making decisions regarding an actual tangible asset from the point of view of evaluating costs such as these.

In other words, this is the viewpoint of the market approach, and at the same time, it can also be said to involve the income approach for business managers, who expect the building to be used as a business. In other words, it is assumed that attention will be paid to the market value. However, it can be understood that besides the actual asset value of the building itself, there are many intangible assets such as the brand assets of the building, the social contribution assets, the intellectual assets accumulated in the building, and the set of process assets (Matsushima, 2004, pp. 64–67, 79–80) that testify to the efficiency and validity of the building operation management. Then, a large value is created when the sum total of these assets is appropriately received by the market evaluation, and it is here that from the management point of view resources are invested, cash flow is maximized, and the business value is increased. Considering building value in this way, in addition to the asset value of the building itself, the market approach and the income approach superimposed on the building lifecycle are indispensable, and that is how renewal activities should proceed strategically. Here, the businessperson's passion for the future arises as a mission full of promise, and we touch upon the roles in projects by explaining the business strategic level by the technological level. However, first we will briefly describe the characteristics of the construction industry in Japan.

A characteristic of the building construction industry in Japan is design and build, and special appointment contract. The party ordering a facility nominates a contractor at an early stage, and the two proceed with the project in consultation. If the method in Europe and America in which design and construction are separated is referred to as "goal-oriented", the method in Japan may be referred to as "mission-driven" (Ohara, 2006). In other words, by having the mission of solving the problems of the party ordering the facility at the beginning, by proceeding with analyzing specific specifications for the facility, the final goal is arrived at, which is the building.

Example 1. This is a project aimed at providing a domestic distribution network for a pharmaceutical manufacturer, based on the order from the president of the client company to "make the world's best distribution center". Taking the keyword "the world's best" to mean that the mission was that the distribution center should set the standard as the leader in the industry, the client commissioned the general engineering company (Company T) to prepare the facility planning and construction. The contract was concluded between the pharmaceutical manufacturer and Company T at a stage when the goal was still unclear, and the project was started. In this way, at an early stage, the two parties proceeded with "system setting = goal setting" by passing through the sequence of mission confirmation, understanding the situation → future predictions → setting the planning parameters, and system concept. The mission was accomplished two and a half years from the start of the project.

However, after 10 years, a major modification to the automated system, which was advanced at the time, was required due to the need to replace the computer, and also the original requirements being out of step with the times. Therefore, Company T was again asked for proposals to solve the problem. By using the budget that was originally intended for equipment renewal costs, a modification to the system so that it could handle another company's products was achieved.

As can be seen from this example, in renewal activities that form a part of business innovation, it is difficult to understand the method of achieving the mission as a technical system with a clear structure (Ohara, 2005, pp. 94, 97) such as the construction of a building. This is because the value sought in renovation is multi-faceted, so repeated human thinking activities to seek out the significance of the mission as [Objectives]→ [Means]→[Activities] while defining them is necessary. Among them, in the development of thinking regarding [Objectives] and [Means] in Soft Systems Methodology (SSM), it is important to focus on new discoveries and perceptions arising from the comparison of "the present" and "the future" (Toda and Iijima, 2004, pp. 44–46, 55–66). This is the confrontation of the present situation with the future concept, the mutual comparison and compatibility between "the reality of the conceptual activity model explained by [Objectives] and [Means] when focusing on the external environment", and "the reality of the actual model of the building as represented by the drawing information when focusing on the existing building". Also, for [Activities], since it is directly connected to the project, taking more specific action is necessary than defining what it is. It is necessary to provide sound practical measures for the tasks to be solved, from the conditions referencing the practicality and the limitations that clarify the framework. The incorporation of information is essential for this translation into reality, but this is discussed later.

3 The Information Value Chain Created by the Standard Project Model of Architecture

In recent building renewal projects, energy efficiency measures, facility management systems using CAFM, and due diligence which contributes to supporting activities that consider a building as a management resource are frequently used. However, the management decisions of managers play an important role while making sure of the effect. In other words, this is just the work of finding the target for building performance on line B or line C in Figure 2, as stated previously. Therefore, further consideration is given to the factors supporting this series of activities and that leads to success, by concentrating on the building value chain.

As shown in Figure 4, the stages of a building project can usually be divided into an upstream planning and design scheme model, a mid-stream building construction and completion system model, and a downstream service model which corresponds to building operation and investment recovery. Also, the value chain of the building standard project model includes "building information", "drawing information", "document information" and other information. However, reusing this information in the service sector for building ancillary technology and service technology and applying it to the evaluation of building performance or improvement can also be defined as building renewal. In other words, it is an important point that the "information embodied and realized in the building" and the "continuous information stock" created by the system models within this value chain can be said to be proof that explains the building. Also, effective utilization of information is essential for solving the problems that will frequently arise in the service sector of the future. In the following examples connected to the

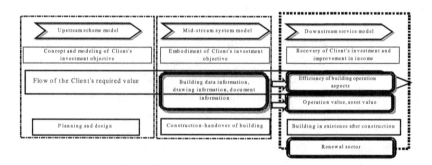

Fig. 4   Building standard project model

service sector business are verified, by firmly structuring them in accordance with the value chain of the building standard project model.

Example 2. This is an example currently in progress in which information in the technical system of a building construction project was structured so that it can be used in the future service sector. The building is a large complex facility that was completed in the late 1990s. A significant characteristic of this facility is that it includes 10 or more companies and five or more facilities management departments. The biggest problem in this regard is how to share information among these participants after completion of construction, and how to conduct business and operate the facility with unity. Therefore, to solve this problem, in parallel with the flow of the building construction project, a "construction drawing integrated drawing control project", a "document control project", etc., were implemented. Also, at the same time, aiming for collection of the results for facilities management, a "Computer-Aided Facility Management (CAFM) development and improvement project" was carried out. An important point here was that the collection of information and integration work was carried out with the consensus of the participants. A framework for forming the overall agreement of several owners was created, so that a common understanding could easily be formed regarding building operational aspects.

Example 3. This is an example in which after a building construction project was completed, strategic building operation was aimed for by reconstructing the information accumulated up to that time as knowledge. The building is a large multi-purpose facility that was completed in the mid-1990s. A feature of the facility is that there is one operating company, and the facility is operated by the facilities management department of virtually one company. Also, the operating company commissioned the building contractor to develop an LCC future prediction model and to provide information on the results to date, for integrated management and efficient allocation of resources for several tens of facilities throughout the country, such as rental income, measures against aging, etc.

In this way, they aimed to create and develop a new business model for their property business for the future by recreating the information for the facility for which 10 years had passed since completion of construction. In addition, a support office of the building contractor was provided in the facility to support the building operations from the time of the construction project.

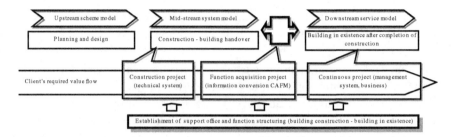

Fig. 5   Implementation example: Project management activity model

What can be understood from these examples is that these projects' activities are organically linked by "information". Also, if these activities are viewed from the viewpoint of the value chain, the following two main points can be understood (see Figure 5):

(1) *These two examples contain three common projects.* These are firstly the normal "construction project" in which a building is constructed. Next, there is the "continuous project" in the service sector carried out by the management and operation activities of the operating companies. This is a continuous project contributing to improvement activities and business changes in order to continuously solve problems due to the effect of the external environment. Then, positioned between these two projects is the "function acquisition project" in which the drawing information and building information created in the construction project is designed and implemented to function in the service sector. However, this project is structured by the introduction of the information conversion tool CAFM which was introduced in the example, and the function given to the role of the support office.

(2) *These three projects are arranged within the value chain of the building.* Through their combination, a system was designed (a combination of systems) that can be used in the "continuous project (management system, business)" in the service sector, by extracting information that can contribute to building renewal from the "building project (technical system)" in the system sector, and reprocessing and converting it (using CAFM as the information conversion tool).

In this activity, an important point is management activities that utilize the value chain. However, accurately understanding the conditions and limitations imposed by the information is an indispensable important factor for carrying out and achieving innovation and improvement activities in the service sector.

4 The Position and Role of Building Renewal in Business Innovation and Improvement Activities

The points made above can be summarized into the following five points:

(1) Because the lifespan of a building is long, the viewpoint of improving value over the entire lifecycle is necessary, and businesses recover their investment through activities that raise the business value in the service sector.

(2) Problems have been found in the relationship between social systems and management systems for building renewal carried out in the management and business realm of businesses, for which the reform business can play a role by utilizing the peripheral technology of a building.

(3) Businesspeople form an idea of the future as a mission, which becomes the mission of the business. From this starting point, innovation and improvement activities are initiated, which are then repeated continuously in accordance with the lifecycle.

(4) For innovation and improvement activities in the building service sector, strategic information utilization mechanisms are necessary for evaluation of assets or costs.

(5) To utilize the information created in a construction project in the service sector such as renewal, an IT system that supports technical processes as an information conversion system is necessary.

5 Application of the Building Renewal Service Model to Business Innovation

Regarding the building renewal service model, two factors that are general rules for application of the model are as follows:

(1) By placing the basis of the information utilization mechanisms in the building standard project model value chain, the service model contributes to effective management execution.

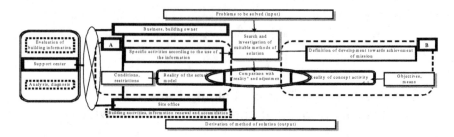

Fig. 6   Service model

(2) For support from the building sector for business innovation and improvement, the service model should emphasize defining the objectives and means to read and solve the mission, and thinking processes that aim at identifying the problems to be solved for the project activities.

Figure 6 expresses the concept of the service model. The conceptual activity model in part B on the right-hand side is the concept formation and development phase, in which the mission is gradually defined by the work of finding the objectives and means. In part A in the left-hand side is the information utilization phase, in which the building that exists in reality as "drawing information", "data information", and "document information" is expressed as a real model. However, this is a condition for giving direction to the limitations and practicality as an overall framework for the work to find the objectives and means, and plays the role of leading to specific activities towards practical problem solving. These activities are the solution of problems that lie hidden in the mission, the work of adjusting the concept activity model and the real model, which contain mutual conflicts. Also, this mechanism has the characteristic that it ensures that new information created by the construction activities of the site office is accurately and rapidly accumulated. Next, the support center can provide the "analysis and diagnosis of the situation" information, and these values circulate, constructing an integrated system.

6   Conclusion

As a background to the dynamic changes towards future-oriented activities in building renewal in Japan, it can be seen that the mission of innovation in companies is acting as a powerful mission within the construction industry. In addition, it goes without saying that the development and realization of a methodology for developing from mission to reality (Ohara, 2006) has resulted in major advances in management technology in the construction industry. A task imposed by this is to be able to contribute to reliably supporting management and improving business value, by increasing the capability of those responsible for executing projects and managers. It is here that we expect the model to be used.

References

Japan Facility Management Promotion Society (ed.) (1998). *Facility Management Guidebook*, 2nd ed., Nikkan Kogyo Shimbun, Ltd.

Matsushima, K. (2004). *MOT Management Studies*, Nikkei BP Publishing Center.

Ohara, S. (2005). Towards system management with total harmony, in *Commemorative Proceedings of "The Challenge of Program Management Contributing to a New Society"*, 1st issue, International Association of Project & Program Management.

Ohara, S. (2006). Mission-driven approach (MDA) of managing complex projects, *Journal of the International Association of Project & Program Management* 1(1), pp. 61–70.

Toda, H. and Iijima, J. (ed.) (2004). *Business Process Modeling*, Juse Press Ltd.

Part 4

Project Management for Knowledge-Based
Development Strategy

Abstract

Innovation and development are key factors to survive and to grow in the global competition. This is accelerated by the strategic thinking that technology, knowledge, and information are vital resources to be involved with performance. In this Part, the main topics of R&D activities are discussed in relation with the advanced styles of project and program management influenced by value creation paradigm. The researchers disclose new views and experiences of projects linked to strategies of competition and cooperation for benefits of speed, time and outcome in the global environment. The contents are given in the following, together with the authors' profiles.

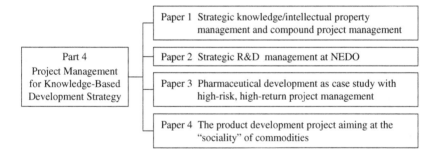

Ellie Okada is well-known as a distinguished scholar in the field of theory and practice of intellectual property rights and strategic R&D management, who gives lectures at Yokohama National University. She is the author of the first paper, which focuses on the relationship between reform and organizations. She refers to the typical issues of discontinuity of innovation and protracted projects due to lack of ideas in R&D management. To break through these issues, she underlines the firm intention of the top leader, the domain sharing of R&D in partnerships, and organizational capability. According to her, these essential elements are systematically presented and compatible with the fourth generation type of project management (KPM) rooted in the third generation (P2M). Her implication is interesting that randomness and serendipity of R&D shall be scheduled in the realm of problem solution in non-linear form of value creation.

Shiro Okazaki and Yousuke Manabe are distinguished engineers and management staff who belong to the R&D public organization of NEDO (New Energy and Industrial Technology Development Organization). They are the authors of the second paper related to R&D program and project management of public and private partnerships. After the guidance of the historical outlook of developments, they introduce comprehensive management and coordination activities for policy-level R&D conducted with the collaboration of government, enterprises and academia. The trinity approach of NEDO is introduced for readers interested in the strategic management for the three stages of technology development, empirical verification, and popularization. Strategic Technology Roadmap (STR) is also used to link public policy intent in the form of scenario introduction, technology overview and roadmap documents and tools to the formulation and implementation for program and project management.

Koji Iwasaki is the author of the third paper. He is a manager at Takeda Pharmaceutical Company, the largest enterprise of the industry in Japan engaged in R&D of the high-risk high-return program and project management for new drug development. The author explains the fundamental process and depicts the complexity of basic structure of clinical trials, modularity, and functional collaboration by multiple teams formed inside and outside the enterprise. This architecture shall be linked to strategy formulation in grand design to be connected to implementation of program and projects systematically. The decision making is made by a steering committee at the top level, and by the program manager at the office for integration and coordination in case critical issues might arise at phases where "go" or "no go" options are selected. The whole framework is congruent with the thinking, framework, and methodology proposed by P2M/KPM.

Ninako Makino is Professor of Business Administration at Momoyama Gakuin University. She proposes a unique view of the relationship between cooperation and competition for product development projects in which "sociality" is deeply engraved. Sociality is the key term used today to signify that the enterprise shall assume social responsibility and trust beyond stakeholders. A spectrum of products are developed, produced, and marketed in the category of sociality observed by frequent appeals to ecology, safety and environmentally friendly functions. Nevertheless, although profiling of product configuration is mandatory for development, it is extremely difficult to hit the market target segment. The author has taken note of the limited capability of a single company to have access to core information resources, and further identified the reasoning in the collaboration of enterprises to be proven by the emergence effects generated in the collaboration case research. The idea is compatible with the thinking and method of KPM paradigm.

Shigenobu Ohara
Professor, Graduate School of Management of Technology
Nippon Institute of Technology

Strategic Knowledge/Intellectual Property Management and Compound Project Management: Theory and Practice

Ellie Okada

Professor, International Graduate School of Social Sciences
Yokohama National University

1   Introduction

This paper discusses ways to improve the effectiveness of reforms by incorporating the perspective of knowledge and intellectual properties into the reform process achieved by the compound type of Program and Project Management (P2M/KPM).

The innovation required at present is discontinuous from past developments. The reform of technologies, as well as systems and rules, is required to achieve these advancements. The systems, rules, mechanisms and procedures shared in an enterprise reflect the normative consciousness among individuals. Thus, any change in systems or rules requires changing people's way of thinking. Changes in the mindsets of workers, inventors, users of intellectual property, consumers who consume innovations and managers who implement innovations are required.

However, KPM of the fourth generation proposes "reform promotion of the enterprise". In order for fourth-generation P2M to succeed, mechanisms that search, analyze and integrate critical knowledge into the process flow are indispensable. This way of thinking is consistent with the idea of "strategic management of innovation competencies and intellectual properties", where "strategic direction of research and development (R&D)" and "learning organization" are key issues.

Fourth-generation KPM is also consistent with the process of corporate reform introducing novel ideas into the pattern of a normal procedure to induce change internally. From an intellectual property perspective, this process can be applied to the conventional cycle of creation, protection and usage by introducing novel ideas or intellectual properties to form a new intellectual foundation or platform. National and public research laboratories and university laboratories are examples of organizations that create novel ideas and intellectual properties.

Thus, it is necessary to consider how to introduce a new idea or intellectual property into the normal business cycle, regardless of whether the project is inside or outside of the organization. That is, we should consider how to incorporate technology elements or newly acquired intellectual platforms, how to develop products and services from them, and how to tie them to the reform of a social system, such as the resource allocation method used in the market.

In this paper, a theoretical framework on "knowledge-based project management linked with the strategy" is presented, and KPM is analyzed in the context of a semiconductor consortium. First, the conceptual framework of intellectual property and corporate reform are constructed. Next, cases of P2M and intellectual property in consortiums are described. Finally, the implications of these examples are discussed. Product/service development in corporations and R&D in national research institutes and universities will be explained in detail in following papers.

2   Knowledge and Intellectual Property in the Context of Corporate Reform

2.1   *Aspects of strategic management of intellectual property*

Strategic management of innovation competency and intellectual property is a management system that directs research and development by incorporating the intellectual property approach into the management decision-making system. Thus, the intellectual property approach to the learning organization mechanism is included in a non-linear process of innovation, where solutions do not necessarily lead from the problem setting in a straight line. This assumes two points — "showing the strategic direction of research and development" and "learning organization".

This management pattern was originally observed in the 1990s, when companies began to suffer from a lack of novel ideas, redundancy in research and development projects, protracted launching of new products, and issues with technology management. KPM is considered to have high compatibility for implementing the corporate reforms of these management systems.

2.2   *Complex systems*

Innovations are usually created through deliberate development of a hypothesis or through a flash of imagination. This is followed by experimentation, with occasional failures or assistance from outside knowledge. During this stage-by-stage process, participants may increase or decrease, and a few unexpected inventions may also be born. This process of innovation can be compared to the process of genetic or natural selection.

These complex systems, originally developed to explain life sciences, were then applied to the phenomena of social sciences, such as the self-organizing economy of cities (see Krugman, 1996). Although the content of the "complex system" changes slightly depending on the field, three common elements remain: (1) existence of a feedback loop; (2) the phenomenon that summation of individual elements are not necessarily the same as the whole; and (3) self-organization (Krugman, 1996).

The author considers that the main characteristic of strategic management of innovation competencies and intellectual properties is the approach by which, based on the company's vision, a set of core competencies and technology element units can be used effectively in a non-linear innovation process. This management approach is considered to be particularly effective for corporate reform, although it is applicable to all types of management situations.

2.3   *Corporate reform*

The main difficulty of corporate reform lies in the fact that non-continuous reform cannot be realized as long as employees are engaged in the established pattern. In such a situation, it is difficult to develop or implement innovative ideas, as attention must be diverted from normal work procedure while the organization is exposed to the heavy competition. It is important to develop or implement innovative ideas and lead them to corporate reform with systematic intention.

2.4   *Reform with systematic intention*

Floyd and Wooldridge (2000) assume the following three patterns of corporate reform: (1) traditional patterns, in which the purpose-means relationship is clear; (2) dialectic patterns, which are composed of two opposing ideas that are integrated into a broader concept (Nonaka and Konno, 2003);

and (3) complex systems, where certain ideas or behaviors spread, interact with other ideas, and integrate into a certain direction of the reformation process. In real-life situations, any of these patterns can be utilized, in any combination.

Based on the above framework, real-life situations have the following three features: (1) a pattern where the relationship between the purpose and means or the problem and solution is predicted, with some uncertainty; (2) a pattern where individuals displaying diverse opinions are integrated into a certain direction (both 1 and 2 require organizational systematic intention); and (3) a pattern where reform occurs in a complex system. Reforms in real-world situations occur through a combination of these three patterns.

In other words, the pattern of knowledge and intellectual property-based development reform is categorized as follows:

(1) Reforms based on a systematic intention with long-term uncertainty
     a. Reform considering purpose-means and problem-solution
     b. Reform that investigates direction while introducing new concepts
(2) Reform by complex systems.

2.5   *Intellectual property exchange*

Here, the author attempts to describe the above patterns from the viewpoint of a new intellectual property program, to introduce a new program (intellectual property for scientific organizations such as universities or public laboratories) using an existing creative method, and to conceptualize a process for enhancing the reform ability of the organization (Figure 1).

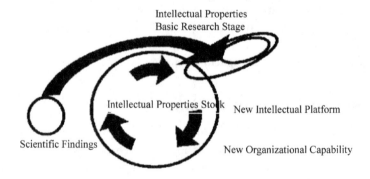

Fig. 1   Scientific findings and new organization capability

For example, the quantum dot has been investigated in the major research laboratories of various domestic and foreign universities, public laboratories and enterprises. When the Fujitsu Corporation, for example, decided to advance to the development phase of the quantum dot research project, the development of the project reached a certain level at which a synergistic effect occurred between the technology units and intellectual properties of the optical communication domain. In another case, the development of biotechnology at Nagoya University for practical use as a raw material for biomass energy was pursued in cooperation with a private company, SCIVAX; the research project in turn added a new business segment for the company.

Thus, intellectual properties born in the basic research stage are shaped to offer the economic society new value, as well as affecting the cycle of creation, protection and intellectual property usage of the sponsoring organization.

2.6 *Management of randomness and serendipity*

When we consider non-continuous reformation, randomness or serendipity is a familiar concept. We think of young research assistants who make mistakes that happen to lead to a novel invention. However, according to corporate researcher Dr. Isaburo Fukawa (Asahi Kasei Corporation), "For enterprises, what is needed is to bring such randomness into the realm of problem-solving, as if it was intended from the very beginning."

It is important to improve the efficiency of the development process by bringing randomness and serendipity into the scheduled problem-solution relation in the non-linear value creation process.

3 Case of Compound-Type P2M and Intellectual Property

3.1 *A case of strategic management of innovation competencies and intellectual properties*

First, a case where a company searches for a strategic direction with regard to intellectual property is examined.

Regarding the practice of an open innovation, the case of SCIVAX is examined. The business domain of this company is to organize a project by using the intellectual property of national research institutes, specifically, nanotechnology and biotechnology, in addition to the nano-type imprint business domain.

This company focused on a genetically modified plant invented by Nagoya University, and structured its intellectual properties from a global perspective. As a result, these intellectual properties were found to be in the same area as those of the molecular structure possessed by BASF, although SCIVAX differs from Pioneer in that they accumulate intellectual property that is strongly connected to the appropriate material.

However, SCIVAX differs from BASF in that they focus on certain plant varieties with specific characteristics (i.e., SCIVAX focuses on the characteristics of promotion speed and tolerance of salinity, whereas BASF applies for many plant varieties with numerous characteristics). After additional detailed examinations were performed, a sugar beet was found to have strong stress-proof characteristics (i.e., heat tolerance and tolerance of salinity) (Figure 2).

IPRs of genetically modified plant invented by Nagoya University
⇒ Bundling, interpreting and rebundling of IPRs by SCIVAX
⇒ Biotechnology fuel business.

In Japan and Europe, the results of Nagoya University's research would have been, at the very least, criticized as a questionable rejection of a potential use for a genetically modified food. However, through previous experience, SCIVAX was aware that the sugar beet could be used for biomass energy. Thus, the company proposed a joint research project to inject the characteristic of "Promotion speed" of rice plants into the sugar beet, and the investment of two trading companies was secured. The only remaining issue is securing a sales network, as the prototype was completed in December 2005. "Biotechnology fuel business" is now formally listed as a new business of SCIVAX.

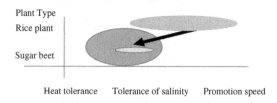

Fig. 2   Open innovation using biotechnology intellectual property rights (IPRs)

3.2 A case of opening-type project management and intellectual property

When considering a national innovation system for improving the competitive edge of a country, the role of the consortium cannot be disregarded. Industrial-government-academic consortiums and industry consortiums are taking charge of numerous projects initiated by national governments.

For example, from a technical perspective, the main issue for semiconductor technology is assumed to be a decrease in the operating speed of LSI due to minimization, power consumption and manufacturing variance. However, from a managerial perspective, technological programs like the process of developing next-generation semiconductor devices, QTAT and energy conservation are the primary issues. In these consortiums, it is important to motivate researchers to invent and innovate in cooperation with each other by using an incentive system of intellectual property.

However, when the international standard is to be formed, the patent platform plays an important role. In these cases, when the owner has the authority to reserve the right of shared purpose, the original exclusivity of the intellectual property right is partly denied. This paper examines both the projects derived from the current Japanese situation and projects resulting from international development.

3.2.1 Semiconductor field

The development of element technology units by private companies began in the mid-1990s as a result of high value-added system of LSI trends in the US and the inflow of low-priced goods from newly developed countries in the semiconductor industry. This competitive pressure was responsible for voluntarily uniting the industry consortium, and inducing cooperation in common ground technology units.

Research consortiums in the semiconductor field were also created in the US and Europe, and these consortiums have the international characteristics at present. The semiconductor consortium SEMATECH was established by the US government in the 1980s to strengthen the competitive advantage of American semiconductor companies; however, it declined government subsidies in the 1990s and instead began to strengthen international cooperation with other countries. In Europe, Ruben University in Belgium established the IMEC to develop cutting-edge technology in the semiconductor field, and currently attracts researchers from around the

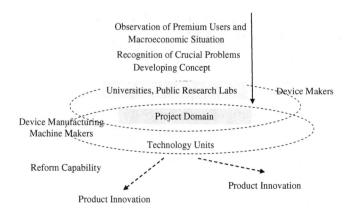

Fig. 3   P2M in consortium

world with its promotion of high-technology industry in Europe. The goal of each consortium is to offer an institution with joint development of infrastructure, common ground technology and next-generation technology.

However, the main project domain of these consortia differs slightly. In Japan, the next-generation semiconductor device process technology platform development program offers many projects, including Millennium Research for Advanced Information Technology, Semiconductor Leading-Edge Technologies, Semiconductor Technology Academic Research Center and Highly Agile Line Concept Advancement. SEMATECH, on the other hand, organizes its projects by dividing the emphasized field into lithography, material development and processing technology. In addition to this regular program, SEMATECH has formed many independent projects such as the Intelligent Manufacturing System (IMS) project, which includes a university, the National Research Institute, as well as existing private companies from all over the world.

IMEC, meanwhile, has planned various projects with a different positioning to SEMATECH. For example, it developed a platform architect, model design and virtual platform design for system C that utilize a common infrastructure for both design and verification. Moreover, spin-off ventures such as CoWARE that execute the intellectual property of the above-mentioned transistor design are also active in the global semiconductor market.

Some international consortiums utilize a common project domain such as material development by nanotechnology, while others develop area-specific projects such as IMEC's development of the platform architect.

3.2.2 Flow of the project

The Japanese HALCA project is an example of an area-specific technological development program that develops next-generation semiconductor
device process by recognizing that the LSI system is a basic technology
indispensable to telecommunication technology today. The organization
aims to develop "technology for device manufacturing machine sharing",
"technology for the multifunction machine" (i.e., processes that manufacture different kinds of thin films in one machine), and "Reduction of RPT
(raw process time)". Their mission is "Ensuring that customer needs are
diversified and processing technology that suits the LSI system characteristic of frequent generation change is achieved".

According to the P2M method, each researcher was allocated a specific
task, and each theme progress management table was set. The work process
was quantified, and expected achievement levels were made available to all
participants. The fact that the work process was made visible had the effect
of making each researcher consider his/her own place in the project.

3.2.3 Continuing issues in intellectual property

One issue for the consortiums is the mutual ownership of intellectual property created in a project by competing enterprises. Thus far, the intellectual property resulting from research projects has been held by the
consortium in the semiconductor consortium in Japan. However, it eventually becomes impossible for the researchers of a participating enterprise
to return to a former enterprise at the ending phase of the project in order
to take care of the intellectual properties they created. Additional problems include a loss of a sense of ownership, and applications for inventions
that do not appear to have a potential use.

3.2.4 Incentives for creation and cooperation in intellectual property policy

In this way, P2M is thought to have an advantage through development
cost reduction, improvement in development speed, and the acceleration of
growth by the team. Such an effect is achieved to give researchers an incentive to create novel intellectual properties by securing their experience
among the consortium members. Additionally, information contamination
can be avoided when device makers and device manufacturing machine
makers work cooperatively.

In addition, to give researchers inventive incentives in a consortium, it is necessary to (1) use the "correct" aspects of intellectual property, while (2) creating cooperative incentives among team members, as the technology developed in a consortium might be disclosed outside the consortium through the customer connection of a team member. In such cases, it is important that inventors direct reprisals not against team members, but against the customer of the team member who is not a direct member of the consortium.

When two or more enterprises own the right, it is necessary to secure all right owners' permission before exercising intellectual property rights. However, as it is unusual to permit the exercise of intellectual property rights towards the customer of a team member, rights are not, in fact, enforced in most real-life situations. The execution of intellectual property rights for consortiums thus becomes impossible as these rights divide the organization, leading to a relatively low business performance.

However, under P2M management, ownership of the intellectual property is given to the firm that sponsored the researcher who created the inventions, access authority is carefully limited among the team members, and access to intellectual properties in terms of rival enterprises are both considered with respect to the incentive of invention and cooperation. Thus, the intellectual property right can be exercised properly, and the contamination of information is avoided. Enterprises joining the project are selected by their intellectual property background, and the technological content, domain and aims are expected to be at the same level among researchers of the participating enterprises. This is the ideal combination between KPM and intellectual property management.

3.2.5 *Telecommunications*

The Mobile Computing Promotion Consortium (MCPC) is a completely different example of fourth-generation KPM in Japan. This consortium is private, and related companies participate on a completely voluntary basis. According to the secretary-general of MCPC, an important point is that, while there is a concrete and practical objective shared among members, there is only a general application of the KPM process.

Member companies vary among telecommunication carriers such as NTT Docomo, KDDI and Softbank; mobile phone manufacturing companies such as NEC, Fujitsu and Panasonic; application software developing companies; and any other companies related to the mobile phone system.

This consortium promotes developments in mobile phone services among member companies, such as One Seg, a service that allows users to watch television content with mobile phones. It is taken for granted that the consortium members share the common platform of mobile phone technology. This consortium also cooperates with US, European and Asian organizations related to mobile phones, including foreign embassies.

The management and development of such a private voluntary association can only be explained by complex theory, as it is completely opposite from the management of national consortiums. Although it is managed on a voluntary basis, member companies actively develop novel services using mobile phones and not only reform their own companies, but also reform the rules and systems for telecommunications usually managed by national governments.

4 Changing the Management Mindset

Management of the mechanism mentioned above, where intellectual properties are managed in the context of KPM, is the method currently in place. However, even if this mechanism is utilized, it cannot function if a manager's consideration pattern or "mindset" is unchanged. It is first necessary to acknowledge that fixed ideas and ways of thinking are no longer relevant and should be replaced; eventually, the whole system may be recognized in an integrated manner.

If, in accordance with Landes and Posner (2003), we also consider the idea stage as intellectual property, then the most important issue for intellectual property management in the context of KPM is how to reform the individual mindsets of those who invent and create application services through intellectual properties.

Psychological attitudes or mental tendencies that motivate an individual reaction to a certain situation, or "interpretations" that are fixed beforehand, are called the "mindset". This word is used to describe the paradigm that individuals or enterprises have during certain periods, especially researchers' patterns of thinking. Once the paradigm is identified, Kuhn (1962) recommends clarifying: (1) what should be observed and examined closely, (2) what questions should be asked, (3) how it should be organized, and (4) how the result should be interpreted. These points represent a chain or flowing pattern of thinking, and are also partly applicable to the business world. Thus, it is necessary for individuals in daily life to acknowledge a certain bias in their way of thinking in order to create reform through fourth-generation KPM.

References

Floyd, S. W. and Wooldridge, B. (2000). *Building Strategy from the Middle*, California: Sage Publications.

Krugman, P. (1996). *The Self-Organizing Economy*, Oxford: Blackwell Publishers.

Kuhn, T. S. (1962). *The Structure of Scientific Revolution*, Chicago: University of Chicago.

Landes, W. M. and Posner, R. A. (2003). *The Economic Structure of Intellectual Property Law*, Cambridge: Harvard University Press.

Nonaka, I. and Konno, N. (2003). *Methodology of Knowledge Creation*, Tokyo: Toyo Keizai Shinpo-sha.

Strategic R&D Management at NEDO (Japanese Public R&D Management Organization)

Shiro Okazaki

Director, Energy Conservation Technology Development Department
New Energy and Industrial Technology Development Organization

Yousuke Manabe

Research and Development, Project Evaluation Department
New Energy and Industrial Technology Development Organization

1   Introduction

The purpose of this paper is to provide an example of project and program management (P2M) formulation and implementation at a Japanese public R&D management organization, the New Energy and Industrial Technology Development Organization (NEDO). P2M is a Japanese approach to project and program management that was developed in 2001 as the first standard guide for education and certification. Specific characteristics of P2M include "mission-driven management of projects" and a program that generally harnesses the complexity of problem solving observed in the interface between technical systems and business models. It has provided a new way to consider less structured and more flexible topics addressing social and business needs compared to the conventional approaches of a well-structured system characterized by explicit goals and definitions. In this context, "project management" means "process management to realize certain goals and missions under certain conditions such as a finite time period, specific tasks and fixed resource constraints".

A "program" is a group of projects integrated under a single mission and, as such, is conceptually at a higher level than a project. In program management, holistic optimization of mission value supersedes the partial value of component projects, and top priority is given to a harmonized, comprehensive concept. Program management offers a pragmatic approach from mission orientation to future reality by developing multiple project models. From this point of view, this paper describes NEDO activities.

2 New Energy and Industrial Technology Development Organization (NEDO)

2.1 *Background*

The New Energy and Industrial Technology Development Organization (NEDO) was established by the Japanese government in 1980 to develop new oil-alternative energy technologies. Eight years later, in 1988, NEDO's activities were expanded to include industrial technology research and development, and in 1990, environmental technology research and development. Following its reorganization as an incorporated administrative agency in October 2003, NEDO is now also responsible for R&D project planning and formation, project management and post-project technology evaluation functions. As an incorporated administrative agency, NEDO is now better able to: (1) manage projects efficiently and effectively, and (2) make decisions independently and with increased accountability. Being an incorporated administrative agency has also allowed NEDO to improve and make more reasonable the terms and conditions of contracts with universities, enterprises and consortiums. For example, it is now possible to have "multi-year contracts", "multiple public solicitations over the course of one year", and to "accelerate, modify, and terminate projects".

Below is a brief history of NEDO as well as its mission. Figure 1 provides an overview of NEDO's organizational structure, and Table 1 shows NEDO's fiscal year 2006 and 2007 budgets.

History

1980: Established (New Energy Development Organization).
1988: Added industrial technology R&D (New Energy and Industrial Technology Development Organization).
1990: Added global environment R&D.
1993: Added promotion of new energy and energy conservation.
2000: Added support for private companies to strengthen international competitiveness.
2003: Reorganized as an "Incorporated Administrative Agency".

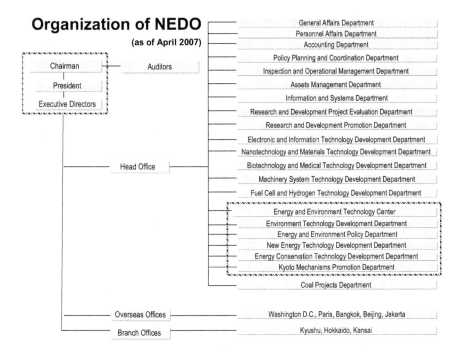

Organization of NEDO

(as of April 2007)

- Chairman — Auditors
- President
- Executive Directors

- Head Office
- Overseas Offices — Washington D.C., Paris, Bangkok, Beijing, Jakarta
- Branch Offices — Kyushu, Hokkaido, Kansai

- General Affairs Department
- Personnel Affairs Department
- Accounting Department
- Policy Planning and Coordination Department
- Inspection and Operational Management Department
- Assets Management Department
- Information and Systems Department
- Research and Development Project Evaluation Department
- Research and Development Promotion Department
- Electronic and Information Technology Development Department
- Nanotechnology and Materials Technology Development Department
- Biotechnology and Medical Technology Development Department
- Machinery System Technology Development Department
- Fuel Cell and Hydrogen Technology Development Department
- Energy and Environment Technology Center
- Environment Technology Development Department
- Energy and Environment Policy Department
- New Energy Technology Development Department
- Energy Conservation Technology Development Department
- Kyoto Mechanisms Promotion Department
- Coal Projects Department

Fig. 1   NEDO's organizational structure

NEDO's Mission

- Strategically prioritize and promote R&D projects on industrial, new energy, energy conservation and environmental technology by means of government, industry and academic cooperation.
- Contribute to solving energy and environmental problems.
- Obtain successful results through flexible operation management and stringent evaluation systems.
- Disseminate information about NEDO's activities and achievements to the public.

2.2   NEDO's role

2.2.1   Promotion of advanced technology R&D

NEDO is Japan's largest public organization for promoting the research and development of advanced industrial, new energy and environmental

Table 1   NEDO's FY2006 and FY2007 budgets (billion yen)

	FY2006	FY2007
R&D Projects	130.6	149.3
• Exploration of Industrial Seeds	6.7	5.9
• Mid- to Long-term/High Risk Research	105.7	125.3[1]
• Support for Practical Application	16.4	16.8
• Others	1.8	1.3
Introduction of New Energy and Energy Conservation	85.0	72.8[2]
• Fields Tests/Overseas Demonstrations	38.5	32.1
• Introduction and Dissemination	41.6	41.4
• Coal Resources Development Projects	4.9	4.6
Acquisition of Emission Reduction Credits through the Kyoto Mechanisms	5.4	12.9
Administrative	8.0	7.9
Total	229.0	216.5[3]

[1] This amount includes some funding for New Energy and Energy Conservation projects.
[2] This amount includes some funding for Mid- to Long-term/High Risk R&D projects.
[3] This amount of duplication in [1] and [2] above (31.7 billion yen) has been subtracted.

technologies. It also actively endeavors to disseminate such technologies. NEDO has no facilities or researchers of its own, as it manages contract research and development activities utilizing a funding allocation mechanism.

2.2.2   Comprehensive R&D management

NEDO focuses on bringing a professional management approach to research and development management, ranging from the cultivation of new technology seeds to the promotion of mid- to long-term projects and support for the development of practical applications.

2.2.3   Coordination of R&D

NEDO provides overall coordination based on an efficient and strategic R&D process so as to achieve superior research results in its projects, which involve the collective efforts of the industrial, academic and governmental

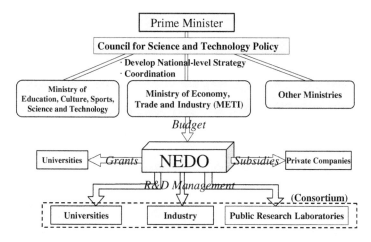

Fig. 2   Japan's R&D promotion scheme

sectors. Figure 2 shows Japan's R&D promotion scheme. Under the Prime Minister and Council for Science and Technology Policy, several ministries carry out R&D activities. NEDO's projects are mainly implemented under its budget provided by the Ministry of Economy, Trade and Industry (METI). NEDO is required to have the ability to coordinate various stakeholders.

2.3   *NEDO's activities*

2.3.1   *Research and development of leading-edge industrial technology*

There is a considerable amount of risk and uncertainty inherent to the development of industrial technology, and consequently, many research fields have not as yet been investigated by the private sector. NEDO undertakes government-funded leading-edge R&D projects that utilize an extensive network involving private sector industries, universities and public research institutes. In addition to national projects, NEDO supports activities over a wide range of development stages, including research that may lead to industrial precursor technologies and commercial development by private sector firms. The R&D fields include:

- Biotechnology
- Information technology

- Nanotechnology
- Environmental technology
- Machinery technology
- Medical technology
- Chemical substance management
- Aeronautical technology
- Robotics technology.

2.3.2   Research, development and dissemination of new energy and energy conservation technologies

The development of new energy and energy conservation technologies is essential for realizing clean energy sources that can help reduce the amount of carbon dioxide and other greenhouse gases released into the atmosphere. NEDO has achieved considerable success in developing innovative technologies for solar energy systems and fuel cell power generation. Through the implementation of field tests and various types of promotion and support projects, it has also played an important role in the introduction and dissemination of new energy and energy conservation technologies throughout Japan. The R&D fields include:

- Fuel cell and hydrogen technology
- Photovoltaic technology
- Biomass technology
- Energy conservation technology.

2.3.3   Introduction and popularization of new energy and energy conservation technologies

In order to effectively and efficiently introduce and popularize new energy and energy conservation programs, NEDO provides integrated support over three development stages: technological development, empirical verification, and introduction and popularization. Through the implementation of field tests and various types of promotion and support projects, NEDO plays an important role in the introduction and popularization of new energy and energy conservation technologies in Japan and abroad. Figure 3 shows the trinity approach of NEDO's activities.

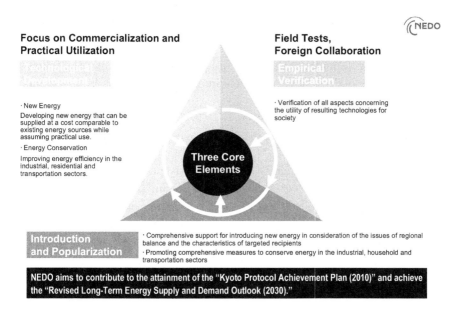

Fig. 3   Trinity approach of NEDO's activities

2.4   *International projects*

Through various projects involving R&D and the dissemination of industrial, energy conservation and new energy technologies, NEDO also undertakes the following international activities.

2.4.1   *Improving technological advantages*

NEDO has the following programs to effectively utilize leading researchers and the capabilities and experience of enterprises in the area of leading-edge industrial technologies:

- A grant program that provides awards to young researchers or teams of young researchers;
- A research program to conduct feasibility studies for international joint research projects;
- A grant program that provides awards to international research teams;
- A cooperative research program that allows foreign-based research institutes and/or private sector companies to participate.

2.4.2   Addressing energy and environmental issues in developing countries

NEDO is using Japanese technology and know-how to conduct the following projects to address energy and environmental problems in developing countries:

- Cooperative research projects with research laboratories in various countries;
- Model projects to demonstrate the effectiveness of new energy and environmental technologies developed in Japan;
- Demonstration projects for photovoltaic power generation systems used under various climatic and social conditions;
- Demonstration projects for stabilized and advanced grid-connected photovoltaic systems to prepare for the future large-scale introduction of new energy solutions;
- Feasibility studies for greenhouse gas emission reduction projects under the Kyoto Protocol's Clean Development Mechanism (CDM) and Joint Implementation (JI) schemes (Kyoto Mechanisms).

2.4.3   Approaches to Kyoto Mechanisms projects

In addition to conducting feasibility studies for Kyoto Mechanisms projects (international cooperative projects to minimize greenhouse gas emissions such as CO_2), NEDO continues to promote support for the creation of Kyoto Mechanisms implementation systems in developing countries. Moreover, using the knowledge accumulated through its projects, NEDO began in 2006 to undertake tasks for the acquisition of Kyoto Mechanisms credits generated by overseas projects that reduce greenhouse gas emissions.

3   Project and Program Formulation and Implementation at NEDO

3.1   Strategic Technology Roadmap (STR)

The purpose of Strategic Technology Roadmap (STR) formulation is as follows:

(1) METI and NEDO seek public understanding by providing an explanation of the perspective, details and achievements of R&D investments.

(2) METI and NEDO seek to understand technological and market trends, prioritize critical technologies, and develop a policy infrastructure for planning R&D projects.

(3) In order to respond to specialized technologies as well as diversified market and social needs, METI promotes alliances across different fields and industries, technology fusion, and coordinated implementation of relevant policies, and also seeks to harness the combined and comprehensive strengths of industry, academia and public institutions.

The STR consists of three elements: (1) Scenario for Introduction, (2) Technology Overview, and (3) Roadmap (Figure 4):

(1) The Scenario for Introduction includes relevant policies that should be dealt with in order to provide the public with the results of R&D in the form of products and services.

(2) Prioritized critical technologies are described in the Technology Overview, together with relevant technological challenges, elemental technologies and desired functions in order to satisfy market and social needs.

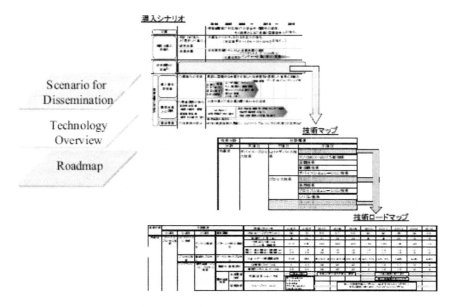

Fig. 4   Structure of strategic technology roadmap

(3) Improvement and progress of elemental technologies generated from R&D, and the enhancement of desired functions, are presented on a time axis as milestones in the Roadmap.

Based on the STR, NEDO formulates projects and programs with a strategic intent.

3.2 *Project and program management process and implementation*

3.2.1 *Project management cycle*

NEDO's project management cycle includes R&D project evaluation and the reflection of evaluation results in future activities. The R&D project evaluation cycle includes a pre-project evaluation, an intermediate evaluation, a post-project evaluation, and follow-up monitoring and evaluation. Figure 5 shows the concept of NEDO's project management cycle.

In an effort to achieve superior research results, NEDO undertakes the following:

- R&D for the purpose of commercialization. If necessary, basic research will be revisited in order to identify breakthroughs.
- Ongoing communication with companies and universities in order to stay abreast of needs in various R&D fields.
- Selection and focus on R&D themes and R&D organizations (companies and universities).
- Identification of crossover applications among different technologies. For example, matching R&D of materials with R&D of electronic devices.

NEDO has also improved contractual terms and conditions to make them more reasonable for R&D organizations (companies and universities). For example,

- Prior to 2003, only single-year contracts were possible. Since 2003, however, multiple-year contracts have been possible, allowing long-term commitments and flexible financing for R&D budgets.

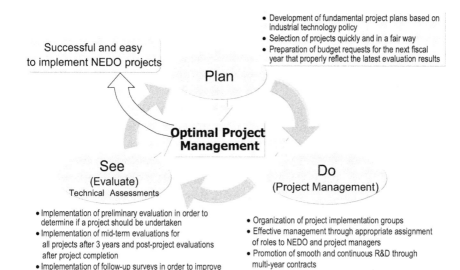

Fig. 5   Plan-do-see approach to optimal project management

- Contractual procedural requirements were simplified to allow R&D organizations (companies and universities) to devote themselves to R&D.

3.2.2   *Pre-project evaluation*

After R&D project planning, NEDO evaluates the adequacy of the project's target, competitor benchmarking, and project formation among players. A pre-project evaluation has the following three phases:

(1)   *Phase 1*
      During pre-screening, NEDO mainly examines a candidate project in terms of its adaptability to NEDO's mission.
(2)   *Phase 2*
      After Phase 1, NEDO evaluates the fundamental scheme of a project in detail.
(3)   *Phase 3*
      After Phase 2, NEDO develops a fundamental scheme for a project. Concurrently, NEDO solicits public opinion by means of an extensive

posting system and considers public comments regarding R&D project planning.

3.2.3 Mid-term evaluation

NEDO evaluates ongoing projects at the midpoint of the research term. For example, in a five-year project, a mid-term evaluation is conducted in the third year. Regarding mid-term and post-project evaluations, the evaluation processes are characterized by external evaluators, open panel discussions involving project participants, simplified evaluation perspectives with sets of criteria, and quantitative evaluation with a simple rating method. This is expected to contribute to ensuring the transparency, explicitness, effectiveness, neutrality and simplicity of the evaluation work. During an evaluation, a project is assessed and evaluated from four perspectives: (1) political positioning and necessity, (2) project management, (3) R&D achievements, and (4) prospects for practical application and other impacts. Mid-term evaluations may result in a modification or termination of projects (Table 2).

Acceleration of a project involves additional research investment in a project that has achieved remarkable achievements of a high level. In order for a project to be accelerated, it is necessary that the project meet one of the following four key conditions:

(1) hold a dominant position compared with global competitors;
(2) rapidly catch-up with a new discovery or new trend;
(3) establish fundamental patents and global standards; and

Table 2   Responses to mid-term evaluation results

	2001	2002	2003	2004	2005	2006
Accelerated	—	—	2	13	3	2
Continued as planned	4	2	12	12	1	1
Modified	16	6	15	6	5	4
Terminated	2	5	2	2	0	0
Total	22	13	29*	29*	6*	5*

* Due to overlapping, sum does not match total.

(4) rapidly undertake R&D on new themes, and cope with changes in R&D trends or social needs.

3.2.4 *Post-project evaluation*

Post-project evaluations are conducted to derive lessons for R&D management. The concepts behind this approach are as follows:

(1) Systematize a concept for NEDO R&D project management to share the same terminology among NEDO staff.
(2) Compile management know-how to share the experiences that NEDO has accumulated.
(3) Provide checklists to all NEDO staff so as not to repeat the mistakes of the past.

The lifecycle of NEDO projects is defined on the basis of six phases, and multi-checkpoints are utilized for project management. The checklists are included for each phase, and checklists for each phase are made available to NEDO staff. Figure 6 shows the R&D evaluation methodology (rating method) for projects.

3.2.5 *Follow-up monitoring and evaluation*

NEDO monitors the post-project activities of project participants to ensure the practical application of R&D results and to assess the impact of national R&D projects. On the other hand, NEDO reviews past post-project evaluations in view of post-project activities and utilizes any resulting feedback for improving R&D management.

NEDO has to demonstrate the benefits of its activities to taxpayers, and outcome surveys are required to show the accountability of its activities. In terms of the benefit of NEDO activities, photovoltaic (PV) technology R&D is one of the most remarkable cases. Solar energy is one of several promising clean energy sources that may contribute to a stable energy supply and mitigate global environmental problems. The Japanese government has thus been promoting PV R&D, production and dissemination through such initiatives as the so-called "Sunshine Project". As a result, Japan is the world leader in PV production and has the second highest installed capacity in the world.

Mid-Term & Post-Project Evaluations

R&D Evaluation Methodology (Rating Method)

1. Either A, B, C or D is given for each perspective by each evaluator.
A: Excellent, B: Good, C: Acceptable, D: Not acceptable
2. An average of evaluator ratings is used as an indicator.
A=3, B=2, C=1, D=0

(Example)

Perspectives for Evaluation	Average	Ratings					
1. Political Positioning and Necessity	2.3	A	A	B	B	B	B
2. Project Management	1.8	A	B	C	B	C	B
3. R&D Achievement	1.5	B	C	C	C	B	B
4. Prospect for Practical Applications and Other Impacts	1.2	B	B	D	C	C	C

How to Summarize the Scores (comparison with other projects)

Score Results of Post-Project Evaluation

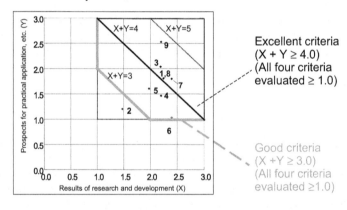

Fig. 6   R&D evaluation methodology

4   Conclusion

NEDO is contributing to the ongoing development of advanced technology. In order to sustain economic development, a number of issues must be considered and addressed. These include the establishment of R&D strategies that emphasize specific targets, the development of methodologies and systems to allow frontrunners to overcome obstacles that hinder the generation of technological innovations, and the practical exploitation of R&D results. These issues need to be addressed in a timely and appropriate manner. From this point of view, project and program management formulation and implementation are particularly essential for NEDO management.

References

NEDO reference materials.

Ohara, S. (2004). *A Guidebook of Project & Program Management for Enterprise Innovation (Revision 2)*, P2M ENAA Committee, PMCC Japan.

Ohara, S. (2005). Profiling mission-driven management for complex projects or programs — Explaining the new framework and its background, IPMA International Congress in Delhi.

Pharmaceutical Development as Case Study with High-Risk, High-Return Project Management

Koji Iwasaki

Manager, Pharmaceutical Development Division
Takeda Pharmaceutical Company Limited

1 Introduction

The process of research and development of new medical pharmaceuticals involves the following steps. A compound that is selected after passing from the initial screening stage (basic genetic research, identification of target molecules, discovery of seed/lead compounds), through drug efficacy evaluation (optimization of pharmacodynamic effect, evaluation of safety), pharmacokinetics and other non-clinical tests, is administered to humans and studied. Normally at this stage, specialists including doctors and pharmacologists as well as non-specialists determine the suitability of the drug, taking ethics into account. The safety and pharmacokinetics of compounds that can be administered to humans are confirmed in a phase 1 clinical trial using healthy adult male volunteers. Then, in phase 2 clinical trials, the dose amount is optimized for efficacy and safety on patients who are to be treated with the compound, and in phase 3 clinical trials the results are verified. Research into industrializing the compound (studies into dosage form, methods of manufacturing, methods of quality control) is started from before the time the drug is administered to humans, and this research proceeds in parallel with the non-clinical and clinical trials.

A Common Technical Document (CTD) that summarizes the results of the non-clinical, clinical and industrial research is prepared, and applications are made to each national and local Competent Authority. After undergoing strict assessment, approval for manufacturing and marketing is obtained, and the drug is marketed (Figure 1).

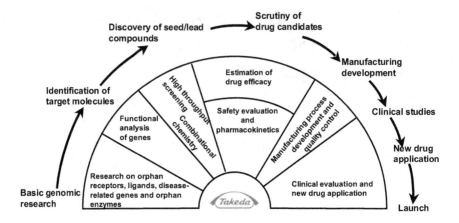

Fig. 1   Research and development process of pharmaceutical products

Note: Research on Orphan Receptors: It is known that the binding of a ligand to a receptor on the cell surface can cause the cell to display various types of bioactivity. Receptors whose ligands have not yet been identified are called orphan receptors. Researching functions of orphan receptors opens up the possibility for discovering novel receptor antagonists or agonists, which are expected to become innovative new drugs. Currently, about half of the world's bestselling pharmaceuticals act on receptors. One of Takeda's approaches in basic research is to study orphan receptors (receptors with unknown functions). Our unique approach consists of using the genetic information for orphan receptors to search for their endogenous ligands. This approach has already led to some significant findings.

Source: Drug Discovery Processes, Takeda Pharmaceutical Company Limited (http://www.takeda.com/research/drug-discovery/article_1050.html).

Therefore, an important point in the clinical development stage, which has an important function of clarifying the product profile, is for management strategy to be able to take the Go/No go decision as early as possible from the viewpoint of cost effectiveness.

2   Pharmaceutical Development as a High-Risk and High-Return Project Management

Pharmaceutical development can be considered to be a program of several organically connected projects to realize the overall mission. By trying to understand how the ambiguity, expandability, complexity and uncertainty, which are basic attributes of the fundamental framework that constitutes the program, apply to the development of new pharmaceuticals, we arrive at the following.

Ambiguities include the fact that the development of new pharmaceuticals is a very public activity that directly affects the health and welfare of the people, so it is not possible to consider pursuing corporate profit alone. Also, each country enforces detailed and strict regulatory requirements for safety, efficacy and quality through their Competent Authority, etc. Regarding expandability, a disease that formerly required surgery could become one that can be completely cured with drugs, as a result of the arrival on the market of a groundbreaking new drug, so that the method of treatment itself changes. Also, there are many examples that have resulted in significant savings in medical costs. Complexities can include the fact that several separate projects, i.e., the basic trials and clinical trials, must be implemented in order to create a new drug, as stated above. Also, regardless of the fact that the development of a new drug requires a large upfront investment, the probability that a candidate compound will pass through the stages where it can be administered to humans to receiving approval from the regulatory Competent Authority is less than 1%, so the uncertainties are very high.

How can program management be used as a method for solving these problems?

3　Program Management and Program Architecture of Clinical Trials

Based on the basic requirements of program profiling and scenarios, program architecture is the grand design of basic structure, total function and basic operability to realize these in program management (Ohara, 2006).

3.1　*Basic structure*

In the basic structure, the program is divided into several projects, and the interfaces and relationships between these projects are coordinated.

In clinical development, the basic structure for each new candidate compound (seed) consists of phase 1 in which the drug is first administered to healthy adults, phase 2 in which the drug is first administered to people having the disease (referred to as patients) to derive the appropriate dose, and phase 3 which verifies the safety and efficacy (Figure 2).

The trials in each phase can be divided into processes such as start-up, implementation control and close-out. The project is executed by a study

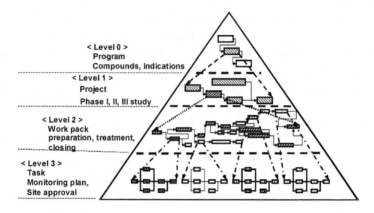

Fig. 2   Basic structure of clinical trial

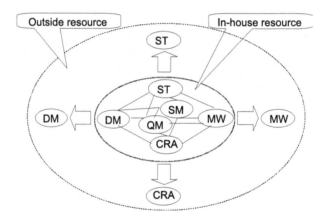

Fig. 3   Members of clinical trial team

manager who manages the project, a monitor (CRA; Clinical Research Associate), a statistical analyst (ST), a data manager (DM), a medical writer (MW) and other members (Figure 3).

3.1.1 *Modularity*

For clinical trials, the processes can be modularized for each stage of progress (Figure 4) for each member, starting with the study manager (SM).

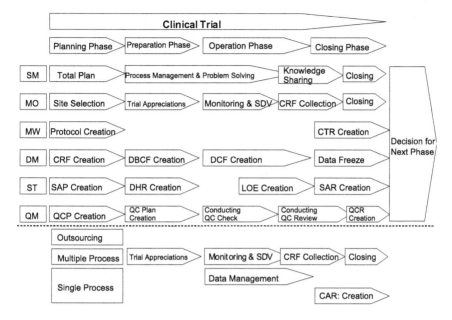

Fig. 4   Modularity of clinical trial project

Notes: SM: Study Manager, Mo: Monitor (CRA), MW: Medical Writer, DM: Data Manager, ST: Statistician, QM: Quality Manager, DBCF: Data Base Clarification Form, ACP: Analysis Clarification Plan, SAR: Statistical Analysis Report, DCF: Data Collection Log Form.

It is possible to visualize the work processes necessary in clinical trials, such as the monitoring process, the data management process, the statistical analysis process, the medical writing process, etc., with a work breakdown structure (WBS) that breaks down the overall work. Each process can be modularized, and modularized processes can be outsourced.

Monitoring work is defined as the inspection by the clinical trial sponsor of the institution implementing the trials, to determine whether the trials are being implemented in accordance with good clinical practice (GCP) and the clinical study protocol, in order to ensure that the clinical trials are carried out properly. Also, the work content of the monitor (CRA) who carries out the monitoring work is prescribed in detail by the standard operating procedures (SOP) of each pharmaceutical company. For each clinical trial, it is possible to visualize the preparation, commissioning, implementation and completion of each process as the start-up, implementation and conclusion processes in project management.

The data management work includes the design of a case report form (CRF) on which the data manager (DM) records the results of the clinical trials, the design of a database for inputting the content of the CRF, a data interface, and an input data edit check program, data cleaning and other processes. These processes can be divided into parts that can be standardized using a template and parts that must be customized for each trial, so these processes are the most clear and modularized.

The statistical analysis work is mainly the analysis of the results of the trial by a statistician based on a statistical analysis plan. This work can be modularized to a certain extent by opening the database structure when using standard statistical methods using package software such as SAS® or similar, simple analysis.

The medical writing work (MW) is mainly preparation of clinical study protocols for clinical trials, clinical study reports and common technical documents (CTD). Templates can be made for these documents, and all or part of these documents can be modularized.

3.1.2   Interface and integration

For overall optimization, it is necessary to clarify the relationships between each module and coordinate their respective interfaces. If each work process is modularized within the monitoring work, these relationships will frequently be clarified. Coordination of interfaces is easy, but if the associated departments or work content is different, this coordination can become difficult.

For example, in the data management work, in the clean-up of the case report forms (CRF), it is necessary to coordinate the interfaces with the monitor (CRA) who visits the medical institution and carries out source document verification (SDV), the quality manager (QM) who checks their content, and the data manager (DM) who standardizes the work using electric data capturing (EDC) utilizing data collecting forms (DCF) and discrepancy lists (DL) with a unified format.

3.2   Total function

3.2.1   Development of basic specification and modular project

The basic specification of pharmaceutical development is the implementation of the series of clinical trials from phase 1 through phase 3 (Figure 5),

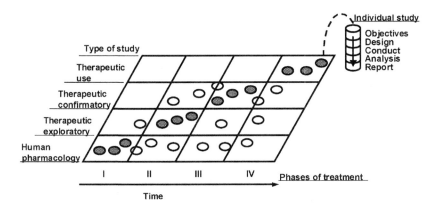

Fig. 5   Correlation between development phases and types of study

Note: This matrix graph illustrates the relationship between the phases of development and types of study by objective that may be conducted during each clinical developing of a new medicinal product. The shaded circles show the types of study most usually conducted in a certain phase of development, while the open circles show types of study that may be conducted in that phase of development but are less usual. Each circle represents an individual study. To illustrate the development of a single study, one circle is joined by a dotted line to an inset column that depicts the elements and sequence of an individual study.

and from the results of the trials to clarify the product profile of the seed compound as a pharmaceutical (ICH Topic E8, 1998).

Developing this into the necessary modular projects, we can broadly classify the trials as standardized clinical trials such as single dose studies, multiple dose studies, proof of concept studies, dose ranging studies, randomized clinical trials and long-term trials, and customized trials for which customization of the seed compound that is to become the product is necessary such as pharmacological studies, and special population studies for the elderly, patients with impaired liver function, patients with renal dysfunction, etc. (Figure 6).

Here, apart from the initial administration during phase 1, several clinical trials proceed in parallel throughout each phase until phase 3. As stated previously, in each clinical trial, the process cycle is preparation, commissioning, implementation and summarizing.

3.2.2   Integration of clinical trial processes

If several clinical trials are proceeding in parallel within the same phase, it can be effective to integrate their processes. For example, in phase 3,

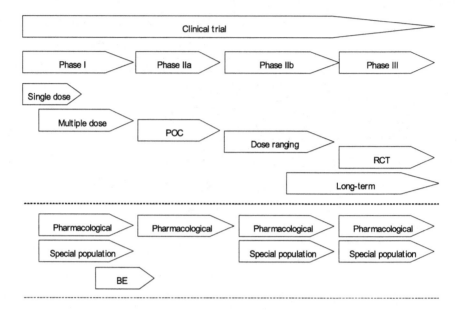

Fig. 6   Example of clinical trial concurrently executed

Notes: POC: Proof of Concept Study, BE: Bioequivalent Study, RCT: Randomized Clinical Trial.

randomized clinical trials and long-term trials proceed simultaneously. In this case, efficiency can be achieved by integrating the work processes of each participant, such as preparation of the clinical study protocol by the MW, arranging the medical institution for carrying out the trials by the CRA, CRF design and DB design by the DM, etc.

3.3   *Basic operability*

For basic operability, a program operation guide and process table (program road map) is created, and by carrying out simulations regarding reduction in progress due to changed circumstances or increases in restricting conditions, etc., taking into consideration the assumed conditions and postulations for the overall scenarios, a design that increases the potential for achieving the program is embraced.

3.3.1   *Program road map*

Before starting a project, the study manager (SM) uses a project management tool such as Microsoft Project® for scheduling each process of the clinical trials and planning resource allocation, to create the program road map. Further, the details of the program road map are communicated to all the stakeholders, including the project members, using a kick-off meeting or similar communication means. When drawing up the overall program concept, it is necessary to allow sufficient time for scenarios that can arise.

3.4 *Grand design*

The grand design is the overall program story, including the restricting conditions, etc., summarized so that the overall optimum can be obtained, prepared by the SM or the project office. In particular, in pharmaceutical development, the results of many clinical trials are summarized, and an application is made to the Competent Authority for approval. Therefore, from this stage, it is necessary to clarify the product profile of the pharmaceutical to a certain extent. To clarify the product profile, it is necessary to accurately determine the requirements of actual medical treatment sites, in addition to scientifically studying the results of animal trials, etc., obtained in the basic research stage. Furthermore, pharmaceutical development takes a long time, e.g., 5 to 10 years, so inferring the circumstances at medical treatment sites 5 or 10 years hence is required. Also, by preparing a decision tree for each of the predicted outcomes that can be obtained from the planned clinical trials, it is possible to visualize in advance the content of decisions at each milestone, and prepare a grand design capable of responding in a timely manner to changes in circumstances.

4 The Future of Clinical Development

4.1 *Organizational correspondence to modularity and globalization*

Here, we consider how a pharmaceutical company responds to changes in the architecture. Pharmaceutical companies are modularizing and globalizing clinical development, which was previously a closed and integral situation (Kneller, 2003). A line axis organization focused on functions such as statistical analysis, data management, clinical development, medical writing, etc., was strong. However, recently, more and more pharmaceutical companies are effectively using project axes based on seed compound or clinical trial units. On the other hand, several problem points have become clear, such as the highly specialized and particular characteristics of each functional organization, and the inability to secure sufficient resources for the project system.

To resolve the conflict between the project axis and the line axis, pharmaceutical companies are appearing with a flexible organizational response, by for example establishing a project management office (PMO) and appointing a core leader. In particular, the core leader is a senior manager experienced as either a line axis leader or a project axis leader. A core leader of this type is not in a position of rivalry in a matrix organization, but plays an important role in forming a cooperative relationship in the organizational culture.

4.2   Creation of program value and the added value of clinical development for the enterprise

Clinical development is the application of a seed compound discovered in basic research to humans, and the clarification of its product profile as a pharmaceutical. In general, two points can be considered regarding creating value as a program.

The first is the limitation to modularization and globalization. In other words, to what extent is it possible in clinical development to modularize each process in several clinical trials proceeding in parallel? Also, how much is it possible to globalize each process? To what extent can pharmaceutical companies visualize clinical development processes, that to date have been closed as corporate secrets, and share each visualized process?

If processes can be visualized, then it is possible to set quality criteria for each process. Then, it would be possible to introduce a development improvement process. In other words, for each project, deliverables are output without changing the quality criteria given for each process, and improvement of problem points in the development process are proposed at the stage of feedback to the overall mission. This can be groundbreaking if the overall mission is reviewed as a result of this improvement process, and the proposals for changing the overall processes are recognized by the owner of the program.

The second point is how to draw up the grand design to realize clinical development as a program, based on basic requirements from scenarios for clarifying the product profile for applying for and obtaining approval from the Competent Authority, by reviewing from a high standpoint and with a broad vision each modularized and globalized project and its processes. As stated previously regarding the characteristics of clinical development, both scientific and ethical decisions are required at pharmaceutical development milestones where there is much uncertainty.

Program management which deals with complex projects can be applied in stages to this problem. Firstly, in defining program management, programs for each pharmaceutical CTD or programs for each therapeutic area can be considered (Figure 7).

In a pharmaceutical-specific CTD program, many non-clinical trials and clinical trials proceed in parallel. In the case of a pharmaceutical in the field of lifestyle-related diseases, it is necessary to strategically verify efficacy and safety over a period of more than five years through a combination of 20 to 30 trials to develop a single drug. A single trial requires from a few months to about a year to implement, and preparation and conclusion also each take several months. Electronic data capture (EDC) is used as the method of electronically collecting the clinical data acquired during the period of implementation of clinical trials.

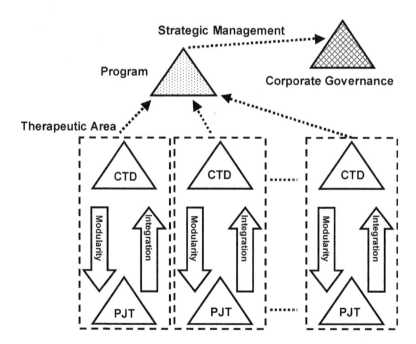

Fig. 7   Strategic drug development using program management
Notes: CTD: Common Technical Document, PJT: Project.

EDC is a system in which the investigator carrying out the clinical trials or the clinical research coordinator (CRC) electronically reports the clinical data to the clinical trials sponsor. Using EDC, clinical trial data can be collected in a timely manner. In the past, paper case reports were used, so it was necessary for the investigator or the CRC to input data to the case reports which were then collected by the monitor (CRA), and the data manager (DM) would input the data in order for the sponsor to obtain the clinical data in detail. However, by introducing EDC, the sponsor has access to the detailed clinical data at the same time that the investigator or CRC inputs data. In this way, it is possible to easily detect the occurrence of adverse events or deviations in the population group during the course of the trials, or detect deviations from the population assumed during planning, or carry out a blind review for efficacy. By using this system, it is possible to carry out adaptive trial design by making small modifications to the plan, so that it is possible to increase the probability of achieving the objectives (Borfitz, 2006; Golub, 2006; Welker, 2007). Also, it is possible to more effectively plan the next trials while the current trial is being implemented. When establishing the plan, program management that integrates the obtained modularized data based on the overall mission is effective (Schindler, 2006).

Furthermore, in a therapeutic area having several pipelines, these pharmaceutical-specific CTD programs can be regarded as development projects, and the overall area can be defined as an area program. In a company having several candidate compounds for treatment of diabetes, each compound is managed, including the value created when the compound is released to the market.

By using the concept of program management integrated with the latest IT technology such as EDC in pharmaceutical development, it is possible to shorten development times, improve development efficiency and gain competitive advantage. Specifically, it is important to improve the accuracy of the grand design as a program. For this purpose, it is necessary to implement the basic structure, total function and basic operability as an accommodating design power. In particular, it is necessary to assign the structure and function by dividing the work into processes and creating the project model based on the strategy and vision, and if necessary, to provide feedback into the overall mission. What is advocated is a knowledge-based system of groundbreaking program management that aims for an effective method of implementing innovation, development and improvement based on global competition in a knowledge-based service society (Ohara, 2007). By practically using this knowledge-based system, it is possible to maintain competitive advantage.

References

Borfitz, D. (2006). Forecast: EDC money-making shifts to phase II trials, *Bio-IT World Magazine*, December, pp. 1–3.

Golub, H. L. (2006). The need for more efficient trial designs, *Statistics in Medicine* 25, pp. 3231–3235.

ICH Topic E8 (1998). General considerations for clinical trials, Note for Guidance on General Considerations for Clinical Trials (CPMP/ICH/291/95), pp. 1–13.

Kneller, R. (2003). Autarkic drug discovery in Japanese pharmaceutical companies: Insights into national differences in industrial innovation, *Research Policy* 32, pp. 1805–1827.

Ohara, S. (2006). Mission-driven approach (MDA) of management complex projects — Demystifying the new framework and its background, *Journal of the International Association of Project & Program Management* 1, pp. 61–70.

Ohara, S. (2007). The fourth-generation type Japanese project management — Synergetic integration of innovation, development and improvement, in *Proceedings of the Second National Conference of International Association of Project & Program Management*, Tokyo.

Schindler, J. (2006). Adaptive clinical trial design: How to lower costs and shorten product development cycles, FDAnews Audio Conference, 31 October.

Welker, J. A. (2007). Implementation of electronic data capture systems: Barriers and solutions, *Contemporary Clinical Trials* 28(3), pp. 329–336.

The Product Development Project Aiming at the "Sociality" of Commodities

Ninako Makino

Professor, Faculty of Business Administration
Momoyama Gakuin University

1 Introduction

Today, environmental problems are very important. Therefore, "environmentally-friendly commodities" are developed in a variety of fields, such as cars and houses. In the household electrical appliance such as refrigerators and washing machines, we also find a lot of "environmentally-friendly commodities".

It is not only "environmentally-friendly commodities" that contain "environmental" considerations as a commodity characteristic. Since all commodities are necessarily related to environmental problems in various ways, for instance energy problems, garbage problems and so on, it can be said that all commodities contain "environment" as a commodity characteristic.

"Safety" can be said to be a commodity characteristic similar to "environment". That is, "environment" and "safety" are the commodity characteristics which indicate the social responsibility to be fulfilled by all commodities.

In this paper, such a commodity characteristic as the social responsibility is called the "sociality" of the commodity. In a word, "sociality" is a characteristic that all commodities should have. When a company notes this "sociality" of commodities, a new business opportunity arises and new competition occurs between the companies.

Up to now, the new competition raised by "sociality" has been watched as the new competition for environmental technology occurred among automakers when the emissions regulation was executed. In this paper, we do not study such a company competition. We study the new type of cooperation between companies that arises when "sociality" of the commodities is pursued (Makino and Asada, 2005). This new type of cooperation between companies has not been studied in the organization relational models of the past (Astley and Fombrun, 1983; Evan, 1972; Levine and White, 1961; Pfeffer and Salancik, 1978; Williamson, 1975).

Although there are some differences in the framework and aspect between the organization relational models mentioned above, they have one common point: in each model of the past, every organization strives to improve its own profit by using cooperation. That is, the purpose of the cooperation is to improve one's own profit by using other parties of cooperation. Such a conventional type of cooperation can be called "bargaining cooperation".

What is the purpose of the new type of cooperation in improving "sociality" of the commodity? The new purpose is to develop the common profits through collaboration with the partner company, and consequentially improving one's own profit.

The important point in this new type of cooperation is that each company does not adhere to its own aspect, but moves from its own aspect to the upper-level aspect. In this new cooperation, a company cannot make its own profit without making the profits of other parties of cooperation. In that sense, the new cooperation can be called a "win–win cooperation".

Here we have two questions. The first question is why such new type of cooperation appears when "sociality" of the commodities is pursued. The second question is connected with the balance between competition and cooperation. In the same industry, how can companies that collaborate deeply compete?

The purpose of this paper is to solve these two questions, using a case study of cooperation concerning product development and sales between companies in the non-fluorocarbon refrigerator industry.

2 The Product Development Project of Non-Fluorocarbon Refrigerators

2.1 The start of the product development project of non-fluorocarbon refrigerators

The company analyzed in this case study is Company A, which is a well-known leading company of the household electrical appliance industry in Japan. This Company A succeeded in developing non-fluorocarbon refrigerators with the cooperation of other companies in 2002.

This case study analyzes this development process of non-fluorocarbon refrigerators. The facts and the quoted comments are based on the hearing investigation executed in Company A (date of the interview: March–April 2004).

Generally, the refrigerator absorbs heat by "refrigerant" (gas for cooling), and keeps the low temperature by "insulation". In the refrigerators, fluorocarbon gas has been used for both this refrigerant and the insulation.

Recently, however, we have understood that this fluorocarbon destroys the ozonosphere when the refrigerator is dumped and the gas is discharged into the air. This is linked to the serious environmental problem of global warming.

Then, the refrigerator using hydro-chlorofluorocarbon for both the refrigerant and the insulation instead of fluorocarbon appeared. Undoubtedly, hydro-chlorofluorocarbon does not destroy the ozonosphere, but we found that this hydro-chlorofluorocarbon is also harmful to global warming. Thus, the development of the "non-fluorocarbon refrigerator" not using hydro-chlorofluorocarbon for the refrigerant and the insulation was needed.

In Germany, which is the leading country in the environmental problems, Foron Co. began the sales of non-fluorocarbon refrigerators with the charge from GP (green peas: environmental groups) and the support of the German government in 1992. This non-fluorocarbon refrigerator, however, also had a big problem related to the hydrocarbon gas used as the refrigerant substituting for the fluorocarbon gas.

For the refrigerant substituting for the fluorocarbon gas, there are a lot of candidates like ammonia, carbon dioxide, and so on. Because the most efficient material is hydrocarbon gas, the hydrocarbon gas is preferred among them. Unfortunately, this hydrocarbon gas is combustible. In 1992, the safety standard concept for a combustible refrigerant applied to the refrigerator had not been established yet.

The safety problem of this combustible refrigerant is a serious problem for the appliance makers. When a fire breaks out in the home, the refrigerator has often been suspected as the first cause of the fire. Therefore, if the refrigerator uses the combustible refrigerant, it would be suspected further as the first cause of the fire.

Moreover, after the Product Liability Law had been enacted in 1995 in Japan, the manufacturers had to bear the accountability of the accident. For instance, Company A manufactures five million refrigerators a year. Therefore, the risk of producing refrigerators that used a combustible refrigerant has become very high for the appliance maker.

Thus, the appliance maker thought as follows:

We should make non-fluorocarbon refrigerators in the future. But, neither a safety standard nor various concerned laws have been maintained yet. Therefore, the consumer might not buy non-fluorocarbon refrigerators. We should not make non-fluorocarbon refrigerators now.

Environmentalists (GP or green peas), however, made an impact on such appliance makers in Japan. The Kyoto Conference on Climate Change (COP3) was held in December 1997, and hydro-chlorofluorocarbon was specified as a material to be restrained. Then, GP sent open letters with the following content to eight appliance makers in Japan in March 1998: "Do you have the plan to produce the refrigerator that uses neither HFC nor HCFC (a kind of the hydro-chlorofluorocarbon gas)?"

Only Company A answered this open letter. Company A began to put in serious efforts to be the earliest to tackle the non-fluorocarbon refrigerators among the eight appliance makers. It changed the refrigerant material to hydro-chlorofluorocarbon in 1993, and the heat insulator material to non-fluorocarbon in 1994.

Due to strong and frequent requests from GP, Company A (the person in charge of the refrigerator sector) could not help promising to GP in December 1999 that the "non-fluorocarbon refrigerators will be put on the market by the end of 2002".

At that time, the members in Company A felt puzzled:

To tell the truth, we were embarrassed, because there were a lot of problems that had to be cleared for non-fluorocarbon refrigerator sales. The failure of the refrigerator is not excused. It will be connected with the lowering reputation of the entire Company A. This decision to start the production of non-fluorocarbon refrigerators was, so to speak, an ultimate decision. Consequentially, the strong appeal of GP became an important incentive to develop non-fluorocarbon refrigerators for Company A. The development of non-fluorocarbon refrigerators would only have taken place four or five years later without the strong appeal of GP.

Development and sales of non-fluorocarbon refrigerators advanced rapidly with the request of GP, as promised by the person in Company A. Company A announced non-fluorocarbon refrigerator sales in October

2002, and began sales in February 2003. The key for the success of this non-fluorocarbon refrigerator development was the new type of cooperation between various organizations.

2.2 The cooperation between various companies led to the success in the development

To develop and sell non-fluorocarbon refrigerators, suppliers had to first guarantee the safety of the refrigerators. The following three measures were adopted for safety of combustible refrigerants in Company A. The first measure was to decrease the amount of refrigerant. Company A has decreased the amount of refrigerant from 100 to 58 grams. The second measure was to design so as not to let the gas leak. Company A has decreased the welding parts of pipes in the cooler. The third measure was to devise the design so as not to ignite when the gas does leak. The refrigerator in Japan used the glass tube heater to defrost automatically. Company A made this glass tube with double glazing.

These technological improvements alone, however, were not enough to realize non-fluorocarbon refrigerator sales. There would be various problems at each stage of the refrigerator lifecycle (from design to recycling) when combustible refrigerant is used. For instance, if combustible refrigerant is used, attention is needed in the stage when the refrigerator parts are recycled. Therefore, to attain non-fluorocarbon refrigerator sales, in addition to technological improvement, suppliers had to deal with the various problems concerning each stage in the refrigerator lifecycle (from design to recycling).

The solutions to the main problems were attained as follows:

(a) *Extraction of problems in each stage of the lifecycle*: A planning committee, subcommittee and working group on each problem were organized with the support of Japan Electrical Manufacturers' Association (JEMA) (its chairman is Company A). Through these organizations, the problems that had to be assumed were extracted and the concrete solutions were analyzed.

(b) *Making the standards and guidelines for safety*: These organizations set the standards and the criteria for safety with reference to an international standard and a Japanese electrical safety law. At the same time, various test methods to verify these standards were concretely examined, and the verification experiments were executed in organizations such as several universities.

(c) *Registration and amendment of various laws*: Various laws are related to each stage of the refrigerator lifecycle (Electrical Safety Law, JIS, IEC, High Pressure Gas Control Law, Fire Service Law, etc.). Of course, tasks set by these laws have to be dealt with. These laws, however, contained several points not suited to combustible refrigerants. The amendment of the Electrical Safety Law became an urgent task for non-fluorocarbon refrigerator sales. So, the refrigerator manufacturers in Japan acted together positively for the amendment of the Electrical Safety Law as follows. First of all, they made an amendment plan based on the standards made at the (b) stage. Next, that amendment plan was admitted in various international and domestic public committees. As a result, when the Electrical Safety Law was revised in Japan in 2002, the safety standard of the refrigerator using combustible refrigerants in the (b) stage was included in a new Electrical Safety Law.

The common point in the above-mentioned (a), (b) and (c) was that the non-fluorocarbon refrigerator manufacturers in Japan attained the success through their cooperation centering on Company A.

Company A considered that "Even if the staff in one enterprise try very hard, it is impossible to extract the problems in the short-term. The problems can be adequately extracted only with the cooperation of specialists in each field gathering from various enterprises."

Thus, Company A decided to gather the specialists from each company into the working group, and to exchange the experiences and opinions among one another:

When the problems of safety standard and the problems of infrastructure like the distribution, the repairs service and recycling were examined, the answer was not found in the case tried by only one company. Because the area of the problems is so wide, they were related to a lot of business organizations. So, by only one company the problems could not be solved.

For instance, it is meaningless for only one company to execute the measure for safety against an explosion, if other companies related to transportation and recycling do not execute the measure for safety. The image of non-fluorocarbon refrigerators worsens when other manufacturers cause the accident. Therefore, all the organizations that are related to non-fluorocarbon refrigerators should execute the measure for safety. This is a task that the whole refrigerator industry should accomplish for the consumer.

The amendment of the law would not have advanced if there had not been cooperation between the public administration, the JEMA secretariat, JET of the certifying association, and all manufacturers. In a word, "the networking of related people was the most important core".

Sales of non-fluorocarbon refrigerators were strongly requested to Company A by GP. Then, other manufacturers who thought "We have to produce non-fluorocarbon refrigerators in the future" gathered around Company A. Company A answered, "After all, the cooperation between the companies is the key to non-fluorocarbon refrigerator achievement".

But, no other manufacturer except Company A was as positive in non-fluorocarbon refrigerator development at that time, because the risk of business was so large for the manufacturer to make non-fluorocarbon refrigerators in the first place.

Why, then, did such manufacturers execute successful cooperation with Company A? The answer is greatly related to the characteristic of non-fluorocarbon refrigerator development itself. We continue to discuss this in the next section.

3 "Sociality" of Commodities and the New Type of Cooperation between Companies

3.1 *The emergence of advanced information in product development*

If companies pursue problems related to the commodity characteristics like "environment" and "safety", they would have to communicate with various external organizations. For instance, if they solve the environmental problem of commodities, they should talk with various consumer organizations.

In this non-fluorocarbon refrigerator development, the appliance makers had to exchange information many times with the JEMA secretariat, the JEMA members and the administrative organizations. Therefore, the appliance makers exchanged information with a lot of organizations and individuals.

Such communication with a lot of organizations and individuals often appears when makers want to solve the problem related to "sociality". The problem of commodities related to "sociality" is very much related to a lot of subjects in the wide range, for instance, the supplier, the consumer and the administrative organizations. Therefore, the solution should satisfy such subjects in various standpoints, and should consist of advanced knowledge that contains various senses of value:

> For instance, when the problems of non-fluorocarbon refrigerator development are pursued, a staff in one company cannot extract the problems adequately. It is important that the specialists in each field from many companies and organizations gather and communicate information adequately in various standpoints.

The most important thing in this communication is that members do not conceal either information or knowledge, as the knowledge to solve the problem cannot emerge without sharing important information with each other.

One of the leading persons in Company A explains the cooperation between the companies as follows:

> Because we companies are competing in the world of business, we sometimes want to outwit other companies. We often think that we do not want to give other companies the acquired information and knowledge. However, it is necessary for the industry that the companies exchange information and cooperate to grapple with the big problem of the environment. Such cooperation will return a big plus to my company.

The innovation of knowledge does not occur in the industry if the companies do not have the spirit of mutual give-and-take:

> To make the challenge succeed, it is most important that companies show the attitude of collaboration in the competition.

What do these comments imply? In these comments, we find the attitude of the company that wants to create new advanced information for the new problems. Such a company does not persist in its own profit only. This was the point of view necessary for the refrigerator industry.

Company A explained the necessity of this cooperation to other manufacturers as follows:

> The development of non-fluorocarbon refrigerators is a problem that should be discussed by the entire industry. We can do anything

by cooperating now. If a company doesn't participate in that cooperation, it will face a big delay in both the knowledge and the cost afterwards.

With this persuasion by Company A, other manufacturers decided to participate in the new cooperation between companies:

For such cooperation, it is very important to share knowledge and sense of values related to the environmental issue between the enterprises. To share sense of values, we always shared all information including overseas information.

As a result, the cooperation of the appliance makers in Japan, which assumes foreign countries to be their rival, has advanced.

Thus, most refrigerator manufacturers in Japan could develop and sell non-fluorocarbon refrigerators within two years from 2000 to 2002. The reason all manufacturers were able to achieve non-fluorocarbon refrigerator development was that they advanced in cooperating.

So far forth, cooperation in the development of parts of refrigerators between appliance makers (for example, development of refrigerator doors) existed for a long time. This conventional cooperation means utilization of the other party to increase one's own profit, otherwise known as "bargaining cooperation".

However, in this non-fluorocarbon refrigerator development, the companies did not think about their own profits only; instead, they wanted to fulfill their responsibility as members of an industry. The range of the problems related to "sociality" of the commodities will broaden further in the information society. Moreover, the relations between those various problems will become more complex.

If "sociality" of the commodities is pursued, advanced information emergence including various senses of value is requested for companies. Such information emergence cannot be executed by one company alone. Planning of the safety standard is the typical example of this case. On that occasion, the companies cooperated to create the solution to "sociality".

To create the solution, the win-win type cooperation that aims at the advantage for the whole of the industry is needed. The company should stand in the superior aspect to the current one, without persisting in its own profit. This is the answer to the first question mentioned in the "Introduction" section. We saw such cooperation in this case study. It can be said that this new cooperation between companies cannot be explained by the conventional models.

3.2 *The strategy for the future*

Here, let us analyze the reason why the win–win cooperation between the companies worked effectively in the non-fluorocarbon refrigerator development problem.

Let us first consider the following assumption. If the characteristic of non-fluorocarbon had become a sales point to consumers, the competition between companies to develop and sell non-fluorocarbon refrigerators might have occurred earlier. If it had been so, the win–win cooperation between the companies might not have happened.

However, it was the actual state at that time that non-fluorocarbon could not become the sales point of refrigerators:

> In questionnaires about environmental issues, a lot of consumers answer that even if it is expensive, they choose a commodity that is good for the environment. However, a lot of consumers actually select the cheapest commodity among the commodities with the same function regardless of whether it is good for the environment.

That is, the characteristic of non-fluorocarbon cannot become the point of a commodity strategy in present Japan:

> The cost of the development of commodities that are good for the environment is very high in general. So, commodities that are good for the environment are rather expensive. They cannot be sold easily. Therefore, it becomes hard for the manufacturers to develop commodities that are good for the environment.

When asking, "Why do you produce commodities that are good for the environment though it is so hard?", the appliance maker answered, "The production of commodities that are good for the environment is necessary now because the environmental strategy is a strategy for the future".

That is, the development of environmental commodities by the manufacturers is a kind of constraint for future consumer behavior, which is a strategy for the future. It is a strategy for the company to adapt to the future society which will value the environmental issue more and more.

It was decided that hydro-chlorofluorocarbon (HCFC) will be abolished in Japan in 2020 by the "Ozonosphere Protection Law". Thus, turning to non-fluorocarbon is exactly a strategy for the future.

As mentioned above, the development of non-fluorocarbon refrigerators was a constraint for the future rather than the present commodity strategy for the refrigerator manufacturer. If it is a present commodity strategy, winning the competition is most important for the company. However, if it is the constraint for the future, solving the problem becomes more important than winning now for the company. In addition, this combustibility refrigerant problem of the refrigerator was quite a new problem, and the risk was very high as mentioned above.

Such developments could not create competition between companies, because the big damage to the refrigerator industry would occur if only one company caused an accident. In other words, even if a company wins in the competition, its own advantage becomes dangerous by the demerit of the other companies occurred by such an accident.

Therefore, cooperating so as not to fail in the industry is more important than increasing one's own benefit. That is, when we have to solve problems related to "sociality" that will be valued in the future, cooperation on product development brings more benefit to each company in the future than the one won in the present competition. This case study can be said to show this fact.

4   Sharing Information and the New Type of Competition between Companies

The new cooperation between companies shown by this case study aims at the benefit of the industry. What kind of competition is carried out between the companies that cooperate like this? How do they compete? This is the second question indicated in the "Introduction" section.

One of the leading persons in Company A said, "Collaboration in the competition is the most important thing". Did Company A share all information with the other companies while collaborating? I asked the leading person in Company A, "For instance, what information do you share with other companies when you plan the design specification while cooperating with them?" He answered the following:

> We shared information on the content of the safety standard, the numerical value that had to be cleared, and the test method of the

safety standard. The companies, however, will not share the solution to the problem of how to achieve this standard in the commodities. This basically becomes an individual problem of each company.

In actual fact, however, this problem was not completely individual for each company. For instance, the appliance makers jointly executed the test to confirm whether non-fluorocarbon refrigerators cleared the safety standard. In that test, each company brought the parts for the safety standard. Also, most parts designed by each company for the safety standard had come out to other collaborating companies before non-fluorocarbon refrigerators were commercialized. As a result, information on clearing the safety standard was shared.

Moreover, because the part makers who produce parts for the environmental problem are limited in Japan, most refrigerator makers use the same parts. What kind of parts each refrigerator maker uses could be easily guessed by information from the part makers.

That is, the companies basically shared information on the standard, the test method and so on for the environment and safety. On the other hand, the companies had decided that they would not share information on the concrete device of a commodity to meet the standard. The above-mentioned comment, however, shows that there was, in fact, no strong motivation to "conceal information the concrete device" in the companies.

Information on the content of the safety standard, information on the numerical value that had to be cleared, and information on the test method of the safety standard are public goods, so these intrinsically have the information characteristic as information to be "shared". Though information on the adaptive measures to the safety standard is peculiar to commodities, such information is undoubtedly related to the "sociality" in commodities. Such information in commodities is a theme that should be cleared by the industry as a whole. Moreover, such a theme has meaning for the industrial strategy of the future. Such information does not become the object of the competition between companies. One of the leading persons in Company A commented, "After all, parts for the environment and safety do not become objects of the competition". Such information gives benefit to each company not by exclusive possession through concealment, but by sharing through communication.

Of course, however, information of the commodities is not only related to "sociality". A lot of other information, for instance, information related to the functionality, design and so on, exists in the commodities. Because the information related to the functionality, design and so on is related to the strategy to capture consumers, it is exactly the object of competition between companies. In this case study, such commodity information was not shared between companies at all.

In this non-fluorocarbon refrigerator development, information related to the "sociality" in commodities was shared and information related to the sales strategy in commodities was concealed between the companies. This way, the companies can execute both cooperation and competition according to the distinction between shared information and concealed information. As shown in this case study, informational cooperation in industries and business competition can coexist in the information society through the information characteristics itself.

5   Conclusion

If the information level of consumers improves, more advanced solutions for the "sociality" of commodities will be requested. Moreover, the relations between organizations related to the "sociality" will become more and more complex. Therefore, the emergence of more wide-ranging and advanced information will be requested for the problem of "sociality". In a word, the cooperation between the companies for the emergence of information might be needed more intensively to share information that contains a lot of the "sociality" for the future. Because "sociality" is an attribute which all commodities contain in some way, such new cooperation between companies in various fields is expected in the future.

References

Astley, W. G. and Fombrun, C. J. (1983). Collective strategy: Social ecology of organizational environments, *Academy of Management Review* 8, pp. 576–587.

Evan, W. M. (1972). An organization-set model of interorganizational relations, in *Interorganizational Decision Making*, edited by Tuite, M., Aldine.

Levine, S. and White, P. E. (1961). Exchange as a conceptual framework for the study of interorganizational relationship, *Administrative Science Quarterly* 5, pp. 583–601.

Makino, N. and Asada, T. (2005). The new inter-firms' collaboration being introduced with the sociality of commodities, *Osakadaigaku Keizaigaku* 54(4), pp. 393–406 (in Japanese).

Pfeffer, J. and Salancik, G. R. (1978). *The External Control of Organizations: A Resource Dependence Perspective*, Harper & Row.

Williamson, O. E. (1975). *Markets and Hierarchies*, The Free Press.

Part 5

Application of KPM
for New Value-Creating Activity

Abstract

Japanese project management harnesses the new project management paradigm. It is crystallized in the context of the KPM rooted from the first version of P2M. This Part 5 guides the essential interpretations of KPM and the new angle to benefits of application findings for value creation driven by dynamic interaction of intelligence and knowledge in uncertain environments.

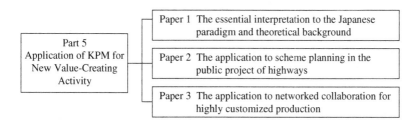

In the first paper, Professor Christophe Bredillet (ESC Lille, France), a distinguished scholar in project management, guides the context why KPM is unique and promising. The author discloses the comparative view on epistemology that the classic paradigm is based on the positivist view, while the Japanese paradigm is based on the constructivist view. Readers may learn here that the essential core of the Japanese paradigm is the insightful type of the mission-driven approach rather than the analytic type. It is the typical thinking for value-creating activity in combination with the mental platform of *ba* which could activate dynamic interaction of knowledge. So, in Part 5, extensive applications are introduced in the arena of public policy in the second paper and public/private partners in the third paper.

Professor Toshinori Nemoto of Hitotsubashi University and Yuki Misui of Takasaki City University of Economics, the authors of the second paper, are the authorities in transportation economics engaged in the national projects in this field. The development in information and communications technologies has made it much less expensive to identify people and objects by means of roadside equipments, such as GPS transceivers, electronic toll collection (ETC) systems, etc. These are fees rather than taxes, and will be effective for financing public projects in the future. The methods to set the socially desirable prices for public projects will be a key issue. Here, the authors explain the complexity of pricing of the public highway project, which is funded by tax by government and tolls paid by users. In general, cost-benefit analysis is applied for project planning. This paper further advances the methodology to the complex project mission by demonstrating simulation. This research may contribute to feasible or optimal toll rate calculation in relation with highway capacity in the long-term scheme model applying KPM thinking.

Professor Hajime Kita and Mikihiko Mori, the authors of the third paper, belong to the Academic Center for Computing and Media Studies at Kyoto University. They are experts in simulation and gaming and hosted an international congress in 2007, and contribute to KPM by guiding the methodology to demystify complexity wherever consensus is formulated and whenever the mission needs to be profiled by visual landscape technique.

The third paper deals with the experiment of a collaboration project for highly customized product and process development by partnership of university, community and enterprises. Suwa/Okaya in Nagano prefecture is well-known for industrial accumulation of precision machinery. Nevertheless, the hollowing out of domestic industry to an Asian shift has been a critical issue for small and medium-sized enterprises in the community. The primary objective of this collaboration was to review the process for highly customized production in network environment. The collaboration had been conducted for crystallizing tacit knowledge accumulated in enterprises in the region.

The networked project team was challenged to a mission of producing frame boxes for personal computers. The project members in distant locations were obliged to exchange opinions frequently on profiling configuration and specification from the design to the manufacture stage of the lifecycle. The development process has been traced for project-based learning and modeling. Readers may be interested in media tools of CAD and groupware, as well as the progressive description of facts in digital and face-to-face communications.

Hideo Yamamoto

Professor, Graduate School of Commerce and Management
Hitotsubashi University

Shikumizukuri vs. One Best (No) Way! Project and Program Management for Enterprise Innovation (P2M): Towards a New Paradigm of KPM?

Christophe N Bredillet

Dean, Postgraduate Programs
Professor of Strategy, Program & Project Management
ESC Lille School of Management

1 Introduction

The purpose of this paper is to investigate the Japanese answer to the 1990s depression, both (1) as a case study of what framework has been developed to address new business challenges and value creation in a complex, ambiguous and uncertain environment, that is, the development of Project and Program Management for Enterprise Innovation (P2M) in Japan (Ohara, 2005a); and (2) in order to expose what are in our view, the underlying theoretical bases supporting this framework, and to draw some theoretical lessons learned which could be helpful to the development of sound PM standards and PM competence model development. This theoretical approach is assumed to be useful to transpose the Japanese experience to other analogical contexts and situations (Gentner, 1983).

2 Where Classical Project Management is No Longer the Answer: Kaikaku Project Management and the Concept of *Shikumizukuri*

In the 1990s, Japanese companies experienced a deflationary depression called the "lost ten years". To survive, and to regain their global competitiveness, they looked for solutions in the *kaikaku* (reforms) of business management, organizations and technology. The companies which utilized the intellectual property of the entire organization were more successful than those which focused only on technological abilities. These successful companies made efforts in the planning and execution of strategic businesses that would change the framework of value creation for the next generation. All these companies applied a new project management paradigm and related framework called Kaikaku Project Management (KPM), composed of 3 K's — *Kakusin* (innovation), *Kaihatsu* (development), and *Kaizen* (improvement). KPM has been developed after P2M but in the extensive roots.

Taking an epistemological approach and promoting project management knowledge is important to solve company-wide issues. Thus, simulation grounded on interdisciplinary approaches, theories based on complex system science, and case studies are useful in explaining the structure, function and behavior of complex, ambiguous, uncertain phenomena in project modeling based on hypothesizing and testing practices.

Ohara (2005b) addressed the question of the need for a new integrative governance framework of program and project management. He cites:

> Man creates an institution or *shikumi* to achieve objectives by organized activity. Localized culture is densely reflected in the *shikumi* framework. At any level of state, society, community and enterprise, rules are enacted in the forms of laws, policies or regulations to effectuate a variety of institutionalized framing or *shikumizukuri* activities to accomplish missions and purposes.

The key Japanese concept is *shikumizukuri* which is composed of the words *shikumi* and *zukuri*. It is a set of contrived framework or architecture used for institutions, business models, systems, or their compounds. *Zukuri* means creation, which signifies framework creation. Creation of value chain for a new undertaking in business is the work of *shikumizukuri*. *Monozukuri* is an often-used term in Japan for manufacturing. *Mono* stands for a product or commodity. Manufacturing is a system of value creation through merchandizing, development, designing, fabrication and procurement. This is a kind of *shikumi*. Entrepreneurs think of innovation of *shikumi* from time to time and apply concepts of *shikumizukuri*. This concept connotes to program management, where compound business models and systems have to be designed to manage a complex mission. *Shikumizukuri* requires integration of a broad range of creativity, know-how, wisdom, technology and knowledge through intellectual insights. This term is popular in the business world as it influences corporate performance. Excellent enterprises are enthusiastic about their original and strategic *shikumizukuri* for innovations.

Before going further, I quote Ohara (2005c):

P2M is the Japanese version of project and program management, which is the first standard guide for education and certification developed in 2001, and KPM is its development. A specific finding of P2M/KPM is characterized by mission-driven management of projects, or a program which harnesses complexity of problem solving observed in the interface between technical system and business model.... The term "mission" is a key word in the field of corporate strategy, where it expresses *raison d'être* or value of business.... Mission is considered as a significant "metamodel representation".... "Project modeling" (*sic*) idea has been introduced in P2M program management.

Thus, KPM takes its roots in P2M and in the concept of *shukumizukuri*.

3 Mission-Driven Approach for Managing Projects in Complex, Ambiguous, Uncertain Environment and Situations: P2M/KPM Main Characteristics

Based on the previous discussion of KPM paradigm, a new Japanese framework for Project and Program Management — called P2M: Project and Program Management for Enterprise Innovation — was developed in 2000–2001, and has been a standard guide for education and certification since its development (Ohara, 2005a). Moving beyond the positivist or analytical paradigm of classical project management, P2M/KPM proposes a framework based on a Mission-Driven Approach and insightful thinking based on a constructivist perspective. This enables solving of complex, ambiguous problems in uncertainty by translating strategic intent (and the resulting mission) into value creation operations and capital recovery through a lifecycle which integrates the scheme, system and service models. In the P2M/KPM context, modeling is a generic approach that integrates multi/interdisciplinary knowledge and methodologies.

In a context where:

- classical project management validity is limited to well-structured socio-technical systems and when mission is explicit,
- complex, ambiguous, uncertain environment involves a new approach, being able to address implicit mission, and

- project definition and the related perception gap between clients and suppliers has to be addressed,

P2M/KPM key characteristics can be summarized as follows:

- Characteristic 1: Mission is shared in ambiguity (adaptive and implicit) rather than with clear definition (explicit) if an innovative view is desired.
- Characteristic 2: P2M/KPM framework addresses implicit mission type and explicit mission type as well.
- Characteristic 3: Mission is a creative output from human insight capability combining rationality and intuition, explicit and implicit, linear and non-linear approaches, divergent and convergent thinking.
- Characteristic 4: Mission is a "meta-model representation" of the future ideality in a complex, ambiguous, uncertain world.
- Characteristic 5: The focus is on "Mission-Driven Approach" project management, which explores and includes value creation activity underpinned by the mission in a complex, ambiguous and uncertain environment.
- Characteristic 6: Modeling is part of P2M/KPM. A program reference model combining three models (scheme, system and service) represents a generic lifecycle from mission to capital recovery through value creation.
- Characteristic 7: Profiling and modeling are core methodologies powered by a combination of human insightful capability and scientific analysis.
- Characteristic 8: Modeling is a generic approach which integrates inter-disciplinary knowledge, methodologies and approaches.

The context and the characteristics aforementioned are related to theoretical insights in the next part of the paper.

4   Some Theoretical Insights about P2M/KPM and Project Management

P2M/KPM moves beyond the classical "process" and "competence" bodies of knowledge (BoKs) and standards proposed by the well-established professional bodies. Industries and professional bodies strive to create an integrated framework, which translates strategic aims into operational processes, thereby improving performance and creating sustained value.

But these BoKs and standards are still mostly based on a positivist paradigm, using linear process views and classical operational research tools when they address "complex project management".

This view is reflected in the developing research and standards which attempt to link strategy, portfolio, program and project management (see, for example, PMI, 2004; Morris and Jamieson, 2004; PMI, 2006a,b; OGC, 2003, 2005; DMO, 2006; GAPPS, 2006).

Our purpose is to provide theoretical insights into P2M/KPM and to develop an understanding of project management as an "entrepreneurial" activity (*vis-à-vis* "operational" activity); and as a mirror (Bredillet, 2004) used for action and reflection, between the mission of the organization and its actual creation of value (for people, organizations and society). This is in the realm of complexity (Richardson, 2005), ambiguity and uncertainty, of interactions between multiple variables; each of them having a specific time horizon and occupying a specific place, playing a specific role and is helpful to transpose the Japanese experience to other analogical contexts and situations (Gentner, 1983).

These developments are grounded in the meta-model and meta-method developed by CIMAP, ESC Lille Research Centre in Project and Program Management. We call for a balanced and integrative epistemological position (constructivism, positivism and subjectivism) and to take into consideration a dual ontological perspective for projects (Heraclitean ontology of "becoming" and Parmenidean ontology of "being"). Further, our work is supported by Complexity Science and the Theory of Systems/Systems Science.

Interestingly, they are fully congruent with what is said about KPM, *shikumizukuri* and P2M, serving as a basis for several joint publications with IAP2M (Bredillet, 2005b; Bredillet and Ohara, 2007) and are reflective of the outcomes of research studies which call for new perspectives for project management (e.g., Cooke-Davies *et al.*, 2007; Leybourne, 2007; Hodgson and Cicmil, 2006; Maylor, 2006; Williams, 2002).

4.1 *Project management as a complex integrative field*

The following discussion is mainly related to contextual issues and P2M/KPM characteristics 1 and 2.

We are surprised by the way the world (organizations, universities and professional bodies) sees project management as a set of methods, techniques and tools which interact with other fields (such as general management, information systems, engineering, etc.) and bring effective (?) ways of solving problems from launching new satellites to new product development, and organizational change. This approach is still positivist. The suitability of this paradigm to solve complex problems has to be questioned. We posit that the understanding of the true nature of project management is hampered by a lack of clear theoretical foundation, lack of clear epistemological stance and paradigm for most research.

This leads to nonsensical advocacy of one's own practice reinforced by the lack of critical thinking by practitioners. They seem to complacently accept seemingly reasonable answers, even if they lead to major failures. Positivism has led in some cases to oversimplification, and in many cases, has obviated against recognition of the complexity and of the relativity of the world. Field research shows that most universities consider project management as a transfunctional discipline and a sub-discipline in construction, engineering, IT or business faculties, and not a discrete discipline. This contributes to reinforcement of positivist paradigm in teaching, research and practice.

4.1.1   *A need for complexity*

Calling to attention the decision making theory and translation of the organization's mission to practice, Kurtz and Snowden (2003) question the following assumptions:

> The assumption of order: that there are underlying relationships between cause and effect in human interactions and markets, which are capable of discovery and empirical verification. In consequence, it is possible to produce prescriptive and predictive models and design interventions that allow us to achieve goals. This implies that an understanding of the causal links in past behavior allows us to define "best practice" for future behavior. It also implies that there must be a right or ideal way of doing things.
>
> The assumption of rational choice: that faced with a choice between one or more alternatives, human actors will make a "rational" decision based only on minimizing pain or maximizing pleasure; and, in consequence, their individual and collective behavior can be managed by manipulation of pain or pleasure outcomes and through education to make those consequences evident.
>
> The assumption of intentional capability: that the acquisition of capability indicates an intention to use that capability, and that

actions from competitors, populations, nation states, communities, or whatever collective identity is under consideration are the result of intentional behavior. In effect, we assume that every "blink" we see is a "wink", and act accordingly. We accept that we do things by accident, but assume that others do things deliberately.

We concur with them and argue that project management is a complex discipline as it deals with complex reality. Citing the law of requisite variety (Ashby, 1958), it is well-known that to control a complex system with n dimensions, you need an $n + 1$ dimensional system. This implies that the available control variety must be equal to or greater than the disturbance variety for control to be possible. In this direction, the following are pertinent to the management of complex situations (programs and projects):

- *The Conant-Ashby Theorem*: Every good regulator of a system must have a model of that system. Implication: The principle prompts one to think through and create a model of what you are teaching/managing/ guiding.
- *The Darkness Principle*: Even though a system is never completely known, it can be managed effectively (black box theory).
- *The Redundancy of Resources Principle*: To minimize the effect of disturbances or noise, the system requires backup systems of critical resources (human and machine) in order to maintain stability. Implications: Plan actions before disturbance or noise happen, because they will.

Project management applications may be seen as coming from some general principles. It needs to integrate both quality ("Be") and quantity ("Have"). It is a process of naming, of revelation, of creation. Thus, our purpose is to defend the proposition that project management has a *raison d'être* in itself; it is both a discipline and an art and contributes to a better understanding of the integrative epistemological position proposed, in which is the very nature of project management.

4.1.2 Project: A polysemic concept

Extending Leroy's perspective to approaching a project by listing its intrinsic characteristics (1994), we present three definitions, chosen to demonstrate the range of different perspectives in the approaching of the project concept.

A project is a temporary endeavor undertaken to create a unique product or service (PMI, 2004; connotes to instrumental perspective); an endeavor in which resources (human, material, financial) are organized in a novel way to undertake unique work with constraints of cost and time (Turner, 1993; connotes to cognitive perspective); a while of actions limited in time and space, inserted in and interacting with the socio-economic environment which is tended towards a goal, and redefining the dialectic between thought and reality (Declerck *et al.*, 1983, 1997; connotes to political perspective).

This illustrates the polysemic nature of the concept of a project (Boutinet, 1996), which gives rise to two underlying visions which have evolved with the development of project management. On the one hand, the development of project management was accompanied by the constitution of codes of practice according to two plans:

(1) An underlying vision which is positivist: experiences and practices lead to standards and rules, standards and rules lead to theories, which lead to paradigms, and all these, according to certain assumptions, are used as a basis for codes of practice, bodies of knowledge.

(2) On the other hand, through projects, man builds reality and the management of projects by its mode of deployment within the ecosystem project/firm/context implies a systemic vision (Declerck *et al.*, 1997). Citing Giambattista Vico (1708), Le Moigne (1995) states, "an 'intelligent' action, 'ingenium', this mental faculty which makes possible to connect in a fast, suitable and happy way the separate things". Thus, the evolution in the use of project management and/or management by projects (Giard and Midler, 1993) and its structuring characteristics suggest a constructivist vision.

4.2   *An epistemological perspective for project management*

Here we address characteristic 3 and some aspects of characteristics 5 and 8.

After Polanyi (1958), we propose an alternative epistemological perspective both to positivism and constructivism. Not separating personal judgment from scientific method, we argue that knowledge creation in project management should integrate classical scientific and symbolic ("fuzzy") aspects. A "reality" can be explained according to a specific point of view and also can be considered as the symbol of higher order (Guénon, 1986) and a more general reality. We argue that the "demiurgic" characteristic of project management involves seeing this field as an open space, without "having" (Have) but rather with a *raison d'être* (Be), because of the construction of "Real" by the projects. It could be considered to be a fundamental explanation of the pre-paradigmatic nature of this field (Kuhn, 1970): the dominant paradigm, source of well-established theory(ies) is *not* to find; the deep nature of project management implies this paradox of being built on moving paradigms reflecting the diversity of the creation process by itself.

This field is thus composed of both quantitative aspects (Have), dependent upon the positivist paradigm where people have few degrees of freedom (example: operational research in network optimization, cost engineering, statistical methods, bodies of knowledge, application of standards, best practices, etc.), and qualitative aspects (Be), dependent upon the constructivist paradigm where people have many degrees of freedom (organizational design, learning, knowledge management, systemic approaches, contextualization of the lifecycle, etc.), some of these aspects being linked together: for example, the creation and evolution of standards seen from the Theory of Convention (social construct) and their application (positivism) (Bredillet, 2002). However, people use methods and tools without understanding the validity of underlying assumptions.

Thus, we envision project management as an integral function: the knowledge field is made up of differential elements, each of them definable. Seen as a whole, it is a transition to the limit. Mathematically, the result of an integral is both quantitatively and qualitatively more than the sum of the parts. Thus, it can be called a system effect: parts A, B and C forming a system S, retaining and losing some of their properties, but gaining some entirely new performances.

From this point of view of the conceptual field of management of projects, like Le Moigne (1995) we argue that there is "inseparability of the knowledge and its representation understood in their distinct activity, the intentional experience of the knowing subject and the groping construction of the subject representing knowledge, this undoubtedly constituting the strong assumption on which are defined teachable knowledge today, both scientific and ordinary" (see below for the role of symbols in the Theory of Convention).

So for us, project management as a knowledge field is both an art and a science, in their dialectic *and* integrative dimensions (close to the "critical-rationalist" and "interactionist" approach of Popper), and thus according to the two epistemological approaches:

(1) The positivist epistemology (materialist–quantitative–Have): "the relation of science to art may be summed up in a brief expression: from Science comes Prevision, from Prevision comes action" (Comte, 1855, Chapter II, p. 43).

(2) The constructivist epistemology (immaterialist–qualitative–Be), with two hypotheses of reference as underlined by Le Moigne (1995): (a) The phenomenological hypothesis — the cognitive interaction between the object or the phenomenon to be known and the subject knowing forms at the same time the knowledge of the object (in "organizing the world") and the mode of development of knowledge by the subject (in "the intelligence organizing itself"); (b) The teleological hypothesis — the intentionality or the finality of the knowing subject, according to its decisive role in the construction of knowledge (phenomenological hypothesis), must be taken into account.

Most of the works on organizational learning, learning organizations, knowledge management, knowledge-creating organizations, etc., are based on a traditional understanding of the nature of knowledge. We could name this understanding the "positivist epistemology" perspective since it treats knowledge as something people, teams, and organizations have. But this perspective does not reflect the knowing found in individual and team practice — knowing (understanding) as an "intelligent" action, "ingenium", as stated by Le Moigne (1995), in calling for a "constructivist epistemology" perspective. The "positivist epistemology" tends to promote explicit over tacit knowledge, and individual knowledge over team or organizational knowledge.

This integrative epistemological approach for project management suggests that organizations will be better understood if explicit, tacit, individual and team/organizational information/knowledge/understanding are treated as four distinct forms (each doing work the others cannot), and information, knowledge and understanding are seen as inseparable and mutually enabling. Thus,

Information is descriptive; it is contained in answers to questions that begin with such words as what, which, who, how many, when and where. Knowledge is instructive; it is conveyed by answers to how-to questions. Understanding is explanatory; it is transmitted by answers to why questions. To understand a system is to be able to explain its properties and behavior and to reveal why it is what it is and why it behaves the way it does (Gharajedaghi and Ackoff, 1984).

4.3 *"Modeling to understand", that is, to do ingeniously!*

The discussion in this section is mainly related to characteristics 4, 5, 6, 7 and 8.

Acting in complex, uncertain and ambiguous management situations involves "Modeling to understand", which is to do ingeniously (Le Moigne, 2003). We introduce the theoretical roots of the design of a meta-model.

Complexity and systemic perspective contend that acting and learning are inseparable. This involves having information (tacit, implicit or explicit), an understanding of the context, the different parameters and variables, their interaction and conditions of change. Thus, we can consider that there is a systemic and dynamic link between mission, management of programs and projects, information, knowledge, learning and understanding for a given context and conditions.

This meta-modeling approach is well-grounded in sound theoretical organizational frameworks. In project management, meta-method is about designing a contextual structure that:

- Provides a place for individuals, project managers and stakeholders to act and learn; the learning integrating the two perspectives, as there is a need for a blend of creative or exploratory learning and application or exploitative learning (Boisot, 1998, p. 116). Having in mind the need for efficiency and effectiveness, a project team acts as a temporary dissipative structure (Declerck *et al.*, 1997, p. 207), generating first entropy (knowledge) creating knowledge with many degrees of freedom, then applying it (entropy reduction by reduction of complexity; Boisot, 1998, pp. 67–68) in the former stage of a project.
- Facilitates this praxis through a specific meta-method, one of the underlying paradigms being that there is a co-evolution between the subject/actor and his or her environment. This involves inseparability between the subject and the object in this observation-action process. This observation-action is related to an epistemo-praxeologic cognition through an observational chain (perception of what is true or

wrong — epistemological subjectivity), a decision chain (decision made founded or unfounded — pragmatical subjectivity), and an effect chain (action fulfilled feasible or unfeasible — praxeological subjectivity). This epistemo-praxeologic cognition involves both partial subjectivity *and* partial objectivity, congruent with our previous alternative epistemological position.

- Enables generating a specific convention (configuration of order) and some kind of stability to cope with uncertainty and ambiguity in a given project's complex situation. The meta-method helps to create a coherent or dissonant framework of symbols, promoting dynamic management practices which are creating adequate initial conditions for decision-making (and thus performance), and transparency (and thus accountability), while being conscious of rational voids.

A mention of underlying theories supporting meta-modeling approach is pertinent here. Two theoretical areas, aligned with our "balanced" epistemological position exposed earlier in this paper, are considered here. This meta-modeling approach is grounded on "N-Learning" vs. "S-Learning" dialectic, a praxeological approach.

4.3.1 *N- vs. S-Learning*

We draw from Boisot (1998) a model grounded on an information perspective and Complexity science, a set of theories describing how complex adaptive systems work. For him (p. 34), knowledge assets emerge as a result of a two-step process: creating knowledge ("process of extracting information from data") and applying knowledge ("testing the insights created in a variety of situations that allow for the gradual accumulation of experiential data"). He defines an Information space (I-Space) according to three dimensions: codification (information codified/uncodified), abstraction (abstract/concrete), and diffusion (diffused/undiffused). The creation and diffusion of new knowledge occurs in a particular sequence (Social Learning Cycle — SLC, p. 59): scanning, problem-solving, abstraction, diffusion, absorption, impacting.

Two distinct theories of learning are introduced as part of the identification of two distinct strategic orientations for dealing with the paradox of value (i.e., "maximizing the utility of knowledge assets compromises their scarcity, and maximizing their scarcity makes it difficult to develop and exploit their utility", p. 90). In neoclassical learning (N-Learning), knowledge is considered cumulative. Learning becomes a stabilizing process. This approach may lead to excessive inertia and fossilization of the knowledge assets. In Schumpeterian learning (S-Learning), change is the natural order of things. Abstraction and codification are incomplete: "Knowledge may be progressive in the sense that successive approximation may give a better grasp of the underlying structures of reality, but it is not necessarily cumulative" (p. 99). S-Learning is more complex than N-Learning, integrating both certainties and uncertainties, and requires an "edge of chaos" culture (p. 116).

4.3.2   *Praxeology*

In project management, learning and practice are integrated into the praxis — hence, the praxeological approach (see the notion of "ingenium" discussed previously). Praxeology is "The science of human action that strives for universally valid knowledge. In all of its branches this science is *a priori*, not empirical. Like logic and mathematics, it is not derived from experience; it is prior to experience. It is, as it were, the logic of action and deed" (von Mises, 1976, Chapter 1, item 6). The name "praxeology" originates from praxis, Medieval Latin, from Greek, doing, action, from prassein to do, practice (*Merriam-Webster Dictionary*). Praxeology is the study of those aspects of human action that can be grasped *a priori*; in other words, it is concerned with the conceptual analysis and logical implications of preference, choice, means-end schemes and so forth. The basic principles of praxeology were first discovered by the Greek philosophers, who used them as a foundation for a eudaemonistic ethics. In the late nineteenth century, the praxeological approach to economics and social science was rediscovered by Carl Menger (1985), founder of the Austrian School, and was later used by Ludwig von Mises (1981).

4.4   *Acting, knowing and learning within projects and programs*

The following developments are principally related to characteristic 5.

"Projects, as strategic processes, modify the conditions of the firm in its environment. Through them, resources and competencies are mobilized to create competitive advantage and other sources of value" (Bredillet, 2005a). Since resources are shared by many organizations, the organization's competencies are the most relevant driver. Thus, through the organization's processes or projects, past action is actualized as experience; present action reveals and proves competencies; future action generates and tries out new competencies (Lorino and Tarondeau, 1998). Competencies (both individual, team and organizational) are at the source of competitive advantage and the creation of value.

We first compare some characteristics of groups and teams. Wenger, McDermott and Snyder (2002, p. 142) draw a comparison between several forms of team organizations: community of practice, formal work group, informal network and project team. There are some fundamental differences between project team, community of practice and *Ba* (platform for the knowledge creation process) (Nonaka, Toyama and Byosiere, in Dierkes *et al.*, 2001, pp. 491–517). They are summarized in Table 1.

To understand the specificity created by the project environment and project team as far as learning is concerned, let us synthesize some of the key perspectives in Table 2.

From Table 2, it is clear that projects, through the way the project team acts (praxis), are a privileged place for learning. Such project-based learning needs to integrate the two perspectives ("Have" and "Be"), as there is a need to create a blend of exploratory learning and exploitative learning (Boisot, 1998, p. 116). Bearing in mind the need for efficiency and effectiveness, a project team first generates information, creating knowledge (adding complexity), and then applies it (reduction of complexity) in the initial stages of a project. The level of knowledge being created will depend of the nature of system project/organization/ environment.

On a larger issue, this praxis is fascinating because all new project teams must solve a unique conundrum: to what degree is the information/knowledge available (past experience, replicable processes, etc.) to complete the project, and to what degree must all knowledge and learning be acquired or "emergent" as a result of the unique nature of the project tasks?

The consequence at the praxis level is twofold. On the one hand, focusing on the "Have" side, there is a need for some form of knowledge — guidance, best practice, standards, etc. — at the individual, team and organizational level. It is important to recognize that such standards have to be seen as largely social constructs, developed to facilitate communication and trust among those who are adopting them, but their evolution is in line with the experiences gained by the users, or because of new developments or

Table 1   Putting in perspective project team, community of practice and *Ba*

Project Team	Community of Practice	*Ba*
Members practice their jobs and learn by participating in the project team	Members learn by participating in the community and practicing their jobs	Members learn by participating in the *Ba* and practicing their jobs
Place where knowledge is created, where members learn knowledge that is embedded, and where knowledge is utilized	Place where members learn knowledge that is embedded in the community	Place where knowledge is created
Need of energy (forming the team) and then learning occurs	Learning occurs in any community of practice	Need of energy in order to become active
Boundary is set by the task and the project	Boundary is firmly set by the task, culture, and history of the community	Boundary is set by its participants and can be changed easily. Here-and-now. Created, function, disappear
Membership fixed for the project duration (temporary nature). May vary depending on the phases of the project	Membership rather stable. New members need time to learn and fully participate	Membership not fixed. Participants come and go
Participants may relate or belong to the project team for the duration of the project, but may belong or relate to the operational/functional organization (department, contractors, suppliers, etc.)	Participants belong to the community	Participants relate to the *Ba*

Table 2   Synthesis of two perspectives ("Have" and "Be") regarding knowledge management, organizational learning and learning organizations

Epistemology	Positivist — "Have"	Constructivist — "Be"
Knowledge Management	Western approach. Codification. Explicit knowledge. Linear thinking. Knowledge market	"Japanese" approach (KPM). Personalization. Tacit knowledge. Dialectical thinking: "synthesizing dialectical thinking", aiming at identifying contradiction and resolving it by means of synthesis or integration, from "compromising dialectical thinking", focusing on tolerating contradiction
Organizational Learning	Single-loop learning. Information theory (knowledge as formal and systematic-hard data, codified procedures, universal principles)	Double-loop learning. Information theory (Nonaka, 1991; Boisot, 1998). System dynamics theory (Senge, 1990; Kim, 1993)
Learning Organization	Neoclassical learning (N-Learning), knowledge is considered cumulative (Boisot, 1998)	SECI cycle, *Ba*, knowledge assets, need for a supportive organization (Nonaka, 1991). Schumpeterian learning (S-Learning), change is the natural order of things (Boisot, 1998)

practices, is vital to avoid any fossilization. On the other hand, on the "Be" side, the need for more creative competence (e.g., some professional certifications are incorporating personal characteristics), flexible frameworks (e.g., use of meta-rules) and organizational structure to enable the sharing of experience is fundamental. In this context, it is interesting to note that KPM has newly introduced the three layers of concepts which are symbolized by *Kakusin* (innovation), *Kaihatsu* (development) and *Kaizen* (improvement). Though cross-functionality of team building has been emphasized in the project management, the lateral level of collaboration is also critical in the program in terms of project linkage. The effective linkage depends more on the mental model of role and competency motivated by leaders of project teams rather than the hierarchy positioning. Dynamic interaction of knowledge interaction is explained to be congruent to *Ba* constructivist theory. KPM intends to explore the enhanced framework of strategy implementation in the form of the hybrid of lateral and cross-functional collaborations.

Considering a learning organization and the necessary support structures, each organization running projects and programs has its own characteristics. Being conscious of the specificity of projects and the underlying assumptions of the concepts, methods, tools and techniques available, should help in the design of an appropriate system for project and program management governance, and efficient and effective strategy implementation.

4.5 *Modeling as "convention" generator*

In P2M/KPM, a mission is considered as a meaningful "meta-model representation" (characteristic 4), and modeling is part of the P2M/KPM program reference model combining three models (scheme, system and service). This represents a generic lifecycle from mission to capital recovery through value creation (characteristic 6). Characteristics 7 and 8 are addressed as well. Meanwhile, P2M/KPM development as such can be seen as a modeling activity. Thus, the previous theoretical and following developments can apply to both P2M/KPM framework development *and* to modeling as part of P2M/KPM. We are focusing here on the latter aspect.

It is thus important to understand that modeling enables the generation of specific "conventions". These conventions are more than organizational or professional bodies' standards.

Bredillet (2002) has introduced an alternative view of standardization, mentioning the difficulties classical microeconomics poses in establishing a theory of standardization that is compatible with its underscored fundamental axiomatic. He has proposed to reconsider the problem from the opposite perspective by questioning the theoretical base and by reformulating assumptions on the autonomy of the choice of the actors. The theory of Convention offers both a theoretical framework and tools, helping one understand the systemic dimension and dynamic structure of standards seen as a special case of conventions.

Gomez and Jones (2000) outline the main characteristics of the Theory of Convention. Starting with the notions such as "deep structure" (Giddens, 1986; Gersick, 1991; Schein, 1980) and "system structure"

(Crozier and Friedberg, 1980; Senge, 1990, 1994), they adopt "this viewpoint that a state of 'un-enlightenment' represents neither a failure nor a consequence of cognitive limitations, but rather that it has a social function, and that it exists because it is essential for the smooth running of relationships in society" (Gomez and Jones, 2000, p. 697). They argue that it could, indeed, constitute a referential notion, making compatible individual calculations and social context, and allowing for their co-construction and co-evolution (Schumpeter, 1989).

Three main notions are discussed before they propose a definition of convention: uncertainty, "rationalization" and the process of justification of the behavior to cope with uncertainty, and rational voids (systems of non-justified beliefs). The rational void is "surrounded by a screen of information which both provides individuals with signals that they share the same assumptions, and also distracts their attention from questioning it" (Gomez and Jones, 2000, p. 700). These signals are also said to operate as symbols.

So, what is a convention? A convention is a social mechanism that associates a rational void, i.e., a set of non-justified norms, with a screen of symbols, i.e., an interrelation between objects, discourses and behaviors. People acting according to a given convention refer to the same non-justified criteria and take for granted the symbolic meaning of signals they receive.

More formally, the concept of convention can be described as follows:

- A convention eliminates a situation of uncertainty where the result of a decision or an action for an agent would be indeterminate by individual calculation alone (Gomez, 1994, p. 95).
- A convention is an evolutionarily stable (Sugden, 1989) element of regularity. It provides a justifying set of norms (the rational void), which makes justification of some choices dispensable, but which gives them sense in the context of a screen of symbols, which relate objects, discourse and behaviors to the same rational void.
- A convention is based on a shared belief. Five criteria, known as Lewis' conditions (Orlean, 1989; see also Lewis, 1969, p. 42) are used to verify this: (1) There is general compliance with the convention. Those who comply are known as adopters; (2) All adopters anticipate that others will also comply (adopt); (3) Everyone prefers compliance with the convention to be general rather than less than general; (4) There could be at least one other alternative regular solution for the problem the convention exists to solve; and (5) These first four conditions are common knowledge.

From this, important consequences related to based (meta-) modeling seen as "convention generator" can be drawn:

- An individual always finds himself within a conventional system of rationalization. An observed behavior is not always in relation to all symbols. It is situated in the screen of symbols, which means that it is linked with some other behaviors or objects, but not the totality of them. This notion of situation is crucial to understand the dynamics of conventions.
- Conventions are stable but not static patterns; evolving, modifying themselves and sometimes disappearing.
- Within any convention, conformism allows individuals to escape the perils of uncertainty.
- Conventions are never completely isolated. If an alternative provides a more coherent set of symbols, the individual can spontaneously escape ambiguity and potential uncertainty by behaving according to this one.
- The more numerous the symbolic signals received by an individual, the higher the probability of finding dissonant signals, and thus to be "attracted" by another convention. Learning plays an ambiguous role in this matter as even the organizational learning process (Argyris and Schön, 1978) can itself be either a new source of conformity and conservatism when it leads to the recognition of only coherent symbolic signals, or a source of non-conformist behavior when it allows an increase in the number of signals that the individual perceives and the probability of encountering dissonance.
- No one individual can change a whole convention, but if everyone acts on it and within it locally, they can contribute to its evolution. This gives precision to the role and the limit of managerial action in organizations. Managers are not planners and decision makers applying a supposedly pure rationality, as they are always included in a social environment which gives both sense and limits to their rationality. They do not choose to act in one convention over another, but rather, as individuals, to escape the inhibiting effect of uncertainty. Once again, for any individual, the fact that the diversity of conventions allows some room for doubt and ambiguity is paradoxically the fact which gives them some freedom for action.
- Convention highlights in particular the important task of symbolic management. This allows us to better understand that management

practices can also be a way of creating coherence, or creating gaps between the hidden and the visible, which leads to dissonance. Management has the subtle task of creating the conditions for routinization and, eventually, deroutinization. In practice, the use of a conventionalist framework leads us to understand organizational situations rather than organizations as an abstract and static whole.

5 Concluding Remarks

Based on the investigation of the Japanese answer to the 1990s depression, we illustrated that classical project management was no longer (but was it

Table 3   Relations between P2M/KPM main characteristics and underlying theories

P2M/KPM Main Characteristics	Theoretical Development
Characteristic 1. Mission is shared in ambiguity (adaptive and implicit) rather than with clear definition (explicit) if an innovative view is desired	PM as a complex integrative field
Characteristic 2. P2M/KPM framework addresses implicit mission type and explicit mission type as well	PM as a complex integrative field
Characteristic 3. Mission is a creative output from human insight capability combining rationality and intuition, explicit and implicit, linear and non-linear approaches, divergent and convergent thinking	Integrative epistemological approach
Characteristic 4. Mission is a "meta-model representation" of the future ideality in a complex, ambiguous, uncertain world	"Modeling to understand", that is, to do ingeniously Modeling as "convention" generator
Characteristic 5. P2M/KPM focuses on a "Mission-Driven Approach" project management, which explores and includes value creation activity underpinned	Integrative epistemological approach "Modeling to understand", that is, to do ingeniously Acting, knowing and learning within projects and programs

(Continued)

Table 3 (*Continued*)

P2M/KPM Main Characteristics	Theoretical Development
by the mission in a complex, ambiguous and uncertain environment	
Characteristic 6. Modeling is part of P2M/KPM. A program reference model combining three models (scheme, system and service) represents a generic lifecycle from mission to capital recovery through value creation	"Modeling to understand", that is, to do ingeniously Modeling as "convention" generator
Characteristic 7. Profiling and modeling are core methodologies powered by a combination of human insightful capability and scientific analysis	"Modeling to understand", that is, to do ingeniously Modeling as "convention" generator
Characteristic 8. Modeling is a generic approach which integrates interdisciplinary knowledge, methodologies and approaches	Integrative epistemological approach "Modeling to understand", that is, to do ingeniously Modeling as "convention" generator

ever?) sufficient to face the challenge of value creation in complex, ambiguous and uncertain situations. We introduced the new Japanese framework (P2M/KPM) based on Mission-Driven Approach project management, and its main characteristics. From this we proposed a theoretical debate and suggested some possible relations between P2M/KPM main characteristics and general theories. Table 3 summarizes the links between them.

In order to tentatively generalize these findings, we suggest that recognition of "complexity, ambiguity and uncertainty", "integrative epistemological approach", modeling and its underlying bases (N- vs. S-Learning, Praxeology), "Acting, Knowing and Learning", and Theory of Convention seem to form a robust theoretical background to the development and content of any framework aiming at addressing the challenge of value creation in complex, ambiguous and uncertain environments and situations.

Beyond P2M/KPM specificity — rooted in the Japanese culture — these theoretical bases may be seen as useful in supporting project (program, portfolio) management frameworks contents, and in their contextual application. Finally, we suggest that organizations and professional bodies would benefit by being more conscious of all the "new" theoretical approaches and of the dynamic at stake in such framework development and design.

Currently, we are investigating what Theory of Convention — and thus, coordination through the relationship between effort convention (focusing on the organization) and qualification convention (focusing on the relationships between the organization and the "market") — could bring and how it could be applied to the analysis and improvement of organizational maturity, another misunderstood topic.

References

Argyris, C. and Schön, D. (1978). *Organizational Learning: A Theory of Action Perspective*, Reading: Addison-Wesley.

Ashby, W. (1958). Requisite variety and implications for control of complex systems, *Cybernetica* 1, pp. 83–99.

Boisot, M. H. (1998). *Knowledge Assets: Securing Competitive Advantage in the Information Economy*, New York: Oxford University Press.

Boutinet, J.-P. (1996). *Anthropologie du Projet*, Paris: PUF.

Bredillet, C. (2002). Genesis and role of standards: Theoretical foundations and socio-economical model for the construction and use of standards, in *Proceedings of IRNOP V*, Renesse, Zeeland, The Netherlands.

Bredillet, C. (2004). Beyond the positivist mirror: Towards a project management 'gnosis', in *Proceedings of IRNOP VI*, Turku, Finland.

Bredillet, C. (2005a). P2M: Toward a new project & programme management paradigm? — The link between strategy, programme & project, *PMCC Journal* March.

Bredillet, C. (2005b). Some reflections about P2M: The place of the mirror, International Association of Project and Program Management (IAP2M) meeting, 30 October, Tokyo.

Bredillet, C. and Ohara, S. (2007). 'Kaikaku' Project Management: Investigating the Japanese answer to the 90s depression, EURAM Conference, Paris.

Comte, A. (1855). *Positive Philosophy*, New York: Calvin Blanchard.

Cooke-Davies, T., Cicmil, S., Crawford, L., and Richardson, K. (2007). We're not in Kansas anymore Toto: Mapping the strange landscape of complexity theory, and its relationship to project management, *Project Management Journal* 8(2), pp. 50–61.

Crozier, M. and Friedberg, E. (1980). *Actors and Systems*, Chicago, IL: University of Chicago Press.

Declerck, R. P., Debourse, J.-P., and Navarre, C. (1983). *La Méthode de Direction Générale: Le Management Stratégique*, Paris: Hommes et Techniques.

Declerck, R. P., Debourse, J.-P., and Declerck, J. C. (1997). *Le Management Stratégique: Contrôle de l'irréversibilité*, Lille, France: Les éditions ESC Lille.

Defence Material Organization (DMO) (2006). *Competency Standard for Complex Project Managers. Public Release — Version 2.0 September 2006*, Commonwealth of Australia (Department of Defence).

Dierkes, M., Antal, A. B., Child, J., and Nonaka, I. (2001). *Handbook of Organizational Learning & Knowledge*, New York: Oxford University Press.

Gentner, D. (1983). Structure-mapping: A theoretical framework for analogy, *Cognitive Science* 7, pp. 155–170.

Gersick, C. (1991). Revolutionary change theories: A multilevel exploration of the punctuated equilibrium, *Academy of Management Review* 16(1), pp. 10–36.

Gharajedaghi, J. and Ackoff, R. L. (1984). Mechanisms, organisms and social system, *Strategic Management Journal* 5(3), p. 289.

Giard, V. and Midler, C. (1993). *Pilotages de Projet et Entreprises: Diversités et Convergences*, ECOSIP, Paris: Economica.

Giddens, A. (1986). *The Constitution of Society: Outline of the Theory of Structuration*, Berkeley, CA: University of California Press.

Global Alliance for Project Performance Standards (GAPPS) (2006). *Framework for Performance-Based Competency Standards for Global Level 1 and 2 Project Managers*, Sydney: GAPPS.

Gomez, P. Y. (1994). *Qualité et Théorie des Conventions*, Paris: Economica.

Gomez, P. Y. and Jones, B. C. (2000). Conventions: An interpretation of deeps structure in organizations, *Organization Science* 11(6), pp. 696–708.

Guénon, R. (1986). *Initiation et Réalisation Spirituelle*, Paris: Editions Traditionnelles.

Hodgson, D. and Cicmil, S. (2006). *Making Projects Critical*, Basingstocke: Palgrave MacMillan.

Kim, D. H. (1993). The link between individual and organizational learning, *Sloan Management Review* Fall, pp. 37–50.

Kuhn, T. (1970). *The Structure of Scientific Revolutions*, Chicago, IL: University of Chicago Press.

Kurtz, C. F. and Snowden, D. J. (2003). The new dynamics of strategy: Sense-making in a complex and complicated world, *IBM Systems Journal* 42(3).

Le Moigne, J.-L. (1995). *Les Epistémologies Constructivistes*, Paris: PUF.

Le Moigne, J.-L. (2003). *Le Constructivisme — Tome 3 Modéliser Pour Comprendre*, Paris: Ed L'Harmattan, Coll. Ingenium.

Leroy, D. (1994). *Fondements et impact du management par projets*, Thèse de Doctorat, IAE de Lille — USTL, 12/94.

Lewis, D. K. (1969). *Convention: A Philosophical Study*, Cambridge, MA: Harvard University Press.

Leybourne, S. A. (2007). The changing bias of project management research: A consideration of the literatures and an application of extant theory, *Project Management Journal* 38(1), pp. 61–73.

Lorino, P. and Tarondeau, J. C. (1998). De la stratégie aux processus stratégiques, *Revue Française de Gestion* 117, pp. 5–17.

Maylor, H. (Guest Ed.) (2006). Rethinking project management, *International Journal of Project Management (Special Issue)* 24(8).

Menger, C. (1985). *Investigations into the Method of the Social Sciences with Special Reference to Economics*, ed. Louis Schneider, trans. Francis J. Nock, New York: New York University Press.

Morris, Peter W. G. and Jamieson, A. (2004). *Translating Corporate Strategy into Project Strategy: Realizing Corporate Strategy Through Project Management*, Newtown Square, PA: Project Management Institute.

Nonaka, I. (1991). The knowledge-creating company, *Harvard Business Review* 69, pp. 96–104.

Office of Government Commerce (OGC) (2003). *Managing Successful Programmes*, Norwich: The Stationery Office.

Office of Government Commerce (OGC) (2005). *Managing Successful Projects with Prince 2*, Norwich: The Stationery Office.

Ohara, S. (2005a). *P2M: A Guidebook of Project & Programme Management for Enterprise Innovation*, Tokyo: Project Management Association Japan. November 2001, Rev 3 October 2005.

Ohara, S. (2005b). Exploring *"Shikumizukuri"* management for holistic harmonization, International Association of Project and Program Management (IAP2M) meeting, 30 October, Tokyo.

Ohara, S. (2005c). Profiling mission-driven management for complex projects or program: Explaining the new framework and its background, IPMA Conference, November, New Delhi.

Orlean, A. (1989). Pour une approche cognitive des conventions économiques. J.-P. Dupuy, ed. L'économie des conventions, *Revue Economique* 2, pp. 241–272.

Polanyi, M. (1958). *Personal Knowledge*, Chicago, IL: University of Chicago Press.

Project Management Institute (PMI®) (2004). *A Guide to the Project Management Body of Knowledge (PMBOK® Guide)*, 3rd ed., Newtown Square, PA: Project Management Institute.

Project Management Institute (2006a). *The Standard for Program Management*, Newtown Square, PA: Project Management Institute.

Project Management Institute (2006b). *The Standard for Portfolio Management*, Newtown Square, PA: Project Management Institute.

Richardson, K. A. (2005). To be or not to be? That is (not) the question: Complexity theory and the need for critical thinking, in *Managing Organizational Complexity: Philosophy, Theory, and Application*, edited by Richardson, K., Greenwich: IAP, pp. 21–46.

Schein, E. (1980). *Organizational Psychology*, Englewood Cliffs, NJ: Prentice-Hall.

Schumpeter, J. A. (1989). *Essays on Entrepreneurs, Innovations, Business Cycles, and the Evolution of Capitalism*, New Brunswick: Transaction Publishers.

Senge, P. M. (1990). *The Fifth Discipline, the Art and Practice of the Learning Organization*, New York: Doubleday Currency.

Senge, P. M. (1994). Building learning organizations, in *Strategy: Process, Content, Context*, edited by De Wit, B. and Meyer, R., Minneapolis, MN: West Publishing.

Sugden, R. (1989). Spontaneous order, *Journal of Economic Perspectives* 3, pp. 85–97.

Turner, J. R. (1993). *The Handbook of Project-Based Management*, London: McGraw-Hill — The Henley Management Series.

Vico, G. B. (1708). *La Méthode des études de notre temps*, Presentation & Traduction par PONS Alain, 1981 (texte de 1708), Paris: Grasset.

von Mises, L. (1976). *Epistemological Problems of Economics*, New York: New York University Press.

von Mises, L. (1981). Praxeology, *The Freeman: Ideas on Liberty* 31(9).

Wenger, E., McDermott, R., and Snyder, W. M. (2002). *Cultivating Communities of Practice: A Guide to Managing Knowledge*, Boston: Harvard Business School Press.

Williams, T. (2002). *Modelling Complex Projects*, Chichester: John Wiley & Sons, Ltd.

Pricing Public Projects with Complexity — Highway Management and Capacity Optimization by Mile-Based Pricing

Toshinori Nemoto

Professor, Graduate School of Commerce and Management
Hitotsubashi University

Yuki Misui

Assistant Professor, Faculty of Regional Policy
Takasaki City University of Economics

1 Introduction

The construction and management of public facilities or public systems such as highways and parks are generally financed by taxes because it is difficult or not cost-effective to collect a fee at every usage of these facilities. The term for this situation in economics is "non-excludability", i.e., non-paying users cannot be excluded from these services. As a result, there is a gap created between the facility usage and the cost sharing among the users; the total usage (or, in turn, the desire to use the facility) will grow excessive, leading to protests of unfair pricing by those users who actually paid the facility cost unproportionally.

However, the development in telecommunications technologies has made it much less expensive to identify people and objects, and thus, to instantly know when a user has entered a space and should be charged a fee. Users in automobiles can be detected by roadside equipment (at least, those in automobiles carrying onboard transponders) or onboard GPS transceivers; electronic toll collection (ETC) systems are a typical example. These are fees rather than taxes, and will, no doubt, be effective for financing public projects in the future.

In this paper, we intend to investigate the methods by which advances in telecommunications can be employed to set the socially desirable prices for public projects, taking highways as a case study.

In the first half of this paper, highway costs are defined and the principles of marginal cost pricing and average cost pricing are introduced, where marginal and average costs derived from road cost function are employed as users' fees. Here, "marginal cost" means the increase in total costs caused by a unit increase in the traffic volume. The significance of these principles is verified from the viewpoint of short-term and long-term optimization. In the latter half of the paper, two simulations are performed to examine the validity of these principles.

2 Theory

2.1 *Average cost pricing and marginal cost pricing under fixed highway capacity*

The road price is defined as the total of the taxes and fees paid by the user upon purchase, possession and use of an automobile, including vehicle holding taxes, gasoline taxes and road tolls, although the user has to bear the vehicle cost and time cost additionally when driving. These taxes and fees are transferred from the users to the government, which appropriates them for maintenance and renewal of the highways (Table 1). Here, it is desirable

Table 1   Road costs

	Fixed Costs	Variable Costs (with Traffic Volume)
Internal Costs		
Road Users	A: Vehicle costs and maintenance	B: Time cost, travel cost
Transferred	C: Vehicle acquisition tax, license fee	D: Gasoline tax, expressway fee, congestion charge, mile-based fee
Highway Administrators	E: Construction cost, maintenance cost (lighting, etc.)	F: Maintenance cost (painting, etc.)
External Costs	G: Landscape destruction, redundancy	H: Congestion, air pollution, noise, traffic accidents

to set a policy for deciding how to set the price and how much of the revenue to allocate to which roads.

The traditional way to finance highways has been to attempt to collect taxes amounting to the total fixed cost E (in Table 1) for constructing the highways plus the variable cost F (i.e., E and F make the total expenses of highway administrators). This principle is called average cost pricing because the average cost multiplied by the traffic volume makes the total cost. However, it is theoretically understood that charging social marginal costs, which include the environmental costs (e.g., air pollution), is the way to obtain the optimal distribution of the resources in the short-term. This approach synchronizes the marginal costs with the users' willingness to pay (marginal benefits).

The principles of average cost pricing and marginal cost pricing are illustrated in Figure 1. The maintenance cost F increases with traffic volume, but the increase diminishes with volume, so the average cost curve of highway administration (AC_{EF}) is concave upward. The average cost curve including external effects (AC_{EFGH}) begins to increase once the traffic volume exceeds the highway capacity and traffic speed drops. Previous research on estimating externalities indicates that congestion cost is the dominant portion of the marginal cost curve (MC_{FH}) (Quinet and Vickerman, 2004). It is known that the line MC_{FH} intersects the line AC_{EFGH} where AC_{EFGH} is at a minimum. If the demand for a given road is D_1, the

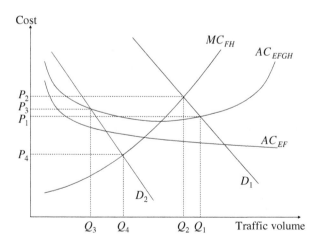

Fig. 1   Average cost pricing and marginal cost pricing

average cost pricing results in a price of P_1 and the traffic volume at this price is Q_1. Marginal cost pricing indicates corresponding values of P_2 and Q_2. At a lower demand D_2, the prices predicted by the average cost and marginal cost pricing are P_3 and P_4 respectively.

The revenue and expenditure of the highway administrators are balanced under average cost pricing, but they are not able to make any preparations against congestion or environmental problems. In addition, the shares of the users are higher in regions where the demand is low. In contrast, marginal cost pricing internalizes the externalities that are caused by congestion and environmental problems. These prices can reduce the traffic volume to the optimal level, but when no congestion occurs, an insufficient price is collected since the price has been set lower than the average cost. The administration is then unable to afford maintenance and renewal, and they have to make up the shortfall from the general revenue source, or abandon some of the renewal works.

Ramsey pricing is a scheme that combines the advantages of marginal cost and average cost pricing. The marginal cost is allocated to each user first, then a shortfall to cover the total cost is allocated in an inverse relation to the price elasticity of the demand by the user. By reducing relatively the share paid by the users who are particularly sensitive to the cost (for example, passenger car drivers are more price-sensitive than truck drivers), large swings in the representation of different groups of users can be avoided. This scheme encourages high prices to users who have no alternative modes; therefore, it must be administered with due care. Thus, it again becomes a political consideration how much to charge each group of user.

Generally, highway administrators in Japan have attempted to maintain an even balance with respect to financing highways by average cost pricing. It still remains for them, however, to introduce Transportation Demand Management (TDM), i.e., to institute fee structures using marginal cost pricing that places higher tolls on routes that suffer environmental problems and lower tolls on less-congested routes.

2.2 *Optimal highway capacity building through social marginal cost pricing*

The previous section on road pricing assumed that the highway capacity is given and fixed, and focused on whether it is more appropriate to adopt short-term marginal cost pricing or short-term average cost pricing. Both pricing theories are, however, lacking in the perspective to see highway capacity as a "variable". To manage the highway network efficiently, it is desirable to increase the highway capacity if demand exceeds supply; likewise, highway capacity should be decreased if supply exceeds demand. It is possible to change the capacity of the highways over some length of time, since road stock has a finite life of a certain number of years.

Mohring (1976) proved this under constant returns to scale; in other words, given a horizontal long-term average cost curve for roads, "the optimal price is set at a short-term marginal cost when the optimal road level is realized." We have applied this idea to propose a new highway planning scheme with mile-based pricing. Under the new planning scheme, when roads are congested, the highway administrator applies a congestion charge to earn excess revenue and invests it in increasing the highway capacity. On non-congested sections, on the other hand, the toll rate set by marginal cost pricing is relatively low; thus, the highway administrator must "give up" maintaining the capacity and reduce the highway capacity according to the revenue shortage level.

We propose a new scheme, under which the long-term optimization of highway capacity can be realized through the short-term marginal cost pricing determined according to transportation demand. Under this new planning scheme, the short-term optimal toll rate is determined as the difference between the short-term social marginal cost ($SSMC$) and short-term private marginal cost ($SPMC$) where the $SSMC$ curve crosses with demand curve. A portion of the toll rate — specifically, the difference between the short-term social average cost ($SSAC$) and $SPMC$ — is necessary for maintenance and renewal of the existing highway capacity (Figure 2). When the $SSMC$ is higher than $SSAC$, the toll revenue exceeds the maintenance/renewal cost. The highway administrator then invests the excess amount to increase the highway capacity (lane-widening, network development, etc.). In the next period, the highway capacity is larger than in the previous period, as a result of the investment in the previous period.

Through repetition of pricing and investment, the long-term optimal highway capacity is realized where the $SSMC$ curve crosses the $SSAC$ curve and the demand curve (Figure 3). On the contrary, when the demand is small, the optimal highway capacity is realized by decreasing the highway capacity (lane-narrowing, network density decreasing, etc.).

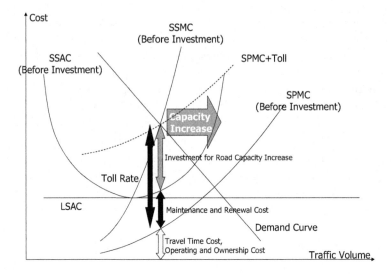

Fig. 2   Cost of roads before investment

Note: SSMC: Short-term Social Marginal Cost; SPMC: Short-term Private Marginal Cost; SSAC: Short-term Social Average Cost; LSAC: Long-term Social Average Cost.

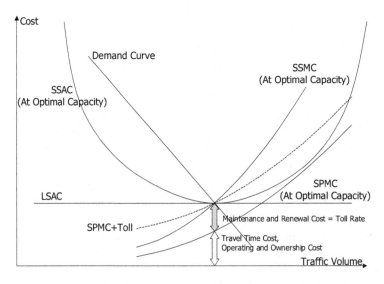

Fig. 3   Cost of roads at optimal capacity

Under the conventional highway planning scheme in Japan, the arterial road network standard or density has been determined in an "engineered" way, which means adequately dealing with the future traffic volume. For example, for the determination of the inter-city arterial road network standard, the "national coefficient theory" has been applied. This theory determines the necessary network density by population, land area, etc. (Imai *et al.*, 1971). For the urban arterial road network, on the other hand, necessary network density and lane numbers have been determined based on the land use and traffic generation density [City Bureau of the (former) Japanese Ministry of Construction, 1992]. These "engineered" methods might be most appropriate during the high-growth period, when no one questions the continuous transportation demand growth.

In the depopulating era that Japan is now facing, however, it is noteworthy to analyze the "economic" aspect of road demand and supply. Economic theory indicates that transportation demand is determined by the price of road use (fuel tax, tolls, etc.), and the price must be set considering the road supply cost. Based on this principle, the price of road use would be high on a costly section of roads both in terms of construction costs and environmental costs, and the higher price would lead to less transportation demand. It is necessary to create a method to estimate the price of road use based on the estimated cost of road construction, maintenance and renewal, so that it is possible to supply the optimal highway capacity through a new planning and financing scheme (a mile-based and social marginal cost pricing).

3   Case 1: More Effective Use of Roads by Discounting Tolls

There have been complaints in recent years that expressways are not fully used due to the high tolls, and simultaneously, that the traffic situation on ordinary roads is deteriorating. Flexible toll rate schemes have been proposed, and there are ongoing social experiments on the discounting of tolls on expressways.

From the viewpoint of minimizing the overall transportation cost, given the present highway capacity, it is recommended to set prices by marginal costs for both expressways and ordinary roads. Thus, when the ordinary roads are congested, it is necessary to introduce a congestion charge on the ordinary roads. However it is not possible to raise the tolls on the ordinary roads. Conversely, it was proposed to reduce the fees on the expressways. The discount for expressway users is expected to have the similar effect as the introduction of a congestion charge for ordinary roads. However, it is not obvious how large the optimal discount is. It depends on the situations on the expressways and the ordinary roads, especially their degrees of congestion.

Therefore, in the following section, we introduce a method for calculating the tolls that minimize transportation costs on parallel expressways and ordinary roads, and justify offering discounts for expressways users with data from social experiments in Hitachi City.

3.1 *Traffic equilibrium model*

A single origin-destination pair is assumed (Figure 4), joined by two parallel routes, a high-speed expressway and an ordinary road. It is also assumed that the total transportation demand between the origin and destination is constant. A toll is paid if Path A is used. The travel time is greater if the user takes Path B instead of Path A, but no toll is paid for Path B. Drivers will choose the path with the lower generalized cost, so equilibrium will be reached between the generalized costs of the expressway and the ordinary road.

If we assume that the transportation demand between the origin and destination is constant, the generalized cost is given in the following expressions: the sum of the travel time cost $(\alpha T \ell)$, the travel cost $(G\ell)$, and the toll (τ). "Generalized cost" means the cost borne by the user of a single vehicle on the highway, whereas "transportation cost", used in the following, means the socially generated cost without transferred cost such as the toll.

Path A: high-speed expressway

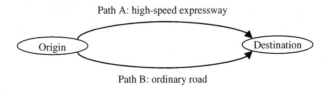

Path B: ordinary road

Fig. 4   Assumed network

$$P_A = \alpha T_A \ell_A + G_A \ell_A + \tau$$
$$P_B = \alpha T_B \ell_B + G_B \ell_B$$
$$G_A = G_A \,(VA), \; G_B = G_B \,(V_B),$$

P_A, P_B: Generalized costs when using Paths A and B (yen)
T_A, T_B: Time consumed per km when using Paths A and B (hour/km)
ℓ_A, ℓ_B: Distances traveled when using Paths A and B (km)
α: Value of time, assumed constant (yen/hour)
G_A, G_B: Costs per km when using Paths A and B, as functions of travel speed (yen/km)
τ: Toll for using Path A (yen).

High traffic volume on a highway results in congestion, lowering the travel speed and increasing the travel time. Therefore, travel time is a function of traffic volume, as follows:

$$T_A = \ell_A/V_A, \; T_B = \ell_B/V_B, \; V_A = V_A(Q_A, \, k_A), \; V_B = V_B\,(Q_B, \, k_B),$$

V_A, V_B: Travel speeds on Paths A and B (km/hour)
Q_A, Q_B: Traffic volumes on Paths A and B (vehicles/hour); traffic volume is constant, so $Q_A + Q_B = Q$
k_A, k_B: Capacities of Paths A and B (vehicles/hour).

The road users select the route that provides the lower generalized cost, so the traffic volumes on Paths A and B reach an equilibrium, where $P_A = P_B$. Solving the above simultaneous equations provides the traffic volumes and the generalized costs on each path.

The total transportation cost and revenue from tolls are given by the following equations. Toll τ is not included in the total transportation cost, since it is a transferred cost.

$$C = (P_A - \tau)\,Q_A + P_B\,Q_B, \; I = \tau Q_A$$

C: Total transportation cost (sum of transportation costs on Paths A and B)
I: Revenue from tolls.

If the toll for Path A is lowered, the cost for Path A is changed, and the equilibrium point for the traffic volume changes, as follows:

$$P^*_A = \alpha T^*_A \ell_A + G^*_A \ell_A + \tau^*, \quad P^*_A = P^*_B$$
$$Q_A < Q^*_A, \ Q^*_B < Q_B$$

τ^*: Toll after discount
P^*_A, P^*_B: Generalized costs of Paths A and B after discount
Q^*_A, Q^*_B: Traffic volumes on Paths A and B after discount.

As a result, the total transportation cost and revenue from tolls change to values C^* and I^*, necessitating the public subsidy of S:

$$C^* = (P^*_A - \tau^*) Q^*_A + P^*_B Q^*_B$$
$$I^* = \tau^* Q^*_A$$
$$S = I - I^*.$$

In the above group of equations, there is a toll for which the total transportation cost is minimized. The transportation cost is represented by a function which increases with the transportation volume; so, when the toll is reduced, the traffic volume on Path A increases by the extent to which the volume on Path B decreases. Here, the benefit due to introduction of the discounted toll is defined as the difference $D \ (=C - C^*)$ in the total transportation cost. The new toll τ is found for which D is maximized.

3.2 Simulation results

Data from a social experiment in Hitachi City were used to examine the effectiveness of a toll rate discount. The reader should refer to Nemoto and Imanishi (2006) for the description and model of the experiment.

3.2.1 Shift of equilibrium point through a toll discount

When the toll is discounted, it shifts the equilibrium point to the right, and the traffic volume on the expressway increases with a commensurate decrease on the ordinary route. The total transportation cost also decreases and reaches a minimum at some toll. The public subsidies used to compensate for the lower tolls also vary. Figures 5 and 6 show the results under the conditions of the experiment in Hitachi City.

Equilibrium points are found in Figure 5 at the intersections of two lines, one representing the generalized cost of using the ordinary road, and the other nearly flat line representing the general cost of the expressway with traffic flow at almost free speeds. At the current toll rate (515 yen), the travel speed on the ordinary road is quite low (i.e., the generalized cost is high). If the toll was reduced to zero, it is expected that all the traffic on the ordinary road could use the expressway, and the total transportation cost would be minimized and the benefit would be maximized. However, we assumed that only 50% of the traffic on the ordinary road can be transferred to the expressway, and then no further transfer to the expressway occurs below a toll of 100 yen (discount rate of 81%). Comparisons of the reduction in transportation cost (i.e., benefit) with the necessary public subsidies showed that the benefit always exceeded the subsidies, for all cases examined.

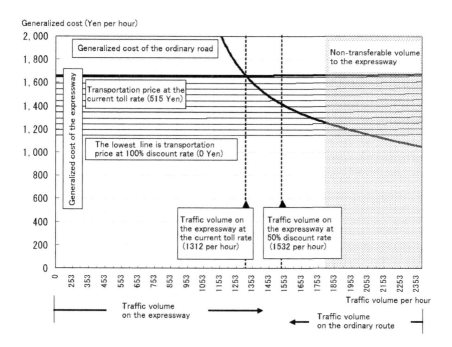

Fig. 5   Toll and generalized cost equilibrium

Note: The lowest line represents a toll of 0 yen; the succeeding lines indicate rising tolls in 50-yen steps.

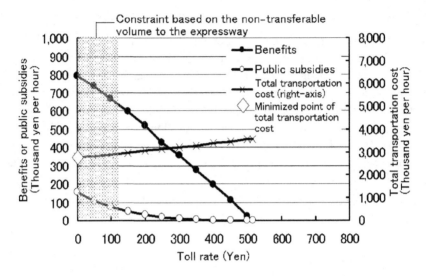

Fig. 6   Toll and total transportation cost

3.2.2   *Effects of toll discount in different degrees of congestion*

A toll discount has varying effects, depending on whether the traffic volume is large or small. The Hitachi model was expanded and we analyzed the effects in cases with different "degrees of congestion of both routes", which means the sum of the traffic volumes on both paths is divided by the capacities of the paths.

When the congestion is high and the toll is lowered, this transfers traffic from the ordinary route to the expressway. The travel speed is almost free, but there is some reduction in speed on the expressway, increasing the generalized cost (see Figure 7). When the congestion reaches 0.9, the toll resulting in the lowest total transportation cost is 200 yen (Figure 8).

3.2.3   *Summary*

This analysis estimated the effectiveness of reducing transportation cost by varying the toll on a high-speed expressway that is parallel to an ordinary route, with the following results:

(1)   An equation was created using observed data to approximate the relation between the traffic volume and travel speed in order to create a model of traffic equilibrium. Variations in traffic were reproduced by varying the toll in this model and calculating the resulting traffic.

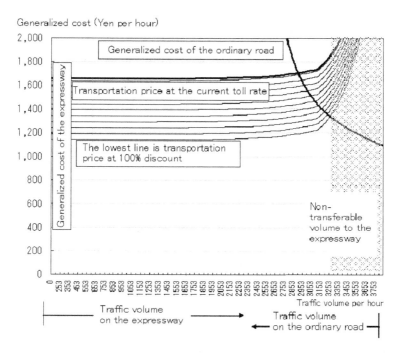

Fig. 7 Equilibrium points for generalized cost at given toll rates at road congestion of 0.9

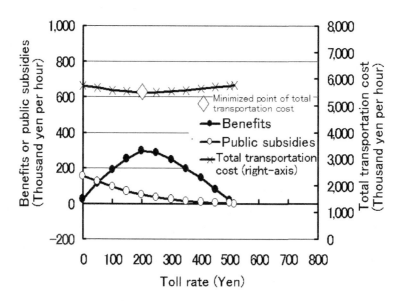

Fig. 8 Relation between toll and benefit at road congestion of 0.9

(2) A financial benefit is realized, reducing the total transportation cost, when tolls on expressways are discounted. The benefit can be greater than the compensation for the shortfall in toll revenue, but this does not hold in all cases; during severe congestion, raising tolls results in a lower total transportation cost.

4   Case 2: Optimal Highway Capacity Building Through Mile-Based Pricing

The purpose of this analysis was to calculate the user's share by mile-based pricing according to the marginal pricing approach, in order to propose a highway planning scheme that provides an optimal highway capacity over the long-term. Here, "optimal highway capacity" means the highway capacity that meets the transportation demand at a minimum cost. The highway capacity is determined from the intersection of the road demand curve with the long-term marginal cost curve. This method appears to be practical for calculating highway capacity that can be efficiently maintained and renewed.

4.1   *Simulation framework*

In this section, we discuss the simulation of optimal highway capacity building based on the financing scheme described in Section 2.2. Assuming there exists some extent of road stock, the purpose of this simulation is to calculate the toll rate based on short-term social marginal cost pricing (SMCP) and also the toll revenue, then to calculate the optimal level of highway capacity given the revenues are to be allocated to maintain and renew the tolled section of the road.

The framework of simulation is shown in Figure 9. First, we set the initial amount of the highway capacity as given. The amount of the highway capacity with the traffic volume (transportation demand) determines the travel speed on the section and finally determines the toll revenue. (This process can be defined as the "Revenue Side" as shown on the left side of Figure 9.) On the other hand, the highway capacity also determines the necessary amount of expenditure to maintain, renew and widen the tolled section. (This is the "Expenditure Side" as shown on the right side of Figure 9.) At the end of each period, we calculate the excess amount (toll revenue minus expenditure for maintenance and renewal) that can be spent to increase the highway capacity (lane widening), and as a result,

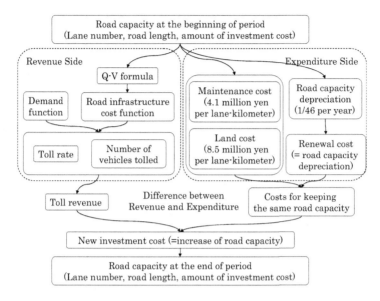

Fig. 9   Framework of the optimal capacity building simulation

calculate the increased amount of the highway capacity at the end of the period, which is the initial capacity for the next period.

The excess amount of toll revenue minus the expenditure will decrease as the number of periods increases, because the toll rate decreases and the expenditure increases as the capacity increases. The excess amount will be zero when the toll revenue equals the expenditure for maintenance and renewal. The highway capacity at this point is defined as "optimal". We will examine how the highway capacity changes through the simulation periods.

We consider the number of lanes, which translates into highway capacity, to be variable. In this simulation, we assumed the tolled section was the only one route, and then we introduced the above definition of highway capacity. Highway capacity could be defined differently if we considered a road network composed of several routes. This point should be examined in the future.

The following sections outline the revenue and expenditure calculations.

4.1.1   *Revenue calculation in the simulation model*

We first need to estimate the cost function of roads and also the transportation demand function to calculate the toll rate based on marginal cost pricing theory. We used the observed data of traffic volume and corresponding travel speed, with reference to the existing studies to estimate the cost function of the road and transportation demand function, respectively.

Regarding the cost function of the road, Small, Winston and Evans (1989) considered that the road cost could be explained by the function below. This equation consists of the infrastructure cost of the road (the first term on the right side) and the total time cost of road users (the second term on the right side):

$$C(q,Q) = aK(Q) + qht(q,Q),$$

where $C(q, Q)$ refers to the cost function of the road. Variables q, Q, $K(Q)$, $aK(Q)$, h, and $t(q, Q)$ refer to hourly traffic volume, highway capacity, construction cost for highway capacity Q, yearly road cost (including maintenance and renewal), unit value of time and travel time function (we calculated travel time as a function of traffic volume), respectively. We first estimated the QV function, which calculates travel speed as a function of traffic volume to estimate the cost function of the road.

Considering the data availability, etc., we applied the observed data of the traffic volume and travel speed of Kosei highway (access-limited, 2-lane highway) to the BPR (Bureau of Public Roads) function to estimate the parameters (Figure 10).

The BPR function is shown as below. $V(Q)$ refers to the travel speed (km/h). V_0, Q and K refer to the free flow speed, hourly traffic volume and hourly traffic capacity, respectively. The estimated variables and parameters, α and β, for Kosei highway are $V_0 = 65$, $K = 800$, $\alpha = 0.15$, $\beta = 4$.

$$V(Q) = 60 \times (1/(V_0 (1 + \alpha (Q/K))^\beta)).$$

Based on the QV function estimated above, we now estimate the cost function of the road as follows:

$$C(n,Q) = I(n) + Qh(L/v(Q)),$$

where $C(Q)$ stands for the total cost function of the road (yen/km·hour), and Q, $I(n)$, n, h, L and $V(Q)$ are the hourly traffic volume (vehicles/hour),

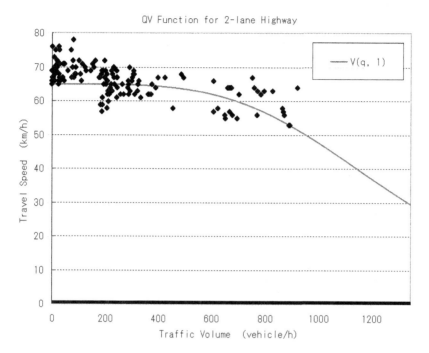

Fig. 10 QV function of Kosei highway

cost function of road development (construction, land acquisition and maintenance) (yen/km·hour), lane number, unit value of time (yen/h), length of tolled road (km) and QV function (km/h), respectively. The variables are set as $I(n) = 66{,}000 \times n$, $h = 3{,}772$, and $L = 10$.

Next, we estimate the (inverse) demand function, based on the past studies such as those of Small and Yan (2001). We assumed the demand function has a linear shape, as shown below:

$$P(TD) = a - b\ TD,$$

where P refers to the generalized cost for road users (yen/vehicle), and TD refers to the transportation demand (vehicles/hour). Both a and b are parameters and are estimated as $a = 4{,}000$ and $b = -3.75$.

We can now calculate the toll rate by marginal cost pricing theory, using the cost function and demand function estimated as above. For example, the initial toll rate is set at 343 yen/10 km, which is the difference of SSMC and SPMC, where SSMC crosses the demand curve P (Figure 11).

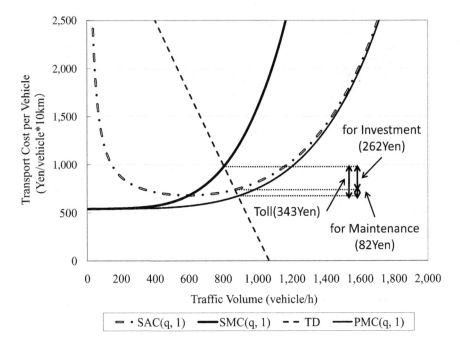

Fig. 11   Calculation of toll rate

Out of the tolled 343 yen, 82 yen (difference between SSAC and SPMC) is the amount to be spent on maintenance, and 262 yen (difference between SSMC and SSAC) is spent on the investment to increase highway capacity.

4.1.2   *Expenditure calculation in the simulation model*

The cost of the road is defined as the cost for maintenance, land and renewal in this model. The unit cost of maintenance is set at 4.1 million yen/km·year, as shown in the Road Bureau and Urban and Rural Development Bureau of Ministry of Land, Infrastructure and Transport (2003).

Second, the unit land cost is set at 8.5 million yen/km, as a result of the average of actual 11 general road works adopted in FY 2005 (140 million yen/km) times typical ground rent (6%). Therefore, the land cost for each period is calculated as the initial highway capacity times unit land cost.

Third, the renewal cost is calculated on the assumption that the duration period of road stock is 46 years (Cabinet Office, 2002) and therefore the capacity would decrease by 1/46 every period without renewal. Hence, the necessary renewal cost for each period is calculated as the initial monetary value of the highway capacity times 1/46.

These three cost items are necessary for each period to keep the highway capacity as it is. The investment cost to increase the highway capacity is set at 287.5 million yen/km·lane. In other words, 287.5 million yen is necessary to add another lane to the section.

4.2 *Simulation results*

4.2.1 *Expanding highway capacity through mile-based pricing*

Simulation results are summarized in Figures 12 to 14.

In the first period, the toll rate is 343 yen [SSMC (1,009 yen) minus SPMC (666 yen)] and the traffic volume (number of tolled vehicles) is 798 vehicles/h. After the second period, the SSMC, SPMC and toll rate decrease gradually, while the traffic volume increases gradually. The toll revenue is about 400 million yen in the first period, but it rapidly decreases as the toll rate decreases.

When we look at the cost components, the maintenance and renewal costs increase gradually, while the investment cost decreases. As the investment cost decreases, the additional number of lanes also decreases

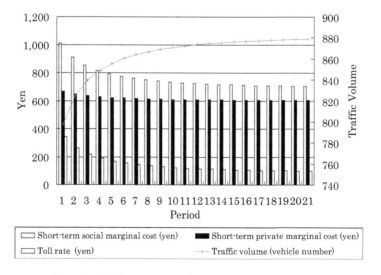

Fig. 12 Toll rate and traffic volume for each period

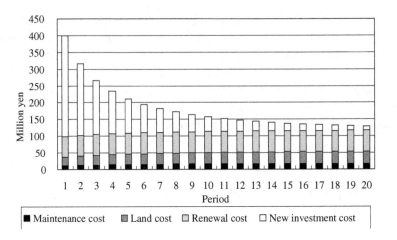

Fig. 13 Use of the toll revenue for each period

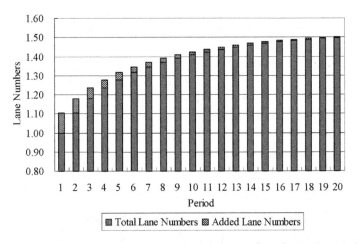

Fig. 14 Total lane numbers and added lane numbers for each period

(0.1 lanes are added in the first period but fewer in the following periods). As a result of this simulation, the initial highway capacity (1 lane for each direction, i.e., a 2-lane highway) will grow by investment to 1.5 lanes in each direction in the 20th period. This is the optimal and convergent capacity of this road.

4.2.2 Summary

In this case study, we test a new road planning scheme to build optimal highway capacity through social marginal cost pricing by applying the concept of Mohring (1976). The traditional argument has focused on the tradeoff issue between "marginal cost pricing theory" and "average cost pricing theory". Although the former calculates the optimal toll rate in the short-term, the latter calculates the optimal toll rate to maintain current capacity; in both cases, the current highway capacity is considered to be given and fixed. This case study, on the other hand, proposes a planning scheme to build an optimal highway capacity in the long-term through the mile-based and social marginal cost pricing.

Furthermore, we tried a simulation based on the model proposed to see how the optimal toll rate and highway capacity is realized throughout the periods. By applying the data obtained from examples of the actual road works in Japan to the cost function of road construction/maintenance and the cost function of time, we observed that the simulation calculated the optimal highway capacity in the future, and thus proved that the proposed planning scheme is feasible.

5 Conclusions

Telecommunications technologies have provided an opportunity to introduce mile-based road pricing which enables us to charge road users depending on the real-time external effects (e.g., congestion). This paper examined pricing theory and pointed out that social marginal cost pricing could be applied both to short-term optimization to manage transportation demand on highways, and to long-term optimization to reach desirable highway capacity.

We conducted case studies to simulate these two optimization processes by introducing data on road cost function, QV function and so on, demonstrating that new financing schemes with mile-based pricing would be feasible and effective.

We recognize, however, that these simulation models contain further issues to be solved. First, we need more simulation analyses by applying other conditions. For example, the optimal road stock does not always converge to a certain level, as shown in the simulation in the second case study. Second, we need more detailed examples of the road cost and price elasticity of transportation demand, etc., to refine the exogenous variables. Finally, although we only examined the case of the fixed demand curve, we also need to examine the appropriate financing and planning scheme for the cases where the transportation demand will change in the future.

Acknowledgments

The authors appreciate the support of Mr. Yoshikazu Imanishi and Mr. Akira Kajiwara from Public Planning and Policy Studies Inc. for model building and simulation analysis.

References

Cabinet Office (2002). *Infrastructure in Japan — Stocks Over Generations* (in Japanese).

City Bureau of the (former) Japanese Ministry of Construction (1992). *Affluent Society and Town/Street Development*, Taisei Publishing (in Japanese).

Imai, Y., Inoue, T., and Yamane, T. (1971). *The Long-Term Planning of Roads*, Gijutsu Shoin (in Japanese).

Mohring, H. (1976). *Transportation Economics*, Cambridge Mels.

Nemoto, T. and Imanishi, Y. (2006). Evaluating the economic effect of expressway toll reductions, *Journal of Transportation and Economics* 66(11), pp. 59–69 (in Japanese).

Quinet, E. and Vickerman, R. (2004). *Principles of Transport Economics*, Edward Elgar.

Road Bureau and Urban and Rural Development Bureau of Ministry of Land, Infrastructure and Transport (2003). *Manual for Cost-Benefit Analysis* (in Japanese).

Small, K., Winston, C., and Evans, C. (1989). *Road Work: A New Highway Pricing and Investment Policy*, Brookings Institute.

Small, K. and Yan, J. (2001). The value of 'value pricing' of roads: Second-best pricing and product differentiation, *Journal of Urban Economics* 49, pp. 310–336.

Projects of Participatory Production and Their Management: Practice in Industrial Accumulation in Suwa

Hajime Kita

Professor, Academic Center for Computing and Media Studies
Kyoto University

Mikihiko Mori

Assistant Professor, Academic Center for Computing and Media Studies
Kyoto University

1   Introduction

"Industrial Accumulation" (IA), which is the accumulation of thousands of small manufacturers in a region, is one of the characteristic structures of Japanese industry. With physical nearness, IA enables manufacturing of various products, and it is one source of the competitiveness of Japanese industry. However, in recent years, manufacturing of mass production has shifted to other Asian countries, especially to China, and a new vision of exploiting the strength of IA is required.

The strength of IA is the flexibility and quickness of production brought about by concentration of various small production platforms in the same region. To cope with the "Asian Shift" of production, some companies in IA are pursuing further sophistication of production technology to keep their competitiveness. In addition to physical nearness of the platforms, utilizing IT such as CAD/CAM and information networks, production with very small lot size and short delivery time has been realized. As a business/market exploiting this strength, trial production for research and development has attracted attention. Beyond such direction of the production, Ohashi and Deguchi have proposed "Highly Custom-Made Production" (HCMP), in which the end users participate directly in the production process and realize the products that meet their individual needs as a vision of a novel industry (Ohashi *et al.*, 2002; Ohashi *et al.*, 2003; Deguchi, 2002).

Taking the vision of HCMP into consideration, the authors have carried out a trial case of collaborative production in which a chassis of personal computer realizing the user's needs is developed by students of a graduate school of Kyoto University and several companies in the IA in Suwa/Okaya area. This paper describes the process of the case and discusses the possibility and problems in participatory production toward HCMP.

2 Participatory Production

For the participation of end users in production, several styles can be taken ranging between mass production and customization (Matsui, 2005). The one most successful and closest to mass production is the BTO (buy-to-order) style taken, e.g., by DELL. Customers can construct products that meet their needs by choosing several options prepared by the producer in advance. An intermediate style is, as taken by TANOMICOMU (http://www.tanomi.com/) by Wedge Holdings Co. in Japan, when a person proposes his/her own idea of products on the web, and if it succeeds in gathering sufficient participants as buyers, the coordinator of the site arranges its production. HCMP proposed by Ohashi and Deguchi is at the other extreme of participatory production. It tries to realize more personalized products through direct collaboration between the user and the manufacturers.

The possible targets of HCMP are trial production for research and development, production for internal use in factories, products that need to adapt to each user in healthcare, and products for hobby use. Considering these targets, the production process has characteristics of conventional production projects in the sense that products are visible and concrete. On the other hand, it resembles software development in the sense that it is highly customized production including requirement analysis, and the weight of project management gets large. Thus, it is important to support the projects with the process knowledge of the project management and utilization of information technologies.

The authors have investigated the above-mentioned issue through real cases of trial products for research in university with the collaboration of companies in the IA in Suwa/Okaya area, one of the active IA in Japan

(Kita *et al.*, 2004a,b; Tomizawa *et al.*, 2003; Kita, 2002). Through these practices, we have obtained know-how in various aspects such as coordination of production projects, distant communication and collaboration, and selection of production technologies suitable to such cases.

Furthermore in recent years, Project-Based Learning (PBL) has attracted attention in higher education, especially in education of engineering. In PBL, the learners are asked to complete some projects of the problem-solving type by themselves, subjectively. PBL is useful for learning the knowledge of the target domain and process knowledge of project management, and self-learning (Kita, 2006). In the participatory production, both the users and manufacturers of the projects face the diversity and novelty of the targets and production activities, and therefore it is important to accumulate and utilize the knowledge in education with the recognition of the participants as learners.

3   Experimental Case

The case reported in this paper is carried out as one of the projects held in FY 2005 in "Information System Design as Co-creation with the Societies, the Initiative for Attractive Education in Graduate School, Graduate School of Informatics, Kyoto University (FYs 2005–2006)".

3.1   *Objectives of the experiment*

Under the vision of HCMP, this project aims at investigating learning opportunities to:

(1) make graduate students have the experience of realizing their needs collaboratively with several companies in IA;

(2) understand the process of design, production and maintenance of the products with distant communication/collaboration among end users and producers of the process innovation;

(3) understand the potential of the vision of a novel industry;

(4) foster capability of project coordination for collaborative production; and

(5) try to think about innovation utilizing the information technologies to support the collaborative production process.

3.2   *Schedule of the case*

This project was carried out in the following schedule:

- 1–17 December 2005: Learning of collaborative production in a seminar style, concept making of the target product at Kyoto University side, visit of a factory in Suwa/Okaya area, and having a meeting to start the project at Suwa/Okaya.
- 18 December 2005–15 January 2006: Discussion and finalize the requirements for design via CSCW.
- 16 January–26 February 2006: Discussion of the design of the product in detail.
- 26 February–25 March 2006: Finalization of the design, trial production and evaluation of the information systems for support of the project, proposal of the improvement.
- 26 March–17 July 2006: Reflection and reporting of the project.

3.3   *Organization for the project*

At the Kyoto University side, as well as Kita and Mori (the authors), Prof. Hiroyuki Matsui of the Graduate School of Business Administration also participated in the project as facilitating faculties of the project. He is also investigating the participatory production using Suwa/Okaya area as the research field (Matsui, 2005). Three graduate students of the Graduate School of Informatics participated, taking the role of the end users. At the Suwa/Okaya side, Industry Network Ltd. (Toshio Ohashi is the president) participated as the coordinator of the project/production. Next Design Co. took part as the mechanical designer, and Kojima Industry took part as manufacturer.

3.4   *Practice of the project*

3.4.1   *Starting phase (1–17 January 2005)*

Since the available time for the project was limited to four months, which was not sufficient to discuss the concept of the target product from scratch, we decided to develop a chassis of personal computer as the target product based on the experience of trial production by Prof. Matsui. Considering the objective of the project, the three graduate students took the roles of the project leader (Student A), a staff for information system and recording of the activities in the project, and a facilitator of the project meetings. During this period, they held five meetings and discussed the concept of the product.

In the beginning, they adopted a concept of "a PC chassis that had flexibility in extension", and the design and parts layout in the chassis were discussed. However, in the fourth meeting, they found that the objective and the concept of the product were not clarified sufficiently. Hence, they forgave this concept and started the discussion again. They discussed what type of PC they really wanted to have. Considering the hobby of Student A was audio, they finally decided to design a PC fit for an audio system. In the fifth meeting, the concept was deepened to a PC fit for the booth of a disc jockey, and they had a rough sketch of a "L-shape chassis".

During this phase, we visited the IA of Suwa/Okaya area, and held a meeting with people from the coordinating and manufacturing companies. The students also visited the precise metal sheet cutting and folding factory to learn the process of manufacturing. During the meeting, the students presented their concept and discussed the problems in manufacturing, budget, timeframe, etc., with the people from the IA. We also decided to use a web-based CSCW tool called GooP designed for management of production projects (Figure 1) for accumulation of information, and to continue discussion via e-mail and web.

3.4.2 Specification phase (18 December 2005–15 January 2006)

During this period, the students made a mock-up model of the conceptual design of the PC chassis with advice obtained from the collaborating members [Figure 2(a)], and also constructed a prototype PC with the parts used for the target product. Further, at this stage, they introduced an extended concept called "L-family". According to this concept, the PC would consist of a large L-shape chassis for the CPU and a small L-shape chassis for the hard disk and optical drives. The built mock-up was sent to Industry Network Co.

At this stage, the students held many off-line and face-to-face meetings to handle the mock-up model and actual parts for the PC. They recorded the meetings with a video since discussion of shape and color is difficult to express in words. However, only the decisions obtained in the meetings were distributed in the mailing list. Photographs and drawings were also used for distant communication.

Fig. 1   GooP: A web-based CSCW tool for trial production

3.4.3 *Design stage (16 January–26 February 2006)*

Based on the mock-up model made by the students, a PC chassis was designed by the professional designer of mechanical systems participating in the project. During the design process, his ideas expressed in 3D CAD were circulated in the mailing list as picture files [Figure 2(b)]. Responding to such information, design in detail was discussed on the mailing list. Off-line discussion was held at the Kyoto University side, and only the decisions were circulated in the mailing list. Thus, recording the discussion in some media was difficult. During this period, the students also bought the parts for a "L-family PC" by themselves and checked the function of the PC.

At this phase, an important problem occurred due to lack of communication. In the specification phase, the students had introduced the concept of a parent-child type two-part model as "L-family". However, it was not well understood by the coordinator and manufacturer (except the designer) at the Suwa/Okaya side. The two-part model ended up costing more than

(a) Paper mock-up model

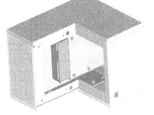
(b) 3D CAD design

(c) Final product PC

Fig. 2   Products in the participatory production project

the initial rough estimation based on the concept of a L-shape PC consisting of only one chassis, and we later had to forego the child chassis for disk drives due to the budget constraint. In this phase, communication was made mainly by the mailing list, but sufficient attention was not paid by all the project members.

One reason for this failure was that important decisions were made only at the face-to-face meetings while visiting Suwa/Okaya, and that e-mail was used only for exchanging data and opinions. Further, the participants of both sides were quite busy with other activities during this period, and messages distributed through the mailing list might not have been read well by all the members.

At the end of this phase, the students visited Suwa/Okaya, and by referring to the blueprint, they decided on the details of the design such as the material and screws used for the chassis. In the meeting, they confirmed and shared decisions, and clarified the tasks that should be done before the next visit.

3.4.4   *Manufacturing phase (27 February–25 March 2006)*

During this period, manufacturing of the PC chassis was carried out based on the design of the 3D CAD. In the previous phase, the design information was shared by data in picture format. However, the students had few experiences of mechanical design and encountered difficulty in examining the cabling and handling of parts in the designed chassis using only the pictures. Hence, we decided to use "e-Drawings" — interactive preview software of 3D CAD data. This improved the process of design confirmation by the students.

While we had previously decided to complete the manufacturing of the chassis at the final meeting, this was delayed since the manufacturing company was too busy. At the final visit to Suwa/Okaya, the students tried to test the assembling of the chassis and confirm the result of manufacturing. The final trial product is shown in Figure 2(c).

3.4.5   *Reflection phase (25 March–17 July 2006)*

After completion of production, the students analyzed the process of the project, and discussed the problems and possible improvements mainly from the viewpoint of information systems. For the reflection of the project, they listed the activities of the participants as much as possible, and made a chart to give graphical representation of the process. Then, by referring to the chart, they discussed the problems that occurred in the project and possible improvements. For listing of the behavior, they used the archives of the e-mail communication and minutes of the face-to-face meetings. The recognized activities were listed on a calendar. They also employed Work Breakdown Structure (WBS), a technique in project management, for visualization of the activities.

This analysis shows that the delay and deterioration of the product were brought about by failure in sharing the decisions circulated on the mailing list, and over-concentration of the work at certain periods. Based on the analysis, the students proposed a concept of an information system for confirmation of decisions in the project, visualization of the project progress, and issuing warnings for completion of assigned tasks to the members. The students and faculties then visited Suwa/Okaya and reported their analysis to the members from the IA, and discussed improvements to the process for participatory production.

The students analyzed the whole process using the archives of the mailing list, minutes of the meetings and other information yielded in the project. Since such information was not well arranged for analysis, this took about 30–40 hours. Information acquisition, accumulation and arrangement of the project in a more systematic manner will help the reflection of the project in the future.

4 Problems and Improvements in the Participatory Production

4.1 *Facilitation in the case and its problems*

With the experience of similar projects (Kita *et al.*, 2004a,b; Tomizawa *et al.*, 2003; Kita, 2002), we have introduced some ideas for facilitation:

- First, the concept of the product and outline of the project was proposed from the user (university) side, and the coordinator roughly evaluated its feasibility. Then, all the project members had a face-to-face meetings to start the project. Previous experiences show that such meetings are very important in constructing mutual trust and understanding the user's needs and the manufacturer's knowledge level in production technology and process. At the same time, the users also have opportunities to learn possible options in production and their constraints. It is difficult to express such information in words or to exchange it over telecommunication media. To encourage such mutual learning, we also conducted visits to the factory by the users. Such face-to-face meetings were also held while fixing the design of the product. Effectiveness of such face-to-face meetings in distant collaboration is also experienced through distance learning programs such as video conferencing system.
- Utilization of information technology for distant collaboration: We used the CSCW tool named "GooP" developed by the Industry Network Co. This tool was developed based on similar distant collaborative production projects, and was designed to accumulate and arrange various sorts of data such as text, pictures, video and CAD data effectively. It also enables smooth communication amongst members belonging to different organizations by combining the Web (a pull/stock type media) and e-mail (a push/flow type media). We also used a video conferencing system and recorded the meetings on a HDD video recorder.

- We asked the users (students) to build a paper mock-up model to share the concrete image of the product.
- We used 3D CAD not only for collaboration between the designer and the manufacturers, but also for that between the users and the designer. Operation of CAD is only done by the professional designer; however, the users gave comments by examining the pictures generated by the CAD software, or by reviewing the design using a preview software. The 3D CAD helped the users since the view given by the 3D CAD is easy to understand for ordinary laymen.
- To make the vision of the product clear and discussion more fruitful, we assigned different roles such as the producer of the product and the facilitator of the meeting to different students.

While such facilitation was mostly effective in this case, we also found several problems:

- In this distant collaboration of production project, vast amounts of information concerning design and discussion on it were circulated in the network. However, the workload to track such information for the project coordinator/facilitator was very high. Consequently, the coordinator who governed the whole budget failed in controlling the design discussed between the end users and the designer, and we had to forego the child chassis of the two-box design.
- Since 3D CAD was a powerful tool for both the professional designers and the end users, the users often proposed ideas to improve the function of the products, and the designer tried to meet their requirements by making the design more complex. However, this raised the cost of manufacturing higher.
- We had experienced several projects of trial products for research use. However, compared with the full-time researchers who participated in such projects as users, students had to carry out many other activities such as course work, part-time jobs, examinations and job hunting in parallel with the project. This may have reduced their motivation to participate in the project. Furthermore, due to differences in lifestyle, it was difficult to find a common time for video conferencing that worked well in the previous projects.
- Even though the users were of graduate school student level, they had a lack of experience in creating concepts of custom products that realized their needs. Hence, they took time for concept making.

In the following, based on findings in this case, we discuss the problems in the participatory production for HCMP.

4.2   *Issues in project management*

In HCMP, we have to deal with many production projects in parallel. We therefore need to manage many projects effectively and reduce the management load of the coordinators. For example, we have to assist the coordinators in gathering the manufacturers and designers to meet the users' needs, and to improve the quality of the projects. Effective monitoring is also needed to enhance awareness of the progress of the projects and to ensure timely contribution from the participants.

Time scheduling of the project will also be a big issue. From the detail design phase to the manufacturing phase, temporal concentration of activities to particular projects may improve the quality of the project since it helps to keep the context of the project among the members.

4.3   *Issues in learning*

In participatory production for HCMP, all the stakeholders face some novel situation, i.e., new target products, their values, production process and technologies to be learnt by the users. Thus, the projects should be operated by considering the participants as learners, and learning should be built in as a key factor in management of the projects. Face-to-face meetings must be facilitated with the aforesaid recognition. While it may be expensive, mutual visits (e.g., visits to the user's site and producer's site) will be helpful. Further, construction of a self-learning environment with e-learning is another important factor. For example, e-learning material giving virtual experience of the participatory production will be useful.

4.4   *Issues in production technologies*

For HCMP, production is done with a very small lot size compared with the conventional mass production. Hence, we need to seek the technology that makes production in a small lot size cheap such as technology for rapid prototyping. Computerized machine tools that accept CAD data will be important tools. Sometimes, such environment makes the manufacturing process directly open to the end users (Gershenfeld *et al.*, 2005). We also need to have choices of module products to achieve the user's needs by combining them.

4.5 *Issues in utilization of information technology*

In the reported case, we utilized various IT tools such as 3D CAD, web and e-mail-based CSCW, and video conferencing. Information technology is the key factor to absorb the diversity in HCMP. We will also need novel concepts of Web 2.0 types. Making the production project open to a wide range of people interested in such activities will be an interesting idea (Tapscott and Williams, 2006). In the management of production process, we have to collect vast amounts of information yielded in the real collaborating world for concept making, design, manufacturing and evaluation, and then accumulate and arrange them in the virtual space. While software for production management does exist, we need to explore CSCW/CSCL tools for project-based learning considering the learning factor of the activities (Akahi *et al.*, 2007; Batatia, 2001). Further, to support information retrieval for matching users and producers in coordinating the projects, to edit effectively the accumulated information for various usages to support information retrieval and evaluation in design, and to generate documents such as manuals for users, repeat production and maintenance automatically utilizing the accumulated information in the project will be the subjects of future study.

5 Conclusion

In this paper, we discussed the possibility and problems in participatory production for highly custom-made production through a case of making a PC chassis with the collaboration of university graduate students and manufacturers in industry accumulation. The case shows the potential of participatory production, and problems in project management, learning, production technology and utilization of information technology. We would like to improve the process through further practice.

References

Akahi, K., Matsuzawa, Y., and Ohiwa, H. (2007). A Course Management System Supporting Project-Based Learning, IPSJ SIG Technical Report, CE-88 (in Japanese).

Batatia, H. (2001). A model for an innovative project-based learning management system for engineering education, CALIE2001, Tunis, 8–10 November.

Deguchi, H. (2002). Open source production system on industrial accumulation, *Organizational Science* 36(2), pp. 38–53.

Gershenfeld, N. *et al.* (2005). *FAB The Coming Revolution on Your Desktop — From Personal Computers to Personal Fabrication*, Basic Books.

Kita, H. (2002). University and industrial accumulation: Collaborative production for research, *Organizational Science* 36(2), pp. 28–37.

Kita, H. (2006). Education in university and project management, in *Proceedings of the IAP2M Spring Conference*, pp. 103–108 (in Japanese).

Kita, H., Miyamoto, Y., and Takei, M. (2004a). Creation of custom-made markets and information technology — From a viewpoint of project support, in *Proceedings of the SICE 34th Research Meeting of SIG System Engineering*, pp. 55–58 (in Japanese).

Kita, H., Kimura, H., Yamazaki, Y., and Deguchi, H. (2004b). Manufacturing of reinforcement learning robots by collaboration of universities and industrial accumulation, in *Proceedings of the SICE 34th Research Meeting of SIG System Engineering*, pp. 25–28 (in Japanese).

Matsui, H. (2005). A feasibility study of the online manufacturing system getting the most of industrial accumulation — The case study of the 17cm PC project, *Keizai-Ronsou* 175(3), pp. 92–108 (in Japanese).

Ohashi, T. *et al.* (2002). Toward a creation of new industry and value, *Organizational Science* 36(2), pp. 15–27.

Ohashi, T., Kita, H., and Deguchi, H. (2003). Creation of a novel industrial platform — Challenges in Okaya, in *Proceedings of the SICE System Integration Division Annual Conference (SICE SI2003)*, pp. 984–985 (in Japanese).

Tapscott, D. and Williams, A. D. (2006). *Wikinomics: How Mass Collaboration Changes Everything*, Portfolio.

Tomizawa, H. *et al.* (2003). The case study of the robot prototyping in the open research & production process from the activities of the SME Coalition Model Working Group, in *Proceedings of the 7th Annual Conference of the Japan Association for Evolutionary Economics*, pp. 358–363 (in Japanese).

Part 6

Project Management Infrastructures for Evolving the Standard

Abstract

Undoubtedly, the project management standard is the principal infrastructure. In the global competition, it is without exemption that social acceptance must be assured for survival, and the endeavors for improvement are sustainable. Part 6 covers five papers as illustrated below.

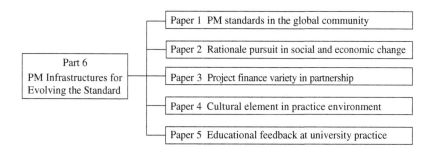

In the first paper, the fair evaluation of standards in the global community is briefed on the first Japanese version of P2M in 2001 as base interpretation. This is further intended to encompass dominant factors affected in the infrastructure. The second paper deals with the outcome of continuous efforts over six years to reflect the improved rationale in social and economic change. Turning to the financing trend, project finance has been observed in a variety of cases in relation with collaboration partnership and risk management, and is studied in the third paper.

The fourth paper introduces the proven outcome of finding cultural factors managed practically in global operations, and is worthy of reading by multinational managers. University is a significant base not only in penetrating standards by education, but also in evolving the standard by joint research. In the fifth paper, six years' practice of education is introduced with evaluated findings. As summarized, Part 6 focuses on the dominant factors which form infrastructure or the environment for betterment of PM standards. The contents are further summarized as follows.

Paper 1: World PM Trends and the Position of P2M in the Global Community

In contemporary society, a variety of types of professionals like engineers, lawyers and accountants perform their specific jobs and duties applying knowledge, skills and disciplines. In order to prove their competencies, they are required to present some evidences of career path and degree of qualification as proven by the reliable authorities. To implement an accreditation system for this purpose, the authorities have to publish standards of knowledge or competence guidelines for public acceptance. Dr. Lynn Crawford, the author of the first paper, is a distinguished researcher acquainted with the world standards of project management. She guides the positioning and contributions of the first Japanese guidelines of P2M established in 2001 in the global community. By citing the renowned standards in the world, readers may be enlightened with the properties of the Japanese standards and their background.

Paper 2: Examples of Changes of Japanese Corporate Business Model: Why is KPM Essentially Important Now?

To bridge thinking from the first version of P2M to the new KPM framework proposed in Part 1, Visiting Prof. Toshihiko Kinoshita of Waseda University, an expert in international economics and finance and author of the second paper, provides distinct rationales in KPM framework faced in relation with economic changes and great reforms (*kaikaku*). His broad, but sharp angle may benefit readers with insightful implications of progress and possibilities in KPM applications. As the paper title suggests, typical examples are quoted and explained in KPM reasoning for why business model changes were needed and successful.

Paper 3: Knowledge of Project Management and Finance in Japan

In the traditional paradigm of project management in the contractor's view, cost management has been a critical subject for cost estimating and budget keeping. On the contrary, KPM underlines the partners' collaboration scheme and the associated financing support in the owner's or sponsor's view. The third paper is written by Masaaki Horiguchi, the head officer of Japan Bank for International Cooperation and an instructor at Teikyo University, who lectures on domestic and overseas finance in Japan. His experience is not only limited to private project financing, but also expands to public financing base of ODA — Official Development Aid. The author endeavors to extend maximum application in limited page regarding project finance as project knowledge and infrastructure angle.

Paper 4: Transcultural Management: Cultural Relevance in Different Industries

This paper presents the new implications to those who run global business operations at enterprises. The author, Prof. Emiko Magoshi of J. F. Oberlin University, applies the famous Trompenaars model of multi-layered cultural structure in global operations in two cases in Europe and the US, with the co-author, Mr. Akio Yamamoto of Kajima Corporation. The model is composed of the outer layer of culture represented by artifacts and products, the mid-layer of culture represented by norms and values, and the inner layer of culture represented by basic assumptions. The proven results and findings in this unique challenge will help international business in multicultural settings to be conducted more smoothly.

Paper 5: Educational Effectiveness and Implementation of KPM in the Cultivation of Human Resource

The author, Dr. Masatoshi Nishio, has been teaching information system and data-oriented approach at Chiba Institute of Technology. Taking into account the circumstance that most graduate students are engaged in system development and management in the ICT industry, a unique policy of education is targeted in the practical training of leadership and management skills guided by P2M and, lately, by KPM standard. The way of implementation is programmed for practical application and debates in team workshop style. In his evaluation, students are trained practically in such a way that leadership is initiated and problem solving capability is fostered to the agenda in practice. The implementation style and evaluation evidence are exhibited for the model of human resource training. It is worthy to note that graduated students are highly appreciated at enterprises.

Masatoshi Nishio
Professor, Faculty of Social Systems Science
Chiba Institute of Technology

World PM Trends and the Position of P2M in the Global Community

Lynn Crawford
Professor of Project Management
Bond University, Australia
and
ESC Lille, France

1 Introduction

In November 2002, the Engineering Advancement Association of Japan and the Japan Project Management Development Committee first launched the P2M, *A Guidebook of Project and Program Management for Enterprise Innovation* and an associated qualification program. This paper considers the positioning and contribution of the P2M in the context of world project management trends and in relation to other standards and qualifications established in the global project management community. Brief case studies of organizations using standards and qualifications in the development of corporate project management capability are presented, and the key strengths and the contributions of P2M to the global community are considered.

2 Trends in the Global Project Management Environment

Projects have been undertaken and managed since the beginning of civilization. However, it was only in the second half of the twentieth century that project management emerged as a distinct field of practice with its own tools, techniques and concepts (Stretton, 1994). Throughout the 1950s, project management developed primarily in the construction, engineering, defense and aerospace industries (Kerzner, 1979) and in the 1960s, the first major project management professional associations were formed.

Throughout the 1980s, interest in and application of project management spread beyond its traditional origins, to a wider range of industries, particularly information technology. In the 1990s, interest in project management grew progressively stronger, with a move towards managing organizations by projects (Gareis, 1992; Dinsmore, 1996) and the application of project management by global corporations on globally distributed projects. While concern for the management of individual projects as the focus of project-based businesses continues and is well addressed by practice standards, application of a project management approach to implementation of strategic change across a wide range of business interests is a trend that arguably presents the major challenges for advancement in project and program management theory and practice.

Developments in the practices and application of project management have taken place within a business environment undergoing fundamental transformation. The Industrial Revolution of the nineteenth century effected transformation from a feudal, agrarian society, with land as the key resource; to an industrial society with capital as the key resource reflected in command and control management and exploitation of human labor and technology through efficiency and process improvement for wealth creation (de Geus, 1997). The industrial era, from the nineteenth century through to the final decades of the twentieth century, was a period of significant but generally continuous and incremental change.

This was the nature of the business environment that shaped the emergence, in the mid-twentieth century, of what is often referred to as Modern Project Management. In this kind of environment, a project, defined as "a temporary endeavor undertaken to create a unique product, service or result" (Project Management Institute, 2004, p. 5) was clearly distinguishable from routine and repetitive processes such as those predominant in manufacturing, finance, administration and service delivery. Highly visible projects were, and remain, the lifeblood of project-based organizations such as those delivering buildings and major infrastructure, usually for clearly identifiable and external clients. Those activities of functional organizations that were acknowledged as projects, such as new facilities and products, were readily differentiated from ongoing business processes.

The latter half of the twentieth century has been described as a period of transition from the Industrial Age to the Information Age (Hames, 1994) or from the Industrial Era to the Knowledge Era (de Geus, 1997), characterized by dramatic and discontinuous change. In this environment, "traditional command-and-control forms of organization that have predominated in twentieth century industry are unable to respond quickly enough to meet the developing demands of consumers and emerging market opportunities: intelligent, networked forms of organization are needed" (Clarke and Clegg, 1998, p. 5).

This scenario gives rise to key opportunities and challenges for project management. A key opportunity is that a project management approach, using temporary, team-based organization to carry out unique endeavors, provides a responsive alternative to traditional command-and-control forms of organization. Hence, there is increasing interest in project management as an approach to enterprise management.

A key challenge is that in a rapidly changing and responsive environment, more and more of the endeavors of organizations are unique and can benefit from being identified and managed as projects. However, these "projects" are often internal, without physical end-products or clearly identified "clients", although they will often have many interested stakeholders both internal and external to the parent organization. In an era of networking, alliances and partnerships, there may not even be a single or clearly identified parent organization, and resources are often shared across multiple projects and, in some cases, multiple organizations.

The expertise that underpins the development of project management practice and standards is founded primarily in the management of clearly recognized and defined stand-alone projects such as those in engineering and construction. These practices were first transferred and minimally transformed by application to information systems and technology projects, but they retain a strong and identifiable legacy from their origins in major engineering projects. They do not recognize or offer a response to the systemic and complex nature of business projects, including implementation of corporate strategy, management of organizations by projects and enterprise innovation.

In this context, P2M, Japan's *Guidebook of Project and Program Management for Enterprise Innovation*, is highly significant as the first national guide, or standard, produced with the support of both government and the project management profession, to directly address the systemic nature of projects in the Information Age, recognizing the importance of integration and the complexity of the relationships between projects and between projects and their environment. It is also significant in that it deals specifically, and in depth, with the concept of programs of projects, a challenge which professional associations such as the Project Management Institute (PMI), International Project Management Association (IPMA), Association for Project Management (APM, UK), and Australian Institute of Project Management (AIPM) were slow to take up. It was not until four years after the first release of the P2M that

PMI released standards for Program and Portfolio Management (PMI, 2006a,b) and began offering a Program Manager certification a year later. The Global Alliance for Project Performance Standards (GAPPS) began working on performance-based standards for Program Managers in September 2005, and in doing so, drew upon the P2M amongst other resources including *Managing Successful Programmes* (Office of Government Commerce, 2003).

The balance of this paper will present a global summary of current project management guides, standards and certification, including the P2M. It will identify the different types of guides and standards and ways in which they are being used by individuals, professional associations and industry in enterprise management and human resource development. The paper will conclude with a review of the current positioning of project management and the contribution of P2M to the future of project and program management and their role in enterprise management.

3 Project Management Standards

Definition of a body of knowledge and the development of guides and standards for practice as a basis for education, training and associated certification or qualification programs are activities generally associated with the formation of a profession. It is therefore not surprising that, associated with growing interest in and application of project management, professional associations such as the Project Management Institute (PMI), International Project Management Association (IPMA), Association for Project Management (APM, UK), the Australian Institute of Project Management (AIPM), and Japan's Engineering Advancement Association and Japan Project Management Association (JPMA) have taken an active role in this area.

Speculating as to the reasons for this interest in standards and certification, Cook (1981) suggested that it may represent a stage in maturity and growth of a professional association; an attempt to establish some form of legitimacy for members; holding of a certificate for purposes of liability or legal concerns; concern for protection of prospective clients or customers by using certification as a means of demonstrating professional competence. Guides and standards can also be seen as a way of making the tacit explicit by formally documenting the accepted "best practices" of practitioners in order to make them more readily transferable to novices.

Enterprises have drawn on these guides and standards, primarily developed by project management professional associations,[1] as a basis for shared project management terminology, corporate project management methodologies and internal accreditation schemes.

Guides and standards have been developed for project management for various purposes, which can generally be classified as:

- **Projects:** knowledge and practices for management of individual projects.
- **Organizations:** enterprise project management knowledge and practices.
- **People:** development, assessment and registration/certification of people.

The most widely known, distributed and used guides and standards for project management are presented in Figure 1, indicating their general focus: projects, organizations or people. They can be further classified as focusing either on knowledge or on description of practices, the latter being primarily in the form of performance-based competency standards or frameworks intended specifically for assessment and development of project management practice in the workplace.

Standards and guides that focus primarily on management of individual projects are essentially knowledge guides, although the latest version of the ICB is more clearly directed at the assessment of competence of people. The P2M is a knowledge guide that deals with management of individual projects, but it extends beyond that to encompass management of multiple projects, programs and enterprise innovation. BS6079 is the British

---

[1] An exception is the development of government-endorsed performance-based competency standards for project management such as those that have been developed with the support of and within the national standards and qualifications frameworks of the United Kingdom, Australia and South Africa. This has occurred outside the direct control of professional associations but generally with their involvement, support and encouragement. For instance, the AIPM strongly lobbied the Australian government for support for development and government endorsement of the Australian National Competency Standards for Project Management in the early to mid-1990s.

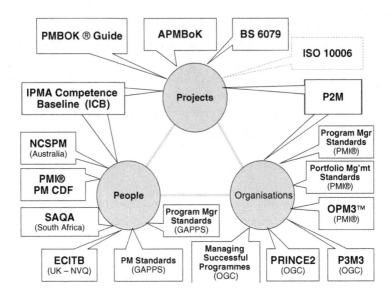

Fig. 1   Most widely recognized, distributed and used project management guides and standards

Standards Board Guide to Project Management (1996) and ISO 10006 is not really a guide to management of projects, but a guide to quality in project management.

- PMBOK® Guide (Project Management Institute: A Guide to the Project Management Body of Knowledge) (Project Management Institute, 2004).
- APMBoK (Association for Project Management Body of Knowledge, UK) (APM, 2006).
- BS6079 Guide to Project Management (British Standards Board, 1996).
- ISO (1997) ISO 10006: 1997: Quality management — Guidelines to quality in project management.
- ICB (IPMA Competence Baseline) (International Project Management Association, 2006).
- P2M: A guidebook of Project and Program Management for Enterprise Innovation (Engineering Advancement Association of Japan Project Management Development Committee) (ENAA, 2001) (now the responsibility of Japan Project Management Association).

3.1 *Organizations*

The P2M can be linked to enterprise or organizational project management through its attention to integration across projects and management of programs of projects and its declared focus on project and program management for enterprise innovation. The PMI Program and Portfolio Management Standards and the OGC's Managing Successful Programmes (MSP) are essentially knowledge guides. PRINCE2 is a methodology. PMI's OPM3™ and the Office of Government Commerce's PMMM are intended as a basis for assessment of organizational project, program and portfolio management practices.

- P2M: A guidebook of Project and Program Management for Enterprise Innovation (Engineering Advancement Association of Japan Project Management Development Committee) (ENAA, 2001) (now the responsibility of Japan Project Management Association).
- Project Management Institute (2006) The standard for portfolio management, Newtown Square, PA: PMI.
- Project Management Institute (2006) The standard for program management, Newtown Square, PA: PMI.
- Office of Government Commerce (OGC) (2003) Managing Successful Programmes, London: TSO (The Stationery Office).
- PMI (2004) Organizational Project Management Maturity Model, Newtown Square, PA: Project Management Insitute.
- Office of Government Commerce (2006) Portfolio, Programme & Project Management Maturity Model (P3M3), London: HMSO.
- Office of Government Commerce (OGC) (2007) Managing Successful Projects with PRINCE2 Manual 2005, 6th edn., London: TSO (The Stationery Office).

3.2 *People*

Except for the GAPPS Program Manager standards, the guides and standards linked in Figure 1 with People are primarily concerned with management of individual or stand-alone projects.

With the exception of the ICB (IPMA Competence Baseline), they are in the form of performance-based competency standards. Performance-based competency standards are specifically designed for assessment and recognition of current competence, independent of how that competence has been achieved. They also encourage self-assessment, reflection and personal development in order to provide evidence of competence against the specified performance criteria. Their format has been developed by governments of Australia, New Zealand, South Africa and the United Kingdom, where they form part of national qualifications frameworks.

- IBSA (2006) Volume 4B: Project Management. In: BSB01 Business Services Training Package Version 4.00, Hawthorn, Victoria: Innovation and Business Skills Australia.
- ECITB (2002) National occupational standards for project management: Pre-launch version September 2002, Kings Langley: Engineering Construction Industry Training Board.
- Project Management Institute (2007) Project Manager Competency Development Framework, Second edn., Newtown Square, PA, USA: Project Management Institute. (PMI states that this is not a standard and is intended for use in professional development of project managers rather than for use in selection or performance evaluation.)
- GAPPS (2006) A Framework for Performance-Based Competency Standards for Global Level 1 and 2 Project Managers, Johannesburg: Global Alliance for Project Performance Standards (available at www.globalPMstandards.org).
- GAPPS Program Manager Standards (in development 2007) (www.globalPMstandards.org).
- SAQA (2005) Further Education and Training Certificate: Project Management — NQF Level 4, South African Qualifications Authority.

The ICB: IPMA Competence Baseline is indicated as having applications to *People*, as it is specifically intended to provide a basis for the International Project Management Association's (IPMA) certification program for project personnel.

4   Project Management Qualifications

Although project management knowledge standards and guides, other than the ICB: IPMA Competence Baseline, do not specify how they will be used as a basis for assessment and recognition of professional competence, the majority do provide an important resource for development of professional project management certification, registration or qualification programs.

Only one of the performance-based competency standards, the Australian National Competency Standards for Project Management, has been adopted as the basis for the certification program of a project management professional association, namely the Australian Institute of Project Management.

The P2M has been designed as a curriculum forming the basis for a project management professional qualification system. It was the first to specifically address the role of program manager.

A summary of project management professional qualifications and associated forms of assessment are shown in Table 1. The highest levels of qualification for both the P2M and the IPMA recognize a program (programme) management role. The AIPM Level 6 qualification, Master Project Director was initially intended for senior and experienced managers or directors of single (complex) projects, but is in practice applied to managers of multiple projects or programs (programmes) of projects.

The Project Management Institute offers three certifications:

- Program Management Professional (PgMP^{SM}) intended for those involved in coordinated management of multiple related projects directed toward strategic business and organizational objectives;
- Project Management Professional (PMP®) intended for those directly involved in managing projects; and
- Certified Associate in Project Management (CAPM®) intended for project team members.

The Global Alliance for Project Performance Standards (GAPPS) aims to develop agreed frameworks as a basis for review, development and recognition of local standards that will facilitate mutual recognition and transferability of project management qualifications. It is intended that the framework and associated standards be freely available for use by businesses, academic institutions, professional associations, and government standards and qualifications bodies globally. Many organizations operate across national boundaries and are thus interested in standards and qualifications that are transferable. Governments, concerned with ensuring an internationally competitive workforce, and individuals, desiring greater mobility, are also interested in the mutual recognition and transferability of qualifications. The GAPPS does not offer certifications or qualifications, but it does develop standards and usage guidelines. These have been developed for two levels of Project Manager (Global Level 1 and Global Level 2) with the levels determined by reference to the Crawford-Ishikura Table for Evaluation Roles (CIFTER), which facilitates evaluation of the

Table 1 Summary of professional qualifications and associated assessment processes

Standard or Guide	Level	Description	Form(s) of Assessment
P2M (*ENAA, JPMA*)	PMA	Program Management Architect	• Interview and essay tests • Experience of at least three projects required
	PMR	Project Manager Registered	• Interview and essay tests • Experience of at least one project required
	PMS	Project Management Specialist	• Written examination
ICB: IPMA Competence Baseline (*International Project Management Association, and member National Associations, e.g., APM*)	Level A	Program or Projects Director	• At least 5 years' experience in portfolio, program or multi-project management • Self-assessment, CV, project list, references • Project report • Interview
	Level B	Project Manager	• At least five years of project management experience, of which three years are in responsible leadership functions of complex projects • Self-assessment, CV, project list, references • Project report • Interview

(*Continued*)

Table 1 (*Continued*)

Standard or Guide	Level	Description	Form(s) of Assessment
	Level C	Project Management Professional	• Evidence of experience, self-assessment • Formal examination with direct questions and intellectual tasks • Workshop or short project report • Interview
	Level D	Project Management Practitioner	• Curriculum Vitae • Formal examination, direct questions and open essays
Australian National Competency Standards for Project Management (*Innovation and Business Skills Australia (IBSA) — Australian Qualifications Framework and AIPM Certification*)	Advanced Diploma	MPD — Master Project Director	• Assessment of portfolio of evidence of competence against the standards by a registered workplace assessor
	Diploma	RegPM — Registered Project Manager	• Assessment of portfolio of evidence of competence against the standards by a registered workplace assessor
	Certificate IV	QPP — Qualified Project Professional	• Assessment of portfolio of evidence of competence against the standards by a registered workplace assessor

(*Continued*)

Table 1   (*Continued*)

Standard or Guide	Level	Description	Form(s) of Assessment
PMBOK® Guide (*Project Management Institute*)	(PgMP^SM)	Program Management Professional	• Application review of work experience by a panel of program managers • Multiple-choice examination including both situational- and scenario-based questions • Multi-rater assessment (MRA)
	(PMP®)	Project Management Professional	• Record of education and experience — 4,500 hours with Bachelors Degree and 7,500 hours without Degree spent leading and directing project tasks • Multiple-choice exam
	(CAPM®)	Certified Associate in Project Management	• 1,500 hours of work in a project team or 23 contact hours of PM education • Multiple-choice exam

management complexity of projects. The GAPPS began working on development of performance-based standards for Program Managers in 2005, with expected release in 2008 (refer to www.globalPMstandards.org).

All qualification programs, except that of the Australian Institute of Project Management (AIPM), include a knowledge-based examination at one or more levels. The P2M and the IPMA qualification processes include interviews, except at entry level (PMS, Project Management Specialist for P2M and Level D, Project Management Practitioner for IPMA).

The assessment process associated with the AIPM's Registered Project Manager program and Australian Qualifications Framework, based on the government-endorsed Australian National Competency Standards for Project Management, requires each candidate for the qualification to prepare a portfolio of evidence of competence, based on the performance criteria specified in the relevant level of the standard for assessment by a Registered Workplace Assessor. These Workplace Assessors must satisfy a registration or qualification process that is just as exacting as that for project management practitioners. They must satisfy government-endorsed standards for Workplace Assessors. A similar assessment process is required for all qualifications based on performance-based competency standards such as those of the United Kingdom (ECITB, 2002) and South Africa (South African Qualifications Authority).

All certification programs summarized in Table 1 include re-certification requirements.

Certification programs, which should be based on guides concerning the standards required in various roles and levels of responsibility, are important in:

- providing project and program management practitioners with guidelines as to the knowledge and practices required for effective performance;
- providing employers and clients with guidance as to the capability of project and program personnel;
- providing project and program management practitioners with recognition that they have the knowledge and experience required for effective performance.

Qualifications based on knowledge tests and records of experience do not provide assurance of ability to apply knowledge and experience effectively. The factors contributing to successful workplace performance are both complex and shifting. There are factors relating to individuals that cannot be effectively captured in standards or measured in examinations, resumes or in interviews, such as personality and behavioral characteristics, values, ethics and motivation. There are also factors relating to context, such as the nature of the project, the nature of the role, resource availability, competence of the project team and extent of organizational support.

Gathering evidence of ability to effectively apply knowledge and consistently deliver results in a range of contexts is a challenge that is beyond the scope of professional qualification programs. For practical reasons, qualification programs must be affordable for applicants, and at the same time, cost-effective for the certifying body to operate sustainably. Associated with this, are limitations to the amount of time that applicants are willing or able to devote to the certification process. The major drawback of the AIPM's very thorough Registered Project Manager process, involving independently registered workplace assessors, is that it can take candidates up to a year to gather evidence, and requires a minimum of six to ten hours and in many cases considerably longer face-to-face time of a Registered Workplace Assessor. Although the process is effective for developmental purposes, it is time- and resource-intensive, and there is no guarantee that the candidate who satisfies the requirements of the assessment process will have the personality characteristics, values, motivation and organizational support to perform effectively under all circumstances.

It is important to recognize the limitations of guides, standards and associated certification and qualification programs. They are valuable in setting benchmarks and providing guidelines for professional development and performance improvement, but must be recognized as only one component in a complex system involving interactions of multiple stakeholders.

Examination of the P2M and descriptions of its development and intended use indicate that there is clear recognition of the complexities involved in building "practical capability" (Ohara, 2001, p. 6). P2M is presented as a guide to building the practical capability required to support "mission-achievement" (ENAA, 2001, p. 2). As for all standards, guides and qualification programs, it is important that the ideals of the P2M Guidebook should not be lost in the desire to gain qualifications. The qualifications should be considered as steps to assist in capability building and encouragement for further development rather than an end in themselves.

Organizations such ENAA, JPMA, PMI, IPMA and AIPM provide an important service to practitioners in providing generic standards, guidelines and qualification programs. These should be seen only as a starting point or resource for building effective individual and enterprise project and program management capability. The following section reviews some of the ways in which organizations are able to contribute to developmental assessment of individual and corporate project and program management capability.

5 PM and Human Resource Development

Lifelong learning is becoming increasingly important for project management practitioners operating at the leading edge of technology, who must be able to actively engage in critical thinking and reflection in order to transform existing knowledge, through creative responses and enhanced decision making, to meet new problem situations (Brookfield, 1987). Professional standards and qualifications can provide baselines for knowledge and practice, but it is the responsibility of each individual to be a reflective practitioner (Schon, 1991) and actively seek opportunities to develop competence, raise benchmarks and rethink "best practice".

Figure 2 models a process for assessment and development of competence. First, current competence needs to be assessed or measured. Guides and standards such as P2M, PMBOK® Guide, Australian National Competency Standards for Project Management or GAPPS can be used as a basis for this entry-level assessment and can be supplemented by

Fig. 2 A model for assessment and development of workplace competence (developed in consultation with Carol Townley, Caliper, UK)

using a range of personality, behavioral and other tests to form a picture of current levels of competence. Requirements of the job role form the basis for identifying the desired level of competence. Developmental needs are represented by the gap between current and desired levels of competence and form the basis for a professional development plan. In the spirit of lifelong learning, reflective practice, career progression and changing workplace requirements, this should be an ongoing developmental process.

Organizations can play an important role in motivating and supporting performance improvement. There are several aspects to this. One is the provision of a supportive environment — a project management culture, top management support, methodologies, systems, tools, recognition and rewards — that encourage effective project and program management performance. The other is the design and implementation of corporate project and program management professional development programs. These should include baseline assessments related to roles and responsibilities, classification of projects and an internal accreditation system to identify development gaps. Individuals, in consultation with supervisors and supported by detailed guidelines, should develop plans to address the identified developmental gaps and work towards their own career goals. Developmental resources and support should be available and may include reading and study guides, web-based support, mentoring and coaching, education and training, and work experience opportunities.

There is value in maintaining an external reference for its internal developmental programs and accreditations through use of and contribution to development of professional standards and benchmarking with other organizations.

6   Significance of P2M in the Global PM Community

The profession of project management is essentially defined by its most widely accepted standards. Current standards, such as the PMBOK® Guide, focusing on knowledge and practices for management of single projects, describe practices and a profession that is firmly lodged at the middle management level of organizations, and research (Crawford, 2000, 2001a) indicates that in the majority of organizations, senior management expects project managers to concentrate on what may be referred to as first-generation project management, managing efficient delivery of results within the established time, cost and quality restraints (Ohara, 2001, p. 4).

Results of two separate research studies indicate that on one hand, less than 40% of senior managers surveyed considered strategy, systems, integration and information management essential knowledge for project managers (Morris *et al.*, 2000), and on the other, increasing levels of use of practices in these areas are associated with a decreasing likelihood of being rated by senior management as a top project management performer (Crawford, 2001b).

Despite the apparent reality of the operational or tactical focus of project management and the reinforcement of this reality through the single project focus of the most widely distributed standards (e.g., PMBOK® Guide), there is considerable rhetoric, echoed in the P2M, promoting the potential contribution of project and program management to corporate strategy implementation (Pellegrinelli and Bowman, 1994) and enterprise innovation. Much recent literature in project management has drawn attention to the limitations of a rational and normative approach, strongly grounded in control theory, that has been dominant in the development of modern project management (Cooke-Davies *et al.*, 2007). This is exemplified in the findings of the UK ESPRC-funded Rethinking Project Management Network, which identified five directions (Winter *et al.*, 2006):

(1) From the Lifecycle Model of Projects and PM to Theories of Complexity of Projects and PM;
(2) From Projects as Instrumental Processes to Projects as Social Processes;
(3) From Product Creation as the Prime Focus to Value Creation as the Prime Focus;
(4) From Narrow Conceptualization of Projects to Broader Conceptualization of Projects;
(5) From Practitioners as Trained Technicians to Practitioners as Reflective Practitioners.

Although initially released several years before the commencement of the Rethinking Project Management Network, the P2M was effectively ahead of its time in reflecting the directions indicated above. The P2M therefore represented the first significant advance towards genuine integration and acceptance of the role of project and program management at the enterprise level. Factors contributing to this significance include:

- It was developed with the support of government, industry and professional associations.

- It gained widespread support for adoption and application within enterprises.
- It was the first guide to:

  — approach enterprise project and program management afresh from the viewpoint of the enterprise rather than drawing on project paradigms developed in the context of large, single, physical projects as the day-to-day business of project-based organizations.
  — directly address program management (rather than focusing only on single projects).
  — recognize and respond to the complexities of fast-moving, multistakeholder environments.
  — recognize and address the systemic nature of projects and programs.

- While other Guides and Standards mention "integration", they use it in reference to integration within a single project; the P2M "is the only standard guide that provides patterns for integration management" (Ohara, 2001, p. 11) across programs and portfolios of projects at enterprise level.
- It heralded a revival of intellectual depth to the field of project management that had been largely lost in the process of codification of knowledge and practices as a means of establishing the boundaries of a project management profession and making membership accessible to a wide constituency.

7   Challenges for P2M

The P2M is a significant contribution to the field of project management and the first guide for project management, recognized by government, professional associations and industry, that directly addressed the issues of enterprise-level project management, taking a systemic view and clearly identifying the role of program and project management in strategy implementation and value creation.

It appears that there is strong support for P2M at enterprise management level in leading Japanese corporations. For P2M to succeed in its stated mission, this level of support must be sustained and strengthened. There needs to be an ongoing partnership that enables the P2M to grow and benefit from feedback as it is applied in practice. Given the apparent reluctance of senior management elsewhere to accept a role for project management at enterprise-level in the strategic and innovative aspects of corporate affairs, maintenance of enterprise-level support for the P2M will be vital.

It is a strength of the P2M that it presents a rich and complex view of project and program management. Although the knowledge guides and performance-based competency standards developed over the last five to ten years are extremely valuable, were excellent when first produced and have filled an important role in making project management accessible to a wider audience, their approach is simplistic and reductionist when compared with the richness and conceptual depth of the P2M. This very strength is, however, a major challenge to the P2M. Widespread adoption of the PMBOK® Guide can be largely attributed to its simple, straightforward approach. It is extremely attractive to a practitioner audience, and particularly to relative novices keen to quickly grasp key aspects of project management knowledge and practice. It may be expected that many will be daunted by the intellectual stimulation and challenge presented by the P2M.

8 Conclusions

Standards and qualifications relating to the management of individual projects are well-developed and are being readily adopted by a wide range of project practitioners and by organizations as a basis for development of corporate capability to manage their project-based operations. Extension of application of project management to non-traditional and arguably "soft" or non-physical service delivery, business change, enterprise management and innovation projects and programs has to date drawn upon standards and qualifications developed initially for the readily recognized projects of project-based businesses such as those in engineering, construction, defense and aerospace.

Development and launch of the P2M at the start of the 21st century is timely, and heralds a new era of project management that elevates the focus of concern from the single project to the program, and from the business as usual operations of project-based organizations to the strategic concerns of enterprise management and innovation. It provides a stimulating platform for further theoretical and practical developments in the field.

P2M has led the world in a fresh approach to development of standards specifically designed for program management, and for the application of project and program management to enterprise-level management and innovation.

References

APM (2006). *Body of Knowledge*, 5th ed., High Wycombe: Association for Project Management.

British Standards Board (1996). *Guide to Project Management: BS6079: 1996*, London: British Standards Board.

Brookfield, S. D. (1987). *Developing Critical Thinkers: Challenging Adults to Explore Alternative Ways of Thinking and Acting*, San Francisco: Jossey-Bass.

Clarke, T. and Clegg, S. (1998). *Changing Paradigms: The Transformation of Management Knowledge for the 21st Century*, London: Harper Collins Business.

Cook, D. L. (1981). Certification of project managers — Fantasy or reality?, in *A Decade of Project Management: Selected Readings from Project Management Quarterly: 1970 through 1980*, edited by Adams, J. R. and Kirchoff, N. S., Project Management Institute.

Cooke-Davies, T. J., Cicmil, S. J. K., Crawford, L. H., and Richardson, K. (2007). We're not in Kansas anymore, Toto: Mapping the strange landscape of complexity theory, and its relationship to project management, *Project Management Journal* 38(2), pp. 50–61.

Crawford, L. (2000). Profiling the competent project manager, in *Project Management Research at the Turn of the Millenium: Proceedings of PMI Research Conference, 21–24 June, 2000, Paris, France*, edited by Slevin, D. P., Cleland, D. I., and Pinto, J. K., Sylva, NC: Project Management Institute, pp. 3–15.

Crawford, L. H. (2001a). Profiles of top project managers: The senior management perspective, in *Proceedings of the PMI New Zealand Annual Conference 2001: Project Success: Putting It All Together, Wellington, New Zealand*, Wellington, New Zealand: PMI NZ.

Crawford, L. H. (2001b). Project management competence: The value of standards, DBA Thesis, Henley-on-Thames: Henley Management College/Brunel University.

de Geus, A. (1997). *The Living Company*, London: Nicholas Brealey.

Dinsmore, P. (1996). On the leading edge of management: Managing organizations by projects, *PM Network* March, pp. 9–11.

ECITB (2002). National Occupational Standards for Project Management: Pre-launch version September 2002, Kings Langley: Engineering Construction Industry Training Board.

ENAA (2001). *P2M: A Guidebook of Project and Program Management for Enterprise Innovation: Interim Translation of Selected Chapters*, Japan: Engineering Advancement Association of Japan.

GAPPS (2006). *A Framework for Performance-Based Competency Standards for Global Level 1 and 2 Project Managers*, Global Alliance for Project Performance Standards (available at www.globalPMstandards.org).

Gareis, R. (1992). *The Handbook of Management by Projects*, Vienna: Manz.

Hames, R. D. (1994). *The Management Myth*, Sydney: Business and Professional Publishing.

IBSA (2006). Volume 4B: Project management, in *BSB01 Business Services Training Package Version 4.00*, Hawthorn, Victoria: Innovation and Business Skills Australia.

International Project Management Association (2006). *ICB — IPMA Competence Baseline Version 3.0*, Nijkerk, The Netherlands: International Project Management Association.

ISO (1997). *ISO 10006: 1997: Quality Management — Guidelines to Quality in Project Management*, International Standards Organisation.

Kerzner, H. (1979). *Project Management: A Systems Approach to Planning, Scheduling and Controlling*, 1st ed., New York: Van Nostrand Reinhold.

Morris, P. W. G., Patel, M. B., and Wearne, S. H. (2000). Research into revising the APM project management body of knowledge, *International Journal of Project Management* 18(3), pp. 155–164.

Office of Government Commerce (OGC) (2003). *Managing Successful Programmes*, London: TSO (The Stationery Office).

Office of Government Commerce (OGC) (2006). *Portfolio, Programme & Project Management Maturity Model (P3M3)*, London: HMSO.

Office of Government Commerce (OGC) (2007). *Managing Successful Projects with PRINCE2 Manual 2005*, 6th ed., London: TSO (The Stationery Office).

Ohara, P. S. (2001). Project management and qualification system in Japan — Expectation for P2M and challenges, in *Proceedings of the International Project Management Congress 2001: Project Management Development in the Asia-Pacific Region in the New Century: 16–21 November, Tokyo, Japan*, Tokyo, Japan: Engineering Management Association of Japan (ENAA) and Japan Project Management Forum (JPMF).

Pellegrinelli, S. and Bowman, C. (1994). Implementing strategy through projects, *Long Range Planning* 27(4), pp. 125–132.

PMI (2004). *Organizational Project Management Maturity Model*, Newtown Square, PA: Project Management Institute.

Project Management Institute (2004). *A Guide to the Project Management Body of Knowledge*, 3rd ed., Newtown Square, PA: PMI.

Project Management Institute (2006a). *The Standard for Portfolio Management*, Newtown Square, PA: PMI.

Project Management Institute (2006b). *The Standard for Program Management*, Newtown Square, PA: PMI.

Project Management Institute (2007). *Project Manager Competency Development Framework*, 2nd ed., Newtown Square, PA, USA: Project Management Institute.

SAQA (2005). Further Education and Training Certificate: Project Management — NQF Level 4, South African Qualifications Authority.

Schon, D. A. (1991). *Reflective Practitioner: How Professionals Think in Action*, Aldershot, England: Arena.

Stretton, A. (1994). A short history of project management: Part one: The 1950s and 60s, *The Australian Project Manager* 14(1), pp. 36–37.

Winter, M., Smith, C., Morris, P. W. G., and Cicmil, S. (2006). Directions for future research in project management: The main findings of the EPSRC Research Network, *International Journal of Project Management* 24(November), pp. 638–649.

Examples of Changes of Japanese Corporate Business Model: Why is KPM Essentially Important Now?

Toshihiko Kinoshita
Visiting Professor, Graduate School of Asian Pacific Studies
Waseda University

"True, Japanese may not be the cradle of Nobel Prize-winning break-through. But consider Total Quality Management, Total Productive Maintenance, and "Just-In-Time" supply chains — all arguably innovations with a far-reaching impact than discoveries that grab the headlines."

— Peter J. Williamson[1]

1   Introduction

I introduce here some successful Japanese firms vigorously reforming themselves in the long-term recession period and a dozen of conspicuous leaders who contributed to such reforms (*Kaikaku*). The challenges which Japanese firms encountered in the period were unprecedentedly deep-rooted. Before 1990, most of the TSE-listed Japanese firms had not been heavily indebted, except real estate business, construction companies, subsidiaries of commercial banks exclusively for housing (*jusen*) and big retailers. On the contrary, they had more than enough cash. Some dozens of "excellent firms" could easily mobilize mid-/long-term money at a relatively cheap cost called as "Japan rate" from international money centers like London and Zurich.

Japanese financial institutions full of liquidity encouraged firms and individuals to borrow money for investment in stock or real estates. Most manufacturers did not borrow money for speculation, however. They had

---

[1] Williamson (2004, p. 51).

been overly equipped in production facilities and overly staffed than the real demands. Their products, either durables or their parts, were very competitive price-wise and quality-wise, however. Manufacturers could newly invest in production at home due to a new law promulgated in the early 1990s, only for rationalization purpose, namely, in a "scrap and build" way so as to improve energy efficiency/material balance and to modernize their production systems for environmental purposes. "Japanese way of management" had been one of the most popular courses in many western business schools.

On the other side, Americans, businessmen in particular, became modest after all. They used to think in the 1960s and 1970s that Japan could hardly catch up to the US by copying the American production system and its IPR. Americans tended to judge that Japan's competitiveness rested on relatively cheap labor and hence, would lose its competitiveness when the level of the averaged wage came to the similar level of the US. But, even when it rose to the same level with those of American workers, prices and quality of Japanese products continued to be competitive — unbelievable, Americans tended to consider. The Japanese yen rate had been appreciated from around ¥240 per US dollar to around ¥120 a year and a half after the Plaza Accord. Japan's *Kaizen* program including Just-in-Time (JIT) system, good services in post-marketing period and the intra-firm training system were obviously superior to the US's. By and by, the confidence in American management was eroding by the mid-1980s.

Some US congressmen brutally destroyed Toyota cars in front of Capitol Hill. Severe trade conflicts continued in the 1990s, including the infamous US-Japan agreement on semiconductors that at least 20% of semiconductors to be used in Japan should be foreign made, virtually the US-made.

However, businessmen were businessmen. They were pragmatic. No small number of American business leaders and their staff visited Japan to study the "secrets" of the strength of the products made in Japan as well as Japanese management. Jack Welch, then Chairman of General Electric (GE), had been one of them. He had many intimate Japanese friends, and tried to induce Japanese good practices to his management, namely conducting a hybrid management. He himself gave much influence to the American business, and later, to Japanese business.

When American businessmen and researchers visited Japan, they learned a lot about how individual Japanese firms produced products "made in Japan" in clean and modernized factories and that workers were well-trained. They concluded that many Japanese firms were superior in quality- and cost-control, teamwork based on OJT and process innovation. They conceptualized the best of their findings into abstract ingredients to make public *The Young Report*, illustrating a new US strategy to strengthen competiveness as a state (Dertouzos *et al.*, 1990). They simultaneously took advantage of such newly induced ingredients mixed with their own superiority such as leadership, openness, flat organization and, above all, the way to make money. This time, they linked such evolution with IT software with enthusiasm. The Japanese were later surprised with such concepts which Americans began to use, and later "taught" the Japanese such terminology as customer satisfaction, TQM, Six Sigma and supply chain management. Those concepts had been originated from Japanese best practices, such as their traditional belief of "every client is God", *kaizen* to total quality control (Toyota's lean production system, or JIT, is one of them) and strong linkage among their group companies (*keiretsu*) and related vendors.

But sharp appreciation of Japanese yen after the Plaza Accord in 1985, adversarial trade agreements on various fields like steel mills, machine tools and semiconductors, and above all the burst of the bubble economy deprived the majority of Japanese firms of their strength for more than a decade. By this time, no small number of European firms had strengthened their competitiveness, such firms as ABB, Siemens, Nokia, Alstrom, Alkantara, Zora, Philips, Unilever, Henkel as well as SAP (Berger *et al.*, 2006). Also, Korean *chaebols* such as Samsung Electronics, LG, Hyundai Motor, Hyundai Heavy Industries and Pohan Steel Mill emerged as very competitive rivals for Japan, EU as well as the US, not only price-wise but quality-wise. The business model of the latter smacks of the revised Japanese version.

By the advent of the 21st century, Prof. Shigenobu Ohara and his team had created a new Japan-specific total management concept: P2M (and later to be renamed as KPM). We questioned circa 2000 why big Japanese manufacturers which still kept high-level technologies could not make enough profits like in the 1980s or like contemporary American firms. We concluded that their conventional business model, based basically on slow decision making on consensus, weak products selection, production-sales strategy depending basically on technological business units, not on marketing unit and lack of meaningful "focus and selection strategy", would no longer be relevant under the quickly changing business environment (Kinoshita, 2005).

Initially, we focused our studies on firms producing plant and machinery such as Ishikawajima Heavy Industries (IHI), Mitsubishi Heavy

Industries (MHI), Kawasaki Heavy Industries (KHI), Hitachi group and Sumitomo Heavy Machinery. It was often said that they had lost price competitiveness in emerging markets not because of weakening quality control, but of "over-specification"; in other words, too expensive due to its super quality from the viewpoint of purchasing power of the overseas buyers, mostly in developing countries.[2] Apparently, as far as the industry is concerned, double-structured markets existed. Japanese big firms such as power companies continued to buy the best of the best quality generators to satisfy Japan's affluent society. They could legally transfer the cost to consumers by a special law subject to accountability. Hitachi, Mitsubishi Heavy Industries and Toshiba used to be beneficiaries, and power companies were one of the biggest implementers of equipment investment every year. However, they could not compete effectively in the international bidding for power generators overseas.

A similar phenomenon had hardly been seen among US firms in the 1970s and even the 1980s, because the power generation/distribution business was mostly unbundled and incorporated to increase competition among them. Thus, electric machinery cost had to be cheap, which enabled their manufacturers to be competitive in the international market. Why, then, did many US "excellent firms" in the manufacturing sector begin to lose competitiveness in the international market? Major reasons were while they targeted to realize total productivity optimization, (a) they continued to produce in mass production and failed in quality control, particularly in durables, and did not meet the matured market where consumers wished to buy many varieties of products with high quality; and (b) they became short-sighted in managing firms. They tended to too easily fire workers for money-making rather than training them well.

On Japan's side, however, a different situation began to emerge. Many Japanese firms continued to try maximizing partial productivity optimization of dozens of business units, but not total productivity optimization for the firm in due consideration of long-term prospects. They seldom adopted the "selection and focus" strategy until the last moment. They could grow well as long as the domestic market grew well. We could hardly observe strong leadership of the CEOs in Japanese firms in the 1980s, with some exceptions like Akio Morita, SONY. To give jobs to all employees

---

[2] The situation has hardly changed dramatically until recently. However, IHI recorded a big deficit due to the lack of cost control in selected projects and the company has to overhaul its management.

and to produce for the non-mass market depending on orders were regarded as a paramount mission (duty) of a firm until the burst of the bubble economy. So, firms could be managed relatively well as far as the CEOs sought consensus and gave due authorization to heads of each business unit. However, when the macroeconomy stopped growth and assets prices precipitated since circa 1990, they had to radically reduce hiring new university and high school graduates, waiting for a "natural decrease" of human resources by the gradual retirement of employees. Most big firms were not forced to decrease regular employees until the end of the 1990s.

Deflation meant in the business world that a firm's total sales amount hardly rises every year. Efforts to cut costs and to adjust from fixed cost to flexible cost reflecting deflation was the primary answer, followed by raising value-added to be created through process innovation, new product creation, branding strategy, shortening "lead time" for developing new products to meet quickening product lifecycle (PLC), and developing new export market, etc. Every firm rushed to the similar directions while assets deflation deteriorated. It did not take long for many firms to encounter the "balance sheet crisis". For banks, that meant an accumulated process of non-performing loans in such areas like real estate business in Japan and big scale retail business like DAIEI. As a new BIS rule was adopted, most of the banks found that their net capital positions were in danger. It led to the financial fiasco in 1997–1998. Popular criticism on financial institutions and competent authorities increased. However, people had to recognize for the government to throw public funds into banks, after all.

Thus, Japan's manufacturing sector, etc., had to survive under such critical situations. To our surprise, however, the break-even point of the Tokyo Stock Exchange (TSE)-listed manufacturing sector continued to lower from over 90 in FY 2001 to 76.4 in FY 2006.

Further, according to *Fortune*, 23 July 2007, out of *Fortune*'s 500 firms, the largest revenues in total country-wise were from 162 US firms, and their total revenues amounted to $7.3 trillion, followed by 67 Japanese firms amounting to $2.4 trillion, and 37 German firms with $1.8 trillion. Out of the best 10 in the US, only three firms (GM, GE and Ford) were manufacturers, but in Japan, seven firms out of the best 10 were manufacturers and the rest were NTT, Nippon Life Insurance and Mitsubishi UFJ financial group.

In other words, the US firms under a different business culture or SWM model could realize quicker recovery through the "radical" reengineering as suggested by Hammer and Champy.

People at large in Japan (and continental Europe) tended to dislike adopting such an American model, thinking that US firms tend to unmercifully fire employees, but that to regard workers and staff as just a kind of merchandise is the last thing for management to do. Likewise, Japanese firms found it extremely difficult to change their traditional business models or "stakeholder's capitalism" overnight.

However, the business environment of Japan saw a dramatic worsening circa 2000 when the IT bubble burst globally. Japan's averaged annual growth rates sank from 3%–4% in the 1980s to no more than 1% in the 1990s and deflation did not stop. Assets deflation, relatively strong yen-rate, aging society, and the strong global pressure to curtail costs and prices on non-brand products led the vicious circle.

Naturally, not all Japanese manufacturing firms were placed in the same condition in the past 20 years or thereabouts. Let us see more closely where big firms, manufacturing firms in particular, were placed, and how smart leaders made success under severe conditions. This will lead us to a conclusion of why KPM is badly required in Japan, even from now.

2   *Kaikaku* Efforts Brought Many Success Stories, But Not in a Uniform Way

Japanese leading manufacturing/engineering firms,[3] among others, have endeavored to adjust to the dramatic socio-political changes at home and overseas, or more precisely, to increase or regain their competitive edge

---

[3] Precisely speaking, engineering firms should not be classified as part of the manufacturing sector. They are based on highly qualified human resources and do not have factories. There are three firms that are exclusively engaged in engineering services, namely JGC Corporation, Chiyoda Corporation (formerly, Chiyoda Chemical and Construction Co.) and TEC (Toyo Engineering Corporation). Other engineering firms are attached to (a) manufacturing business like steel, chemical and machinery; (b) construction; (c) power company; and (d) others. Many of them are export-oriented and tend to conduct with Japanese trading houses and manufacturing firms as a group. Are they "fabless" companies? Broadly speaking, yes. But they are so by their nature. Those "fabless" firms classified as (D) are Japan-based multinationals and have relocated most of the manufacturing jobs overseas. Engineering firms are not multinationals, though they may have subsidiaries overseas to supplement their jobs. They also conduct domestic business like factory automation. Our study on P2M began initially on manufacturing and engineering firms. Hence, I include those firms here.

and to realize higher ROE or other management criteria. Some did idealistically and some did it fairly. Naturally, there are lots of firms still fighting for better positions, and some failed and went bankrupt or were taken over. Objectively speaking, as to the averaged ratio of success stories out of total TSE-listed firms, the manufacturing sector ranks first compared with other industries, like services industries.

I sense that most of the successful manufacturing companies evolved their business models flexibly during the period, not because they were just forced to do so, but because leadership was correctly taken. Anyhow, their efforts resulted in higher profits in some years, and stock prices jumped up as a whole. The keywords applied here are "restructuring" and "total optimization".

While the struggle for existence has intensified, new senses of value such as global environmental consideration, respect for intellectual property rights (IPR), corporate governance (CG) or compliance, and emphasis on the corporate social responsibility (CSR) have spread in the business world as well as the society as a whole. Successful firms are leading in these fields as well.

In the use of updated combined revenues, profits and other management criteria as well as current stock market values, plus the business model changes of TSE-listed firms, I classify the pattern of success stories into the following categories:

(A) Those firms which could basically continue to increase sales amount/profits despite the "lost decade" by various strategies, e.g., Toyota, Canon, Sharp, Shin-Etsu Chemical, Sumitomo Chemical, Takeda Pharmaceutical, Kao, Denso, Ricoh, Komatsu, Nintendo, JGC Corporation, Mitsubishi Corporation, Sumitomo Corporation.

(A') Those firms which could not continue to increase sales amount/profits, but have managed fairly well throughout the period, e.g., Honda, Suzuki Motor, Kyocera, Wacoal, Omron, Mitsubishi Electric, Toray, Nintendo, Olympus, Rohm, Horiba, Murata Manufacturing, Aishin Seiki, FUJIFILM, Casio Computer, Kikkoman, Bridgestone, Shimano, Shiseido, Asahi Glass, Daikin, TDK Corp., FANUC, NIDEC (Nippon Densan), Asterallas Pharma, Daiichi-Sankyo, Mitsubishi Gas Chemical, Mitsubishi Chemical, HOYA.

(B) Those firms which once recorded huge losses during the "lost decade", but with the crisis as a springboard, have revived after restructuring and other efforts, e.g., Matsushita Electric (Panasonic), Chiyoda Corporation, Nissan.

(C)   Those firms which had been regarded as "sunset industry", but have revived after long-term restructuring efforts, e.g., New Nippon Steel, JFE Steel, Sumitomo Heavy Industries.

(D)   So-called "fabless" manufacturers whose production centers are relocated to mostly overseas with their Headquarters as the R&D center or "mother factories", e.g., Mabuchi Motor, Keyence (a maker of touch panel/FA sensor), Minebear (a miniature ball bearing maker).

(E)   Those firms which changed their business model radically and made considerable success or in its transition, e.g., Nihon Yusen, Shosen-Mitsui, Mitsubishi Corporation, Sumitomo Corporation, Toshiba.

Firms exemplified in (A) which continued to increase sales/profits and those (A') which could not continue to increase sales/profits but basically performed well in the "lost decade" are not small in number. You might question why. Indeed, the business conditions surrounding them at that time were the historically severest. They made all efforts and earned victories; for instance, some of them captured bigger foreign market by localizing production and producing more environmentally friendly brand goods by revised Japanese management.

Among the firms exemplified in (B), Panasonic is a typical case. There were many similar cases in the US like GE.

Of the firms exemplified in (C), we could hardly see similar cases in the US reengineering industries.

Conversely, firms exemplified in (D), which have mostly depended on offshoring their products with their headquarters in Japan as planning centers and mother machine centers, are not as many, and the scale of their sales/profits are relatively small in the case of Japan. We can hardly find in Japan such a big retailer like Wal-Mart which exclusively depends on the products made in China, though we see various types retailers like UniQuro (First Retailing), minimarts or even 100-yen shops. This means that the national market of Japan has been segmented into small pieces.

Let me introduce here some of the strong leaders in Japan who emerged in the "lost decade" and led their firms to the right direction. Their names, faces and their characters have been nation-widely known including in some other countries. They made challenging decision making at their risk. Most of them had worked in the US for a certain period and were well-acquainted with the advantages and disadvantages of Anglo-American-type management. They evolved their business model to a hybrid type, leaving the advantage of their own corporate culture to produce and sell, and to keep good relations with employees, vendors and other stake-holders, after big in-house battles in most cases. We have scarcely observed so many charismatic business leaders in the 1970s and 1980s, when the Japanese economy went relatively well. Strong leadership was not necessary, with a few exceptions. Even their successors, who, after being promoted to CEOs, look far less popular and charismatic among the general public. This is, as I understand, due to the fact that the worst period of the Japanese economy has passed, and those who had to make the breakthrough decision at the worst time are those deserving popular respect. The only exception is Atsutoshi Nishida, Toshiba. He was promoted to President in 2005 and has deployed a gallant three-year program, seemingly full of dramas. Toshiba looked a stand-still firm for a long time, but is evidently changing to a new giant company for nuclear generation and power semiconductor. Nishida aims at becoming No. 1 in producing power semiconductors by FY 2009, which ranks the third now in the world.

Below is a list of some selected great business leaders in the "lost decade":

- Okuda, Hiroshi (Former Chairman), Toyota
- Mitarai, Fujio (Chairman), Canon
- Nakamura, Kunio (Chairman), Matsushita or Panasonic
- Takeda, Kunio (Chairman), Takeda Pharmaceutical
- Sakane, Masahiro (President), Komatsu
- Machida, Katsuhiko (Chairman), Sharp
- Inamori, Kazuo (Honorary Chairman), Kyocera
- Sakurai, Masamitu (Chairman), Ricoh
- Kanagawa, Chihiro (Chairman), Shin-Etsu Chemical
- Nishida, Atsutoshi (President), Toshiba
- Suzuki, Osamu (Chairman), Suzuki Motor
- Mimura, Akio (President), New Nippon Steel
- Nagamori, Shigenobu (President), NIDECO.

3   Some Success Stories

3.1   *Toyota Motor*

So much has been written on Toyota that there is no need to go into details. But one sure thing is that the Toyota model, whose spirit is often called *Toyotaism*, has not yet been made into a general model, although

Toyota Production System (TPS) has been widely educated and adopted by many international companies — not only auto sectors, but also even in some service sectors. For instance, surprisingly, Wipro, one of the world's top Indian IT software houses, is to input voluntarily the core ingredient of TPS (Hamm, 2007) in its new software making.

At the time of the oil shock in the 1970s which shook firms all over the world, Toyota was among the first to escape from the predicament. (However, in reality, it was the history of trial and error.) Toyota also overcame the drastic appreciation of the yen from the second half of the 1980s onward by such measures as direct investment for local production and Toyota-type automation making use of the best mix between robots and human resources, not aiming at no-man factory. The MIT team wrote that total productivity of some European and American automobile companies that used as many robots as possible and promoted full automation fell rather than rose. The secret of Toyota, if any, is how to maintain a sense of impending crisis. For instance, Toyota began to flatten the organization so as to make quick decision-making. Okuda said that the worst was not to change. He took leadership to decide the following principles: (1) to produce cars near the consumers, (2) to develop and produce environment-friendly cars (Prius, for instance), and (3) to reciprocate more to shareholders by increasing ROE. Further, education of people and efficiently linking it to the development/production system is the most important factor for the company. Toyota's consolidated pretax profit in FY 2006 was ¥1.6 trillion (some US$14.3 billion), and its real time value of shares at the end of the year was larger than the sum of US Big-Three. ROE was high at 14.7%.

Toyota has tried to introduce similar management and production systems in their overseas operation centers. In advanced nations such as the US, localization of personnel is also substantially underway. Then President Mr. Cho stated:

> Toyota has been dealing with human resources development, the key for future growth, always having a sense of impending crisis. Beliefs and senses of value for management at Toyota inherited as "tacit knowledge" were arranged and collected in "the Toyota way 2001". It was then deployed to overseas business entities as well as inside the firms at home. At the same time, in advancing "globalization of management", Toyota appointed locally recruited personnel to the top of overseas business entities and appointed five foreigners as the

executive managing directors of the Toyota, Japan. Taking such measures as establishing "Toyota Institute" in 2002 as a training organization of the resource people who will support a global Toyota evolving around the "Toyota way", we have been deeply committed to the establishment and innovation of the system and structure to develop people.

Indeed, Toyota can be called an A-student in the sense that it is raising people with desirable action characteristics through daily work and education, and preventing an arrogance of executive members and precedent principle ("bureaucratization"), while linking to the management which aspires to total optimization including expansion of local production.

There are two main reasons why Toyota has been popular in the US after the 1990s. One is that Toyota did not save funds for future investment to expand the limit of energy resources, such as hybrid cars. Another is the keen perception of the firm on international politics, especially US politics. Much is mentioned about Toyota's offshore production. The fact that Toyota understands the political situation of countries such as the US well, and that it sets up operations in and has acted with caution taking the situation into consideration deserves special mention. There may be a view that it is natural for any company to act in a similar way by experiencing such an incident. However, the truth of the matter is that the following points seem to be largely influencing Toyota's actions: Toyota's top leaders assumed such important posts as Japan Federation of Economic Organizations (*Nippon Keidanren*), and they were confronted by internal politics of the US, Europe and other nations, and fierceness of Western economic diplomacy based on such politics. It is not from altruism that Toyota entered a corporate joint venture (NUMMI) with America's biggest car manufacturer, GM, and made efforts to expand sales of GM cars in Japan. It is supposed to be from a viewpoint that if GM management would feel cooperation with Toyota is desirable, it will stabilize Toyota's activity base in the US.

3.2 *Canon*

Canon has long kept its high brand value in digital cameras and printers, and aims to further multiply products and services in future use of IT. Focus and selection has been well-observed and is one of the top earners in Japan. The company has tried to produce key components and key devices for itself successfully.

Fujio Mitarai, Chairman of Canon as well as KEIDAREN, who announced the plan in November 2004 to build the most automated plant in Oita Prefecture, Kyushu and to have them assume different roles than China in the future, also clearly states that "Canon will not fire human resources". (Canon will protect employment for life, but will conduct severe evaluation and transfer positions.) Of course, there were more than a few Japanese companies that literally reduced its personnel or encouraged voluntary redundancy with a special bonus-added system in the last 10 years. However, these measures were taken at a sluggish pace inconceivable by American corporate culture. Behind this was the characteristic of Japanese business that has been longlasting since the end of the war; if it means escaping the bankruptcy of businesses, even the major trade unions tend to cooperate especially strongly with an increase in productivity and cooperate in across-the-board reduction in salaries and bonuses. (This difference in corporate culture between Japan and the US poses a large problem when Japanese companies aim to develop overseas.)

3.3 *Sharp*

Sharp has not developed well as a multinational. Its domestic market share is conspicuously high compared with its overseas market share in LCD TV, solar battery, etc. Sharp's strategy has been "Focus and Selection", and it depends little on outsourcing from overseas.

In order to make total optimization possible, first, a cross-divisional project team system is strongly encouraged to break down sectionalism as much as possible. In the electric/electronics industry, for example, Sharp has used its mobility derived from not being the largest company as its strength. Sharp Co., under the command of then CEO Katsuhiko Machida, has established an efficient system over a long period of time in which new products are made in project teams. Thus, it has made numerous hit products such as LCD TV, solar battery, and new types of home appliances like environment-friendly refrigerators and air-conditioners. Now, severe competition in the market for LCD TVs has forced manufacturers to form new alliances. Sharp, Toshiba and Sony have allied in producing/supplying LCD panels. Sharp is also to sell LCD panels to LG Electronics, Korea. Sharp decided to build a new big plant of the 10th-generation LCD jointly with Sony in 2009 in Sakai City, Osaka. The surrounding area will be a huge LCD production complex. Sharp already owns the 8th-generation integrated LCD production system in Kameyama City, Mie Prefecture, near to the affiliated key devices manufacturers, to keep production know-how secret and to reduce cost.

In ultra major companies, especially conglomerate companies that have many unrelated divisions, such agile cross-functional cooperation is extremely difficult. They have a tendency to waste time. Recently, at major plant manufacturers, moves to cut off engineering divisions (to split-up firms or subsidiaries) are underway. But even if split-up firms were to take place, in case individual split-up firms cannot be independent financially, the possibility of cases similar to non-split-up firms happening is high. Nevertheless, now that we have entered the era in which global capital logic penetrates, it is apparent that the status quo cannot be maintained. Recently, it is ICT-related firms that are trying to aggressively deal with the predicament using P2M-type approach. It is an interesting phenomenon to make efforts to use a qualification system for improving the efficiency of work and as the basis for career development.

3.4 *Matsushita (Panasonic)*

Matsushita has a unique corporate culture. Prof. Tadao Kagono, who has conducted research on the management of Japanese companies for many years, studied the management technique that the company has applied in Japan, Malaysia and other countries. He is seeking the origin of its competitive power in its "simple honesty". However, Matsushita (and its group) has not maintained competitive power by "simple honesty" alone. Naturally, Matsushita implements the basics of *Monozukuri*. On top of that, the firm has thoroughly pursued cost reduction, reformed the organization and the distribution system, and carried out total *Shikumizukuri* which included an acute sense for international politics. That is why the company was also able to immediately recover from failure.

The company had recorded huge operating losses of ¥211.8 billion, and the ordinary loss of ¥537.8 billion for the consolidated statements in the FY2001. In the face of this greatest management crisis since the end of the war, the new President Kunio Nakamura encountered numerable entangled problems. McInerney (2007) describes him as "a highly structural thinker". Much effort had been done, but without good results. His task, therefore, was to "Create" new things and to "Destroy" old impediments in such ways as: (a) fundamental shift to predominance of the Sales Division from predominance of many Production Divisions in selecting new products and their specification; (b) making "V products", utilizing the technologies other companies do not have; (c) personnel reduction; (d) reorganization and expansion of sales network (including making of super pro shops in FY2003); (e) strategic alliance with a Chinese company TCL; and (f) sales strategy of unique products for overseas markets. The number of personnel reduced by the middle of 2005 starting from the term ended March 2002 reached 27,000 in total by paying special retirement bonuses, and across the company staff rationalization seems nearly to be completed. However, this does not mean that the company has stopped its effort for staff rationalization. It has started to put out a call for early retirement, aiming to reduce 1,000 employees by July 2005, equivalent to 6% of the whole personnel at the semiconductor company, a separate company spun off.

Thus, the extremely relentless "Nakamura revolution" has so far been very successful. Namely, the operating profit for the FY2003 was ¥195.5 billion, an increase of 54.5% from the previous year. For FY2004, it recorded ¥308.5 billion, an increase of 57.8% from the previous year. Domestic sales increased by 32% in the fiscal year. For overseas sales, Asian countries such as China grew, and the Appliance Division increased its operating profit by 47%. However, ROE as of the end of FY2006 was no more than 5.64%, and its stock price amounted to ¥2,445 as of the end of 2007, only reaching some 80% of its stock price of ¥3,070 at the end of March 2000. Reform is still in the middle of the way. Nakamura said, however, that the age of the "Creation and Destruction" of the company was over, and handed the CEO position over to Fumio Otsubo in 2006. Otsubo announced that the company names (Matsushita and Panasonic) would soon be integrated to one: Panasonic. This has shown the company's determination to become a real multinational. The prices of electric and electronic products, however, continued to fall, and the market for Plasma TV, to which the firm has invested huge money rather than to LCD TV, would be less prospective than LCD TV in the long run. Otsubo has to change gears and the firm would need new global alliances and M&As in many products. One good news was that the firm acquired the highest number of patents in the world in 2007. The firm has decided to set up a factory in Russia and an R&D center in China.

4 Some Notes on Unsuccessful Manufacturing Cases

World famous Japanese manufacturers like Sony, Nissan, Toshiba, Hitachi, Mitsubishi Heavy Industries and IHI are not included as examples of success stories. Why not? It depends. But one sure thing is that they could not realize total optimization, despite their high-quality assets, due to one reason or another.

Sony, still one of the most popular Japanese manufacturers and holding a special position in the international entertainment business, has apparently lost its "Sony-likelihood" which used to make consumers enthusiastic. It seems that the management tried to run to short-term profit making and saved necessary investment in manufacturing after the too-diversified distribution of its resources in the 1990s. Its profits recorded well below the anticipated level, causing a "Sony shock" in April 2003, which led to the freefall of most of TSE stock prices. Accordingly, the CEO was changed to an American. Although Sony's brand image is still high globally, products of such rivals like Apple (iPod), Nintendo (game machine and software named Wii), Dell (PC), Canon (digital camera) and Panasonic/Sharp (TV) are harshly competing with Sony's products, and to raise profits is far from easy. The company is endeavoring to "focus and select" its business. In September 2007, it was reported that Sony was planning to exit from developing highly qualified semiconductors (LSI called as "cell") for its own game machine PS-3, and to procure them from a joint venture to be set up with Toshiba. Sony's production facility is to be bought by Toshiba. Sony intends to invest the money to develop the high-qualified picture sensor and CMOS to be used in the new mobile phone. This is just a part of the new reform of Sony. It will not be easy for the company to regain its past glory.

Then, on to Nissan. It was only yesterday when Nissan's CEO, Mr. Carlos Goesen, was praised as a hero for leading the most successful and quick recovery. It is a pity for Japan that the reform plan led by a foreign CEO could not end in Japan with a big success story. Otherwise, foreign firms would show more interest in joining and reviving Japanese "problematic firms". Why then has Mr. Goesen's reform stumbled? Few professionals predicted the eventual failures of Goesen's grandiose strategy jointly developed by Nissan's staff. Initially, Goesen's approach (reform plan) was widely accepted by existing executives and employees of a half-bankrupt Nissan with a brilliant history. His grand plan consisted of three parts. One was to close an inefficient factory in Saitama Prefecture to reduce employees by paying extra bonuses and so on; secondly, to change procurement policy completely; thirdly, to design, develop and produce new-type of Nissan cars which the company had not been able to do due to financial reasons.

He closed the firm without being bothered by the local community (he had a hard time doing the same in the Netherlands some years ago due to the strong resistance of the local community). Many employees left the firm silently. So, the start-up proceeded as he had planned.

As for the second agenda, he had been convinced that the prices of parts and components traditionally procured locally, mainly through Nissan's "group companies", were too expensive for a European standard. He tried to make more efficient use of the market mechanism in the bidding/awarding process. Hence, many existing suppliers in the Nissan group were either thrown out or fell to the similar positions with "non-group" companies with a relatively small number of exceptions, which made a great contrast with the cases of Toyota and Honda. He also changed in the contract negotiations with steel mills the long-term procurement share of steel, namely, increased the share for NNS and decreased that for JFE, the traditional main supplier to Nissan. Steel suppliers in an oligopolistic industrial structure in Japan decide the scale of their long-term equipment investment in due consideration to their commitments to their clients.

To make the story short, Nissan's sales rose beyond the plan just after Goesen became the CEO, and the procurement cost reduced sizably. Nissan's profit rose abruptly. Media at home and overseas praised Mr. Goesen by saying that no other person but he, a newcomer, could effectively cut redundant costs related to vested interests. But, over time, this observation proved to be not necessarily true. Most vendors for Nissan became exhausted by the ever-lasting "free competition". Efforts to reduce prices and improve quality would not be reciprocated forever, they thought. The company found that it could not procure the best-quality parts. Accordingly, many complaints were made of the company on the quality of its cars. A similar story followed in other areas. Nissan wished to procure more steel to increase car production, but JFE refused to increase the volume beyond its commitment, while NNS had no capacity to supply more steel to Nissan than its commitment. Thus, Nissan wasted the opportunity to produce more cars when the sales went well. Goesen would have never anticipated that the Japanese economy would revive in several years, and that the demand and supply conditions would change quickly from a "buyer's market" to a "seller's market" in the Japanese auto sector.

He could not realize the opportunity to produce a completely updated Nissan model, either. While he increased dividend share, he did not allocate enough resources to R&D and equipment investment to create real innovation. His new strategy is to sell small cars for very cheap prices in India and China. Nobody can predict what the result will be.

Let us look at Hitachi, MHI and IHI, then. Their technology levels are still one of the best. However, they could not flexibly change their business models under the global pressure. They could not get rid of bureaucratization either, partly because their main client has been the government. Quality has been deemed more important than price. Their products have often been regarded in developing countries as "too expensive though the quality is excellent", namely, to be "over-specification" for their purchasing power. Naturally, some of their business units could be revived if the management were to be done cleverly, but the first thing to do is to change the mindset of the executives and employees.

Now, Toshiba's turn. Toshiba used to be a respectful company, having high-quality technology. At that time, executives of such companies like GE and Samsung visited Toshiba frequently to learn its way of developing high technologies. But, as does often happen in such companies full of success stories with a long history, equipped with excellent technology in dozens of business units like Hitachi, MHI and IHI, Toshiba could not keep up with the pace of the quickly deteriorating situation of the Japanese economy and the dramatic change in world business environment. However, this changed all of a sudden when Atsutoshi Nishida assumed the CEO position. He decided to focus resources on nuclear generation, LSE (Nand-type flash memory, etc.) and other limited areas. Toshiba bought Westinghouse (WH), one of the largest owners of the technology nuclear generating system. It is a kind of speculation. Media and critics tended to say that Toshiba spent too much money, which might paralyze the company itself. However, due to worsening global environmental problems, most of the countries of the world, including the US, China, Japan, India and Russia, must depend on nuclear power generation. From this viewpoint, Toshiba's huge investment to merge Westinghouse, which has strong connections with the US and other governments, looks reasonable. Toshiba Group already received four orders for nuclear generation system from the US and China. Further, Nishida decided to exit from production of HD-DVD players and recorders. This decision will save a huge amount of money. A good news for the company is that Toshiba extended its profit record again as of the end of September 2007.

5 A Note on Some Excellent Firms in the Services Industry

Services industries are not included in the preceding classification due to the fact that Japanese economic recovery this time was largely led by the manufacturing sector. On this opportunity, however, I wish to note that such industries like trading business (e.g., Mitsubishi Corporation, Mitsui Corporation, Sumitomo Corporation) and marine transport (e.g., Nihon Yusen, Shosen Mitsui) have largely increased sales amount and profits as well by changing their business model. Trading houses which used to work mainly on trading business have changed their business style to overseas investors mainly in the field of energy and natural resources. They have adopted "risk-adjusted performance measurement" (RAPM), or more simply, "risk-return assets ratio", as one of the most crucial management indicators. Marine transport firms used to depend largely on domestic clients in Japan as a hub and the majority of crews were Japanese. They changed their business model, as a big increase in volume of marine transport has moved to China. They set up completely updated global marine transportation management with IT-controlled, high-quality services in the use of many foreign crews.

6 Architecture Theory and Points for Reconsideration

In Japan, the management mind is gradually changing. Nonetheless, there are still industries that are very proud of maintaining their traditional mind. Most of the major firms in the above-mentioned heavy industry have a commonality in their large fixed capital investment. These companies have comprehensive high technologies in production, assembly and engineering that embody the world's preeminent "integrated and approximation (*suriawase*) type" architecture. And yet, they accept not being able to achieve high ROI and ROA and to have low stock prices ranging from 100 to 300 yen level as of the end of 2004. It is apparent that on the one hand, there are radical changes in the world's cost structure, unique and multifaceted group structure within which it is difficult for synergy to work, and a considerably large stable market. On the other hand, several elements have delayed disengagement from the existing situation. These include the special circumstances of the industry in which the needs of the overseas market with rapid changes differed from those of domestic products and simultaneous pursuit of them both becomes difficult, the strong linkage with the local society resulting from clusterization of industry ("castle town"), and fragile financial structure. Moreover, it is a fact that because foreign capitals have not aggressively entered as in the cases of automotive industry and financial industry, "outside pressure" for consolidation, reorganization and external direct investments were small in spite of the low market price of these firms.

This is obvious at a glance when one compares the situation of Japanese and Western plants/specialized engineering firms. There were 67 major Western plant engineering firms in 1985, but the number has sharply declined to 49 in 1990, and then to 17 famous firms in 2001 including Bechtel, Fluor, Foster, Feeler, GE, Siemens, ALSTOM and ABB. In the meantime, MW Kellog, a typical process engineering firm, was taken over by Dresser, while Lummus Crest, a dominant engineering firm for ethylene process, became a subsidiary of ABB. And yet in Japan, although major plant engineering firms suffered a "Winter era for the plant" in the late 1980s, they recovered their wind due to the demand boom for plants in Asia in the 1990s during the bubble economy age that followed. Once again today, they are increasing their order intakes due to a global shipbuilding boom and making of the LNG base. Major players have not changed very much. However, financially speaking, their market value has been declining after 1996 due to order intakes at unreasonable prices resulting from excess competition in the middle of the 1990s. On the other hand, specialized engineering companies that have little fixed capital in Japan and that have depended mainly on external demand for their development (that have "open module type" architecture) such as JGC and Chiyoda Chemical have skillfully used their high engineering technologies demonstrated in constructing facilities including LNG plants and outsourcing. They have expanded their order intakes for large projects, morphing into companies with high earning capacity.

P2M, the new knowledge system transmitted from Japan, was initially developed as a result of a survey research at the study group of Engineering Advancement Association of Japan (headed by Shigenobu Ohara, currently Professor at the Nippon Institute of Technology).

The main purposes of the study group were to let Japanese plant engineering companies suffering from these structural changes have a sense of responsibility as entities (sense of mission) and to have them think of the optimum solution for the company as a whole and not the partial optimized solution. It was also to quantify tacit knowledge (explicit knowledge) within firms and to make them into true corporate assets. Following its verification, a new twist was added, and it has developed into a P2M qualification accreditation system widely known both in Japan and overseas.

Even the Toyota group that enjoyed a large amount of profit amounting to ¥1.75 trillion for the term FY2004, ending March 2005, has largely made revisions to its conventional "seniority-based payment system and lifetime employment" and has embarked on accepting contract workers and temporary employees extensively. Overseas production ratio, or overseas production amount (OPA)/OPA + domestic production amount, is rising, but yet, failures of foreign operations are not allowed. The Japanese technical system can be brought in, but localization of human resources, goods, money, design and engineering are unavoidable. Amid this situation, mistakes in production are gradually increasing. A new issue of how to cover such unprecedented risks is emerging.

Furthermore, as an element that makes Japanese-style management more complex and difficult, a product lifecycle (PLC) can be mentioned. In such changes taking place, the number of companies that are setting with confidence long-term financial targets that had been considered a characteristic of Japanese firms is decreasing. Such super excellent firms as Toyota and Canon have the luxury to continue with it, but pressures from foreign shareholders and others that put emphasis on relatively short-term profits have a tendency to increase. Firms struggling with the management have abandoned long-term management targets and have fallen into living on a day-to-day basis.

7 Concluding Remarks

We may be able to conclude that the perennial successful companies or successful companies after severe restructuring must keep a sense of crisis to avoid being bureaucratic in their efforts to optimize their value-added activities while conquering to conduct for partial optimization. Japanese firms can grow and contribute to the world in their own way.

References

Annual reports of selected companies.

Berger, S. *et al.* (2006). *How We Compete: What Companies Around the World are Doing to Make It in Today's Global Economy?*, New York: Currency Bookdata.

Dertouzos, M. *et al.* (1990). *Made in America: Regaining the Productive Edge*, Cambridge, MA: Harper perennial, The MIT Press.

Hamm, S. (2007). *Bangalore Tiger: How Indian Tech Upstart Wipro is Rewriting the Rules of Global Competition*, The McGrawhill Corporation.

Kinoshita, T. (2005). Revitalizing Japanese economy/firms and appropriateness of P2M approach, A revised and translated version in 2006, of his paper (Japanese version) published as a special study report by Project Management Certification Center (PMCC), Tokyo.

McInerney, F. (2007). *Panasonic: The Largest Corporate Restructuring in History*, NY: St. Martin's Press.

Williamson, P. (2004). *Winning in Asia: Strategies for Competing in the New Millennium,* Harvard Business School Press.

Knowledge of Project Management and Finance in Japan

Masaaki Horiguchi
Instructor, Faculty of Economics
Teikyo University

1   Introduction

1.1   *Required level of knowledge of project management*

Regarding the type of finance for projects, the focus has shifted from Corporate Finance, which depends on the credibility of a project's implementers (Sponsors), to Project Finance, which depends solely on the cash flow of a project. This tendency has already had an impact on the field of Project Management, as the required knowledge of Project Management has changed in accordance with the type of finance. This paper discusses how finance for projects impacted the knowledge of Project Management in Japan in terms of finance for overseas projects, and describes the required knowledge of Project Management in these cases.

1.2   *Finance for domestic projects*

Why is finance for overseas projects used to illustrate changes in the knowledge required for Project Management? In Japan, finance for projects has traditionally been the Corporate Finance approach. Finance opportunities are extended to "Sponsors" who are responsible for the funding; this tendency has been strengthened in domestic projects. In this view, the function of Project Management is to ensure completion of a project on schedule and within the budget. Consequently, the management of finance and/or funding of domestic projects is limited to overseeing budgets, costs and earned values.

1.3 *Finance for overseas projects in Japan*

For overseas projects in Japan, however, finance that depends on the value of the project instead of Sponsor credibility has been realized and implemented, although there are still many cases of funds procured by corporate financing.

After World War II, the Japanese government supported its exporters through the Export Import Bank of Japan, a government financial institution established in 1950. The Export Import Bank of Japan, now the Japan Bank for International Cooperation (JBIC), grants the financing of export projects. In accordance with Japanese economic development, JBIC financing for overseas projects has been diversified from the support of exports to the support of imports, the development of natural resources and overseas investments, and international economic cooperation. However, JBIC bases its financing of overseas projects upon careful review of these projects — a principle known as "project-based finance". Thus, the object has not been to extend export financing to Japanese exporters and investment financing to Japanese investors, but to support projects on their own merits. However, in some cases, financing still depends on Sponsor credibility as securities.

1.4 *Importance of project management*

In reviewing and monitoring the feasibility of the projects concerned, it is natural that the success of Project Management is a matter of keen interest for stakeholders, including financial institutions such as the JBIC. In accordance with changes in finance types indicative of the diversification of overseas projects in Japanese economic development, i.e., from export finance to economic cooperation finance, the role of Project Management should also be updated. In addition, the required knowledge of Project Management should be expanded from the basic concepts of Quality, Cost and Delivery (QCD) to include evaluation of financial results and project investment, as well as designing project schemes for maintaining financial independence, creating project value, and risk management.

1.5 *Project-based finance in Japan*

However, project-based finance in the manner of JBIC has not attained popularity as a general financing scheme. Private commercial banks in

Japan continue to favor the corporate finance approach, which depends primarily on Borrowers' assets. It is said that such financial practices contributed to the cumulative amounts of non-performing debts during the "Bubble" economy. In reviewing the treatment of non-performing debts after the collapse of the "Bubble", the necessity of separating financing for projects from Borrowers' total assets has increased in importance.

Historical trends in JBIC financing for overseas projects are shown in Table 1. Resource Development Finance and Project Finance are diversified into Export, Import and Investment Finance, according to their funding objectives.

1.6 *Purpose*

In this paper, I aim to demonstrate changes in the required knowledge of Project Management in Japan using JBIC's approach for financing overseas projects, and the knowledge level of Project Management currently required will be discussed with regard to finance type.

2   Knowledge of Project Management for Finance for Overseas Projects (First Stage)

2.1 *Finance for plant export*

JBIC financing is popular with Japanese exporters, particularly those exporting plants to developing countries. Since the 1960s, when export of plants on deferred payment bases was popularized, JBIC extended financing

Table 1   Trends in JBIC financing for overseas projects

Finance	FY1960	FY1970	FY1980	FY1990	FY2000	FY2006
Export	80	397	416	40	174	76
Import	0	33	9	194	321	8
Investment	8	68	216	496	524	890
Others	14	37	286	857	67	76
Total	102	536	926	1,587	1,086	1,050

Note: Data are the amount of commitment (in billion yen) in international financial operations, excluding economic cooperation operations (ODA loans). FY = Fiscal Year (April to March).

to Japanese suppliers (so-called "Suppliers' Credit") by allowing the transfer of deferred payment claims as security. Risks in this stage are risk to completion/delivery of plants, risk of deferred payment of debtors (commercial risk) and risk of future political instability in the debtors' country (political risk). Successful Project Management realizes the completion/delivery of plants and obtained credibility for debtors by securing guarantees from buyer-side banks and governments. If JBIC and Nippon Export Import Insurance (NEXI), which currently handles export insurance, are sufficient in obtaining an explanation from the Exporters, financing is successful.

Next, in accordance with the enlargement of plant export, buyers receive JBIC financing directly; government organizations and banks on the import side also utilize JBIC financing by taking the risk of buyers, known as "Buyers' Credit" or "Bank-to-Bank Loans". In such cases of export Project Management, the QCD factors and explanations of Buyer credibility/guarantees of security are the same as for Suppliers' Credit. In the finance of plant export, risks after delivery are transferred to JBIC and NEXI. Consequently, it is sufficient, in principle, for exporters to utilize Project Management until delivery, although the Borrowers' responsibility to Suppliers' Credit remains.

In financing the export of ships, JBIC extends long-term finance on a deferred payment basis by taking a ship mortgage and the long-term charter contracts' claim as security. In this case, Project Management of Japanese exporters involves the completion and delivery of the ship as well as confirmation of the registration of the ship mortgage and transfer of claims in charter contracts, even though the eligibility of ship mortgage and creditability of charter parties have already been checked by JBIC and NEXI.

2.2   *Project management for finance for plant export*

Project Management for plant export financing, as noted above, is, in principle, responsible for completing the delivery and managing the budget, costs and earned values of the project.

3   Knowledge of Project Management for Finance for Overseas Projects (Second Stage)

3.1   *Financing Japanese investment projects*

In the latter half of the 1980s, following the high valuation of the Japanese yen, Japan's international competitiveness had decreased; in its place, foreign direct investment by domestic companies became a major factor in Japanese overseas projects. Accordingly, JBIC financing of Japanese investment projects increased.

For investment loans, it is important to calculate projections for the projects in question. In Project Management for investors, the most important issue is whether the project will create value in the operations stage, after completion of the project facility. The Project Management knowledge required in this case is analyzing and estimating the strength of value creation in the project, by adding to the base of QCD. This involves an evaluation of the value to be created from the project, as well as the return from investment. In this stage, to add to the financial projection of the project, it is necessary to evaluate the future project value in terms of the present value to find the net value. Project Management in this case involves studying the feasibility of a project from technical, financial and funding points of view, otherwise known as a Feasibility Study.

After confirming the expected level of value creation, the Sponsor should decide whether or not the project will start. For project funding, many Sponsors attempt to secure financing from JBIC, which supports Japanese overseas investment as a national policy. After reviewing a project, if JBIC standards for projected future value and the risks of debt service payment are satisfied, and the project is fit for support, JBIC will extend financing. This financing comes with a guarantee of the Sponsor for the Borrower's payment (debt service); this guarantee is usually taken by JBIC as a security. The knowledge of Project Management required is an analysis of project feasibility and evaluation of value creation of the project; that is, to utilize a Feasibility Study.

3.2 *Development of proposal business in export of plants*

In the last few decades, export of Japanese plants has stagnated due to a decline in Japan's international economic competitiveness. In order to improve the export of plants, Japanese industry has attempted to expand the proposal business by which contractors desiring to promote the export of plants propose candidate projects to customers. For example, a Japanese plant manufacturer may propose the rehabilitation of old power plants and explain the feasibility of completion from a technical and commercial perspective. In this case, Project Management of the proposing party involves explaining the proposal using a Feasibility Study.

3.3 *Review of loans for official development assistance (ODA)*

The JBIC, which now includes the former Overseas Economic Cooperation Fund (OECF), has extended Yen Loans as one form of Japanese ODA to developing countries. Such Yen Loans are primarily in the form of project loans, and there are numerous processes for cultivating, planning, implementing and monitoring these project loans. Project Management for these loans has been preceded by qualified consultants in accordance with the guidance on the implementation institutions of JBIC. The guidance appears to contain numerous concepts of the Feasibility Study.

3.4 *Project management for investment projects, business proposals for plant export, and ODA loan projects*

The knowledge of Project Management required for investment projects, business proposals for plant export and ODA loan projects further develops the knowledge of the QCD base. The Feasibility Study analyzes the project in terms of technical and financial points, including funding. While technical points may differ with respect to the business contents of a project, the financial points of a Feasibility Study are fortunately standardized to a certain level. The main financial items covered in a Feasibility Study are an analysis of investment amounts and construction and operation plans, as well as the reporting of financial statements during the construction and operation period. It also includes an evaluation of the results of financial statements, business accomplishments, return on investment and risk management using an extensive analysis, such as a Sensitivity Analysis.

4 Knowledge of Project Management for Finance for Overseas Projects (Third Stage)

4.1 *Finance for resource development projects*

JBIC financing for resource development projects is primarily directed towards large development areas such as coal, natural gas and iron. Such financing has evolved from the advance payment method to support joining, to project transactions such as investing equity. With the subsequent increase in funding for projects, it has been difficult for JBIC to take

Sponsor guarantees as security. Thus, JBIC has extended Project Finance for certain resource development projects by taking the cash flow to be raised from the projected earnings of projects, such as long-term export contracts for resources, as security. In such cases, it is required to first acknowledge the values to be created from a project and then to maintain a secure cash flow by avoiding and/or mitigating risks related to the project, by structuring contracts among stakeholders by monitoring the performance potential of their contracts, and by risk management. However, since this stage of Project Management requires specialists in resource development projects, it has not expanded to more general fields.

4.2 Finance for privatized infrastructure projects

Since the 1980s, following the privatization of infrastructure fields and the mitigation of debt burden by the governments of developing countries, demand for Project Finance for privatizing infrastructure projects has increased. This type of Project Finance has extended to "green field" projects in Asian countries and to rehabilitation projects for existing infrastructure ("brown fields") in Latin American countries. Project Finance methods have been popularized from specialized fields like resource development to more generalized sectors in infrastructure. JBIC has been a pioneer in Japanese Project Finance by extending a variety of Project Finance options.

4.3 Project management in projects funded by project finance

The knowledge of Project Management required for projects funded by Project Finance adds to the knowledge of the first and second stages to verify the possibility of financial independence of projects, which is maintained by structuring contracts among stakeholders and by risk management. JBIC performs due diligence for projects to secure a stable cash flow from projects. In such cases, Project Management should be required for due diligence only. Because Project Finance depends only on cash flow from the project, the financial institution must conduct a thorough and detailed study of the project and confirm stable repayment of the loan.

4.4 Expansion of project finance into other areas

Finance based on Project Finance has recently been expanded to domestic projects. For example, the law of Private Finance Initiative

(PFI) in Japan, effected in 1999, promotes the use of private business methods including funding in infrastructure. Such projects usually request the use of Project Finance. Additionally, bidders who want to invest in a PFI project should create proposals that verify the feasibility and the financial independence of the project. In these cases, Project Finance means independent and more effective funding that does not use the Sponsor's assets and credibility. If Project Finance is available for projects, Project Management should secure the most effective type of funding.

5   Conclusion

In conventional Project Management, the target is the accomplishment of QCD, and the financial aspects of Project Management are limited to the budget, costs and earned value management. Currently, in Japan, the knowledge of Project Management required for financial aspects involves more knowledge than that of the QCD base (first stage). Already, knowledge for the second stage (Feasibility Study) and third stage (Project Finance) is being utilized (Ohara, 2005). In one qualification examination for Project Management (Project Management Specialist (PMS)), knowledge of Project Finance Management is required (PMAJ Web.). The knowledge of Project Management currently required in Japan is summarized as follows:

5.1   *First stage (QCD base)*

Project Management from a financial perspective should involve the knowledge of managing the budget, costs and earned value (Ohara, 2005; PMI, 2004).

5.2   *Second stage (feasibility study level)*

Adding to the knowledge in the first stage, Project Management should involve knowledge of analyzing the future value of projects. Proficiency in financial/accounting fields is not sufficient; a knowledge body for analyzing future values and return on investments is required (Ohara, 2005; ADB, 2005; UNIDO, 1991; Callahan *et al.*, 2007).

5.3 *Third stage (project finance)*

Adding to the knowledge in the first and second stages, Project Management should involve structuring for financial independence and contract schemes using risk management, and successfully introduce Project Finance from financial institutions (Ohara, 2005; Yescomb, 2002). Since Project Finance is the most effective type of funding, the knowledge of Project Management for Project Finance contributes to better relationships among concerned stakeholders. However, as this level of knowledge of Project Management appears to be difficult for Project Managers to master, extensive and thorough educational programs in Project Finance are required.

References

Asian Development Bank (ADB) (2005). *Financial Management and Analysis of Projects*, Manila, Philippines: ADB.

Callahan, K. R., Stetz, G. S., and Brooks, L. M. (2007). *Project Management Accounting — Budgeting, Tracking, and Reporting Costs and Profitability*, Hoboken, USA: John Wiley & Sons, Inc.

Japan Bank for International Cooperation (JBIC) (http://www.jbic.go.jp).

Ohara, S. (Representative Author) (2005). *A Guidebook of Project & Program Management for Enterprise Innovation*, Volumes 1 and 2 Translation, Project Management Association of Japan (PMAJ) (http://www.pmaj.or.jp/ENG/index.htm).

Ohara, S. (Representative Author) and Project Management Professional Certification Center (PMCC) (now integrated to PMAJ) (2004). *A Guidebook of Project & Program Management for Enterprise Innovation*, Volumes 1 and 2, Tokyo, Japan: PHP (in Japanese).

Project Management Association of Japan (PMAJ) (http://www.pmaj.or.jp).

Project Management Institute (PMI) (2004). *A Guide to the Project Management Body of Knowledge*, 3rd ed. (PMBOK Guide), Newtown Square, USA: PMI.

United Nations Industrial Organization (UNIDO) (1991). *Manual for the Preparation of Industrial Feasibility Studies*, Vienna, Austria: UNIDO.

Yescomb, E. R. (2002). *Principles of Project Finance*, San Diego, USA: Academic Press.

Transcultural Management: Cultural Relevance in Different Industries

Emiko Magoshi

Professor, College of Business Management
J. F. Oberlin University

Akio Yamamoto

Senior Manager, Building Construction Management Division
Planning Department, Kajima Corporation

1 Introduction

Business operations are increasingly becoming global and companies with overseas business now employ personnel of different nationalities and with diverse cultural backgrounds. Under these circumstances, the influence of national culture on business strategies and practices has become less significant. Will national culture cease to exert influence on international business? In this paper, we examine the concept of culture in an attempt to determine which layers of culture are most difficult to transcend and which ones can be overcome by using various means including project and program management (P2M/KPM).

We begin by reviewing some previous research on transcultural management and then present three studies that investigated the role of culture in international business.[1] The purpose of the first study was to compare the role of national and corporate cultures at Japanese multinational companies. The purpose of the second study was to compare how local and overseas employees working at a high-tech US company perceive corporate culture, management and other related issues. The third study was a case study of a Japanese construction company with rich experience in doing mega-projects overseas. The construction industry is unique in that it can be classified as belonging to both service and manufacturing industries. We argue here that for consumer electronics and IT companies, national culture is becoming less and less important,

---

[1] The first two studies were conducted by the first author, Emiko Magoshi; the third study was conducted by the second author, Akio Yamamoto.

whereas for construction companies, the role of national culture remains significant. In this paper, we also discuss the differences in the relevance of culture to different industries and companies.

2   Review of the Literature

2.1   *What is culture?*

Bartlett and Ghoshal (1998) created a new concept of *transnational company*, which goes beyond the concept of multinational, international or global entities. Today, companies operating in the global market have to deal with different nationalities, gender and age groups as well as diverse ways of thinking and behavioral patterns of their employees and customers. Hofstede (1991) calls these thinking and behavioral patterns of individuals a *mental program* or *software of the mind*, and defines them as culture in a broad sense of the term. Along these lines, a multitude of attributes including those described above can be considered as culture.

We believe that companies with worldwide operations encompass all kinds of culture and that their business practices need to accommodate all these diverse cultures. Thus, we propose to call the management of such companies *transcultural*.

Trompenaars (1995) described culture as a multi-layered structure (see Figure 1). The outer layer represents explicit culture, or the artifacts and products of human existence such as language, food, buildings, art

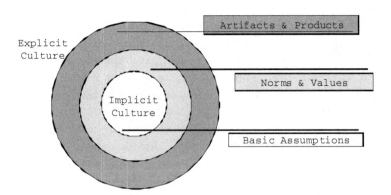

Fig. 1   Structural layers of culture

Source: Trompenaars (1995, p. 51).

and fashion. The layer in the middle represents societal norms and values including laws, social frameworks and the beliefs shared by members of the same cultural group. The inner layer is implicit culture, or basic assumptions including behaviors, thoughts and other things that members of the same cultural group take for granted and follow without thinking.

2.2 *The role of culture in management*

Most studies on culture and management have focused on the differences between national cultures as well as on how these differences affect business practices. For example, using the results of a survey of more than 110,000 managers of IBM in 50 countries, Hofstede (1991) identified the well-known five dimensions of culture to contrast business cultures in different countries. Trompenaars (1993) also conducted a survey of 15,000 employees in several dozen multinational companies in 50 countries and produced seven dimensions of culture. Although Hofstede's research is generally considered stronger in predictive validity, both authors have placed similar emphasis on national culture. On a smaller scale, England (1995) undertook a survey of a representative sample of 5,000 workers in the US, Germany and Japan to compare the workers' work-related values. He developed a work centrality index showing large gaps in attitudes among the employees in the three countries.

Adler (1997) advocated cultural synergy in multicultural settings. In an attempt to minimize the negative impact of multicultural factors and to maximize their benefits, she explained how synergistic effects could be obtained in a multicultural environment. Hayashi (1985) proposed the concept of *cross-cultural interface management*, which assumes the existence of a cross-cultural interface between two cultural groups and the presence of an interface manager serving as a contact point and a mediator between the two groups.

However, other works have shown less influence of national culture on business. For example, Langhoff (1997) introduced the notion of *psychic distance*, which refers to a cultural distance between a firm and its markets. He posited that the effects of cultural bias may be most significant when a firm exports to culturally close, rather than culturally distant, markets. Pahlberg (1997) interviewed managers working in the headquarters and subsidiaries of several Swedish multinationals in 13 countries and concluded that cultural distance did not cause problems in the relationship between the headquarters and the subsidiaries. Yasumuro (1993) has argued that over and above national culture, corporate culture and personal traits play an important role in the management of multinationals. He proposed developing a knowledge base of companies encompassing different cultures.

3   Study 1

3.1   *Overview*

This study is based on research conducted at a subsidiary of Sony Corporation[2] in France (Sony France), a subsidiary of the Bank of Tokyo (BOT)[3] in Luxembourg, and a subsidiary of another Japanese bank, Bank A (BA, a pseudonym), in Luxembourg. The purpose of this study was to examine whether national culture has become less important in international business. More specifically, this study compared the role of national vs. corporate culture in international business. Data were collected in the summer of 1993 when the first author visited Sony France, BOT Luxembourg and BA Luxembourg. Interviews were conducted with four Japanese expatriates and three local managers of the three companies, and additional data were collected from 53 employees using a questionnaire.

To measure employees' perception of culture and management, the questionnaire covered the following nine groups of questions: (1) intra-company communication, (2) degree of difficulty in communication, (3) problems in communication, (4) transparency of management, (5) degree of localization (defined as the number of local employees and their positions as compared to the number and positions of Japanese expatriates), (6) access to information, (7) degree of satisfaction, (8) global-mindedness, and (9) degree of motivation of personnel. The questionnaire contained 35 Likert-scale items: 25 were addressed to both Japanese expatriates and local employees, and 10 were addressed separately to each of these two groups of respondents.

3.2   *Assumptions and analysis*

Based on the interviews with Japanese and local managers, an assumption was made that in companies with long overseas experience, national culture would have less influence on business operations, whereas corporate culture

---

[2] Sony Corporation is a big Japanese consumer electronics company.

[3] The Bank of Tokyo has since merged with Mitsubishi Bank to form Tokyo-Mitsubishi Bank.

would take on a more important role. It was also assumed that a high degree of global-mindedness of a company and a high degree of motivation of its personnel would have a positive effect on diminishing the "mental distance" between Japanese expatriates and local employees. The term *mental distance* refers to the distance between the minds of employees. The interviews also indicated that a high degree of localization greatly benefited the morale of the personnel. Thus, it was hypothesized that employees of the companies surveyed in the study perceived corporate culture as being more important than national culture.

Responses obtained in the survey were analyzed separately for the three companies surveyed and for the Japanese expatriate vs. local employees. Responses obtained from the employees of the three companies represented differences in the perception of corporate culture; responses obtained from the Japanese expatriate vs. local employees represented differences in the perception of national culture.

3.3 *Results*

The study found differences in opinion between the employees of the three companies surveyed on five out of the nine groups of questions (or 71%), namely on (1), (3), (4), (5) and (7). Differences were observed on 75% of the questions. In contrast, differences in opinion between Japanese expatriates and local employees were found on only 45% of the questions.

These results indicate greater differences in opinion between the employees of the three companies than between Japanese expatriates and local employees. They suggest that corporate culture may play a more significant role in business than national culture. This study also found that the differences in opinion between Japanese expatriates and local employees were minimal at Sony. At BOT, these differences were greater than at Sony but much smaller than at BA. Similar trends were observed for global-mindedness and motivation. These results support the hypothesis that employees of the companies surveyed in the study perceived corporate culture as being more important than national culture.

4 Study 2

4.1 *Overview*

This study is based on research conducted during the first half of 1997 at a US-based high-tech company. The company is headquartered in the US, maintains overseas offices in 14 countries, and operates in 48 countries throughout the world. It has 900 employees. It is a highly localized company with most overseas offices run by local staff. The purpose of this study was to compare mental distance between employees working in the headquarters and those working in the company's domestic regional offices as well as between employees working in the headquarters and those working in the company's overseas offices in Europe, Asia and Oceania. Data were collected through interviews with three executive officers and a questionnaire administered to 170 managers and professionals. Of these, responses were obtained from 88 people, producing a response rate of 52%.

The questionnaire consisted of 49 Likert-scale items that focused on nine broad themes: corporate culture, management, corporate social responsibility, communication, competitive advantage, work satisfaction, cooperation at work, motivation, and value placed on work and family.

Descriptive statistics including mean, median, mode and standard deviation were calculated for each statement separately for the respondents from the headquarters, for the respondents from the regional offices, and for the respondents from the overseas offices. Additional data were collected on the respondents' age, gender, nationality, educational level, professional status, years of service and job description.

4.2 Assumptions and analysis

Global corporations such as the company described above operate in multiple markets in the world and hire people with diverse cultural backgrounds. As a result, they are characterized by a high degree of heterogeneity both externally and internally, and the physical distance between their headquarters and overseas offices is inevitable. While the physical distance can gradually be overcome by advances in information technology, the distance between the minds of employees may be harder to bridge. This mental distance resulting from differences between different people's values and cultures can impede the successful management of global corporations. We assume, however, that in corporations with management practices based on global perspectives and systems, this mental distance can be overcome.

The study compared responses obtained from the Headquarters (HQ), US regional offices (REs) and overseas offices (OVs). It was hypothesized that if the mental distance between the HQ and OVs was equal to or smaller than that between the HQ and REs, then by implementing transcultural management and sharing corporate values, global corporations could reduce both physical and mental distances among their employees. The following hypothesis was formulated: Mental distance between the HQ and OVs is equal to or smaller than that between the HQ and REs.

Principal factors extraction with varimax rotation was performed and the following nine factors were extracted: F1, corporate culture; F2, management; F3, corporate social responsibility; F4, communication; F5, competitive advantage; F6, satisfaction level at work; F7, cooperation at work; F8, motivation; and F9, value placed on work and family.

4.3 *Results*

Differences in opinion between the HQ and REs were greater than between the HQ and OVs for the following six factors: corporate culture, management, communication, work satisfaction, cooperation at work and motivation.

Thus, six out of the nine factors indicated a greater mental distance between the HQ and REs than between the HQ and OVs. Therefore, the hypothesis was supported. These results are in stark contrast to many earlier published findings such as those of Hofstede (1991), which found a cultural gap between different countries and national cultures. The present findings indicate that this may not be so and that the mental distance between the HQ and REs may be greater than that between the HQ and OVs, even though both the HQ and REs are located in the same country.

There are several possible explanations. First, the company investigated in this study is engaged in high-tech business and it is possible that national culture may have a smaller effect on this type of business than on other types. Second, many overseas offices of this company are headed by local managers with MBAs from US universities, which indicates that they may be familiar with US business norms and practices. This may help maintain smooth communication between the HQ and overseas offices. Third, both regional offices and overseas offices share similar marketing concerns, whereas the HQ appears to be more preoccupied with technical concerns. As a result, RE and OV employees may feel closer to one another than to the HQ. Fourth, the HQ may not fully understand the needs of local markets in the US or overseas, which would cause RE personnel to feel isolated from the HQ. Fifth, significant cultural diversity exists within the US itself. Also, regional offices in the US are less tolerant of the HQ when there is a lack of understanding on the part of HQ personnel or when there are delays in feedback from the HQ. They are likely to expect speedy action from the HQ, whereas overseas offices are more tolerant of delays as the physical distance is unavoidable. Finally, top management at the HQ includes directors and executive officers from Europe and Asia, who take part in the decision making process. This may help disseminate corporate objectives among international staff and maintain coherence in a diverse workforce.

These results suggest that by taking advantage of state-of-the-art information technology and by implementing a management system with a global perspective and transcultural mindset, companies with global operations can overcome both physical and mental distances among their culturally diverse employees and motivate them to contribute to their company to the best of their ability.

To conclude this part of the paper, contrary to previous research, the two empirical studies described above indicate that national culture may be becoming increasingly *unimportant* in international business, especially in the fields of consumer electronics and IT. These studies suggest a possible decline in the role of national culture on the corporate arena.

We believe that the companies surveyed in these studies were able to overcome the negative impact of national culture because they were able to minimize cross-cultural barriers in the outer layer of culture as well as in the mid-layer of culture, through standardization of products, clarification of business processes, utilization of IT and the sharing of objectives. As for the inner layer of basic assumptions, the Japanese companies surveyed here succeeded in minimizing its impediments by pursuing localization vigorously and by nurturing the international mindset of the Japanese expatriates.

We will see in the next part of this paper how Japanese construction companies are tackling this problem. It is our impression that Japanese construction businesses are more heavily influenced by both the mid-layer and the inner layer of culture than are the industries surveyed in the studies described above, because of the way construction business is conducted and of the work behavior of front-line managers and operators. In the next section, we present a case study of a Japanese construction company doing business overseas.

5   Case Study of a Japanese Construction Company

Construction businesses have a greater dependence on regional and local factors, and it is common to use local contractors and suppliers in construction projects based on the project's location. Construction businesses are different from other industries operating overseas in that there is a greater involvement and presence of Japanese managers. This tends to create opportunities for cultural conflict in project execution. The cultural diversity of local people involved in specific projects further exacerbates the problem.

5.1 *Overview*

This study surveyed four construction projects (A, B, C and D) in the Middle East, Asia and Europe, carried out by a major Japanese contractor between 1980 and 2000. Results indicate that cultural issues were highly significant in these projects and that cultural issues play a significant role in Japanese construction businesses working overseas.

In order to visualize the complexity of cultural influence in each project, six cultural indices were used: nationality, ethnic group, religion, language, percentage of women, and percentage of Japanese expatriates in a project team. These cultural indices were scored on a scale from 1 to 5 as shown in Table 1. They are shown in radar charts as illustrated in Figures 2 and 3. A higher score indicates greater cultural complexity.

5.2 *Findings*

5.2.1 *Strong local presence and resistance to change*

The construction workers involved in the overseas projects investigated in this study came from different nationalities, ethnic groups and religious backgrounds. Their work behavior tended to be governed by their cultural norms, and it was normal for many to follow their own style of management and business customs. When Japanese management style was used in a project, some local workers showed resistance towards external forces

The cultural complexity of a construction project is the lowest in Japan since all scores are 1s or 2s, and there is no expatriate input in a homogeneous working environment.

Fig. 2   Homogeneous culture of Japanese domestic projects

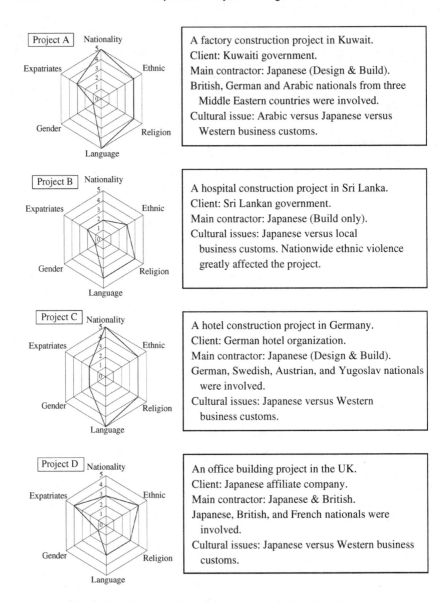

Project A

A factory construction project in Kuwait.
Client: Kuwaiti government.
Main contractor: Japanese (Design & Build).
British, German and Arabic nationals from three
Middle Eastern countries were involved.
Cultural issue: Arabic versus Japanese versus
Western business customs.

Project B

A hospital construction project in Sri Lanka.
Client: Sri Lankan government.
Main contractor: Japanese (Build only).
Cultural issues: Japanese versus local
business customs. Nationwide ethnic violence
greatly affected the project.

Project C

A hotel construction project in Germany.
Client: German hotel organization.
Main contractor: Japanese (Design & Build).
German, Swedish, Austrian, and Yugoslav nationals
were involved.
Cultural issues: Japanese versus Western
business customs.

Project D

An office building project in the UK.
Client: Japanese affiliate company.
Main contractor: Japanese & British.
Japanese, British, and French nationals were
involved.
Cultural issues: Japanese versus Western business
customs.

Fig. 3   Brief description of project and their cultural patterns

seeking to change their traditional systems. Under such circumstances, even most capable and experienced project managers in Japan may lose confidence and face depression or dilemmas in overseas projects due to the difficulty in adapting to new environments and business culture.

Table 1　Definition of cultural indices and scores

Culture Index	Score	Description of Ranking 1–5	Culture Index	Score	Description of Ranking 1–5
Nationality	1	One nationality	Language	1	Single language is used
	2	Two nationalities		2	Two languages are used
	3	Three nationalities		3	Three languages are used
	4	Four nationalities		4	Four languages are used
	5	More than five nationalities		5	More than five languages are used
Ethnic Group	1	Single ethnic groups	Gender (Percentage of women in a project team)	1	No women (100% men)
	2	Two ethnic groups		2	Women 5% or less
	3	Three ethnic groups		3	Women 6%–10%
	4	Four ethnic groups		4	Women 11%–15%
	5	More than five ethnic groups		5	Women more than 15%
Religion	1	Single religion	Expatriates (Percentage of Japanese in a project team)	1	Less than 5% expatriates
	2	Two religions		2	5%–10% expatriates
	3	Three religions		3	11%–15% expatriates
	4	Four religions		4	16%–20% expatriates
	5	More than five religions		5	More than 20% expatriates

5.2.2　*A limited learning curve in cultural understanding*

Construction projects are one-off, purpose-made contracts, and each project is unique and different in terms of location, organization and operational style. Project participants often change as the work progresses, which makes it difficult to sustain a certain level of cultural understanding in a project team throughout the project period. Overcoming barriers in cross-cultural management in overseas projects may take more time due to the more complex nature of such projects.

5.2.3 *Cultural barriers are more complex in overseas projects*

In overseas projects, cultural issues are more complex because the background of people involved in these projects is more diverse. A project team needs to liaise with people representing different stakeholders, and it is necessary to overcome cross-cultural problems at different levels. There may be different cultural barriers at the top, middle and operational levels of management, depending on the degree of complexity of cultural backgrounds of employees involved in each project and the particular project's management policy.

5.3 *Solutions*

Below, we describe possible solutions to the above problems. These solutions are based on the use of project and program management (P2M).

5.3.1 *Excellent communication skills, mutual trust and respect*

To achieve and maintain the best output, core members of an amalgamated project team need to have excellent communication skills, mutual trust and respect, and create a balanced mix of individuals so that the group's motivation can promote creativity and dynamic ideas for a positive outcome.

In Project A, local foremen who had achieved good work performance were praised in front of other employees, and their high motivation positively affected other workers. In Project B, a local senior manager (a former Army Captain), who was fluent in three languages and had a profound understanding of Japanese business customs and culture, played a major role in the recruitment of local staff, public relations and liaison with other parties to resolve complicated local problems. In Project C, a Swedish subcontractor directly employed workers from former Yugoslavia, and their foremen, who were fluent in German, effectively communicated with other key members of the project team to bridge language barriers.

5.3.2   *A hybrid management approach for project teams*

To achieve better performance in a changing work environment, a hybrid management approach can be implemented by core team members to enhance day-to-day communication and detect any sign of potential misunderstanding or conflict before it turns into a problem.

In Project D, a daily early-morning meeting of core senior members from each team was introduced for the last six months of the project. Participants discussed outstanding problems and everybody made a commitment to the common goal of the project, headed by a Japanese director. In Project B, the workers' monthly pay period was changed to a weekly pay period, and the pay day was moved to Monday to minimize unexcused employee absences. After the completion of the project, the main contractor helped some of the best-performing employees find jobs in the hospital they had built.

5.3.3   *Hybrid management at the operational level*

In a complex project environment, small misunderstandings may trigger conflicts or confrontation among various groups of people. For this reason, key persons in each group need to communicate with other group leaders in daily operations and try to detect potential problems. Hybrid management is an effective method of bridging cultural barriers between different groups. In a hybrid management relationship, it is important to respect and trust each other and not to push one-sided views on another person. Hybrid management can be achieved not only at the top and middle levels of management, but also at the operational level.

In Projects A and C, employees represented five nationalities and there was a need for interpreters and translators for communication. There were also difficulties in cross-cultural communication and understanding. To solve these problems, various get-together functions were organized by the main contractor during the projects to improve communication and understanding among the staff and workers. Sometimes, face-to-face communication was more effective than e-mails.

In Project D, local supervisors with overseas work experience became leaders in organizing multi-service groups of people with different cultural backgrounds. The supervisors treated the cultural norms of each group as important and were able to control the groups without any major confrontations.

The above case study indicates that there may be a big cultural gap between the homogeneous Japanese people and the multicultural people of the Middle East, Europe and many Asian countries. In overseas construction projects, local people often show strong resistance towards external forces seeking to change their traditional systems. Our results support the earlier finding that culture remains a serious barrier to productive work in overseas construction companies.

6 Conclusion

When people of different nationalities and with different cultural backgrounds become an amalgamated team, they can create a highly dynamic, flexible and productive environment. To achieve and maintain the best output, core team members need effective communication skills, mutual trust and respect. The strength of Japanese mid-level managers is widely recognized in Japan. If they can show similar capabilities in overseas construction projects, if they can implement Japanese project and program management (P2M), and if they can create a culture of hybrid management in business, there is a good chance that construction companies will be able to overcome cultural problems. We believe that Japanese P2M can be an effective means for contractors to expand their construction projects worldwide.

We conclude from the findings that by minimizing cross-cultural barriers in the outer layer of culture (i.e., artifacts and products), as well as in the mid-layer of culture (i.e., norms and values), international business in multicultural settings can be conducted more smoothly. These barriers can be minimized through standardization of products, clarification of business processes, utilization of IT and the sharing of objectives. The inner layer of culture representing basic assumptions is much more difficult to tackle as it involves the very basic personality and behavior of personnel. The construction industry appears to be more heavily influenced by both the mid-layer and the inner layer of culture than are other industries described in this paper because of the way construction business is conducted and of the behavior and attitude of front-line managers and operators. Overcoming cultural differences is the *sine qua non* of success for the construction industry, which symbolizes the strength of the Japanese manufacturing technology. This, we believe, will also enable the construction industry to help developing countries develop high-quality, solid infrastructure.

References

Adler, N. (1997). *International Dimensions of Organizational Behavior*, Ohio: South-Western College Publishing.

Bartlett, C. A. and Ghoshal, S. (1998). *Managing Across Borders: The Transnational Solutions*, Boston: Harvard Business School Press.

England, G. W. (1995). National work meanings and patterns-constraints on management action, in *Cross-Cultural Management*, edited by Jackson, T., Oxford: Butterworth Heinemann.

Hayashi, K. (1985). *Cross-Cultural Interface Management*, Tokyo: Yuhikaku.

Hofstede, G. (1991). *Cultures and Organizations*, London: McGraw-Hill.

Langhoff, T. (1997). The influence of cultural differences on internationalization processes of firms, in *The Nature of the International Firm*, edited by Björkman *et al.*, Copenhagen: Handelshojskolens Forlag.

Pahlberg, C. (1997). Cultural differences and problems in HQ-subsidiary relationships in MNCs, in *The Nature of the International Firm*, edited by Björkman *et al.*, Copenhagen: Handelshojskolens Forlag.

Trompenaars, F. (1993). *Riding the Waves of Culture*, London: Nicholas Brealey Publishing.

Trompenaars, F. (1995). Resolving international conflict: Culture and business strategy, *Business Strategy Review* 7(3).

Yasumuro, K. (1993). Cultural diversity and tacit management theory, in *Global Management and Innovation Strategies*, edited by Yano, S., Tokyo: Chikura Shobo.

Educational Effectiveness and Implementation of KPM in the Cultivation of Human Resource

Masatoshi Nishio

Professor, Faculty of Social Systems Science
Chiba Institute of Technology

1 Introduction

Today, society is changing at an unprecedented speed. Educational institutions also have no choice but to adapt to trends in the world at large, and the roles expected of universities are becoming more diverse. Chiba Institute of Technology continues to engage in campus-wide efforts to adapt to these environmental changes. One such step was to establish new faculties and departments in 2001; and new classes are being developed in this context.

The essential missions of a university are research and education. Each university has attempted to achieve a balance between both of these missions while upholding its own traditions. With the evolving needs of society, research has become increasingly sophisticated and complex; meanwhile, there is also a strong expectation that universities will produce human resources who will be useful to society. To survive amidst the rigorous demands of society in the present era, it is necessary for each university to achieve some sort of distinctiveness.

As indicated in the example of program management described in Chapter 3 of *Introduction to P2M* by Shigenobu Ohara (2002), universities ought to engage in campus-wide endeavors to address the question of how a university should evolve in the future. However, the magnitude of the barriers between ideals and present-day realities has made this difficult to achieve. Generally speaking, I am convinced that applying the concepts of KPM can open up new possibilities in the field of research as well as education. However, in this paper, I will limit the scope of discussion to the field of university education.

For persons involved in university education, it is possible to regard each class as an individual project, and each subject as a program or a set of interrelated projects concerning that subject, with the individual classes making up its curriculum. When multiple subjects are related to each other, they can be considered as a compound program. Classes, including both lecture classes and practicums, can be regarded as projects and programs. In addition, the activities of a seminar operated within a laboratory unit can also be considered as a program which combines many projects. While the authority for appropriate management of these projects and programs lies with university professors, I believe that it is of great importance to implement university education in accordance with the concepts of KPM.

I will leave the question of the scope of application of the concepts of KPM as a topic for future study. I personally have been directly involved in three types of programs based on the concepts of KPM in the field of education. In this paper, I will discuss the results of implementing these programs.

2 University Programs for Human Resource Cultivation

2.1 *Seminar implementation*

2.1.1 *Aims of a seminar*

In general, the term "seminar" refers to a type of class in which a small group of students conducts research, makes presentations and holds discussions under the guidance of a professor. However, in this paper, I will use the term "seminar" in its broader sense, referring to all of the activities of a laboratory.

The basic aims of a seminar are as follows:

(1) to foster independence, initiative and cooperation;
(2) to develop skills for planning, investigation and analysis (problem finding) as well as problem solving capabilities;
(3) for each student to select his own research topic in the field of information systems development and operation, and to engage in planned, stepwise efforts culminating in a graduation thesis. Any topic is acceptable, so long as the student is interested and capable of pursuing it with initiative.

In addition to the above seminar aims, the following can also be adopted as clearly defined goals. These were pronounced last year by the Ministry of Economy, Trade and Industry as fundamental abilities for all members of society (MITI Small Committee, 2006):

- *Positive action: The ability to step out ahead.*
  This includes the ability to step out and work with tenacity even at the risk of failure, along with independence, initiative and practical ability to get things done.
- *Thinking: The ability to think things through.*
  This includes the ability to think things through when there is a problem, along with problem finding skills planning skills and creativity.
- *Teamwork: The ability to work in a team.*
  This includes the ability to cooperate with a variety of people toward a goal, along with the ability to express oneself, listening skills, flexibility, the ability to assess a situation, self-discipline and stress management skills.

2.1.2   Seminar management

We introduced KPM as a way of linking the above seminar aims and fundamental abilities for members of society, and established the following educational goals in seminar management:

- Cultivating independent creativity;
- Cultivating an overall perspective through systematic endeavors;
- Cultivating skills for project execution based on cooperation and collaboration.

Each of the activities conducted within a laboratory unit — practicums in management and information systems, graduation research and seminars (in the narrow sense of the word) — are considered as programs and projects; and seminar management, which encompasses all of these programs and projects, is considered as a compound program.

2.1.3   Information systems education

In the curriculum of our department, students acquire a basic understanding of information technology (IT) in classes on computer literacy and information literacy and in practicums on the fundamentals of information processing and other subjects; and they obtain general knowledge concerning information systems in classes on the fundamentals of information systems and management information systems (see Section 3.1). In practicums in the field of management information science which are pursued within the laboratory unit, students work on projects to develop information systems that draw on and consolidate all of their previous learning. The purpose of this experience is for students to acquire practical skills and insights regarding IT (see Section 3.2).

2.1.4 Graduation research

Based on the following considerations, students work on individual projects for about a year and a half, culminating in a graduation thesis:

(1) This is a major project in which students must submit (deliver) a graduation thesis (the product) with a quality that is satisfactory to the stakeholders (supervising professor of the laboratory, professors of other laboratories, and students), and complete its presentation and defense by the assigned deadline (delivery time).
(2) Although this is basically an individual project, all of the students share the common goal of completing their own graduation theses under the constraints described above in (1).
(3) Therefore, it is important for each individual to arrive at the final destination by attaining each milestone on a planned basis.

Each student pursues his graduation research independently, according to several milestones established annually by the laboratory. The subject of evaluation is the graduation thesis, which is the deliverable, as well as the process of conducting the graduation research. The graduation thesis must satisfy certain criteria; and the same applies to the process of conducting the graduation research.

2.2 CRM system

Customer relationship management (CRM), or the management of building and maintaining relationships with customers, has received a great deal of attention in recent years in marketing and other fields. Relationship management, one field of knowledge of P2M, also deals with this as a way of rebuilding relationships with customers (Project Management Introductory Development Survey Committee, 2001). In the case of CRM in the manufacturing field, the goal is to maximize customer value; meanwhile, in the case of CRM in the field of university education, students are the customers, and the goal is to build and maintain relationships with the customers, based on the aim of cultivating human resources who will play a useful role in society. For a university to survive in the present era, now that open enrolment has become a reality as a result of declining birthrates, the key is to provide thorough attention to each of many students and to obtain their satisfaction.

CRM opportunities in the Nishio laboratory include type 1 lecture classes (management information systems), type 2 lecture classes (fundamentals of information systems), type 1 practicums (seminars in the narrow sense), type 2 practicums (practical experience in the field of management information science), graduation research, dormitory lodging for seminar students, social gatherings of seminar participants and e-CRM system (laboratory website).

In the lecture classes, problems encountered in the practicums are solved. In addition, students are expected to share their opinions so that the class is not merely one-way communication from the professor. Teaching assistants (TAs) also provide support, explaining the material from a student's perspective. This is a reliable way to contribute to the growth of TAs participating in the classes, in addition to that of the students hearing the lectures.

Students are given opportunities to contribute synergistically to each other's growth in practicums and through discussions in the seminar's dormitory. Meanwhile, the instructors also communicate to the students as needed, in order to maintain and strengthen relationships between the instructors and students.

In graduation research, students are primarily expected to cultivate the abilities listed as items (1) and (2) in Section 2.1.1. Therefore, few restrictions are placed on graduation research, and each seminar student can pursue independent research on the topic of his or her own choice. However, students are periodically given opportunities to give presentations. This helps them develop the fundamental abilities which are needed by members of society, as they are able to cultivate the presentation skills which are essential in the working world, while also gaining an opportunity to engage in discussions with other seminar students.

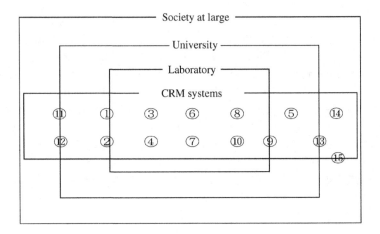

Fig. 1   CRM systems in seminar management

Notes: (1) Type 1 lecture classes (management information systems); (2) Type 2 lecture classes (fundamentals of information systems); (3) Type 1 practicums (seminars in the narrow sense); (4) Type 2 practicums (practical experience in the field of management information science); (5) Classes on other subjects; (6) Graduation research; (7) Dormitory lodging for seminar students; (8) Social gatherings of seminar participants; (9) Open campus; (10) e-CRM system (laboratory website); (11) Job-seeking activities; (12) Internships; (13) Club activities; (14) Part-time employment; (15) Other specific efforts or venues.

The e-CRM system (laboratory website) not only serves to provide information on the laboratory to outsiders, but also includes bulletin boards where laboratory participants can hold discussions or where instructors can post messages. Effective use of this tool can help students develop the fundamental abilities which are needed by members of society. There is also an e-learning system for lecture classes and a computer-aided instruction (e-CAI) system for practicums, where students can study on their own.

CRM systems are considered to encompass all of the venues that involve students, as shown in Figure 1, in addition to those described above (Oohashi, 2007).

3   Implementation of University Education Programs

3.1   *Implementation of lecture classes*

In the Department of Management Information Science, Faculty of Social Systems Science (formerly the Engineering Management Department, Faculty of Engineering), in order to provide a foundation of specialized knowledge in information technology, I teach a class in the fundamentals of information systems for second-year students and a class in management information systems for third-year students. Since students who have no practical experience may not be interested solely in one-way lectures on specialized fundamental knowledge, I also provide guidance regarding national qualification examinations in the field of IT, including the qualifications of Fundamental IT Engineer and Junior Systems Administrator. I chose a fundamental IT engineering textbook (Nakane, 2006) for my class on management information systems, and a reference book for junior systems administrators (Fujisaki, 2006) for my class on the fundamentals of information systems; and I have adopted a student-participation model for my classes (Nishio *et al.*, 2006).

We developed the project model shown in Figure 2, using architecture management with regard to unified program management (Project Management Introductory Development Survey Committee, 2001). Figure 3 shows the flow of classes in the current academic year.

3.2 *Implementation of practicums*

Since the mission of a university is to produce the kinds of human resources that are needed by society, it is desirable for universities to cultivate practical skills and human qualities, in addition to providing students with the knowledge needed for their classes.

Those who conduct university classes must consider the questions of what kinds of knowledge are necessary, what kinds of human resources are needed by society, and how to most effectively educate students in order to achieve these purposes. Based on this view, every year, I have conducted an educational project class with a data-oriented approach (DOA, a method of building data-oriented information systems) for students of different backgrounds.

Setting goals for the educational service project			Scheme model
Scenario of educational service strategies	Schedule scenario	Evaluation scenario	
Educational service strategy plan	Schedule plan and execution, part I	Evaluation plan	System model
Implementation of educational service strategies	Schedule execution, part II	Implementation of evaluation	Service model

Fig. 2   Project model

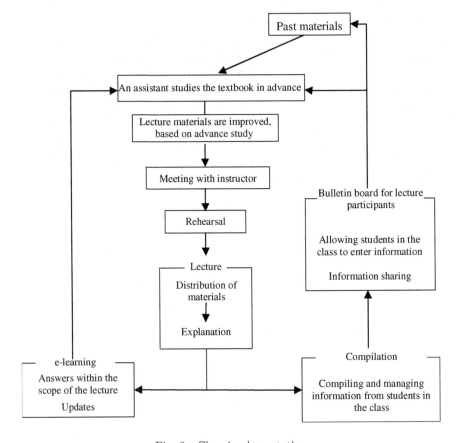

Fig. 3   Class implementation

In this DOA educational project, students form groups of four to five persons (see Figure 4) and use DOA techniques to analyze and reconstruct the assigned system. The overall purpose is to develop the kinds of human resources that are needed by society.

During the first month of the class, I use a classroom lecture format. During the same time period as the classroom lectures, each group separately selects one of the systems that has been assembled by previous DOA educational projects, conducts a requirement analysis on that system, proposes a reconstructed system to the users (laboratory alumni) and an instructor acting in the role of project owner (PO), and obtains their agreement. Next, each group selects persons to be responsible for each work category, prepares a project plan and makes its first interim presentation

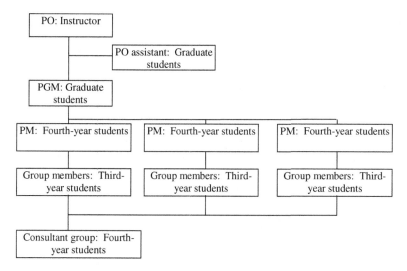

Fig. 4　Organizational structure of the DOA educational project

during the fifth week. The purpose of the two interim presentations is for each group to evaluate its progress on the project up to that time, and to analyze any schedule delays or problems. Next, the group prepares the interim deliverables of the DOA project: a conceptual database structural diagram, an information process flow (IPF) chart, and a schematic process flow (SPF) chart. Finally, the group uses Microsoft Access for implementation. Each group delivers its reconstructed system and report (project record) to the users and PO. At that time, the users and group members evaluate the project and make their final presentation (Nishio *et al.*, 2007).

3.3　*Implementation of seminar management program*

Seminar activities begin before the summer vacation of third-year students, after the students have been assigned to laboratories. In the seminar in the narrow sense of the word, the basic procedure is that students assigned to the laboratory each pick a research subject and give periodic presentations on their own research, with discussions. These presentations are led by students according to a predetermined schedule in the second half of the third year and first half of the fourth year. The seminar in the narrow sense is closely related to each student's graduation research project and information systems development project.

The graduation research project is implemented with the following chronological milestones:

(1) Student-led seminar presentation during third-year summer vacation;
(2) Research presentation in the seminar's dormitory before the end of summer vacation;
(3) Presentation in the seminar (narrow sense) during the second half of the third year;
(4) Third-year interim poster presentation;
(5) Presentation in the seminar (narrow sense) during the first half of the fourth year;
(6) Fourth-year interim presentation and defense;
(7) Submission of graduation thesis; presentation and defense.

4 Effectiveness of the University Education Program

4.1 *Evaluation of lecture classes*

The results of a survey on the students' level of satisfaction with the class on fundamentals of information systems in the second half of the 2006 academic year are given in Table 1.

In each category, the level of satisfaction with the class was found to be higher than anticipated. For classes conducted earlier, during the fifth and sixth periods, more students reported a low level of satisfaction; while for classes conducted later, during the ninth and tenth periods, fewer students reported a low level of satisfaction. This trend has been observed in every survey (Ujino and Nishio, 2007).

4.2 *Evaluation of practicums*

4.2.1 *Evaluation of practical experience in management information science (DOA educational project)*

Table 2 shows the results of a survey of 11 seminar undergraduate students concerning their level of satisfaction with the class. Each item is ranked on a scale of 1 to 5 (5: Yes; 4: Somewhat agree; 3: Neither agree nor disagree; 2: Somewhat disagree; 1: No).

For the students to learn about information systems themselves and to use that knowledge to build information systems, they need hands-on experience in addition to simply learning from textbooks. In a variety of situations that arise during the project, they need to correct their own

Table 1　Survey on satisfaction with the class on fundamentals of information systems in the second half of the 2006 academic year

		5th and 6th periods	9th and 10th periods
General	Your general satisfaction with this class, on a scale of 1 to 5	3.4	3.7
Content of class	Is the content easy to understand?	3.0	3.5
	Is the content unified and cohesive?	3.6	4.0
	Does the content match the plan for this class (syllabus)?	3.6	4.1
	How does the class compare to your expectations and interest level before taking it?	3.2	3.6
Teaching method	Is it easy to read from the blackboard, projector, etc.?	3.5	3.5
	Is the class conducted at an appropriate speed?	3.4	3.6
	Can you hear the instructor's voice and words clearly?	2.7	3.1
	Does the instructor check on the students' level of understanding?	2.8	3.1
	Are you provided with the assignments and other materials needed for advance study or review?	3.0	3.5
Environment	How is the situation regarding students whispering among themselves, arriving late and leaving early?	3.2	4.1
	Is the classroom size appropriate for the number of students in the class?	4.1	4.4
General	Your general satisfaction with this class, on a scale of 1 to 5	3.4	3.7

misconceptions and perform additional study in areas of inadequate understanding. It is apparent that the students have acquired a great deal of knowledge through this process, which ultimately results in the submission of an information system, the deliverable of the project. In addition to learning about the construction of a specialized information system, the students clearly have also gained knowledge about projects and the importance of teamwork, and cultivated interpersonal communication skills and other capabilities that are essential in society but cannot be learned in an ordinary lecture class.

Table 2   Survey on satisfaction with the class on practical experience in management information science

	Average response
1. Did you participate actively in this class?	4.1
2. Was the content of this class easy to understand?	3.3
3. Did the approach reflect determination of the students' level of understanding?	3.1
4. Was the class useful for improving your understanding, capabilities, knowledge and skills?	4.5
5. Are you generally satisfied with this class?	4.0

Source: Investigation results of class satisfaction by students, Chiba Institute of Technology (2006).

Table 3   Survey on satisfaction with the seminar class

	Average response
1. Did you participate actively in this class?	4.3
2. Was the content of this class easy to understand?	3.6
3. Did the approach reflect determination of the students' level of understanding?	3.5
4. Was the class useful for improving your understanding, capabilities, knowledge and skills?	4.3
5. Are you generally satisfied with this class?	4.0

Source: Investigation results of class satisfaction by students, Chiba Institute of Technology (2006).

4.2.2   Evaluation of the seminar in the narrow sense

As shown in Table 3, the average responses for questions 1, 4 and 5 are high, indicating a positive result with regard to the level of customer (student) satisfaction.

4.3   Evaluation of the graduation project

As shown in Table 4, this project seems to have been useful in gaining independence and problem solving skills, since it consists of individual work. The responses to questions 5 and 6 indicate a good level of satisfaction.

Table 4   Questionnaire on graduation research

		Average response
1.	Was the graduation research useful in developing greater independence?	4.6
2.	Was it useful in developing initiative?	3.6
3.	Was it useful in developing cooperative skills?	3.4
4.	Was it useful in developing problem solving skills?	4.1
5.	Are you satisfied with the graduation research?	3.7
6.	Are you satisfied with the support provided by instructors?	3.9

Source: Oohashi (2007).

Table 5   Overall evaluation of seminar management

		Average response
1.	Was the seminar management useful to you in acquiring positive action capabilities (independence, initiative and practical ability to get things done), or the ability to step out and work with tenacity even at the risk of failure?	4.4
2.	Was the seminar management useful to you in acquiring the ability to think things through when there is a problem (problem finding skills, planning skills and creativity)?	4.1
3.	Was the seminar management useful to you in acquiring teamwork capabilities (the ability to express oneself, listening skills, flexibility, the ability to assess a situation, self-discipline and stress management skills), or the ability to cooperate with a variety of people toward a goal?	4.1

Source: Oohashi (2007).

4.4   *Overall evaluation*

Table 5 shows the results of a questionnaire survey of 14 seminar undergraduate students and one second-year student in the master's program regarding their overall evaluation of seminar management.

The average responses were 4.4 for question 1 and 4.1 for questions 2 and 3, indicating a high level of satisfaction for all three items. This result is very important in attaining the ultimate goal of CRM in education, which is to cultivate the kinds of human resources that are needed by society. It indicates that the seminar was useful in helping students gain the fundamental skills needed by members of society. The fact that each individual is aware of having achieved personal growth is an indication that positive relationships were developed between instructors and students.

Of course, the supervising professor of a seminar should not be satisfied merely with a positive evaluation by the students. However, based on the following, it is concluded that the introduction of KPM has shown educational effectiveness:

- The laboratory has cohesive strength (capability to carry out a project).
- The students are able to adapt well to companies in their job-seeking activities (overall perspective).
- All of the students engage in graduation research activities with initiative and attain a certain level (independent creativity).

5 Conclusion

I have described a program with attention to active class participation by students, in which students work on a project in both lecture classes and practicums for one semester.

It is, of course, desirable to endeavor to further improve the level of awareness regarding individual graduation research projects. In addition, in the area of project-based seminar management, which is a strength of this laboratory, further effort is needed to enhance the cooperative relationships among members and to heighten the effects of synergy based on friendly rivalry.

Everyone connected to a university shares the common goal of cultivating the kinds of human resources that are needed by society. However, in reality, there is no guarantee of being able to produce these kinds of human resources without fail; and the only way to survive in a challenging environment is to work with each individual in an effort to achieve this goal. It is increasingly necessary to conduct educational projects for the cultivation of human resources, with missions and goals that have been clearly defined on the basis of KPM, and to maintain a process of continuous improvement in response to new environmental changes.

Because the educational environment changes year-by-year, new class endeavors in response to these changes are necessary each year. There is a limit to what instructors can accomplish alone, regardless of what outstanding classes they may devise; it is also essential for students to participate in classes with motivation and initiative. Instead of the simple formula of teaching by instructors and learning by students, my aspiration is to continue to move ahead with a participatory model in which students are given opportunities to teach, notwithstanding the high level of risk involved.

Acknowledgments

This study was performed with the participation and cooperation of the students and alumni of my seminar. I would like to express my sincere appreciation for everyone's cooperation.

References

Fujisaki, K. (2006). *Preliminary System Administrator Basic Text*, Tac LTD.

MITI Small Committee (2006). Interim study report on fundamental abilities for all members of society.

Nakane, M. (2006). *Basic Information Technology Standard Text*, Ohm Inc.

Nishio, M. *et al.* (2006). Educational project in university based on P2M, *Journal of International Association of Project & Program Management* 1, pp. 29–39.

Nishio, M. *et al.* (2007). An execution example of educational DOA project based on platform management, in *IAP2M Proceedings of Second National Conference 2007*, pp. 69–98.

Ohara, S. (2002). *Introduction to P2M*, H&I publication.

Oohashi, K. (2007). Study on CRM in laboratory operations, B.Sc. Thesis, Faculty of Management Science, Chiba Institute of Technology.

Project Management Introductory Development Survey Committee (2001). *P2M Project & Program*, Engineering Enhancement Association of Japan.

Ujino, T. and Nishio, M. (2007). Study on strategy of class management based on P2M, in *IAP2M Proceedings of Second National Conference 2007*, pp. 120–121.

Index

Printed in the United States
By Bookmasters